W9-ANV-851

The FIFTH DIRECTORY *of* PERIODICALS

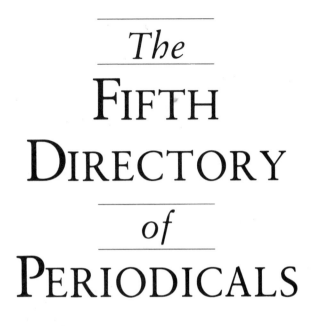

The
FIFTH
DIRECTORY
of
PERIODICALS

Publishing Articles on
American and English Language and Literature,
Criticism and Theory,
Film, American Studies, Poetry and Fiction

By Richard G. Barlow

Swallow Press/Ohio University Press
Athens

Swallow Press/Ohio University Press books are printed
on acid-free paper ∞

ISBN 0-8040-0958-9
ISBN 0-8040-0962-7 pbk.

Library of Congress Catalog Card Number 65-9218 (ISSN 0070-6094)

General Editors

DONNA GERSTENBERGER & GEORGE HENDRICK

CONTENTS

I. Literature Journals

Mosaic: A Journal for the Interdisciplinary Study of
    Literature
The Nabokovian
The Nathaniel Hawthorne Review
The New York Review of Books
Nineteenth-Century Contexts
Nineteenth-Century Literature
Nineteenth-Century Prose
Nineteenth-Century Studies
Nineteenth Century Theatre
NMAL: Notes on Modern American Literature
Notes and Queries
Notes on Contemporary Literature
Papers of the Bibliographical Society of America
Papers on Language and Literature: A Journal for Scholars and
    Critics of Language and Literature
Par Rapport: A Journal of the Humanities
Persuasions: Journal of the Jane Austen Society of North
    America
Philological Quarterly
Phoenix
PMLA: Publications of the Modern Language Association of
    `America
Poe Studies/Dark Romanticism: History, Theory,
    Interpretation
Prose Studies: History, Theory, Criticism
Proteus: A Journal of Ideas
Pynchon Notes
Queen's Quarterly
RE: Artes Liberales
Reading Medieval Studies
Records of Early English Drama Newsletter
Religion and Literature
Renaissance and Reformation/Renaissance et Réforme
Renaissance Drama
Renaissance Papers
Renaissance Quarterly
Renascence: Essays on Value in Literature
Res Publica Litterarum: Classical, Medieval, Renaissance Studies
Research Opportunities in Renaissance Drama

THE THOMAS HARDY JOURNAL
THE THOMAS HARDY YEARBOOK
THE THOMAS WOLFE REVIEW
THE THOREAU SOCIETY BULLETIN
TRANSACTIONS OF THE SAMUEL JOHNSON SOCIETY OF THE NORTHWEST
TRISTANIA: A JOURNAL DEVOTED TO TRISTAN STUDIES
TSE: TULANE STUDIES IN ENGLISH
TURN-OF-THE-CENTURY WOMEN
TWENTIETH CENTURY LITERATURE: A SCHOLARLY AND CRITICAL
    JOURNAL
TWENTIETH CENTURY VIEWS
UNIVERSITY OF MISSISSIPPI STUDIES IN ENGLISH
UNIVERSITY OF TORONTO QUARTERLY: A CANADIAN JOURNAL OF THE
    HUMANITIES
THE UPSTART CROW: A SHAKESPEARE JOURNAL
VIATOR: MEDIEVAL AND RENAISSANCE
VICTORIAN LITERATURE AND CULTURE
VICTORIAN NEWSLETTER
VICTORIAN PERIODICALS REVIEW
VICTORIAN POETRY
VICTORIAN STUDIES: A JOURNAL OF THE HUMANITIES, ARTS AND
    SCIENCES
VICTORIANS INSTITUTE JOURNAL
VIRGINIA QUARTERLY REVIEW: A NATIONAL JOURNAL OF LITERATURE
    AND DISCUSSION
VIRGINIA WOOLF MISCELLANY
THE VISIONARY COMPANY: A MAGAZINE OF THE TWENTIES
THE WALLACE STEVENS JOURNAL
WALT WHITMAN QUARTERLY REVIEW
THE WELLSIAN
WESTERN HUMANITIES REVIEW
WILLA CATHER PIONEER MEMORIAL NEWSLETTER
WILLIAM CARLOS WILLIAMS REVIEW
THE WINESBURG EAGLE: THE OFFICIAL PUBLICATION OF THE SHERWOOD
    ANDERSON SOCIETY
WOMEN'S STUDIES: AN INTERDISCIPLINARY JOURNAL
THE WORDSWORTH CIRCLE
WORLD LITERATURE TODAY: A LITERARY QUARTERLY OF THE UNIVER-
    SITY OF OKLAHOMA
WORLD LITERATURE WRITTEN IN ENGLISH

II. CRITICISM AND THEORY JOURNALS

III. FILM JOURNALS

CAMERA OBSCURA: A JOURNAL OF FEMINISM AND FILM THEORY

CINEASTE: AMERICA'S LEADING MAGAZINE OF THE ARTS AND POLITICS OF THE CINEMA

CINEMA

CINEMA JOURNAL

FILM: MONTHLY JOURNAL OF THE BRITISH FEDERATION OF FILM SOCIETIES

FILM & HISTORY

FILM COMMENT

FILM CRITICISM

FILM DOPE

FILM QUARTERLY

FILMS IN REVIEW

IMAGENES: PUBLICATIÓN SEMESTRAL DE TEORÍA, TÉCNIA, CRÍTICA Y EDUCACIÓN ACERCA DE LA IMAGENE EN MOVIMIENTO

THE JOURNAL OF FILM AND VIDEO

JOURNAL OF POPULAR FILM AND TELEVISION

JUMP CUT: A REVIEW OF CONTEMPORARY MEDIA

LITERATURE/FILM QUARTERLY

MONTHLY FILM BULLETIN

PERFORMING ARTS RESOURCES

POST SCRIPT: ESSAYS IN FILM AND THE HUMANITIES

QUARTERLY REVIEW OF FILM STUDIES

SCREEN

SHAKESPEARE ON FILM NEWSLETTER

VARIETY

THE VELVET LIGHT TRAP

WIDE ANGLE: A FILM QUARTERLY OF THEORY, CRITICISM, AND PRACTICE

IV. LANGUAGE AND LINGUISTICS JOURNALS

ADFL BULLETIN

AMERICAN SPEECH: A QUARTERLY OF LINGUISTIC USAGE

ANNUAL REVIEW OF APPLIED LINGUISTICS

ANTHROPOLOGICAL LINGUISTICS

APPLIED PSYCHOLINGUISTICS

BABEL: INTERNATIONAL JOURNAL OF TRANSLATION

THE BILINGUAL REVIEW/LA REVISTA BILINGÜE

V. AMERICAN STUDIES

VI. FICTION AND POETRY JOURNALS

THE ARMCHAIR DETECTIVE
BLACK WARRIOR REVIEW
CAROLINA QUARTERLY
CONJUNCTIONS: BI-ANNUAL VOLUME OF NEW WRITING
CREATIVE MOMENT
CUMBERLAND POETRY REVIEW
THE DENVER QUARTERLY
FANTASY REVIEW
FIELD: CONTEMPORARY POETRY AND POETICS
FORMATIONS
THE GEORGIA REVIEW
THE GETTYSBURG REVIEW
HIGH PLAINS LITERARY REVIEW
HIGGINSON JOURNAL
THE HOLLINS CRITIC
THE HUDSON REVIEW
INTERIM
THE IOWA REVIEW
IRONWOOD
THE KENYON REVIEW
KENTUCKY POETRY REVIEW
THE LITERARY REVIEW: AN INTERNATIONAL JOURNAL OF
    CONTEMPORARY WRITING
MID-AMERICAN REVIEW
THE MINNESOTA REVIEW
THE NEW CRITERION
NEW ENGLAND REVIEW AND BREAD LOAF QUARTERLY
NEW LAUREL REVIEW
NEW LETTERS: A MAGAZINE OF FINE WRITING
NEW ORLEANS REVIEW
THE NORTH AMERICAN REVIEW
NORTHWEST REVIEW
THE OHIO REVIEW
ONTARIO REVIEW
PARNASSUS: POETRY IN REVIEW
PARTISAN REVIEW
PEMBROKE MAGAZINE
THE PLATTE VALLEY REVIEW
PLOUGHSHARES

ACKNOWLEDGMENTS

I WISH TO THANK Donna Gerstenberger and George Hendrick, the general editors, for their kindness in allowing me to continue the work which they began in 1959. They have been most helpful and kind in providing suggestions regarding the preparation of this update of *The Directory*.

I am indebted to the late Suzanne Comer who read an early version of the manuscript and who made numerous helpful comments regarding the form of the entries. I wish to thank Professor Charles Harris, Chairperson of the Department of English at Illinois State University, for helpful suggestions regarding the division of journal categories and for the use of the Illinois State University Department of English copy of the *Third Directory*. Professor Stanley Renner also provided me with the use of his copy of the *Second Directory*. I want to acknowledge Professor Harrison T. Meserole, who read the introduction carefuly, provided critical help regarding some of the entries, and suggested bibliographical changes that improved the manuscript.

I thank my wife, Lois Ann Barlow, for her assistance in typing letters of request for information, for help in preparing the index, and for her patience while the manuscript was in progress.

PREFACE

THE FIFTH DIRECTORY OF PERIODICALS: Publishing Articles on American and English Language and Literature, Criticism and Theory, Film, American Studies, Poetry and Fiction came into existence as a result of the continuing need for a reasonably priced reference tool where scholars in the humanities could locate journals to which they could submit manuscripts for possible publication. *The Fourth Directory of Periodicals*, published in 1974 by Donna Gerstenberger and George Hendrick, provided a large selection of periodicals, but it has been out of print and unavailable for some time. Since 1974, many new journals have come into existence, arriving almost as rapidly as the old ones have departed. New emphases on film, women's studies, literary theory, interdisciplinary approaches to literature, children's literature, comparative literature, and the expansion of foreign language studies account in part for the proliferation of these journals.

Journal publishing, once confined to a few well-known periodicals in each academic field, has expanded to the point that the growth of specialized journals, which were once the preserve of the large, established universities, has opened opportunities for more authors to publish. The chances for many scholars to publish good scholarship have improved now that less well-known state universities and small, private schools have entered the publishing business.

Every scholar gradually acquires some knowledge of the principal periodicals in her or his field. While it is impossible to know all of the possible forums for a finished research article, *The Directory,* through its successive revisions, has been a helpful aid over the years in placing scholarly manuscripts. Its use has been well established since Professors Gerstenberger and Hendrick published *The First Directory* in 1959. Since then, *The Directory* has become an institution in the world of academic publishing and an indispensable aid to scholars. The format first adopted has proved its worth through successive updates. In fact, this format has become so familiar that it seems to have provided the basic pattern for specialized directories by many other scholars, and a number of university graduate classes in research and bibliography have long utilized *The Directory* as an introduction to the necessary professional enterprise of scholarly publishing. Many professors, graduate students, librarians, and managers of bookstores are among those willing to testify to its usefulness.

As in its previous updates, *The Fifth Directory* lists a considerable number of regularly published journals on literature and language, but in undertaking this revision, I have changed the organization of the book and expanded its scope. Instead of listing all the entries seriatim, as in *The Fourth Directory,* I have now organized the journals into six general categories: (1) Literature Journals, (2) Criticism and Theory Journals, (3) Film Journals, (4) Language and Linguistic Journals, (5) American Studies Journals, and (6) Fiction and Poetry Journals. While I recognize that the assignment of journals into categories represents a somewhat arbitrary act of classification, and a number of journals could have been placed in more than one category, users of *The Fifth Directory* can consult the index for complete clarification of the scope of each journal. Also, in a short introductory essay, I discuss some aspects of form in the preparation of journal manuscripts before submission to an editor for consideration. These remarks are intended for beginning scholars who may find them useful. Most older scholars are well aware of the mechanics of preparing manuscripts for publication.

More periodicals, journals, and magazines are listed in *The Fifth Directory* than in any previous update, especially in the categories of literature, film, language and linguistics, and American studies. I have not, however, listed specialized periodicals, such as alumni magazines, state historical society bulletins (or quarterlies), or undergraduate literary magazines which are restricted to on-campus contributors. Some periodicals, which are not, strictly speaking, focused on American and English language and literature but which might be of interest to scholars in the history of ideas, are included, as have numerous periodicals in the modern foreign languages, since these journals, in addition to carrying articles on language, sometimes publish essays on comparative literature. I also include several little magazines which occasionally carry critical articles.

Although most editors of periodicals to whom requests for information were sent answered my queries, some did not. Some of the journals from which limited information was available are listed on the grounds that their presence makes *The Fifth Directory* more complete and answers the question of the scholar who is considering one of these journals as a possible place of publication. In every instance, I have provided as much information as possible for those who might find it useful.

One of the new features of *The Fifth Directory* is the "Table of Contents" which lists the periodicals in each of the six sections in alphabetical order. The entries are thus arranged alphabetically by the titles of the journals. A comprehensive Index also lists the journals under subject headings from "Aesthetics and Theory" to "W. B. Yeats."

The "Key to Entries" below describes the kinds of journal data a reader of *The Fifth Directory* can expect to find in each entry. Through paragraphing, the major blocks of information are provided for each journal. Thus, the reader who desires to locate quickly a certain type of information about a certain journal (e.g., *Major Field(s) of Interest*) can, if familiar with *The Fifth Directory's* system, find it without reading the complete contents of each entry.

KEY TO ENTRIES

ENTRIES ARE ARRANGED ALPHABETICALLY, excluding *A* and *The*. Thus *The Evelyn Waugh Newsletter* will be found under *E*. Each entry contains the following information: the name of the journal, its editorial address, price on a yearly basis unless otherwise specified, year of founding and sponsor, major field(s) of interest, manuscript information, payment, indexes, and policy regarding copyright and reprinting. If the journal is a member of the Council of Editors of Learned Journals (CELJ), an asterisk (*) precedes the name of the journal.

Unless specifically indicated within the entry, the journals do not:
(1) Restrict contributions to subscribers or members.
(2) Desire solicited manuscripts only.
(3) Have special religious or political biases.
(4) Carry creative, nonscholarly material.
(5) Desire more than one copy of a manuscript.
(6) Publish a bibliographical issue.

INTRODUCTION

THE FIFTH DIRECTORY OF PERIODICALS is intended to serve scholars in the humanities as a reference guide to a number of scholarly journals to which they may submit manuscripts for publication. The necessity of having specific information about the various journals that will accept scholarly manuscripts is of more than passing interest to those who may consult the resources contained in this book, for most scholars recognize the importance of publishing the results of their research in order to establish their academic careers. The necessity of academic publishing, its justification and its art, is beyond serious doubt today; it is an inescapable fact of life that most professors (and those with appointments in research centers) are expected to disseminate the results of their research inquiries. Those who do publish find that it can lead to conference invitations, leaves of absence, promotions, and regular increases in salary.

Many university administrators and faculty also claim that there is a strong relationship between publishing research and effective teaching. A number of academic deans believe that research and scholarly publishing, when integrated into the area in which a faculty member is teaching, improve a professor's effectiveness. Good teaching is important, but it must be backed by and supported with good scholarship. Of course, scholarly journals are most often the means by which academic authors publish the results of their research, and most editors rely largely or entirely on unsolicited manuscripts from scholars as the source of research which they publish in their journals. Authors and editors are therefore jointly involved in the enterprise of writing, submitting, evaluating, and publishing the most important research and best commentary on literary texts, pedagogical issues, and professional concerns that are raised by the reading, teaching, and explicating of American and English language and literature, criticism and theory, film, American studies, poetry and fiction.

Because publication of scholarship in academic journals is a cooperative venture, professional collaboration between authors and editors is central to its process. It is evident that authors need editors to evaluate and to publish their manuscripts, while editors cannot produce journals or periodicals without the interest and trust of authors who submit manuscripts for consideration. Authors expect that their manuscripts will be read with fair and impartial judgment, will be objectively and critically evaluated, and will be returned by the editor of a journal in a timely manner with respectful written notification that the articles has been accepted for publication or rejected. If the article is rejected, an author hopes that the editor will provide the reasons, and some journals do, in fact, return copies of referees' comments.

On the other hand, if a manuscript is rejected, there are often good reasons. The manuscript is not suitable for publication in the journal in question; it violates the journal's restrictions on subject matter or methodology; it pays no attention to limitations on length, or it ignores the periodical's requirements for style. Some other reasons why scholarly manuscripts are rejected by the editors of journals to which they are sent are that: (1) Space is available for only the best papers submitted. (2) The facts stated in the paper are already known. (3) The author does not know the facts about the subject. (4) The conclusions are not justified by the reasoning or by the evidence provided. (5) The paper is not based upon first-hand research or observation. (6) The paper is intended for oral delivery and not for publication. (7) The material in the paper is poorly organized. (8) The subject matter is not suitable for the readers of the journal. (9) The material is not sufficiently condensed. (10) The author has tried to dress-up the facts in an elaborate and ornate style. (11) The writing is ungrammatical, verbose, and obscure. (12) The same point-of-view is not retained throughout the manuscript.

An author who has spent long hours conducting research, formulating his or her thoughts about a subject, and writing and revising a manuscript for publication, wants to feel sure that it receives serious evaluation by fair, knowledgeable, efficient, and capable readers. Usually, this is the case. Sometimes, however, an editor may seem indifferent to an author's concerns or appear to treat a manuscript slightingly. Authors and editors do not always communicate closely with one another during the period in which manuscripts are being evaluated. The review process can provoke questions about the selection procedures and the fairness of the ways in which manuscripts are evaluated, especially if a manuscript is rejected. Sometimes there is room for appeal. If, for example, an author feels that his or her manuscript has not been evaluated fairly and it has been submitted to a journal that belongs to the Council of Editors of Learned Journals (CELJ), the author can appeal a negative decision by writing to the president of the Council of Editors of Learned Journals, care of the Modern Language Association, and request that any dispute be adjudicated.

Information on the preparation of scholarly manuscripts is thoroughly covered in *The MLA Style Manual*, Third Edition (1985) and its student-oriented version, the *MLA Handbook for Writers of Research Papers*, Third Edition (1988), either of which may be purchased from the MLA, 10 Astor Place, New York, NY 10003–6981 and in *The Chicago Manual of Style* (13th Edition), which may be ordered from the University of Chicago Press, 5801 Ellis Avenue, Chicago, Illinois 60637. These handbooks are the most commonly used style manuals in the literary field, although there are many other excellent manuals. It should be noted that in the advice given regarding the preparation of scholarly manuscripts, they differ in important ways. Some journal editors require the older *MLA Style Sheet* (Second Edition) or the *MLA Style Sheet* (Revised Edition). These style manuals should be consulted unless the journal in question specifies another kind of style manual.

Editors of scholarly journals (and their policies) change regularly. Editors have the right—indeed, it is widely believed the obligation—to outline through a statement of editorial policy, the specific conditions under which they will accept manuscripts for consideration, the criteria they require be met for publication, the physical preparation of the manuscript they desire, and the kinds of evaluations manuscripts must undergo in order to be accepted for publication. Most journals publish such statements regularly. For example, a statement of editorial policy appears in every blue issue of *PMLA* that describes the types of articles the journal publishes and the requirements for submission, although it says little about the selection procedures. Periodically, then, the editor of *PMLA* will publish a column discussing the ways in which an article travels the path to publication (see *PMLA*, Volume 102, Number 1, January 1988).

Many authors are unaware of the demands on an editor's time and resources that require them to process many manuscripts in addition to their other duties. In the preparation of manuscripts to be submitted for publication, authors often do not follow instructions. Most journal editors expect authors to follow the directions in the appropriate style manual carefully, and careful writers will also take the time, before submitting a manuscript to a particular journal, to read its most recent issue and to determine its special features, its range of styles, the nature of its illustrative material, and its editorial policy before they submit a manuscript.

It may surprise some authors that journal editors refuse many scholarly manuscripts offered to them for publication that appear, from the evidence in the footnotes, to have been the product of substantial scholarly research and that contain serious contributions to knowledge. These articles are rejected simply because, as submitted, they do not reflect minimal professional levels of clarity or cogency. After several readings, the editor (or the referees) is unable to discover what point the author is trying to convey, or the information being conveyed is presented in a manner that is not compelling to a knowledgeable and critical reader. Too many researchers prepare a manuscript with less commitment than they devoted to conducting the research. Their minds are full of the subject, and they know every detail about it. But they do not present it in an attractive and readable form. They assume that readers will be impressed solely by the nature of the information they are presenting. But before a manuscript is likely to be accepted, it must be shaped and formed so that the information it contains can be understood with ease and certainty by those who are its likely readers. The manuscript must be submitted in its most attractive form.

Some writers have an intuitive sense of form. Without conscious thought, they are aware of the divisions and subdivisions of their material, and they put ideas in proper order naturally. Others find it desirable to write themselves into their subjects, as it were, and later to juggle the pieces into a logical arrangement. Most publishable articles share certain qualities of form, and while there are no formal conventions about writing scholarly articles in the humanities *per se*, most research articles that are published in scholarly journals are organized so that form enhances content. Occasionally an article that is generally regarded as bad work will be published, but more often good articles that contain substantive research and that would be useful to those with interest and knowledge of the subject are rejected because the form in which they are submitted does not present the content in a clear and attractive manner. The writer does not realize that editors and readers are not willing to spend time and effort puzzling out the meaning of work that is not immediately clear or that is not written properly the first time.

With a little thought and some care, writers can present research material in its most compelling form as serious and interesting contributions to knowledge, in which form and content work well together. Journals always want to publish new information, new facts, fresh interpretations, innovative critical approaches, well-argued evaluations, and different theories based on new ideas which add to the existing aggregate of knowledge or to the better understanding of a field or some part of it. Such articles are and must be welcome, so long as editors and readers can clearly and easily understand what is written. In other words, readability is a prime consideration in making a scholarly article acceptable for publication.

Most readers are not impressed by elaborate sentence constructions and excessive verbiage presented in an unorganized manner. Invariably, editors will reject a manuscript in which there is good material but the material is submitted in a form that readers must work unnecessarily hard to understand. This is true even though, as a general rule, the interest and importance of a piece of research lie either in the new facts which it discloses or the methods by which they have been brought to light—or both. To these prior considerations, the manner of manuscript presentation may be subordinate, but good presentation will help greatly in getting a paper accepted while bad presentation may prevent it from being considered. It was for this reason that *The MLA Style Sheet* came into existence in 1951: manuscripts were being rejected by editors that were acceptable in every respect except as to *form*.

Assuming other professional concerns are satisfactory (i.e., the article presents original and significant material; it is appropriate for the journal; it conforms to specified limitations on length; it has been prepared according to the style manual requirements; and—if the journal does not accept duplicate copies—it is an original typescript), prospective contributors to learned journals may wish to consider the following advice before they submit a manuscript to an editor for consideration:

(1) The manuscript should have a title that focuses the reader on the nature of the research and clearly indicates what the article is about. Cryptic titles should be avoided, and the title should not be used to attract attention to itself.

(2) The introduction to the article should be written with great care since it is critical to the success of the article. No matter how familiar a reader is likely to be with a field (and indeed many readers are likely to have a considerable knowledge, not only of a particular period in which they have expert knowledge, but also of English or American literature as a whole or of linguistics or film), the introduction should clearly explain the nature of the research and indicate what the writer hopes to accomplish in presenting the material. The introduction should indicate to readers why they should bother to read what the writer has to say. Facetious opening references should be avoided, since they at best annoy and at worst offend the reader whose good will the writer seeks to obtain.

(3) The article should be easy to read. The writing should reflect organization that is clear and simple to follow. Readers should be able to understand, for example, how the article's opening relates to its ending. They should be able to see easily the connections and relations between the parts. Above all, they should be able to follow the progression of ideas and the thread of logic that connects one point to the next and that relates the points to the article's controlling idea(s).

(4) Only a minority of readers are likely to be experts in the particular field in which the article is focused, and very few can be expected to possess the minute knowledge that the writer, who has been devoting his

or her time to the study of the field, has or ought to have. Authors should therefore be careful to document references and support general statements and conclusions, unless they are accepted critical commonplaces in the field. Authors should also verify the accuracy of all quotations. In so far as possible, they should state facts in logical order and as simply as possible, although chronological order may not always be the best way to present facts.

(5) References, citations, and quotations should be precise and complete, and they should follow the style of the journal concerned. *The MLA Style Manual* is explicit with regard to documentation, footnote logic, and footnote numbers, as is *The Chicago Manual of Style,* which also provides a complete discussion of documentation for scholarly articles. In the current *MLA Style Manual* (1985), the Modern Language Association (MLA) has radically changed the style of documentation for learned papers from what had been the standard for most books and learned journals in the humanities since the first edition of the *MLA Style Sheet* appeared in 1951. Instead of indicating the source of quotations and citations in footnotes and endnotes, the MLA system now uses a parenthetical style of documentation much like that used in *Publication Manual of the American Psychological Association* (APA). The MLA Committee on Research Activities believes that this new system of documentation will help scholars achieve consistency, clarity, precision, economy, and comprehensibility, and that it will help to bridge the gap that has existed between the documentation system of the humanities and those of other academic disciplines.

(6) Articles should be focused on the research. Any tendency to digress should be avoided, unless the digression is necessary to illustrate a point or to provide background for an argument. When a digression is necessary, the writer should make it clear that it is a digression and, when the end has been reached, note its relevance to the subject. The writer should then make it quite clear the return to the main course of the argument.

(7) Manuscripts should be as long as necessary but as short as possible. Research articles should avoid trendy language, bureaucratic jargon, and technical words. Readers are more likely to respond positively to clear and effective expressions than to obscure, verbose, or vague statements. Very few readers will appreciate (or tolerate) literary ornamentation or verbal rodomontade in research articles.

(8) The author should attempt to avoid the use of literary paraphrases and wordy or ambiguous expressions, such as "it is generally admitted that," "there can be no doubt that," "it is well known that." If such expressions are used, authorial responsibility should be placed on at

least one other source by means of a reference or documentation. Qualifying adverbs and abstract nouns, such as *rather, quite, somewhat,* can usually be omitted without sacrificing much meaning.

(9) Before writers begin to conduct research, they should establish whether the work breaks new ground on the subject, or whether this work has not been done before by someone else. A researcher should not be disappointed if an editor rejects an article which conveys information that scholars in the field already know. The publication of certain work in one area does not necessarily eliminate or preclude similar work from being considered, but publishable articles should represent new additions to knowledge or fresh critical appraisals based on new scholarly study.

(10) Authors should not try to be humorous or cute. Humor is enjoyed in its place, but nothing infuriates a reader who is looking for plain statements of fact more than untimely humor. In other words, the subject of the research should not be treated with levity.

(11) Whenever a journal's submission policy is in doubt, authors should write an inquiry to the editor. A prospective contributor should also examine carefully a recent issue of the periodical under consideration, not only for the style of its present contents and footnote form, but also to see whether the research being considered for submission is compatible with the general nature of the journal's contents. If the journal publishes articles in the field of the same length and scope, then it may be appropriate for the manuscript that the author is considering submitting. If, on the other hand, the research seems substantially different from or foreign to the subjects that are written about in the journal, the author may be better advised to reconsider submitting the manuscript. The editor of a journal may find the argument in a submission reasonably persuasive, but may still reject the manuscript because its content does not have a specific enough connection with the editorial intent of the journal to warrant publication in its pages. The editor may recommend submitting the article to a journal that more closely specializes in the kinds of material about which the author is writing. For example, a source study on Shakespeare, submitted to *The Huntington Library Quarterly,* may be more suitable for *Notes & Queries* or *The Explicator,* both of which specialize in this kind of research.

(12) For articles written in a language other than English, authors are urged to use the language in which they can write most effectively. Perfect language fluency is essential, especially with articles or quotes written in French or Spanish. The printer is not expected to know foreign languages and usually cannot decipher foreign words written by hand. If type is not clean, the printer may not be able to distinguish "e" or "o." Type or print

all corrections legibly above the lines involved. Never write anything in the margins.

(13) For spelling, hyphenation, determinations of foreign words, etc., consult *Webster's Third New International Dictionary of the English Language*.

(14) Contributors to special departments, especially reviewers of books and films, should study the typographical arrangements of the journal in question carefully. When writing a review, for example, the following data must always be furnished: author's name(s) (last name first), title of book, place of publication, publisher, date of publication, number of pages in the case of a book, size and rpms or ips in the case of discs or tapes, and price (in the currency of the country of publication).

(15) Authors should avoid gender-specific language or other usages that may offend readers. The use of "he," "his," etc. (or "she," "her," etc.) is acceptable to many editors only when referring to a definite individual.

(16) If an article is accepted, the editor may wish to consult with the author about changes in the manuscript. Authors should provide a full address, including postal codes and country.

(17) Submission of an article or note implies that it has not been published elsewhere. Authors are responsible for obtaining written permission to publish material (quotations, illustrations, etc.) for work of which they do not own the copyright.

(18) All manuscripts must, of course, be typed and double-spaced. Send the manuscript of the article or note, loose and flat, by first-class mail. Transmittal correspondence should include a self-addressed envelope with sufficient return postage (S.A.S.E.) to cover the return of the manuscript to the sender in the event that it cannot be accepted for publication. In the case of foreign periodicals, enclose International Reply Coupons.

I. LITERATURE JOURNALS

*A/B: Auto/Biography Studies

English Department, University of Wisconsin-Whitewater, Whitewater, WI 53190–1790. Rates: $15 per year individuals. $45 per year institutions. Founded 1985. Sponsored by The Joyce and Elizabeth Hall Center for the Humanities, University of Kansas, Lawrence, KS 66045–2967. Published 2 times per year.

Major Field(s) of Interest: The journal deals with all aspects of autobiography, biography, diaries, letters, and other life-writings, as well as with relations between life-writings and other forms of literature. The journal accepts material from all periods and all languages, but articles must show a clear connection to theory and practice. Journal reviews books, but book reviews are usually solicited.

Manuscript Information: Articles of 10–25 double-spaced typed pages. Notes up to 500 words. Book reviews of 1,500–2,000 words. Style: MLA with endnotes. 2 copies of manuscript required. Journal requires 1 copy on computer disc (WordPerfect 4.2, 5.0) if article is accepted. Report in 3–6 months. Rejected manuscripts returned with S.A.S.E.

Payment: 2 copies of the journal.

Copyright: By the journal. Reprint rights granted with permission.

ADE Bulletin

10 Astor Place, New York, NY 10003–6981. Rates $15 per year individuals. $30 per year institutions. Founded 1962. Sponsored by the Association of Departments of English. Published 3 times per year.

Major Field(s) of Interest: The journal publishes essays and surveys dealing with professional, pedagogical, curricular, and departmental issues in English studies and matters affecting Departments of English.

Manuscript Information: Articles of 2,500–7,500 words. Book reviews of 1,000–4,000 words. Style: MLA. 2 copies of manuscript required. Report in 2–3 months. Rejected manuscripts returned with S.A.S.E.

Payment: 4 copies.

Copyright: By the Association of Departments of English. ADE freely grants reprint rights to authors.

*The Age of Johnson: A Scholarly Annual

c/o Professor Paul J. Korshin, Department of English, University of Pennsylvania, Philadelphia, PA 19104. Rates: $25 per year individuals. $50 per year institutions. Founded 1984. Sponsored by the University of Pennsylvania. Published annually.

Major Field(s) of Interest: The scope of the journal is the age of

Samuel Johnson (1709–1784) and his contemporaries, roughly the years from 1730–1810. The journal welcomes contributions on all aspects of the period including essays on English literature, culture, and the arts that deal with the period of Johnson's primary influence and the eighteenth century. Journal reviews books, but all book reviews are solicited.

Manuscript Information: Articles of 25–65 pages in length. Book reviews of 5–15 pages. Style: Chicago with endnotes. Report in 3 months. Rejected manuscripts returned with S.A.S.E.

Payment: 1 copy of the volume and 25 free offprints.

Indexed In: MLA International Bibliography.

Copyright: By the journal. Authors may reprint with permission.

*ALLEGORICA

Department of English, Texas A&M University, College Station, TX 77843. Rates: $10 per year in North America. $12 per year elsewhere. Founded 1976. Sponsored by the Department of English, Texas A&M University. Published annually (Spring).

Major Field(s) of Interest: A journal devoted primarily to making available to scholars literal translations of Medieval and Renaissance literary works and documents that heretofore have been available only in their original languages or in outmoded or inadequate English translations. The journal will also publish scholarly articles on Medieval and Renaissance topics from the Early Christian period through the Rococo, as well as book reviews on pertinent topics. The editor invites the submission of translations and articles, as well as suggestions concerning the documents that most need to be made available in translation.

Manuscript Information: Articles and translations up to 40 pages. Styles *MLA Style Sheet* (Revised Edition). All extensive foreign language quotations should be translated in footnotes. Translators should send a xerox copy of the original for copyright purposes. Report in 3 months. Rejected manuscripts returned with S.A.S.E.

Payment: Offprints.

Copyright: By the Department of English, Texas A&M University.

AMERICAN BENEDICTINE REVIEW

Assumption Abbey, Richardson, ND 58652. Rates: $10.00 per year. $10.50 per year foreign. Sponsored by Abbeys and Priories of the American Cassinese Federation of Benedictines. Published quarterly.

Major Field(s) of Interest: Research articles on the theory and history of the religious life (Christian and monastic), theology, science, and the humanities. The journal is particularly concerned with the religious aspects of the arts and sciences.

Manuscript Information: Articles of 15–30 pages. Style: MLA. Submit original manuscript. Report in 4–5 months. Rejected manuscripts returned with S.A.S.E.

Payment: Offprints.

Indexed In: Catholic Periodical Index, MSL.

Copyright: By the journal and the author. Permission to reprint required.

AMERICAN BOOK COLLECTOR

The Moretus Press, Inc. P. O. Box 1080, Ossining, NY 10562–1080. Rates $33 per year individuals. $47 per year institutions. Founded 1932. Published monthly except July.

Major Field(s) of Interest: The journal solicits articles on first editions, Americana, illustrated and children's books, fine printing, printing and publishing history, and the many byways of book collecting. Author bibliographies are especially welcome. The journal reviews books.

Manuscript Information: Articles of 1,000–2,500 words. Notes up to 200 words. Book reviews of 750–1,000 words. Style: Chicago. Prefer no footnotes. Submit original typescript and send 200–word summary in advance to the editor. Report in 6–10 weeks. Rejected manuscripts returned with S.A.S.E.

Payment: On publication, $50 per 1,000 words.

Indexed In: MLA International Bibliography, Book Review Index, ARTbibliographies Modern, Reference Source, Reference Services Review.

Copyright: By The Moretus Press. Authors may acquire all rights on request.

THE AMERICAN BOOK REVIEW

Publications Center, Campus Box 494, University of Colorado, Boulder, CO 80309–0494. Rates: $18 per year individuals. $23 per year institutions. Sponsored by the University of Colorado Publications Center. Published bimonthly.

Major Field(s) of Interest: The journal publishes book reviews of novels, literature, poetry, and theory from small, alternative, university, and women's presses. Please send query and sample review first.

Manuscript Information: Reviews up to 3 double-spaced typed pages, although there may be exceptions. Style: None. No footnotes. Report in 6–8 weeks. Rejected manuscripts returned with S.A.S.E.

Payment: $50 upon publication.

Copyright: By the journal. Permission to reprint is required.

AMERICAN IMAGO: A PSYCHOANALYTIC JOURNAL FOR
CULTURE, SCIENCE, AND THE ARTS
Department of English, Rutgers University, P. O. Box 5054, New
Brunswick, NJ 08903-5054. Rates: $33 per year. Founded 1939. Sponsored by the Association for Applied Psychoanalysis and Rutgers University. Published quarterly.

Major Field(s) of Interest: The major focus of the journal is the interrelationship of psychoanalysis and culture and the applications of psychoanalysis to the humanities. The journal publishes essays in many fields if they are oriented psychoanalytically to the subjects in which it specializes.

Manuscript Information: Articles of 20-40 pages. Style: MLA with endnotes, Chicago, or APA. 3 copies of manuscript required. Report in 2-3 months. Rejected manuscripts returned with S.A.S.E.

Payment: 20 copies.

Indexed In: MLA International Bibliography.

Copyright: By Johns Hopkins University Press. Authors may reprint with permission.

*AMERICAN LITERARY HISTORY
Department of English, University of Wisconsin, Madison, WI 53706.
Rates: $24.50 per year individuals. $46.00 per year institutions. Founded
1989. Sponsored by the Department of English, University of Wisconsin,
Madison. Published quarterly.

Major Field(s) of Interest: Critical and scholarly articles on literary history, rhetorical theory, literary theory, major figures, philosophy, history, cultural studies, and drama. Journal reviews books.

Manuscript Information: Articles of 20-40 pages. Book reviews up to 10 pages. Style: MLA. 3 copies of manuscript required. Report in 1-4 months. Rejected manuscripts returned with S.A.S.E.

Payment: 2 copies plus 25 offprints.

Indexed In: MLA International Bibliography.

Copyright: By the journal. No charge to reprint.

AMERICAN LITERARY REALISM, 1870-1910
Department of English, University of New Mexico, Albuquerque, NM
87131. Rates: $25 per year domestic. $31 per year foreign. Founded
1967. Sponsored by the English Department, the University of New
Mexico, and the McFarland Publishers. Published 3 times per year.

Major Field(s) of Interest: Critical, biographical, and bibliographical articles, notes, and reviews that concentrate on American writers active between 1870 and 1910. Journal reviews books and publishes notes.

Manuscript Information: Articles of 5,000 words; reviews of 1,500 words. Style: MLA, Second Edition. Notes should follow text. 2 copies of manuscript required. Prepare manuscript for blind submission. Report in approximately 3 months. Rejected manuscripts returned with S.A.S.E.

Payment: 2 copies of the journal and 10 offprints of the article.

Indexed In: Abstracts of English Studies.

Copyright: By McFarland & Company, Inc. for Volume 19, Number 1 and forward. Reprinting is on a fee basis with permission from the publisher.

AMERICAN LITERATURE: A JOURNAL OF LITERARY HISTORY, CRITICISM, AND BIBLIOGRAPHY

404 Perkins Library, Duke University, Durham, NC 27706. Rates: $20 per year individuals, $35 per year institutions. Founded 1929. Sponsored by the American Literature Section of the Modern Language Association and Duke University Press.

Major Field(s) of Interest: Historical, critical, scholarly, and bibliographical articles on American literature. Articles should represent additions to knowledge or fresh critical appraisals based upon scholarly study. Journal reviews books, but unsolicited books reviews are not accepted.

Manuscript Information: Articles up to 30 pages. Notes up to 1,500 words. Book reviews up to 500 words. Style: *MLA Style Sheet* (1977) with endnotes. Submit original manuscript, double-spaced throughout including quotations and footnotes. Leave ample margins on every page and place footnotes on separate sheets following the text. Report in 3–4 months. Rejected manuscripts returned with S.A.S.E.

Payment: 1 copy of the journal and 50 offprints. No reprints for book reviews.

Indexed In: Abstracts of English Studies, America: History and Life, Arts and Humanities Citation Index, Book Review Digest, Book Review Index, Current Book Review Citations, Current Contents, Historical Abstracts, Humanities Index, Index to Book Reviews in the Humanities, Literary Criticism Register, MHRA Annual Bibliography of English Language and Literature, MLA International Bibliography.

Copyright: By Duke University Press.

AMERICAN PERIODICALS: A JOURNAL OF HISTORICAL, CRITICAL, AND BIBLIOGRAPHICAL COMMENTARY

Department of English, University of North Texas, P. O. Box 5096, Denton, TX 76203–5096. Rates: $15 per year (includes membership in the Research Society for American Periodicals). Founded Fall 1990. Sponsored by the Journals Division of the University of North Texas

Press and the Department of English, University of North Texas. Published annually.

Major Field(s) of Interest: The journal is an annual publication devoted exclusively to scholarship and criticism relating to any aspect of American magazines and newspapers: scholarly, literary, bibliographic, historical. Journal reviews books in the subject area.

Manuscript Information: Articles of 2,500–6,500 words. Book reviews up to 500 words. Style: MLA. Prefer footnotes to be parenthetical. 2 copies of manuscripts preferred along with a diskette specifying the word processing system. Report in 60 days. Rejected manuscripts returned with S.A.S.E.

Payment: None.

Indexed In: MLA International Bibliography, MHRA.

Copyright: By the journal. Reprint with permission only.

THE AMERICAN SCHOLAR

1811 Q Street, N.W., Washington, D.C. 20009. Rates: $21 per year. Founded 1932. Sponsored by the United Chapters of Phi Beta Kappa. Published quarterly.

Major Field(s) of Interest: The journal is interested in articles on subjects in the arts, sciences, social sciences, and literature of general interest. The journal is a general intellectual quarterly focused on current affairs, the culture scene, politics, the arts, religion, and science. Articles should be written in a clear unpedantic style for an intelligent audience. Journal reviews books.

Manuscript Information: Articles of 3,000–4,000 words preferred. Book reviews of 1,500–2,000 words. Style: Chicago. Report in 2 weeks–2 months. Rejected manuscripts returned with S.A.S.E.

Payment: Up to $500 for articles, $100 for book reviews, $50 for poems plus 3 copies of the issue for articles and poems and 2 copies for book reviews.

Indexed In: Readers' Guide.

Copyright: By the author. Reprinting by permission only.

AMERICAN TRANSCENDENTAL QUARTERLY: A JOURNAL OF NEW ENGLAND WRITERS

Department of English, University of Rhode Island, Kingston, RI 02881–0812. Rates: $20 per year. Founded 1969. Sponsored by the University of Rhode Island. Published quarterly.

Major Field(s) of Interest: The journal is interested in authors and literary works of nineteenth-century American culture and society as well as nontechnical articles on all aspects of New England.

Manuscript Information: Articles of 3,000–7,000 words. No length restrictions on notes. Style: MLA. Report in 2–4 months. Rejected manuscripts returned with S.A.S.E.

Payment: Copies.

Copyright: By the University of Rhode Island.

ANAIS: AN INTERNATIONAL JOURNAL

P. O. Box 276, Becket, MA 01223. Rates: $7.50 per year. Foreign $8.50. Sponsored by the Anais Nin Foundation. Published annually.

Major Field(s) of Interest: Critical biographical material about Anaïs Nin and her circle, Henry Miller, Otto Rank, Antonin Artaud, et al., both in the United States and Europe. The journal is also interested in women's studies, psychology, diary writing, modern novel, French and Japanese literature surrealism, and film. Suggest that contributors query editor before submitting manuscripts since all submissions are arranged with the editor. The editor invites suggestions for suitable material. Journal reviews books, but all book reviews are solicited.

Manuscript Information: No length restrictions on articles, notes, or book reviews. Style: See publication for content and style. Report in 1 month. Rejected manuscripts returned with S.A.S.E.

Payment: Copies.

Indexed In: American Humanities Index, MLA International Bibliography.

Copyright: By the editor. Permission from the editor required.

*ANALYTICAL & ENUMERATIVE BIBLIOGRAPHY

Department of English, Northern Illinois University, Dekalb, IL 60115. Rates: $12 per year individuals. $17 per year institutions. Founded 1977. Sponsored by the Bibliographical Society of Northern Illinois. Published quarterly.

Major Field(s) of Interest: Scholarly articles, notes, and book reviews on the bibliography (enumerative, descriptive, historical, analytical), textual criticism, and publishing history of English and American literature.

Manuscript Information: No length limitations on articles, notes, or book reviews. Style: Prefer MLA, but any standard documentation style is accepted. Report in 1–2 months. Rejected manuscripts returned with S.A.S.E.

Payment: 5 copies.

Indexed In: MLA International Bibliography, ABELL, YWES.

Copyright: By the author. Acknowledgement required in reprinting.

ANNUALE MEDIAEVALE
Department of English, Duquesne University, Pittsburgh, PA 15282.
Founded 1960. Sponsored by Duquesne University. Published annually.

Major Field(s) of Interest: The journal publishes articles that provide
new insights into all aspects of medieval literature and culture.

Manuscript Information: Articles up to 10,000 words. Style: MLA.
Report in 2 months. Rejected manuscripts returned with comments with
S.A.S.E.

Payment: Offprints.

Copyright: By the journal.

ANQ: A QUARTERLY JOURNAL OF
SHORT ARTICLES, NOTES, AND REVIEWS
Department of English, University of Kentucky, Lexington, KY 40506.
Rates: $14 per year. Founded January 1988 (formerly AMERICAN NOTES
AND QUERIES, founded 1962). Sponsored by the Department of English,
University of Kentucky. Published quarterly.

Major Field(s) of Interest: The journal prints short articles and notes
based on new bibliographical, biographical, linguistic, lexicographical,
and textual research in English and American language and literature. It
also publishes reviews of critical studies. The journal concentrates increas-
ingly on reviews of new editions, reference works, and scholarly bibliographies. The journal also publishes queries related to scholarly research;
replies to queries should be sent to the editor for publication in future
issues.

Manuscript Information: Articles up to 1,600 words in length. Reviews of 300–800 words. Style: MLA (1988). Report within 4 weeks.
Rejected manuscripts returned with S.A.S.E.

Payment: 2 copies of the issue.

*Indexed In: Book Review Index, The Year's Work in English, Annual
Bibliography of English Language and Literature, MHRA, MLA Interna-
tional Bibliography, Victorian Studies, American Literary Scholarship,
Old English Newsletter, Review of Reviews.*

Copyright: By the journal.

*ARIEL: A REVIEW OF INTERNATIONAL ENGLISH LITERATURE
Department of English, University of Calgary, 2500 University Drive,
NW, Calgary, Alberta, T2N 1N4, Canada. Rates: $12 per year individu-
als. $18 per year institutions. Founded 1970. Sponsored by the Univer-
sity of Calgary. Published quarterly.

Major Field(s) of Interest: Comparative critical studies of international English Literature. The journal seeks to give global representation

to literatures in the English language through critical and scholarly studies, original poems, and poems in translation.

Manuscript Information: Up to 5,000 words in length for articles. Style: *MLA Style Sheet* (Second Edition). Report in 1 month. Rejected manuscripts returned with S.A.S.E. and Canadian stamps or International Reply Coupons.

Payment: Copies.

Indexed In: Humanities Index, MLA International Bibliography, Arts and Humanities Citation Index, Canadian Literature Index, Bowker Serials Bibliography.

Copyright: By the Board of Governors, the University of Calgary.

ARIZONA ENGLISH BULLETIN

English Department, Box 6032, Northern Arizona University, Flagstaff, AZ 86011. Rates: $20 per year individuals. $25 per year institutions. Sponsored by the Arizona English Teachers Association. Published annually.

Major Field(s) of Interest: The journal is interested in essays that address problems in English and language arts education, K–16, research and theory on literary subjects. The journal also publishes essays on personal opinion and poetry and fiction. Check current issues for upcoming themes.

Manuscript Information: Articles up to 15 pages. Style: MLA and APA. Report in 8–10 weeks. Rejected manuscripts returned with S.A.S.E.

Payment: 2 copies.

Copyright: By the journal.

*THE ARNOLDIAN: STUDIES IN VICTORIAN NON-FICTION PROSE

English Department, U.S. Naval Academy, Annapolis, MD 21402. Rates: $8 per year individuals. $20 per year institutions. Founded 1973. Sponsored by the U.S. Naval Academy. Published semiannually.

Major Field(s) of Interest: The journal publishes short articles, notes, and bibliographical material relating to the works of Matthew Arnold and Victorian nonfiction. It also publishes essay-reviews on subjects unrelated to Arnold and his circle, but focuses on Victorian literature. The journal is especially interested in material related to mid-Victorian nonfictional prose. Journal reviews books.

Manuscript Information: Articles of 25–30 double-spaced pages. Notes of 2–3 pages. Book reviews of 500–1,000 words. Style: MLA with endnotes. 2 copies of manuscript requested. Report in 4–12 weeks. Rejected manuscripts returned with S.A.S.E.

Payment: Copies.

Bibliographical Issue: "Review of Scholarship" published annually.
Indexed In: MLA International Bibliography. LITIR Database.
Copyright: By the author. Reprints approved on request.

AVALON TO CAMELOT

P. O. Box 6236, Evanston, IL 60204. Rates: $20 per year. Founded 1983. Alan Lupack, Editor. Published irregularly.

Major Field(s) of Interest: The range of Arthurian studies from ancient Celtic lore through medieval romance to contemporary literary and cinematic interpretation. The search for the historical Arthur in history and archaeology and the art historical aspect of the legend are regularly included. Journal reviews books.

Manuscript Information: Articles from 750–1,500 words. Book reviews up to 750 words. Notes up to 150 words. Style: Chicago. 2 copies of manuscript required. Report in 90 days. Rejected manuscripts returned with S.A.S.E.

Payment: Copies.
Copyright: By the journal.

THE BAKER STREET JOURNAL:
AN IRREGULAR QUARTERLY OF SHERLOCKIANA

11333 Big Bend Boulevard, St. Louis, MO. 63122. Business Office: Fordham University Press, University Box L, Bronx, NY 10458–5172. Rates: $15 per year; $17 foreign. $5 single copy. Founded 1946. Sponsored by The Baker Street Irregulars and Fordham University Press. Published quarterly.

Major Field(s) of Interest: Articles about Sherlock Holmes and the Sherlockian Scene, the Sherlock Holmes canon, Conan Doyle, and Victoriana as they related to Holmes. Also news from the Scion Societies of The Baker Street Irregulars as well as reviews of Sherlockian books. Each issue carries reviews written in-house, news, and notes. While BSJ carries (and encourages) a wide variety of serious literary criticism of the Sherlock Holmes canon, much of its contents comprise the peculiar intellectual pastime known as Sherlockian Higher Criticism. Prospective contributors may be well-advised to consult a sample issue to discover the nature of such criticism.

Manuscript Information: Articles from 500–3,750 words. Style: New MLA documentation form preferred, but consult latest issue for sample. Report in 6–8 weeks. Rejected manuscripts returned with S.A.S.E.

Payment: 5 copies.
Copyright: By The Baker Street Irregulars. Write to the publisher for permission to reprint.

THE BARBARA PYM NEWSLETTER
Department of English, University of Tulsa, 600 South College Avenue,
Tulsa, OK 74104–3189 or Drawer F, St. Bonaventure, NY 14778. Rates:
$10 per year individuals. $12 per year institutions and overseas. Founded
1981. Sponsored by the editors: Mary Anne Schofield and Doreen A.
Saar. Published 2 times per year.

Major Field(s) of Interest. Articles and essays which critically examine Pym's works and those of her circle. Journal reviews books.

Manuscript Information: Articles up to 10 pages. Notes up to 250
words. Book reviews up to 2 pages. Style: *MLA Style Manual.* Report in
8–10 weeks. Rejected manuscripts returned with readers's comments
with S.A.S.E.

Payment: 2 copies.

Indexed In: MLA International Bibliography.

Copyright: By the editors.

*BIOGRAPHY: AN INTERDISCIPLINARY QUARTERLY
Department of English, University of Hawaii, Honolulu, HI 96822.
Rates: $20 per year individuals. $24 per year institutions. Founded 1978.
Sponsored by the Center for Biographical Research. University of Hawaii.
Published quarterly.

Major Field(s) of Interest: Articles, essays, and reviews in the field of
biographical scholarship. The journal acts as a forum to stimulate the
criticism and theory of life-writing by presenting new information, sharper
definitions, fresh interpretations, and well-argued evaluations. The journal
welcomes contributions from all points of view on all topics concerning
life-writings, but articles linking biography to aesthetics, historiography,
the other arts, and general concepts in the social sciences and sciences are
especially encouraged. The journal publishes an annual bibliography.

Manuscript Information: Articles of 2,500–7,500 words. Notes of
250–1,000 words. Book reviews of 250–1,000 words. Style: "of the
writer's profession." 2 copies of manuscript required. Report in 2–3
months. Rejected manuscripts returned with S.A.S.E. Abstracts are encouraged and included in the table of contents.

Payment: 5 copies of issue.

*Indexed In: MLA International Bibliography, American Humanities
Index, ABC, Ulrich.*

Copyright: By the Biographical Research Center. Reprints granted
without charge provided 2 copies of reprint are given.

*BLAKE/AN ILLUSTRATED QUARTERLY

Department of English, University of Rochester, Rochester, NY 14627 or Department of English, University of California, Berkeley, CA 94720. Rates: $20 per year individuals. $40 per year institutions. Founded 1967. Sponsored by the University of Rochester, Department of English. Published quarterly.

Major Field(s) of Interest: Scholarly and critical material on the life and work of William Blake and certain of his contemporaries and followers. The journal publishes news, essays, notes, discussion, and bibliographical tools, reviews, queries, and reproductions of Blake's works. Journal reviews books, but unsolicited book reviews are not accepted.

Manuscript Information: Articles over 14 pages. Notes up to 14 pages. Book reviews no longer than 10 pages. Style: *MLA Style Manual* with endnotes. 2 copies of manuscript required. Report in 2–3 months. Rejected manuscripts returned with S.A.S.E.

Payment: Copies.

Indexed In: MLA International Bibliography, MHRA Annual Bibliography, The Romantic Movement: A Selective and Critical Bibliography, American Humanities Index, Arts and Humanities Citation Index, Current Contents.

Copyright: By the journal. Journal freely gives permission to reprint.

THE BOSTON REVIEW

33 Harrison Avenue, Boston, MA 02111. Rates: $15 per year individuals. $18 per year institutions. Founded 1975. Sponsored by the Boston Critic, Inc. Published bimonthly.

Major Field(s) of Interest: Critical articles on literature, the arts, and culture with an emphasis on American literature and writers. The journal considers material on music, dance, theater, painting, film, and photography. Submissions should be suited to an audience of authors, scholars, and members of the literary community, and be well-written, concise, and respectful to the generalist. Nonfiction submissions may be concerned with any subject informing the realm of contemporary culture. The journal has some preference for short poems. Journal reviews books.

Manuscript Information: Articles of 1,500–5,000 words. Book reviews up to 800 words. Style: Chicago. Report in 6–8 weeks. Rejected manuscripts returned with S.A.S.E.

Payment: Ranges from $50 to $500 plus copies.

Indexed In: Book Review Index, Gale Research Company, Index of American Periodicals.

Copyright: The journal acquires first serial rights on accepted pieces. The copyright automatically reverts to the author after publication.

*BUCKNELL REVIEW: A SCHOLARLY JOURNAL OF
LETTERS, ARTS AND SCIENCES
9 Bucknell Hall, Bucknell University, Lewisburg, PA 17837. Rates: $21
per issue. Founded 1949. Sponsored by Bucknell University. Published
biannually.

Major Field(s) of Interest: A scholarly interdisciplinary journal, each
issue is devoted to a major theme. Recent and forthcoming issues are devoted to special topics and contain papers solicited from eminent scholars
or from those known to be working in the field. This policy will continue for the foreseeable future.

Manuscript Information: Articles of 20–25 double-spaced pages.
Style: Chicago with endnotes. Report in 6–8 weeks. Rejected manuscripts returned with S.A.S.E.

Payment: 1 copy of the issue.

Copyright: By the journal.

BULLETIN OF BIBLIOGRAPHY
Meckler Publishing, 11 Ferry Lane West, Westport, CT 06880. Rates:
$75 per year. Founded 1895. Sponsored by Meckler Publishing. Pub-
lished quarterly.

Major Field(s) of Interest: All issues are bibliographies on a wide
range of topics in the humanities and social sciences. Journal welcomes
submissions on topics of general interest that contain material not accessible through published sources. Bulletin publishes book reviews.

Manuscript Information: Articles up to 60 pages in length. Notes of
100 words. Book reviews up to 1,000 words. Style: MLA, Chicago. 2
copies of manuscripts required. Include a brief introduction outlining
scope of article and citing previous bibliographical research on the subject. Report in 4–6 weeks. Rejected manuscripts returned with S.A.S.E.

Payment: Copies.

Indexed In: American Literature, Annual Bibliography of English
Language and Literature, Bibliographical Index, MLA International Bibliography, Victorian Studies, Year's Work in English, American History
and Life, Historical Abstracts.

Copyright: By Meckler Publishing. Reprinting by author is permitted.

THE BULLETIN OF THE WEST VIRGINIA ASSOCIATION
OF COLLEGE ENGLISH TEACHERS
Department of English, Marshall University, Huntington, WV 25701.
Founded 1955. Sponsored by Marshall University and the West Virginia
Association of College Teachers of English. Published annually.

Major Field(s) of Interest: The journal publishes papers and book reviews in all traditional areas of scholarship and criticism in all periods. Journal reviews books.

Manuscript Information: Articles up to 5,000 words. Book reviews of 400–800 words. Style: Chicago or MLA. Report in 2–5 months. Rejected manuscripts returned with S.A.S.E.

Payment: Copies.

Copyright: By the author.

THE BYRON JOURNAL

Department of English Language and Literature, University of Liverpool, P. O. Box 147, Liverpool, L69 5BX, England. Rates: $12 per year individuals. $10 per year institutions. (U.S. members order through the Byron Society, The American Committee, 259 New Jersey Avenue, Collingswood, NJ 08108.) Rates include membership in The Byron Society. Founded 1973. Sponsored by The Byron Society, Byron House, 6 Gertrude Street, London, SW10 OJN, England. Published annually.

Major Field(s) of Interest: Scholarly and critical articles, essays, and book reviews about the life and works of the English Romantic poet, Lord Byron (1788–1824) and his literary circle. Articles on related Romantic topics will also be considered. Preference will be given to those which contain new material or offer new insights and to those which are less than 6,000 words. Journal reviews books. Books for review should be sent to the Review Editor, Department of English, University of Leicester, Leicester, LE1 7RH, England. Contributors are restricted to members of The Byron Society.

Manuscript Information: Articles of 10–15 typed pages. Notes up to 4 pages. Book reviews up to 500 words. Style: *MHRA Style Sheet* with footnotes at end of article. Report in 3–6 months. 2 copies of manuscript required. Rejected manuscripts are returned only if there is a specific request to do so and correspondence includes S.A.S.E.

Payment: 1 copy of publication.

Indexed In: MLA International Bibliography, Keats-Shelley Bibliography.

Copyright: By The Byron Society. No reprints are permitted.

THE BYRON SOCIETY NEWSLETTER

Byron Society, American Committee, 259 New Jersey Avenue, Collingswood, NJ 08108. Rates: Included in membership in The Byron Society. Founded 1973. Sponsored by The Byron Society.

Major Field(s) of Interest: General information articles, notes, news items, scholarly profiles, seminar and tour reports about The Byron Society and about the English Romantic poet Lord Byron and his literary circle.

Manuscript Information: Articles of 8–25 double-spaced typed pages. Notes of 2–5 pages. News items ("fillers") 3–6 paragraphs. Style: *MLA Style Sheet.* Footnotes, where needed, should be parenthetical. Contributors restricted to The Byron Society.

Payment: 5 copies of issue.

Indexed In: Keats-Shelley Bibliography.

Copyright: By the newsletter.

THE CAMBRIDGE QUARTERLY

c/o The Forbes Mellon Library, Clare College, Cambridge, CB2 ITL, England. Rates: $13 per year members. $19 per year institutions. Founded 1965. Sponsored by the Oxford University Press. Published quarterly.

Major Field(s) of Interest: Articles and reviews on English, American, and classical European literatures primarily, but also on any subject of interest to the general reader. Journal reviews books.

Manuscript Information: No restrictions on length for articles. Book reviews of 2,000–3,000 words. See copy of journal for style. 3 copies of manuscript required. Report in 2–3 months. Rejected manuscripts returned with S.A.S.E.

Payment: Copy of the journal and offprints.

Copyright: By the journal.

THE CEA CRITIC

CEA Publications, Department of English, Youngstown State University, Youngstown, OH 44555-0001. Rates: $25 per year (includes CEA FORUM). Founded 1939. Sponsored by the College English Association, Rochester, NY. Published 3 times per year.

Major Field(s) of Interest: The journal publishes articles that focus on literary texts: fiction, poetry, nonfiction prose, and film, and literature or composition essays that focus on classroom activities. The journal is also interested in articles that apply critical theory to what and how teachers teach in university classrooms.

Manuscript Information: Articles of 15–25 typed pages. Style: MLA with endnotes. 2 hard copies plus WordPerfect 5.1 or ASCII file on IBM-compatible disk. Report in 2 months. Rejected manuscripts returned with S.A.S.E.

Payment: 3 issues of the journal.

Copyright: By College English Association. Permission to reprint freely granted.

The CEA Forum

CEA Publications, Department of English, Youngstown State University Youngstown, OH 44555–0001. Rates: $25 per year (includes The CEA Critic). Founded 1939. Sponsored by the College English Association, Rochester, NY. Published 2 times per year.

Major Field(s) of Interest: The journal publishes opinion pieces on professional and pedagogical issues, information and opinion on the state of the profession, critical problems facing the discipline and the positing of possible solutions, and discussion of innovations, changes, and advancements in the teaching of English. The journal also publishes announcements of coming meetings and news items.

Manuscript Information: Articles up to 6 typed pages. Style: MLA with endnotes. 2 copies required plus WordPerfect 5.1 or ASCII file on IBM-compatible disk. Report in 6 months. Rejected manuscripts returned with S.A.S.E.

Payment: 3 copies of the journal.

Copyright: By the College English Association. Permission to reprint freely granted.

CCTE Studies

Conference of College Teachers of English, Department of English. University of North Texas, P. O. Box 13827, Denton, TX 76203. Rates: $5 per year. Founded 1935. Sponsored by the Conference of College Teachers of English (CCTE). Published annually.

Major Field(s) of Interest: Articles on literature and teaching literature, including submissions on critical theory, genre, and style. The journal also publishes articles on rhetoric, composition, and technical writing, including submissions on stylistics, linguistics, and writing pedagogy. The journal also publishes articles on creative writing.

Manuscript Information: Articles of 2–10 double-spaced pages. Style: MLA. 3 copies of manuscript required. Submit 3 copies of a 100–word abstract. Contributors must be members of CCTE and paper must have been read at CCTE convention and not have been previously published. Report in 2 months. Rejected manuscripts returned with S.A.S.E.

Payment: 5 copies.

Copyright: By CCTE. Authors are freely granted permission to reprint with usual credit line.

*The Centennial Review

312 Linton Hall, East Lansing, MI 48824–1044, Rates: $10 per year. Founded 1956. Sponsored by the College of Arts and Letters, Michigan State University. Published 3 times per year.

Major Field(s) of Interest: Articles concerned with the interrelations among the disciplines, cultural study, and social implications of the natural and physical sciences, social sciences, humanities, and arts. The journal avoids extremes of specialization and popularization. Authors should attempt to convey the results and implications of specialized study in a language understandable to persons in all fields of the liberal arts. Articles may deal with particular scholarly methods, research techniques, or intellectual attitudes, elucidate interrelationships between established or chronically exclusive disciplines, or set forth historical or critical perspectives on current problems and ideas. Journal reviews books.

Manuscript Information: Articles of 17–30 pages. Book reviews up to 750 words. Style: MLA with parenthetical documentation and list of works cited. 2 copies of manuscript required. Report in 2–3 months. Rejected manuscripts returned with S.A.S.E.

Payment: 2 copies of the issue plus 1 year's subscription.

Indexed In: Abstracts of English Studies, American Bibliography, Slavic and East European Studies, American History and Life, American Humanities Index, Arts and Humanities Citation Index, Current Contents, Arts and Humanities, Granger Annuals, Historical Abstracts, Index of American Periodical Verse, Indiana Book Review, Review of Humanities Language and Language Behavior Abstracts, MLA International Bibliography.

Copyright: By the journal. Permission to reprint granted freely by the journal with permission of the author.

THE CHARLES LAMB BULLETIN

9 Dale View Gardens, Crawcrook, Ryton Tyne and Wear, NE40 4ED, England. Rates: £8 British. $40 per year individuals. £12 British. $21 per year institutions. Founded: New Series 1972. Sponsored by The Charles Lamb Society, London. Published quarterly.

Major Field(s) of Interest: The journal publishes articles and notes on the life, work, and times of Charles Lamb and his circle and appropriate aspects of the English Romantic movement in literature and the arts. Journal reviews books.

Manuscript Information: Articles of 5,000–6,000 words. Notes of 500–1,000 words. Book reviews up to 1,000 words. Style: MLA with notes at end of article. Report in 1 month. Rejected manuscripts returned with S.A.S.E.

Payment: 6 copies of the Bulletin.

Copyright: By The Charles Lamb Society. Permission to reprint granted on request by the author or the author's representatives.

*THE CHAUCER REVIEW: A JOURNAL OF MEDIEVAL STUDIES
AND LITERARY CRITICISM
117 Burrowes Building, Pennsylvania State University, University Park, PA 16802. Founded 1966. Sponsored by the MLA Chaucer Group. Published quarterly.

Major Field(s) of Interest: Scholarly and critical studies on Chaucer and other Middle English authors.

Manuscript Information: Articles of 15–30 pages. Notes from 2–7 pages. Style: MLA. Translate extensive foreign language quotations in footnotes; identify citations of medieval works appearing in a collection according to the division of the original and the volume and page (or column) of the collection. Submit typescript. Report in 6 months.

Payment: Offprints.

Copyright: By Pennsylvania State University.

CHILDREN'S LITERATURE: AN INTERNATIONAL JOURNAL, INC.
Department of English, U–25, University of Connecticut, 337 Mansfield Road, Storrs, CT 06269–1025. Rates: $40.00 per year cloth. $13.95 per year paper. Founded 1972. Sponsored by The Modern Language Association Division on Children's Literature and the Children's Literature Association. Published annually.

Major Field(s) of Interest: The journal welcomes comparative, critical, and theoretical studies of all aspects of children's literature in all periods. The journal is less interested in explication of specific texts than it is in studies with broader implications or in articles which incorporate the theoretical with the specific. Journal reviews books.

Manuscript Information: Articles of 25–30 double-spaced pages. Book reviews of 3–6 pages. Style: MLA with endnotes double-spaced. 2 copies of manuscript required. No dot-matrix printouts. Submit original typescript and 1 copy. Word count on manuscripts and short contributor's note are requested. Report in 2–4 months. Rejected manuscripts returned with S.A.S.E.

Payment: 1 copy of the journal and 1 unbound offprint.

Indexed In: MLA International Bibliography.

Copyright: By the Children's Literature Association. Permission to reprint must be requested.

CHILDREN'S LITERATURE ASSOCIATION QUARTERLY
Department of English, University of Calgary, 2500 University Drive, N.W., Calgary, Alberta, T2N 1N4, Canada. Rates: $40 per year. Founded 1979. Sponsored by the Children's Literature Association. Published quarterly.

Major Field(s) of Interest: The journal considers articles on all aspects of scholarly research on children's literature and related aspects of the field: analysis of texts, theory, pedagogy, children's folklore, illustrations in children's books, and the teaching of children's literature. The journal includes a Bulletin Board page that prints notices of conferences, awards, scholarships, and library resources useful to readers. Journal reviews books.

Manuscript Information: Articles of 3,000–5,000 words. Book reviews of 250–3,000 words. Style: *MLA Handbook For Writers of Research Papers* (Second Edition). All notes are endnotes (see *Handbook,* 5.8.4.). 2 copies of manuscript required. Report in 2 months. Rejected manuscripts returned with S.A.S.E.

Payment: 1 copy of the issue in which the article appears.

Copyright: By the Children's Literature Association. Reprinting may be granted upon request.

*CHRISTIANITY AND LITERATURE

Department of English, Seattle Pacific University, Seattle, WA 98119. Rates: $15 per year individuals. $20 per year institutions. Founded 1951 as a newsletter and 1973 as a quarterly journal. Sponsored by the Conference on Christianity and Literature. Published quarterly.

Major Field(s) of Interest: Devoted to the scholarly exploration of how literature engages Christian thought, experience, and practice. The journal publishes articles in all areas and periods of literature with an emphasis on the relationship between literature and Christianity. Although the journal presupposes no particular theological orientation, it respects an orthodox understanding of Christianity as an historically defined faith. Contributions appropriate for submission should demonstrate a keen awareness of their own critical assumptions in addressing significant issues of literary history, interpretation, and theory. Journal reviews books, but unsolicited book reviews are not accepted.

Manuscript Information: Articles of 4,000–9,000 words. Book reviews up to 1,500 words. Style: MLA (1985) with "Works Cited." 2 copies of manuscript required. Report in 3 months. Rejected manuscripts returned with S.A.S.E.

Payment: 2 copies of the issue. Offprints at modest fee.

Indexed In: MLA International Bibliography, MHRA.

Copyright: By the Conference on Christianity and Literature. Authors are freely granted permission to reprint with the usual credit line and acknowledgement.

*Cimarron Review

205 Morrill Hall, Oklahoma State University, Stillwater, OK 74078–0135. Rates: $12 per year ($15 in Canada). Founded 1967. Sponsored by the College of Arts and Sciences, Oklahoma State University. Published quarterly.

Major Field(s) of Interest: Articles on arts and letters from any period. The journal also publishes poetry and nonfiction. Journal reviews books. Journal does not print religious or political material.

Manuscript Information: No length restrictions for articles and non-fiction. Book reviews up to 500 words. Style: MLA. Report in 6–8 weeks for fiction and nonfiction; 4 weeks for poetry. Rejected manuscripts returned with S.A.S.E.

Payment: 2 copies of the issue plus 1 year's subscription.

Indexed In: MLA International Bibliography, Index of American Periodical Verse, The International Directory of Little Magazines, The American Humanities Index.

Copyright: By the Board of Regents, Oklahoma State University. Reprint permission granted freely upon request.

*Classical and Modern Literature: A Quarterly

CML, Inc., P. O. Box 629, Terre Haute, IN. 47808–0629. Rates: $16 per year individuals. Founded 1980. Published quarterly.

Major Field(s) of Interest: The journal publishes articles that explore the interrelationship between classical and modern literature. Journal reviews books.

Manuscript Information: Articles up to 25 pages. Notes of 3–5 pages. Book reviews up to 5 pages. Style: Chicago. 2 copies of manuscript required. Report in 3 months. Rejected manuscripts returned with S.A.S.E.

Payment: Offprints.

Indexed In: Book Review Index. MLA International Bibliography, Literary Criticism Register, and others.

Copyright: By the journal. Reprint rights granted free.

*CLIO: A Journal of Literature, History, and the Philosophy of History

Indiana University-Purdue University, Fort Wayne, IN 46805. Rates: $15 per year individuals. $40 per year institutions. Founded 1971. Sponsored by Indiana University-Purdue University at Fort Wayne. Published quarterly.

Major Field(s) of Interest: CLIO is the only English-language quarterly that deals with three interrelated topics: literature as informed by historical understandings; historical writings considered as literature; philosophy of history, speculative and analytic. The journal is also interested in speculative philosophy of history and in particular with the thought of Hegel from various perspectives and interdisciplinary applications.

Manuscript Information: Articles of 4,000–10,000 words. Notes of 100–300 words. Book reviews up to 1,200 words. Style: Chicago. 2 copies of manuscript required. Submit original typescript plus 1 copy. Report in 3 months. Rejected manuscripts returned with S.A.S.E.

Payment: 2 copies of the journal. Offprints available at modest fee.

Indexed In: Historical Abstracts, America: History and Life, Western Historical Quarterly, The Philosopher's Index, Community Development Abstracts, Language Behavior Abstracts, Sociological Abstracts, Abstracts of English Studies.

Copyright: By the journal. Full rights granted author for reprinting.

*CLUES: A JOURNAL OF DETECTION

Popular Culture Association, Bowling Green University, Bowling Green, OH 43403. Rates: $12.50 per year. Founded 1980. No sponsor. Published 2 times per year.

Major Field(s) of Interest: The journal is devoted to detection in the widest sense of the word and as evidenced in all the media and in all aspects of culture. Journal reviews books.

Manuscript Information: Articles of 15–20 pages. Notes of 1–2 pages. Book reviews of 1–2 pages. Style: MLA (Revised Edition) with footnotes embedded in the text. 2 copies of manuscript required. Report in 3 months. Rejected manuscripts returned with S.A.S.E.

Payment: 25 offprints.

Copyright: By the journal. Permission to reprint is granted upon request.

*COLLEGE COMPOSITION AND COMMUNICATION

1111 Kenyon Road, Urbana, IL 61801. Rates: $12 per year (NCTE membership is a prerequisite). Founded 1950. Sponsored by The National Conference on College Composition and Communication of the National Council of Teachers of English. Published quarterly.

Major Field(s) of Interest: The journal publishes articles dealing with the theory, practice, history, and politics of composition and its teaching at all college levels. It also is interested in research into the processes and teaching of writing, the preparation of writing teachers, and the relationship of literature, language studies, rhetoric, communication theory and other fields to composition. Journal reviews books, but all book reviews are assigned by the editor.

Manuscript Information: Articles of 3,500–6,500 words. Book reviews up to 500 words. Style: MLA but use month as well as year in citing journals. A brief author's guide is also available. 4 copies of manuscript required. Send original and 3 copies. Report in 6–8 weeks. Rejected manuscripts returned with S.A.S.E.

Payment: 2 copies of the journal. Offprints are available from the printer.

Indexed In: Annual Bibliography of English Language and Literature, Book Review Index, Current Contents, CIJE, Educational Index, Index to Book Reviews in the Humanities, Language and Language Behaviors.

Copyright: By the National Council of Teachers of English. Authors are granted permission to reprint with credit line.

College English

Department of English, University of Massachusetts-Boston, 100 Morrissey Blvd., Boston, MA 02125-3393. Rates: $35 per year individuals (includes NCTE membership). $40 per year institutions. Founded 1938. Sponsored by the National Council of Teachers of English. Published monthly (September through April).

Major Field(s) of Interest: Articles in which scholars address a broad cross section of the profession. Appropriate subjects are literature (including nonfiction), linguistics, literacy, critical theory, reading theory, rhetoric, composition, drama, pedagogy, and professional issues. Journal reviews books, but all book reviews are commissioned by the editor.

Manuscript Information: Articles up to 30 double-spaced typed pages. Book reviews up to 750 words. Style: MLA with no footnotes. 2 copies of manuscript required. Report in 16 weeks. Rejected manuscripts are not returned.

Payment: 2 copies of the issue.

Indexed In: MLA International Bibliography, Current Contents, CIJE, Annual Bibliography of English Language and Literature, Education Index, ERIC, Exceptional Child Education Resources, Index to Book Reviews in the Humanities.

Copyright: Reverts to author upon publication.

*College Literature

544 New Main, West Chester University, West Chester, PA 19383. Rates: $15 per year individuals. $18 per year institutions. Founded 1974. Sponsored by West Chester University. Published triannually.

Major Field(s) of Interest: Articles dealing with British, American, and comparative literatures that are most commonly taught in American colleges and universities and form a loose canon of Western culture. It encourages a variety of approaches to textual analysis and criticism (including political, feminist, and poststructuralist) on English and American literature in addition to Eastern literatures, minority and Third World literatures, oral literature, and interdisciplinary studies (such as anthropology and literature, computers and literature, literature and film). The journal is most receptive to articles which deal with a single literary work. Occasionally, it will publish articles which deal with a cluster of short pieces, or with a single literary idea or movement, or with some particular social or philosophical aspect of literature. Journal reviews books.

Manuscript Information: Articles of 20–30 pages. Notes of 10–15 pages. Book reviews up to 5 pages. Style: MLA with endnotes. 3 copies of manuscript required. Report in 3–4 months. Rejected manuscripts returned with S.A.S.E.

Payment: 1 copy plus 10 offprints.

Indexed In: American Humanities Index, Arts and Humanities Citation Index, Slavic and East European Studies, Research in Word Processing Newsletter, The Year's Work in English Studies, Abstracts of English Studies, Literary Criticism Register, MLA International Bibliography.

Copyright: By the journal. Reprint with permission only.

COMITATUS: A JOURNAL OF MEDIEVAL AND RENAISSANCE STUDIES
Center for Medieval and Renaissance Studies, 212 Royce Hall, UCLA, Los Angeles, CA 90024–1485. Rates: $9.00 per year individuals. $12.50 per year institutions. Founded 1970. Sponsored by the University of California, Los Angeles Center for Medieval and Renaissance Studies. Published quarterly.

Major Field(s) of Interest: Interdisciplinary articles on Medieval and Renaissance literature or any area of Medieval and Renaissance studies which has some bearing on literature, e.g., iconography. Articles are selected by the editorial board consisting of UCLA doctoral students and faculty. Journal reviews books.

Manuscript Information: Articles up to 30 pages maximum. Book reviews up to 750 pages. Style: Chicago. 2 copies of manuscript required. Submit original typescript on non-erasable bond. Lengthy passages in languages other than English should be translated in the text with the original language confined to the notes. Report in 90 days. Rejected manuscripts returned with S.A.S.E.

Payment: None. Offprints may be ordered at nominal rates.

Copyright: By the Regents of the University of California, Los Angeles.

COMMENTARY

American Jewish Committee, 165 East 56 Street, New York, NY 10022. Rates: $39 per year. Founded 1945. Sponsored by the American Jewish Committee. Published monthly.

Major Field(s) of Interest: The journal aims to meet the need for a periodical of significant thought and opinion on Jewish affairs and contemporary political, social, and cultural issues in line with the American Jewish Committee's program to enlighten and clarify public opinion and problems of Jewish concern, to fight bigotry and protect human rights, and to promote Jewish cultural interests and creative achievements in America.

Manuscript Information: Articles of 3,000–7,500 words. Book reviews up to 1,500 words. Style: Chicago. Report in 2 weeks. Rejected manuscripts returned with S.A.S.E.

Payment: 2 copies of the issue plus $500 to $1,000 for articles. $350 for reviews.

Indexed In: Readers' Guide, Book Review Digest, Public Affairs Information Service, Index to Jewish Periodicals, ABC Pol Sci, Historical Abstracts, Religion Index One: Periodicals, Political Science Abstracts, America: History and Life.

Copyright: By the American Jewish Committee. Copyright reverts to author for a small charge.

COMMONWEAL

15 Dutch Street, New York, NY 10038. Rates: $36 per year. Founded 1924. Sponsored by Commonweal Foundation. Published bi-weekly except Christmas-New Year's and July and August.

Major Field(s) of Interest: The journal reports and analyzes current developments in religion, national and world politics, literature, scholarship, and the arts. Journal reviews books.

Manuscript Information: Articles of 1,200–3,000 words. Notes up to 150 words. Book reviews up to 900 words. Style: None. Report in 3 weeks. Rejected manuscripts returned with S.A.S.E.

Payment: 4 copies plus 3¢ a word.

Indexed In: Reader's Guide to Periodical Literature, Catholic Periodical Index, Index of American Periodical Verse, Book Review Digest, Book Review Index.

Copyright: By the journal. Permission to reprint required.

*COMMUNICATIONS FROM THE INTERNATIONAL BRECHT SOCIETY
P. O. Box 7353, Wake Forest University, Winston-Salem, NC 27109.

Rates: $25 per year individuals (includes membership in the IBS). $35 per year institutions. Founded 1971. Sponsored by the International Brecht Society, Inc. Published 2 times per year (January and July).

Major Field(s) of Interest: The journal publishes articles, interviews, conference reports, production reviews, announcements, notes, inquiries, official IBS business, MLA, and ATHE reports, etc.—anything pertaining to the work or life of Bertolt Brecht (1898–1956) with an emphasis on his impact on modern theater.

Manuscript Information: Articles of 12–15 double-spaced pages. Notes of 10–12 pages. Style: MLA with endnotes preferred. Report in 1–2 months. Rejected manuscripts returned with S.A.S.E.

Payment: 2 complimentary copies. More upon request if available.

Indexed In: MLA International Bibliography, Theatre Research Data Center, Germantistik.

Copyright: By the journal. Contents may be reprinted with written consent.

THE COMPARATIST: JOURNAL OF THE
SOUTHERN COMPARATIVE LITERATURE ASSOCIATION

Department of English, Virginia Commonwealth University, Richmond, VA 23284–2005. Rates: $12 per year individuals and institutions. Founded 1977. Sponsored by the Southern Comparative Literature Association. Published annually.

Major Field(s) of Interest: The journal publishes articles in the field of comparative literature with a special emphasis on cross-cultural and interliterary relations. The journal is interested in comparative study of literary and cultural movements, literature and the arts, East-West literary exchanges, transAtlantic and interAmerican literary relations as well as literary criticism, methodology, theory, genre, and period studies. Journal reviews books and accepts papers in English, French, and Spanish. Contributors must be members of the Southern Comparative Literature Association at the time of publication.

Manuscript Information: Articles of 5,000–10,000 words. Book reviews of 800–2,500 words. Style: MLA with endnotes and list of works cited. 2 copies of manuscript required. Report in 2–4 months. Rejected manuscripts returned with S.A.S.E.

Payment: Offprints.

Indexed In: Citation Index, Bibliography International, EBSCO, Humanities Index, Literary Criticism Register, and others.

Copyright: By the journal. Authors are granted permission to reprint with usual credit line.

*COMPARATIVE DRAMA

Department of English, Western Michigan University, Kalamazoo, MI 49008. Rates: $12 per year individuals. $22 per year institutions. Founded 1967. Sponsored by the Department of English, Western Michigan University. Published quarterly.

Major Field(s) of Interest: Drama of all countries and all periods with special interest in medieval drama. The journal is interested in critical studies which are international in spirit and interdisciplinary in scope. Methodology is generally comparative. Journal reviews books, but book reviews are solicited.

Manuscript Information: Articles of 15–35 pages. Notes of 10–14 pages. Book reviews of 2–4 pages. Style: MLA (1970). A style sheet is available from the editors. Scholars wishing to submit articles are advised to examine several recent issues prior to submission. Report in 2–6 weeks. Rejected manuscripts returned with S.A.S.E.

Payment: 2 copies of the issue plus offprints.

Indexed In: MLA International Bibliography.

Copyright: By the journal. Authors may reprint without fee. Other reprint nonexclusive rights assigned upon payment of $100 per article.

COMPARATIVE LITERATURE STUDIES

Department of Comparative Literature, The Pennsylvania State University, 434N Burrowes Building, University Park, PA 16802. Rates: $20 per year individuals. $28 per year institutions. Founded 1963. No sponsor. Published quarterly.

Major Field(s) of Interest: Comparative articles in literary history, the history of ideas, critical theory, relationships between authors, and literary relations within and beyond the Western tradition. One of its regular issues every 2 years concerns East-West relationships. Journal reviews books.

Manuscript Information: Articles of 15–18 pages. Book reviews of 5–6 pages. Style: *MLA Style Manual* (1985) with endnotes, which does not use a "Works Cited" list. 2 copies of manuscript required. Report in 3–4 months. Rejected manuscripts returned with S.A.S.E.

Payment: 25 free offprints for articles. 10 free offprints for book reviews.

Indexed In: H. W. Wilson Company Book Review Index, Information Access Company.

Copyright: By The Pennsylvania State University.

CONNOTATIONS: A JOURNAL FOR CRITICAL DEBATE

Westfälische Wilhelms-Universität, Department of English, Johannisstr.

12–20, 440 Münster, Germany. Rates: Europe DM 53. U.S. and all other countries: $40. Founded 1991. Sponsored by Westfälishche Wilhelms-Universität, Münster/Germany. Published 3 times per year.

Major Field(s) of Interest: The journal wants to encourage scholarly communication in the field of English literature from the Middle English period to the present. It focuses on the semantic and stylistic energy of the language of literature in a historical perspective and aims to represent different approaches. Each issue consists of articles and a forum for discussion. The forum presents research in progress, critical hypotheses, responses to articles published in the journal and elsewhere, or to recent books (instead of the traditional reviews), as well as author's answers to reviews.

Manuscript Information: Articles up to 12,000 words. Responses up to 4,000 words. Style: *MLA Handbook*, 2nd or 3rd edition with notes at end of article. 1 copy of manuscript required plus disk in DOS/Word-Perfect if possible. Report in 2–8 weeks.

Payment: 1 copy and 20 offprints.

Copyright: By the journal. Reprint by arrangement.

*CONRADIANA: A JOURNAL OF JOSEPH CONRAD STUDIES

Department of English, Box 4530, Texas Tech University, Lubbock, TX 79409. Rates: $16 per year individuals. $28 per year institutions. Founded 1968. Sponsored by the Department of English, Texas Tech University. Published 3 times per year (January, May, September).

Major Field(s) of Interest: The journal welcomes articles, notes, and book reviews on any aspect of the life, works, and influence of Joseph Conrad. All submissions must relate in some way to the novelist. Journal reviews books.

Manuscript Information: Articles of 10–40 typescript pages. Notes of 2–10 pages. Book reviews of 2–15 pages. Style: Chicago. 2 copies of manuscript required. Manuscripts should be submitted in hard copy as well as on IBM-Compatible discs, preferably as ASCII files. Report in 60–90 days. Rejected manuscripts returned with S.A.S.E.

Payment: 2 copies of issue and 20 offprints.

Indexed In: Abstracts of English Studies, American Humanities Index, Index to Book Reviews in the Humanities, MLA International Bibliography, Twentieth-Century Literature.

Copyright: By the journal. No charge to author for reprinting and permission granted pro forma.

CONTEMPORARY LITERATURE

Department of English, Helen C. White Hall, 600 N. Park Street, University of Wisconsin, Madison, WI 53706. Rates: $20 individuals. $49 institutions. Founded 1960. Sponsored by the University of Wisconsin Press. Published quarterly.

Major Field(s) of Interest: Articles on all forms of twentieth-century literature, with emphasis on the period from World War II to the present with reviews of scholarly and critical books in the field. Journal specializes in interviews with both established and rising poets and novelists. Journal reviews books, but reviews are solicited.

Manuscript Information: Articles up to 30 manuscript pages. Book reviews up to 1,500 pages. Style: 1985 *MLA Style Manual.* Explanatory footnotes only, placed at end of manuscript. Bibliographical documentation in Works Cited list. Report in 3 months. Rejected manuscripts returned with S.A.S.E.

Payment: 5 copies of issue.

Indexed In: MLA International Bibliography.

Copyright: By the University of Wisconsin Press.

CRITICAL QUARTERLY

Department of English, The University, Manchester M13 9PL, England. Rates: $40 per year. Founded 1959. Sponsored by Manchester University. Published quarterly.

Major Field(s) of Interest: Particular, though not exclusive, interest in twentieth-century literature and poems and fiction by writers known and unknown, all of which will receive sympathetic attention. Journal reviews books.

Manuscript Information: Articles from 3,000–5,000 words. Book reviews of 800–1,000 words. Style: MLA. Report in 30 days. Rejected manuscripts returned with S.A.S.E. or International Reply Coupons.

Payment: Offprints.

Copyright: By the author.

*CRITIQUE: STUDIES IN MODERN FICTION

Heldref Publications, Helen Dwight Reid Educational Foundation, 4000 Albermarle Street, N.W., Washington, D.C. 20016. Rates: $39 per year. Founded 1958. Sponsored by Heldref Publications. Published quarterly.

Major Field(s) of Interest: Essays on contemporary fiction from any country. The journal gives special consideration to critical work on the fiction of writers who are alive and without great reputations.

Manuscript Information: Articles of 2,500–8,000 words in length. Style: MLA with endnotes. See journal for example. 2 copies of manuscript required. Submit original typescript. Report in 6–8 weeks. Rejected manuscripts returned with S.A.S.E.

Payment: 2 complimentary issues.

Indexed In: Abstracts of English Studies, Humanities Index, MLA International Bibliography, International Bibliography of Periodical Literature, International Bibliography of Book Reviews, Institute of Scientific Information, Arts and Humanities Citation Index.

Copyright: By Heldref Publications. Authors freely granted permission to reprint with usual credit line.

CSL: The Bulletin of the New York C. S. Lewis Society

419 Springfield Avenue, Westfield, NJ 07090. Rates: $10 per year. Founded 1969. Sponsored by the New York C. S. Lewis Society. Published monthly.

Major Field(s) of Interest: The journal publishes notes and essays on C. S. Lewis and his writings and on the literary and religious issues which he treated. It prefers essays that are not mere hagiography of Lewis. Work is preferred that analyzes some phase of his life or work. Articles selected by readers and by the editor on the basis of quality of writing and contribution to Lewis studies. Journal reviews books.

Manuscript Information: Articles of 2,000–3,000 words. Notes up to 300 words. Book reviews up to 1,000 words. Style: Chicago. Footnotes should be placed at the end of article and kept to a minimum. Report in 6–8 weeks. Rejected manuscripts returned with S.A.S.E.

Payment: 5 copies of the Bulletin.

Indexed In: Literary Criticism Review.

Copyright: By the journal. Permission to reprint is usually allowed.

The D. H. Lawrence Review

Department of English, University of Delaware, Newark, DE 19716. Rates: $14 per year individuals. $20 per year institutions. Founded 1968. Sponsored by the University of Delaware. Published 3 times per year (Spring, Summer, and Fall).

Major Field(s) of Interest: The journal publishes criticism, scholarship, and bibliography on D. H. Lawrence and his circle of literary acquaintances. Occasional special numbers are devoted to particular areas of Lawrence's work or to other figures associated with him. An annual bibliography appears in the Fall issue. Journal reviews books.

Manuscript Information: Articles of 15–25 pages. Notes of 5–15 pages. Book reviews up to 4 pages. Style: MLA. 2 copies of manuscript required. Report in 3 months. Rejected manuscripts returned with S.A.S.E.

Payment: 2 free copies of journal plus 12 offprints.

Indexed In: MLA International Bibliography, Abstracts of English Studies, MHRA.

Copyright: By the journal. Reprinting by permission only.

Dada/Surrealism

Department of French, Graduate Center, City University of New York, 33 W. 42 Street, New York, NY 10036. Rates: Request from Department of Comparative Literature, University of Iowa, Iowa City, IA 52242. Founded 1971. Sponsored by the Association for the Study of Dada & Surrealism. Published annually.

Major Field(s) of Interest: Articles on all topics and techniques related to the field of the avant-garde.

Manuscript Information: Articles of 8–15 pages. Notes of 1–2 pages. Style: MLA. 2 copies of manuscript required. Quotes may be printed in languages other than English, but translations should be provided. Report in 2–4 months. Rejected manuscripts returned.

Payment: Offprints.

Copyright: By the author and the Association for the Study of Dada & Surrealism.

*Dalhousie Review

Sir James Dunn Building, Suite 314, Dalhousie University, Halifax, Nova Scotia, B3H 3J5, Canada. Rates: $15.00 per year individuals plus $6.50 for postage outside of Canada. Founded 1921. Sponsored by Dalhousie University. Published quarterly.

Major Field(s) of Interest: Journal invites contributions of articles in such fields as history, literature, political science and philosophy as well as prose fiction both from new and established writers. Journal reviews books.

Manuscript Information: Articles up to 5,000 words. Book reviews of approximately 500 words, but more important reviews may contain 1,000 words. Less important books can be "noticed" in as little as 75–100 words. Style: MLA. 2 copies of manuscripts preferred. Journal would like submissions of articles to be on IBM or IBM-compatible diskettes. Report in approximately 6 months. Sometimes longer. Rejected manuscripts returned with S.A.S.E.

Payment: 2 complimentary copies and 15 offprints.

Indexed In: Canadian Index, Index to Periodical Fiction, Canadian Magazine Index.

Copyright: By the publisher and by the author. Fee for use is 10¢ per word which is shared with the author.

*Dickens Quarterly

Department of English, University of Massachusetts, Amherst, MA 01003. Rates: $15 per year. Founded 1970 as *Dickens Studies Newslet-*

ter; 1984 as *Dickens Quarterly.* Sponsored by the Office of the President, University of Louisville. Published quarterly.

Major Field(s) of Interest: Articles about the life, times, and literature of Charles Dickens. The Dickens Checklist appears in each quarterly issue. Journal reviews books.

Manuscript Information: Articles of 15–20 pages. Notes of 10–15 pages. Book reviews of 6–8 pages. Style: MLA Style Manual (1985) with parenthetical citation plus endnotes. 2 copies of manuscript required. Report in 3 months. Rejected manuscripts returned with S.A.S.E.

Payment: 2 complimentary issues of the journal. Offprints are available.

Indexed In: MLA International Bibliography, Literary Criticism Register.

Copyright: By the Dickens Society. Authors must request permission to use elsewhere.

*DICKENS STUDIES ANNUAL: ESSAYS ON VICTORIAN FICTION

Room 1219, Graduate School and University Center, City University of New York, 33 W. 42nd Street, New York, NY 10036. Rates: $45 per year. Founded 1970. Published yearly.

Major Field(s) of Interest: Essay and monograph-length contributions on Charles Dickens as well as on other Victorian novelists and on the history or aesthetics of Victorian fiction. Journal reviews books.

Manuscript Information: Articles of 3,750–30,000 words (15–120 typewritten pages). Book reviews of 3,750–10,000 words. Style: MLA. 2 copies of manuscript required. Original typescript is preferred. Report in 3–6 months. Rejected manuscripts returned with S.A.S.E.

Payment: 25 offprints.

Indexed In: MLA International Bibliography.

Copyright: By AMS Press, Inc. Authors may use their work in their own books.

THE DICKENSIAN

The Dickens House, 48 Doughty, London, WC1N 2LF, England. Rates: £7.50 per year individuals UK. £8.50 per year elsewhere. £9.50 per year institutions UK. £11.00 per year institutions elsewhere. Founded 1905. Sponsored by the Dickens Fellowship. Published 3 times per year.

Major Field(s) of Interest: Articles on the work and life of Charles Dickens and on the literature, art, and culture of the Victorian period. Journal reviews books.

Manuscript Information: Articles of 2,000–5,000 words. Book reviews of 500–600 words. No length restrictions on notes. Style: MLA. Report in 3 months. Rejected manuscripts returned.

Payment: Offprints.

Copyright: By the author.

DICKINSON STUDIES: EMILY DICKINSON (1830-86), U. S. POET
4508 38th Street, Brentwood, MD 20722. Rates: $40 individuals for 3 years. $80 institutions for 3 years worldwide. Founded 1968. Sponsored by the editor: Frederick L. Morey. Published 2 times per year (June and December). See HIGGINSON JOURNAL, Section VI.

Major Field(s) of Interest: Scholarly articles, notes, and queries on the life and work of Emily Dickinson. Journal reviews books.

Manuscript Information: Articles up to 2,000 words. Notes up to 300 words. Book reviews up to 600 words. Style: Chicago or MLA. Report in 2–3 weeks. Rejected manuscripts returned with S.A.S.E.

Payment: None. Copies cost $4 each.

Copyright: By the editor. Copyright reverts to the author for all reprints.

DIME NOVEL ROUNDUP: A MAGAZINE DEVOTED TO THE
COLLECTING, PRESERVATION AND LITERATURE OF THE OLD-TIME
DIME AND NICKEL NOVELS, LIBRARIES AND POPULAR STORY PAPERS
87 School Street, Fall River, MA 02720. Rates: $10 per year. Founded 1931. No sponsor. Published bimonthly.

Major Field(s) of Interest: A very specialized publication in the area of popular literature, the journal publishes articles on dime novels, boys' and girls' series books, story papers, and paperback publications of the nineteenth and early twentieth centuries. Journal reviews books.

Manuscript Information: Articles of 3,000–4,000 words. Notes of 175–200 words. Book reviews up to 500 words. Style: MLA. Submissions must be typed and double-spaced. Report in 1–2 months. Rejected manuscripts returned with S.A.S.E.

Payment: 5 copies of the journal.

Indexed In: MLA International Bibliography.

Copyright: Not copyrighted.

*DORIS LESSING NEWSLETTER
Department of English, Mills College, 5000 MacArthur Boulevard, Oakland, CA 94613. Rates: $10 per year individuals. $12 per year for libraries. $14 per year overseas. Founded 1976. Sponsored by the Doris Lessing Society. Published 2 times per year (Fall and Spring).

Major Field(s) of Interest: Articles, essays, and bibliography on any aspect of Doris Lessing's work or life. Contributors must be members of the Doris Lessing Society. Journal reviews books.

Manuscript Information: Articles up to 5,000 words. Notes up to 1,500 words. Book reviews up to 2,000 words. Style: MLA. 2 copies of manuscript required. Report in 2–4 months. Rejected manuscripts returned with S.A.S.E.

Payment: 3 copies of issue.

Indexed In: MLA International Bibliography.

Copyright: By the journal. Material can be reprinted upon request.

THE DRAMA REVIEW

51 West 4th Street, Room 300, New York, NY 10012. Founded 1955. Sponsored by New York University School of the Arts and MIT Press. Published 4 times per year.

Major Field(s) of Interest: The journal documents contemporary and historical trends in full range of the performing arts. Journal reviews books.

Manuscript Information: Articles of 15–25 typescript pages. Book reviews up to 250 words. Style: Journal & Associated Press. Manuscripts should include author's address and social security number. Report in 2 weeks. Rejected manuscripts returned with S.A.S.E.

Payment: Offprints.

Copyright: By the journal.

DREISER STUDIES

English Department, Indiana State University, Terre Haute, IN 47809. Rates: $6 for 2 years (4 issues). Founded 1970. Sponsored by the Department of English, Indiana State University. Published 2 times per year (Spring and Fall).

Major Field(s) of Interest: Critical and bibliographical studies involving Theodore Dreiser. Annual bibliography in Spring issue. Journal reviews books.

Manuscript Information: Articles up to 7,500 words. Book reviews up to 1,000 words. Style: MLA. Report in 2 weeks.

Payment: 5 copies of the journal.

Indexed In: MLA International Bibliography, MHRA.

Copyright: By the journal. Reprinting with permission of the editor.

EARLY AMERICAN LITERATURE

Department of English, CB# 3520, Greenlaw Hall, The University of North Carolina at Chapel Hill, Chapel Hill, NC 27599–3520. Rates:

$12 per year individuals. $16 per year institutions. Founded 1966. Sponsored by the MLA Division of Early American Literature to 1800 and the University of North Carolina at Chapel Hill, Department of English. Published 3 times per year.

Major Field(s) of Interest: American literature through the early national period to about 1830. Occasionally, the journal includes historical and critical analysis, editions, and bibliographies. Journal reviews books.

Manuscript Information: Articles of 20–30 pages. Notes of 3–15 pages. Book reviews of 1–5 pages. Style: MLA with footnotes at end of essay. Report in 6 months. Rejected manuscripts returned with S.A.S.E.

Payment: 10 copies of published essay.

Indexed In: MLA International Bibliography.

Copyright: By the author. Permission to reprint required from both author and editor.

*EDITH WHARTON REVIEW

Department of English, Long Island University, Brooklyn, NY 11201. Rates: $10 per year individuals. $15 per year institutions and foreign. Founded 1984 as the EDITH WHARTON NEWSLETTER; 1989 as the EDITH WHARTON REVIEW. Published semiannually (Spring and Winter).

Major Field(s) of Interest: The journal is mainly interested in short interpretative studies of Edith Wharton's work, life, and background. Occasionally, the journal publishes biographical studies. Journal reviews books, but book reviews are solicited.

Manuscript Information: Articles of 1,500–6,000 words. Notes of 500–2,000 words. Book reviews of 500–2,000 words. Style: MLA. 3 copies of manuscript required. Submit original typescript and 2 copies. Report in 6 months. Rejected manuscripts returned with S.A.S.E.

Payment: 2 copies of the issue.

Indexed In: MLA International Bibliography, American Literary Scholarship.

Copyright: By the journal. Authors are freely granted permission to reprint with usual credit line.

*EDITORS' NOTES

Department of English, University of Rhode Island, Kingston. RI 02881. Rates: $30 per year (includes membership in CELJ). Founded 1981. Sponsored by the Council of Editors of Learned Journals. Published 2 times per year (Spring and Fall).

Major Field(s) of Interest: The journal publishes articles of interest and concern to editors of learned journals, chiefly in the field of the humanities. It is concerned with survival problems, budgets, desktop publishing, electronic mail, announcements of editors' sessions at MLA, and conventions of other professional organizations. As the official journal of the Council of Editors of Learned Journals (CELJ), it is a specialized journal directed primarily to editors of literary journals, bulletins, newsletters, series, and their editorial staffs.

Manuscript Information: Articles of 2,500–3,000 words. Notes of 250–300 words. Style: MLA. 2 copies of manuscript required. Report in 4–6 weeks. Rejected manuscripts returned with S.A.S.E.

Payment: 2 copies of the journal.

Indexed In: Abstracts of English Studies, MLA Abstracts.

Copyright: By the editor of the journal and CELJ.

*EIGHTEENTH-CENTURY FICTION

McMaster University, 321 Chester New Hall, Hamilton, Ontario, L8S 4L9 Canada. Rates: In Canada: $25 per year individuals. $38 per year institutions. Founded in 1988. Sponsored by McMaster University. Published quarterly.

Major Field(s) of Interest: ECF is devoted to the historical and critical investigation of all aspects of imaginative prose written from 1660–1832. Comparative studies are particularly encouraged. Languages of publication are French and English. Journal reviews books.

Manuscript Information: Articles up to 6,000 words. Book reviews up to 1,000 words. Style: Chicago. Report in 3 months. Rejected manuscripts returned with S.A.S.E.

Payment: 2 copies plus 20 offprints.

Indexed In: MLA International Bibliography.

Copyright: By the journal, but *ECF* permits reprinting.

*EIGHTEENTH-CENTURY LIFE

Department of English, College of William and Mary, Williamsburg, VA 23186. Rates: $19 per year individuals. $31 per year institutions. Founded 1973. Sponsored by the College of William and Mary. Published 3 times per year.

Major Field(s) of Interest: Articles, notes, and documents in all areas of eighteenth-century European life, especially literature, history, philosophy, social studies, nontechnical science, art, religion, and music. Journal reviews books.

Manuscript Information: Articles of 15–35 pages. Notes of 3–10 pages. Book reviews of 2–5 pages. Review-Essays of 8–20 pages. Style: Chicago with endnotes. 3 copies of manuscript required. Original and 2 copies. Report in 3–4 months. Rejected manuscripts returned with S.A.S.E.

Payment: 2 copies of the issue.

Indexed In: ABC-CLIO, Abstracts of English Studies, Abstracts of Popular Culture, Arts and Humanities Citation Index, British Humanities Index, ISI, Literary Criticism Register, MHRA Annual, Religion Index One.

Copyright: By the Johns Hopkins University Press.

*EIGHTEENTH-CENTURY STUDIES

Department of English, University of California, Davis, CA 95616. Rates: $52 per year. Founded 1967. Sponsored by the American Society for Eighteenth-Century Studies. Published quarterly.

Major Field(s) of Interest: All aspects of the eighteenth century, especially those of interest to interdisciplinary scholars, such as European and American history, arts, science, and politics, or that are of general interest to scholars working in other disciplines. Occasionally, the journal publishes special issues dedicated to a particular subject, such as art history or the French Revolution. Journal reviews books.

Manuscript Information: Articles up to 6,500 words. Book reviews up to 1,000 words. Style: Chicago with endnotes. 2 copies of manuscript required. Report in 6 months. Rejected manuscripts returned with S.A.S.E.

Payment: 2 copies of the journal for articles plus 20 tearsheets. 10 tearsheets for book reviews.

Copyright: By the American Society for Eighteenth-Century Studies. Permission to reprint is granted to author with credit line.

ELH

The Department of English, Johns Hopkins University, Baltimore, MD 21218. Rates: $19 per year individuals. $55 per year institutions. Founded 1935. Sponsored by the Johns Hopkins University Press. Published quarterly.

Major Field(s) of Interest: Critical contributions in English and American literature of all time periods. Critical articles preferred; explication, source studies, etc. are suitable insofar as they contribute to a critical understanding of major texts. Journal reviews books.

Manuscript Information: No length restrictions within reason. Style: *MLA Style Sheet.* Submit double-spaced manuscripts including notes. Report within 30 days. Rejected manuscripts returned with S.A.S.E.

Payment: 25 offprints.

Indexed In: Abstracts of English Studies, Arts and Humanities Citation Index, Current Contents, Eighteenth Century: Current Bibliography,

Humanities Index, International Index of Periodicals, Legal Contents, Literary Criticism Register, MLA International Bibliography.
Copyright: By the Johns Hopkins University Press.

ELLEN GLASGOW NEWSLETTER

Ellen Glasgow Society, Randolph-Macon College, Ashland, VA 23005. Founded 1974. Sponsored by the Ellen Glasgow Society. Published 2 times per year (March and October).

Major Field(s) of Interest: Short, factual articles about Ellen Glasgow and her contemporaries on the Richmond literary scene and news about scholarship and publications. Journal reviews books.

Manuscript Information: Articles of 200–4,000 words. Book reviews up to 1,000 words. Notes of 200–500 words. Style: MLA. Report in 2–6 months. Rejected manuscripts returned.

Payment: Copies.
Copyright: By the author.

EMBLEMATICA: AN INTERDISCIPLINARY JOURNAL
FOR EMBLEM STUDIES

Department of German, McGill University, 1001 Sherbrooke West, Montreal, Quebec, H3A 1G5, Canada or Department of French & Italian, University of Pittsburgh, 1328 Cathedral of Learning, Pittsburgh, PA 15260 U.S.A. Rates: $30 per year individuals. $55 per year institutions. Founded 1986. Sponsored by McGill University. Published semiannually.

Major Field(s) of Interest: The journal serves as a forum for researchers working in the field and as a clearinghouse for information on the subject of emblem studies. To that end, the journal publishes, in addition to essays, various kinds of documentation, reviews and review-articles, bibliography, notes and queries, research and conference reports, and notices of forthcoming conferences and publications. The journal is open to studies originating in any of the humanistic disciplines (literary studies, art history, intellectual history, etc.) and to studies utilizing any critical approach or methodology with rigor. The determining criterion in selection of articles for publication is their contribution to the better understanding of the field or some part of it.

Manuscript Information: No limitation on length of articles. Book reviews up to 3 pages. Style: MLA (1977). 2 copies of manuscript required. Authors are expected to provide high-quality glossy prints of any illustrations. Report in 3–4 months. Rejected manuscripts returned with S.A.S.E.

Payment: Offprints.

Indexed In: MLA *International Bibliography.*

Copyright: By AMS Press. Authors receive permission to reprint with usual credit.

*English: The Journal of the English Association

The Vicarage, Priory Gardens, London, W4 1TT, England. Rates: $75 per year. Founded 1952. Sponsored by the English Association. Published 3 times per year (Spring, Summer, Autumn).

Major Field(s) of Interest: Journal publishes critical, scholarly, and theoretical essays in all areas of English literature on major English figures of critical interest. Journal reviews books, but all book reviews are commissioned.

Manuscript Information: No restrictions as to length of articles. Book reviews up to 2,000 words. Style: Endnotes, as few as possible. Report in 3–4 months. Rejected manuscripts returned with S.A.S.E.

Payment: 4 copies.

Indexed In: A.E.S., MLA *International Bibliography.*

Copyright: By the English Association. Authors can reprint free of charge provided there is an acknowledgement.

The English Journal

200 Norman Hall, University of Florida, Gainesville, FL 32611. Rates: Subscription and membership rates available from National Council of Teachers of English, 1111 Kenyon Road, Urbana, IL 61801. Sponsored by the National Council of Teachers of English. Published monthly September through April.

Major Field(s) of Interest: Articles on English and education. Journal reviews books, but book reviews are commissioned.

Manuscript Information: Articles of 10–12 pages. Style: MLA. 2 copies of manuscript required. Report in 90 days. Rejected manuscripts returned with S.A.S.E.

Payment: 2 copies of issue. Offprints may be purchased at modest fee.

Copyright: By the National Council of Teachers of English.

English Language Notes

Campus Box 226, University of Colorado, Boulder, CO 80309. Rates: $18 per year individuals. $35 per year institutions. Founded 1963. Sponsored by the Department of English, University of Colorado. Published quarterly.

Major Field(s) of Interest: The journal is interested in short articles and scholarly notes that pertain to all areas of English and American literature and language. Criticism and explication should arise out of historical, biographical, and bibliographical facts, and work unsupported by this kind of evidence is not accepted. Articles and notes should be aimed at an audience with literate, scholarly interest and should not be focused sharply on a highly technical subject with only a limited, specialized technical audience. Journal reviews books.

Manuscript Information: Articles of 1–25 pages. Notes up to 1 page. Book reviews of 500–1,000 words. Style: MLA with endnotes or when appropriate in parentheses in the text. 2 copies of manuscript required. Report in 3–4 months. Rejected manuscripts returned with S.A.S.E.

Payment: 2 copies of the issue. Offprints by arrangements.

Copyright: By the Board of Regents, University of Colorado.

*ENGLISH LITERARY RENAISSANCE

Department of English, University of Massachusetts, Amherst, MA 01003. Rates: $20 per year individuals. $25 per year institutions. Founded 1971. Sponsored by the Department of English and the Graduate School, University of Massachusetts. Published 3 times per year.

Major Field(s) of Interest: Essays, studies, texts, and bibliographies on the intellectual context and literary achievements of English Renaissance literature (1485–1668). The journal publishes a "Recent Studies" section on some Tudor or Stuart author in each issue, and it likes varied approaches to literature, giving equally serious attention to all of them. Rare texts and manuscripts are especially welcome, and illustrations (xeroxes acceptable) should be submitted on separate pages. Essays on rare texts should treat provenance.

Manuscript Information: Articles of 10–50 pages. Style: *MLA Style Sheet* (2nd Editon) with no "Works Cited." Texts should retain old-spelling with variants and annotations submitted on separate pages. Introductions, tables of variants, and necessary glosses should accompany manuscripts. 1–3 manuscripts required. Report in 8–10 weeks. Rejected manuscripts returned with S.A.S.E.

Payment: 5 copies of the journal. Offprints at cost.

Indexed In: Review of English Studies (England), *Bibliographie International de l'Humanise et de la Renaissance* (Geneva), *Bulletin Signaletique, Section Literaire 523 of the Centre de Documentation Sciences Humanities* (Paris), *MLA International Bibliography, Sidney Newsletter, Shakespeare Newsletter, Milton Quarterly, Christianity and Literature, Humanities Citation Index.*

Copyright: By the journal. Authors can reprint with permission. Others can reprint with permission and after paid fee (shared equally with author).

ENGLISH LITERATURE IN TRANSITION (1880–1920)

Department of English, University of North Carolina at Greensboro, Greensboro, NC 27412–5001. Rates: $13 per year individuals. $15 per year elsewhere. Founded 1957. Privately owned. Published quarterly.

Major Field(s) of Interest: The journal publishes essays on fiction, poetry, drama, or subjects of cultural interest in the 1880–1920 period of British literature. This excludes Joyce, Woolf, D. H. Lawrence, Yeats, and James. The journal also publishes book reviews, secondary and primary bibliographies on the literary culture of Britain during this period.

Manuscript Information: Articles of 20–25 Pages. Book reviews of 1,000–1,200 words. Style: Chicago with endnotes. 2 copies of manuscript required. Report in 3 months. Rejected manuscripts with S.A.S.E.

Payment: 2 copies plus offprints.

Indexed In: MLA International Bibliography, Literary Criticism Register, Abstracts in English, Annual Bibliography of English Language and Literature, Bibliographical Index, Index to Book Reviews in the Humanities, The Year's Work in English Studies.

Copyright: By the journal.

ENGLISH MISCELLANY: A SYMPOSIUM OF HISTORY, LITERATURE AND THE ARTS

Via Zanardelli, 1, 00186 Rome, Italy. Founded 1950. Sponsored by Ed. de Storia & Leteratura. Published annually.

Major Field(s) of Interest: Articles on English literature, art, music, foreign influences on English literature, and English influence on foreign literatures.

Manuscript Information: Articles up to 50 typescript pages. Style: MLA. Report in 2–4 months. Rejected manuscripts returned with S.A.S.E.

Payment: Copies.

Copyright: By the journal.

THE ENGLISH RECORD

Learning Center, Niagara University, NY 14109. Rates: $25 per year individuals. $15 per year students and retired. $40 per year overseas. Founded 1950. Sponsored by the New York State English Council. Published quarterly.

Major Field(s) of Interest: The journal invites manuscripts on all aspects of English, literature, composition, English Education/Theory and Pedagogy, and research reports. Journal reviews books.

Manuscript Information: Articles up to 10–15 double-spaced, typed ·

pages. Book reviews up to 500 words. Style: *Revised MLA Style Sheet.* Incorporate documentation within the text whenever possible. 2 copies of manuscript required. Report in 6 weeks. Rejected manuscripts returned with S.A.S.E.

Payment: Copies.

Copyright: By the New York State English Council.

*Envoi: A Review Journal of Medieval Literature

602 Philosphy Hall, Columbia University, New York, NY 10027. Rates: $27.50 individuals. $55.00 institutions. Founded 1987. Sponsored by the Department of English and Comparative Literature and Columbia University. Published twice yearly.

Major Field(s) of Interest: Envoi is both a literary and scholarly journal, specializing in the timely review of recent titles in medieval literature and culture. Its intent is to provide a forum for friendly discussion for medievalists to keep up to date on interesting and important developments in the field. It concentrates its focus on questions of poetry, narrative, genre, and other areas of literary interest. *Envoi* is basically a review journal. It does not publish original scholarship except for review essays. Each issue includes review essays, full-length book reviews, brief notices, and "Books Received" section.

Manuscript Information: 12–25 double-spaced typed pages for review essays. 6–12 pages for reviews. 2–4 pages for brief notices. Style: Request "Guidelines on Review and Notice Format" from the editor. 2 hard copies of manuscript plus computer disk. Although no unsolicited manuscripts will be accepted, Envoi welcomes suggestions for reviews and review essays.

Payment: None.

Copyright: By AMS Press, Inc. Reprint allowed for educational or research projects which are not for profit.

Erasmus in English

University of Toronto Press, Front Campus, Toronto, Ontario, M5S 1A6, Canada. Founded 1970. Sponsored by the University of Toronto Press and Social Sciences and Humanities Research Council of Canada. Published annually.

Major Field(s) of Interest: Provides information about the progress of the *Collected Works of Erasmus* and about Erasmus studies in general. The journal serves as a clearinghouse for information and a forum for articles, notes, and reviews related to Erasmus studies. Journal reviews books.

Manuscript Information: No length restrictions on articles, notes, or book reviews. Style: MLA or Chicago. Submit original double-spaced typescript. Report in 3 months.

Payment: Offprints.

Copyright: By the University of Toronto Press.

*ESQ: A JOURNAL OF THE AMERICAN RENAISSANCE

Department of English, Washington State University, Pullman, WA 99164–5020. Founded 1955 as the EMERSON SOCIETY QUARTERLY; became ESQ in 1972. Sponsored by the Department of English, Washington State University. Published quarterly.

Major Field(s) of Interest: Articles focused on nineteenth-century American literature. Journal is devoted to all aspects of the Romantic Transcendental tradition emanating from New England, of which Emerson is a principal figure. The journal's coverage, however, encompasses influences upon and responses to mid-century Romanticism generally from Charles Brockden Brown to Henry James, from Philip Freneau to E. A. Robinson, but also extends throughout the century to encompass its origins and effects. Articles include critical essays, source and influence studies, biographical and bibliographical studies of all figures in the century as well as more general discussions of literary theory, literary history, and the history of ideas. Journal reviews book, but most reviews are solicited or commissioned as review-essays. A special feature is the publication of essays reviewing groups of related figures and topics in the field, thereby providing a forum for viewing recent scholarship in broad perspectives.

Manuscript Information: No restriction as to length of articles or book reviews. Style: Chicago. 2 copies of manuscript required. Manuscripts must be typed on an IBM Selectric or printed on a letter-quality printer in letter gothic, courier, or prestige elite typeface with unjustified right margins preferred. Report in 2–4 months. Rejected manuscripts returned.

Payment: 2 free copies. Offprints available at modest fee.

Indexed In: MLA International Bibliography, ALS.

Copyright: By the journal. Authors are freely granted reprint permission.

EUDORA WELTY NEWSLETTER

Department of English, University of Toledo, Toledo, OH 43606. Rates: $2 per year North America. $3 per year elsewhere. Founded 1977. Sponsored by the Department of English, University of Toledo. Published 2 times per year (Winter and Summer).

Major Field(s) of Interest: Bibliographical scholarship on Eudora

Welty, including short bibliographic notes, checklists of writings by and about Welty, queries from Welty scholars and collectors, and information about collections and acquisitions of Welty materials.

Manuscript Information: Articles of 4–5 double-spaced pages. Notes up to 1,600 words. Style: Modified MLA. Place footnotes in text when possible. Report in 1–2 months. Rejected manuscripts returned with S.A.S.E.

Payment: 3 copies.

Copyright: Not copyrighted. Copyright application on individual notes will be applied for if author requests.

*THE EUGENE O'NEILL REVIEW

Department of English, Suffolk University, Beacon Hill, Boston, MA 02114. Rates: $10 per year individuals. $15 per year institutions. Founded 1977 as THE EUGENE O'NEILL NEWSLETTER, 1989 as THE EUGENE O'NEILL REVIEW. Sponsored by Suffolk University and the Eugene O'Neill Society. Published semiannually.

Major Field(s) of Interest: Articles, news notes, and queries on the life, works, associations, influences, and legacy of Eugene O'Neill. The journal publishes illustrated reviews of productions, reviews about plays and the playright, reviews of books about the plays, and abstracts of articles published about O'Neill elsewhere. An annual bibliography is published in MODERN DRAMA.

Manuscript Information: No length restrictions on articles, notes, or book reviews. Style: MLA with parenthetical references in text and list of works cited. Journal prefers limited use of footnotes and only for tangential commentary. 2 copies of manuscript required. Include biographical data of author. Report in 1–2 months. Rejected manuscripts returned with comments.

Payment: 2 copies of the issue.

Indexed In: MLA International Bibliography.

Copyright: By the journal. Reprinting permitted with appropriate acknowledgement.

EVELYN WAUGH NEWSLETTER

English Department, Nassau Community College, State University of New York, Garden City, NY 11530. Rates: $8 per year. Founded 1967. Sponsored by the Evelyn Waugh Society. Published 3 times per year (Spring, Autumn, Winter).

Major Field(s) of Interest: The journal is interested in any material related to any aspect of the life and literary works of Evelyn Waugh. Short articles, notes, and news items designed to stimulate research are welcome, and creative work is accepted if it is related to Waugh's life or work. Journal reviews books.

Manuscript Information: Essays of 200–800 words. Notes of 50–200 words. Book reviews of 200–350 words. Style: *MLA Style Sheet.* Incorporate footnotes into the text. 2 copies of manuscript required. Report in 4–6 weeks. Rejected manuscripts returned with S.A.S.E.

Payment: 3 offprints.

Bibliographical Issue: Every year in the Autumn issue.

Indexed In: MLA International Bibliography, Literary Criticism Register, American Humanities Index.

Copyright: By the author.

THE EXPLICATOR

Heldref Publications, 4000 Albermarle Street, N.W., Washington, D. C. 20016. Rates: $41 per year. Founded 1941. Sponsored by The Helen Dwight Reid Educational Foundation. Published quarterly.

Major Field(s) of Interest: The journal welcomes any short, concise, contributions relevant to *explication de texte* in prose or poetry. Short queries are also welcome. Not acceptable are materials concerned with genesis, parallelism, or biography, unless directly related to interpretation of text. If the literary work explicated is short enough, also enclose two copies of it for reprint. Provide translations with foreign works. If the text is not yet in the public domain, please include bibliographical data as an aid in securing reprint permission.

Manuscript Information: Articles of 1–3 pages preferred. Style: *The MLA Style Sheet* (2nd Edition) with endnotes. 2 copies of manuscript required. Report in 2–4 months. Rejected manuscripts returned with S.A.S.E.

Payment: Contributors of comments (not queries) will receive 2 complimentary copies of the issue.

Indexed In: MLA International Bibliography, Humanities Index.

Copyright: By Heldref Publications. Copyright Clearing Center for additional copies.

EXPLORATION

Department of English, San Diego State University, San Diego, CA 92182. Founded 1973. Sponsored by the MLA, Special Session on the Literature of Exploration & Travel. Published annually.

Major Field(s) of Interest: Articles on exploration and travel in literature. Journal publishes essays, reviews, and documents related to real, imaginary, or spiritual exploration or travel.

Manuscript Information: Articles from 3,000–10,000 words. Book reviews up to 1,000 words. Style: MLA. 2 copies of manuscript required. Include an abstract. Report in 6 months. Rejected manuscipts returned with S.A.S.E.

Payment. Copies.

Copyright: By the author.

*EXPLORATIONS IN RENAISSANCE CULTURE

Box 44612, USL Station, Lafayette, LA 70504. Ratest $5 per year for individuals and libraries. Subscriptions to *EIRC* are included in members' annual SCRC dues. Founded 1974. Sponsored by the South-Central Renaissance Conference and Levy Humanities Series. Published annually.

Major Field(s) of Interest: An interdisciplinary journal in the humanities, EIRC publishes articles in all areas of Renaissance studies including literature, history, art, music, and history of science.

Manuscript Information: Articles of 12–25 double-spaced typescript. Style: MLA. Old MLA for endnotes. 2 copies of manuscript required. Contributors must be members of the South-Central Renaissance Conference. Report in 6–12 weeks. Rejected manuscripts returned with S.A.S.E.

Payment: 4 copies of journal and 15 offprints.

Indexed In: MLA International Bibliography.

Copyright: By the journal. Permission to reprint freely granted.

EXTRAPOLATION: A JOURNAL OF SCIENCE FICTION AND FANTASY

Department of English, Kent State University, Kent, OH 44242. Rates: $15 per year individuals. $25 per year institutions. Founded 1959. Sponsored by Kent State University Press. Published quarterly.

Major Field(s) of Interest: Historical, critical, and bibliographical study of science fiction and fantasy. The journal also reviews scholarly books in this area of study. Articles are selected based on evaluation by the editorial board. Notes are also accepted.

Manuscript Information: Articles up to 25 pages in length, Book reviews of 3–4 pages. Style: MLA parenthetical documentation with Works Cited List. 2 copies of manuscript required, Report in 6–8 weeks. Rejected manuscripts returned with S.A.S.E.

Payment: 2 copies.

Bibliographical Issue: List of annual Science Fiction scholarship in fall issue.

Indexed In: MLA International Bibliography, Year's Scholarship in Science Fiction.

Copyright: By Kent State University Press. Must request permission to reprint.

*THE FAULKNER JOURNAL

Department of English, Ohio Northern University, Ada, OH 45810. Rates: $9 per year individuals. $15 per year U. S. libraries and all foreign subscribers. Founded 1985. Sponsored by Ohio Northern University. Published biannually (Autumn and Spring).

Major Field(s) of Interest: The Journal focuses on scholarly criticism of William Faulker. Journal reviews books.

Manuscript Information: Articles of 2,500–7,500 words. Notes of 300–1,000 words. Book reviews up to 200 words. Style: MIA (2nd Edition). 2 copies of manuscript required. Report in 6 weeks. Rejected manuscripts returned with S.A.S.E.

Payment: 2 copies of the journal.

Copyright: Ohio Northern University.

FIFTEENTH-CENTURY STUDIES

Marygrove College, Detroit, MI 48221. Rates: $25 per year. Sponsored by the Fifteenth-Century Symposium. Published annually.

Major Field(s) of Interest: Articles on fifteenth-century literature, history, culture, and language.

Manuscript Information: No restrictions as to length on articles or book reviews. Style: MLA or Chicago. Request guidelines and format sheet. 2 copies of manuscript required. Report in 1–3 months. Rejected manuscripts returned with S.A.S.E.

Payment: Copies.

Copyright: By the editors.

THE FLANNERY O'CONNOR BULLETIN

English Department, Box 44, Georgia College, Milledgeville, GA 31061. Rates: $5 per year individuals. $6 per year institutions. Founded 1972. Sponsored by the English Department, Georgia College. Published annually.

Major Field(s) of Interest: Critical articles concerned with the fiction and thought of Flannery O'Connor. No bias as to critical approach, and new angles are encouraged. The journal prefers critical, biographical, and source studies. Journal reviews books.

Manuscript Information: Articles of 15–20 pages. Notes of 2–3 pages. Book reviews of 3–5 pages. Style: MLA. 2 copies of manuscript required. Report in 3–4 months. Rejected manuscripts returned with S.A.S.E.

Payment: 3 complimentary copies of the issue.

Indexed In: Abstracts of English Studies, MLA International Bibliography.

FOCUS ON ROBERT GRAVES AND HIS CONTEMPORARIES

The University of Maryland, European Division, Department of English, APO New York, NY 09102 or The University of Maryland, English Department, Im Bosseldorn 30, 6900 Heidelberg, F. R. Germany. Rates: Unknown. Founded 1972. Sponsored by The University of Maryland, European Division. Published 2 times per year (November and May).

Major Field(s) of Interest: The major purport of the journal is to offer scholars of Robert Graves a place to publish their discoveries and speculations. The journal accepts articles and notes on Robert Graves and World War I literature as well as articles on the literature of all combatant nations. Journal reviews books.

Manuscript Information: Articles of 500–2,500 words. Notes up to 500 words. Book reviews of 500–1,500 words. Style: *MLA Style Manual.* 2 copies of manuscript required. Report in 3 months. Rejected manuscripts returned with S.A.S.E.

Payment: 2 copies of the journal.

Indexed In: MLA International Bibliography.

Copyright: By the journal.

*FRANK NORRIS STUDIES

Department of English, Florida State University, Tallahassee, FL 32306–1036. Rates: $10 per year. Founded 1986. Sponsored by the Frank Norris Society, Inc. Published twice per year: Spring and Fall.

Major Field(s) of Interest: Informational articles—critical, biographical, textual, and historical—concerning the American novelist Frank Norris. Journal also publishes articles and notes concerning other figures related to Norris. Journal reviews books.

Manuscript Information: Articles up to 3,000 words. Notes: 500 words plus. Books reviews up to 700 words. Style: *MLA Style Sheet* (1968). 2 copies of manuscripts required. Report in 1 month. Rejected manuscripts returned with S.A.S.E.

Payment: 10 copies of journal.

Copyright: By the Frank Norris Society. Permission to reprint by the author at no cost.

FRONTIERS: A JOURNAL OF WOMEN STUDIES

Mesa Vista Hall 2142, University of New Mexico, Albuquerque, NM 87131. Rates: $16 per year individuals. $33 per year institutions. Founded

1975. Sponsored by the Frontiers Publishing, Inc. Published 3 times per year.

Major Field(s) of Interest: A feminist journal that publishes significant contributions to scholarship in the social sciences, feminist theory, and literary criticism. The journal focuses on regional and multicultural approaches to women's lives. Issues often have a cluster of articles addressing a specific theme, although the journal welcomes unsolicited contributions, including those that are interdisciplinary and collaborative. The journal also considers poetry, short stories, photographs, and book reviews.

Manuscript Information: Articles up to 40 double-spaced pages. Book reviews of 3–15 pages. Style: Chicago. 2 copies of manuscript required. Manuscripts must not have been published elsewhere in entirety or in part. Author's name should appear on title page only. Notes should follow text. Report in 3–6 months. Rejected manuscripts returned with S.A.S.E.

Payment: 2 copies.

Copyright: By the journal unless first North American serial rights are required by the author prior to publication.

GENRE

Department of English, 760 Van Vleet Oval, University of Oklahoma, Norman, OK 73019. Rates: $14 per year individuals. $27 per year institutions. Founded 1968. Sponsored by the University of Oklahoma. Published quarterly.

Major Field(s) of Interest: The journal publishes articles dealing with questions of genre in relation to the interpretation of major literary texts, historical development of specific genres, and theoretical discussion of the concept of genre itself. Journal reviews books.

Manuscript Information: Articles of 25–30 typewritten pages. Book reviews up to 10 pages. Style: *MLA Style Sheet* (1984). 2 copies of manuscript required. Report in 3 months. Rejected manuscripts returned with S.A.S.E.

Payment: 2 copies of the issue and 5 offprints.

Copyright: By the University of Oklahoma. Permission to reprint is required.

*GEORGE HERBERT JOURNAL

English Department, Sacred Heart University, Fairfield, CT 06432. Rates: $7 per year individuals. $15 per year foreign and institutions. Founded 1977. Sponsored by Sacred Heart University. Published semiannually.

Major Field(s) of Interest: The journal publishes essays, notes, and book reviews on the life and writings of the seventeenth-century poet George Herbert (1593–1633) as well as on seventeenth-century poetry in general (particularly metaphysical poetry), including special issues on figures other than Herbert. Journal reviews books, but book reviews are assigned.

Manuscript Information: Articles up to 25 pages. Notes up to 25 pages. Book reviews of 4–8 pages. Style: Chicago. 2 copies of manuscript required. Upon acceptance for publication, the journal requests that manuscripts be submitted on IBM compatible diskette if possible. Report in 3–4 months. Rejected manuscripts returned with S.A.S.E.

Payment: 2 complimentary copies of issue plus 5 offprints.

Indexed In: Abstracts of English Studies, Etudes Anglaises, MLA International Bibliography, Literary Criticism Register, Review of English Studies.

Copyright: By the journal. Permission to reprint granted free with acknowledgement.

GEORGE SAND STUDIES

Hofstra Cultural Center, Hofstra University, Hempstead, NY 11550. Rates: $8 per year individuals. $10 per year institutions. Founded 1974. Sponsored by the Hofstra Cultural Center. Published annually.

Major Field(s) of Interest: Articles on all aspects of the life and works of George Sands.

Manuscript Information: Articles up to 3,500 words. Style: MLA. Report in 2 months. Rejected manuscripts returned with S.A.S.E.

Payment: Copies.

Copyright: By the journal.

HAMLET STUDIES: AN INTERNATIONAL JOURNAL

"Rangoon Villa," 1/10 West Patel Nagar, New Delhi 110 008, India. Rates: $18 per year. Founded 1979. Sponsored by the editor: R. W. Desai. Published 2 times per year (Summer and Winter).

Major Field(s) of Interest: The journal welcomes articles, notes, book reviews, and reports on any aspect of *Hamlet:* interpretive, stage and film versions of the play, the influence of *Hamlet* on other works, *Hamlet* in translations, the reception of *Hamlet* in other countries. It includes a digest of articles on the play in other journals and comments by readers. Journal reviews books.

Manuscript Information: Articles up to 6,000 words. Notes up to 2,000 words. Book reviews up to 2,000 words. Style: Chicago and MLA Report in 3 months. Rejected manuscripts returned with S.A.S.E.

Payment: Copies.

Indexed In: MLA International Bibliography, World Shakespeare Bibliography, Abstracts of English Studies.

Copyright: By the journal.

HARVARD LIBRARY BULLETIN

Harvard University Library, Wadsworth House, Harvard University, Cambridge, MA 02138. Rates: $35 per year. Founded 1947. Sponsored by Harvard University Library. Published quarterly.

Major Field(s) of Interest: General journal of the humanities with emphasis on the collections of the Harvard University Library and the significance of those collections to scholarship.

Manuscript Information: Articles of any length. Notes of 500–1,000 words. Style: Chicago and old MLA Style Sheet. Report in 3 months. Rejected manuscripts returned with S.A.S.E. Authors are urged to inform the editor if the text of a paper is in machine-readable form.

Payment: 50 free offprints. Additional offprints may be ordered.

Copyright: By the President and Fellows of Harvard College. Reprint rights remain with the authors.

THE HEMINGWAY REVIEW

Department of English, Ohio Northern University, Ada, OH 45810. Rates: $6 individuals. $9 institutions. Founded 1970. Sponsored by Ohio Northern University. Published 2 times per year.

Major Field(s) of Interest: Articles of interest about and literary criticism of Ernest Hemingway. Journal reviews books.

Manuscript Information: No restrictions on length. Average submission is about 5,000 words. Style: *MLA Handbook,* 2nd edition. Submit original typescript. Report in 6 weeks. Rejected manuscripts returned with S.A.S.E.

Indexed In: MLA International Bibliography.

Copyright: By the journal.

THE HENRY JAMES REVIEW

Department of English, Louisiana State University, Baton Rouge, LA 70803–5001. Rates: $17 individuals. $28 institutions. Founded 1979. Sponsored by the Louisiana State University and The Henry James Society. Distributed by the Johns Hopkins University Press for the Henry James Society. Published 3 times a year.

Major Field(s) of Interest: Essays and notes on all aspects of the life and work of Henry James, including an annual analytic review of James studies.

Manuscript Information: No limit on length. Style: MLA. Report usually in 3 to 5 months, omitting summer months. 2 copies required; submit original manuscript.

Payment: 2 copies of issue.

Indexed In: Abstracts of English Studies, MHRA Annual Bibliography, MLA International Bibliography.

Copyright: By the Johns Hopkins University Press.

THE HOPKINS QUARTERLY

English Department, St. Michael's College, 81 St. Mary Street, Toronto, Ontario, M5S 1J4, Canada. Rates: $8 per year (US) for US and foreign. Founded 1974. Sponsored by the International Hopkins Association. Published quarterly.

Major Field(s) of Interest: Articles, notes, reviews on the life and thought of Gerard Manley Hopkins and his circle: Robert Bridges, Richard W. Dixon, and Coventry Patmore. Journal reviews books.

Manuscript Information: No restrictions as to length of articles, notes, or book reviews. Style: MLA with endnotes. 3 copies of manuscript required. Report in 6 months. Rejected manuscripts returned with S.A.S.E.

Payment: 10 offprints and 2 issues.

Copyright: By the editor. Permission to reprint usually granted.

*HUMOR: INTERNATIONAL JOURNAL OF HUMOR RESEARCH

English Department, Arizona State University, Tempe, AZ 85287-0302. Rates: $45 per year individuals (includes subscription plus membership in the "International Society for Humor Studies.") $75 per year institutions. Founded 1988. Sponsored by the International Society for Humor Studies. Published quarterly.

Major Field(s) of Interest: The journal presents a forum for high-quality research on humor as an important and universal human faculty. Having emerged as an interdisciplinary field, humor research draws upon a wide range of academic disciplines including anthropology, computer science, history, linguistics, literature, mathematics, medicine, philosophy, psychology, and sociology. It publishes original contributions on inter-disciplinary humor research, studies on humor theory, studies of humor research methodologies, applications of one or more disciplines to the study of humor, applications of humor research to one or more disciplines, studies of humor technology, and humor material databases. Journal reviews books.

Manuscript Information: No length restrictions on articles, notes, or book reviews. Style: Chicago. 4 copies of manuscript required with 200–

word abstract. Report in 6 months. Rejected manuscripts returned with S.A.S.E.

Payment: 4 free copies of journal.

Indexed In: MLA International Bibliography.

Copyright: By the journal. After publication, the author is free to reprint with credit to Mouton de Gruyter.

*THE HUNTINGTON LIBRARY QUARTERLY

Henry E. Huntington Library and Art Gallery, 1151 Oxford Road, San Marino, CA 91108. Rates: $25 per year. Sponsored by Huntington Library Publications. Published quarterly.

Major Field(s) of Interest: The journal publishes scholarly articles in the research areas of the Huntington Library collections, concentrating particularly on the literature, history, and art of the sixteenth to eighteenth centuries in Britain and America. Interdisciplinary articles are especially welcome. The journal also publishes extensive reviews of books on the culture and society of the period, and some of the more important recent acquisitions to the collections are described in an Intramuralia section at the end of each issue. Articles are frequently illustrated from rare items in the library. Journal reviews books.

Manuscript Information: No particular length restrictions for articles or notes. Book reviews of 500–2,500 words. Style: Chicago. 2 copies of manuscript required. Report in 8–12 weeks. Rejected manuscripts returned with S.A.S.E.

Payment: 2 copies of the issue and 3 offprints.

Indexed In: Historical Abstracts, Humanities Index, America: History and Life, MLA Abstracts of Articles in Scholarly Journals, American Humanities Index, Abstracts of English Studies, Index to Book Reviews in the Humanities, Literary Criticism Register.

Copyright: By the Huntington Library. Author reprint rights are granted automatically.

THE INDEPENDENT SHAVIAN

The Bernard Shaw Society, Inc. (formerly the New York Shavians), P. 0. Box 1373, Grand Central Station, New York, NY 10163–1373. Rates: $15 per year (includes membership in The Bernard Shaw Society). Sponsored by The Bernard Shaw Society, Inc. Published 3 times per year.

Major Field(s) of Interest: Articles which explore Bernard Shaw and items which relate to his life and works. Journal reviews books.

Manuscript Information: No restrictions on length of articles, notes, or book reviews. Style: *MLA Handbook.* Report in 1 month. Rejected manuscripts returned with S.A.S.E.

Payment: Copies.
Copyright: By the author.

INTERNATIONAL FICTION REVIEW

Department of German and Russian, University of New Brunswick, Box 4400, Fredericton, New Brunswick, E3B 5A3, Canada. Rates: $10 per year individuals. $12 per year institutions. Founded 1974. Published 2 times per year.

Major Field(s) of Interest: The journal publishes articles on contemporary international fiction and authors as well as scholarly reviews of recently published novels and scholarly works on international fiction. Journal reviews books.

Manuscript Information: Articles up to 12 pages. Essays up to 6 pages. Book reviews up to 2 pages. Style: *MLA Style Sheet.* Footnotes according to *York Press Style Manual.* 2 copies of manuscript required. Report in 6–8 weeks. Rejected manuscripts returned with S.A.S.E.

Payment: None.

Indexed In: MLA International Bibliography, An Index to Book Reviews in the Humanities, American Humanities Index, Arts and Humanities Citation Index.

Copyright: By the journal.

JACK LONDON NEWSLETTER

Department of Foreign Languages and Literatures, Faner Hall, Southern Illinois University, Carbondale, IL 62901. Rates: $10 per year. Founded 1967. Sponsored by the editor: Hensley C. Woodbridge. Published 3 times per year.

Major Field(s) of Interest: Biographical material and critical articles on the lives and works of Jack London and Jesse Stuart, reviews of their books, and reviews of works about them.

Manuscript Information: Articles up to 5,000 words. Book reviews up to 1,000 words. Style: MLA Style Sheet. Report immediately. Rejected manuscripts returned.

Payment: None. Copies of the journal available at reduced price.

Copyright: No copyright.

*JAMES DICKEY NEWSLETTER

DeKalb College, 2101 Womack Road, Dunwoody, GA 30338. Rates: $5 per year individuals. $10 per year institutions (in US). Founded 1984. Sponsored by DeKalb College. Published twice annually: Fall and Spring.

Major Field(s) of Interest: Provides a forum for information on the works, bibliography, and biography of James L. Dickey. Journal also publishes a limited amount of new poetry. Articles selected by editor review in the Fall. Book reviews are usually solicited.

Manuscript Information: Articles up to 10 single-spaced pages or about 5,000 words. Notes of any length. Book reviews of 100–500 words. Style: MLA. 1 manuscript copy required. Report in 2 weeks or sooner. Rejected manuscripts returned with S.A.S.E.

Payment: 5 copies of issue.

Indexed In: MLA International Bibliography, Humanities Index.

Copyright: Journal retains first rights only.

*JAMES JOYCE QUARTERLY

University of Tulsa, 600 South College Avenue, Tulsa, OK 74104–3189. Rates: $14 per year individuals. $15 per year institutions. Founded 1963. Sponsored by the University of Tulsa. Published quarterly (November, February, May, August).

Major Field(s) of Interest: The journal concentrates on all aspects of James Joyce, his life, works, and time. It publishes comparative studies, research-oriented scholarship, bibliographical and biographical articles and collector's notes as well as modern critical theory as related to Joyce. Journal reviews books.

Manuscript Information: Articles of 20–25 pages. Notes of 1–6 pages. Book reviews up to 5 pages. Style: MLA (1977 edition) with endnotes. Please follow "Notes to Contributors" inside back cover of journal. 3 copies of manuscript required. Rejected manuscripts returned with S.A.S.E.

Payment: Copies of the issue free. Extra copies available at reduced rate.

Indexed In: MLA International Bibliography, Abstracts of English Studies.

Copyrights: By the University of Tulsa. Permission to reprint is granted with credit line.

JOHN CLARE SOCIETY JOURNAL

The Old Vicarage, Tibberton, North Droitwich, Worcestershire, WR9 7NP, England. Rates: Free to members of the Society. £3 to non-members. members. Sponsored by Eastern Arts. Published annually in July.

Major Field(s) of Interest: Articles about the life and works of the poet John Clare (1793–1864) and his context. Journal reviews books.

Manuscript Information: Articles up to 3,000 words. Book reviews up to 500 words. Notes up to 500 words. Style: MLA with footnotes at end of article. 2 copies of manuscript required. Report in 4–8 weeks. Rejected manuscripts returned with S.A.S.E.

Payment: 3 copies of the issue.

Copyright: By the John Clare Society. Authors are freely granted permission to reprint with the usual credit line.

*JOHN DONNE JOURNAL: STUDIES IN THE AGE OF DONNE

Box 8105, North Carolina State University, Raleigh, NC 27695–8105. Rates: $8 per year individuals. $16 per year institutions. Founded 1982. Sponsored by the Department of English, North Carolina State University. Published quarterly.

Major Field(s) of Interest: In addition to studies of later sixteenth and seventeenth-century poetry and prose in England, the journal is interested in publishing short notes, announcements, and descriptions of manuscripts, texts, and documents. Journal reviews books.

Manuscript Information: Articles of 20–50 pages. Book reviews up to 2,000 words. Style: *MLA Style Sheet.* 2 copies of manuscript required. Report in 2–3 months. Rejected manuscripts returned with S.A.S.E.

Payment: 50 offprints.

Indexed In: MLA International Bibliography.

Copyright: By the journal.

JOHN O'HARA JOURNAL

P. O. Box 106, Pottsville, PA 17901. Founded 1978. Sponsored by the editor. Published 2 times per year (Winter and Summer).

Major Field(s) of Interest: Articles and essays on the work and life of John O'Hara, critical work on twentieth-century American literature (excluding drama), and original poetry and short fiction. Journal reviews books.

Manuscript Information: Articles of 3,000–10,000 words. Book reviews of 500–750 words. Style: MLA preferred. 2 copies of manuscript required. Report in 1–2 months. Rejected manuscripts returned with S.A.S.E.

Payment: Copies.

Copyright: By the author.

*JOURNAL OF BECKETT STUDIES

Department of English, Florida State University, Tallahassee, FL 32306. Rates: $18.50 per year individuals. Founded 1976. Sponsored by John Calder Publishers, Ltd., London. Published semiannually.

Major Field(s) of Interest: Scholarship and criticism on Samuel Beckett and his circle, contemporary drama, critical theory, photographs of productions, and theatrical reviews. Journal reviews books.

Manuscript Information: Articles of 15–25 pages. Notes of 3–5 pages. Book reviews of 3–5 pages. Style: MLA preferred. Endnotes. 2 copies of manuscript required. Report in 3–6 months. Rejected manuscripts returned with S.A.S.E.

Payment: 1 copy of journal.

Indexed In: MLA International Bibliography.

Copyright: Journal holds first publication rights only.

*JOURNAL OF BRITISH STUDIES

Duke University, 104A West Duke Building, Durham, NC 27708. Rates: $47 per year individuals. $55 per year institutions. Founded 1961. Sponsored by the North American Conference on British Studies. Published quarterly.

Major Field(s) of Interest: Interdisciplinary articles in all areas of British studies and all fields of British literature, Colonial history, art, and culture, including British history. Journal reviews books, but book reviews are commissioned.

Manuscript Information: Articles up to 10,000 words. Review-essays of 8–10 pages. Style: Chicago with endnotes. 2 copies of manuscript required. Report in 2–3 months. Rejected manuscripts returned with S.A.S.E.

Payment: 2 copies of the issue and 1 year's free subscription. Offprints available for a fee.

Indexed In: Historical Abstracts.

Copyright: By the North American Conference on British Studies. No reprints without permission.

JOURNAL OF ENGLISH

Department of English, Sana'a University, P. O. Box 1247, Sana'a, Yemen Arab Republic. Founded 1975. Sponsored by Sana'a University. Published annually.

Major Field(s) of Interest: Articles on English literature, language, and linguistics. Journal reviews books.

Manuscript Information: Articles of 15–20 pages. Notes of 800–1,000 words. Book reviews of 1,000–1,500 words. Style: None. 2 copies of manuscript required. Include a brief biography of the author. Report in 4–6 weeks. Rejected manuscripts returned.

Payment: Copies.

Copyright: By the journal.

*JOURNAL OF ENGLISH AND GERMANIC PHILOLOGY

Department of English, University of Illinois, 608 South Wright Street, Urbana, IL 61801. Rates: $17.50 per year individuals. $35.00 per year institutions (add $3.00 for foreign addresses). Founded 1897. Sponsored by the University of Illinois Press, University of Illinois Department of English, and the University of Illinois Department of Germanic Languages and Literatures. Published quarterly.

Major Field(s) of Interest: English, German, and Scandinavian literatures and languages of all periods in all phases of scholarly investigation and critical interpretation. No methodological approach is preferred, but the journal is best known for historical and philological studies. Journal reviews book, but all book reviews are solicited.

Manuscript Information: Articles of 10–35 pages. Book reviews of 3–5 pages. Style: The "old" *MLA Style Sheet.* Footnotes at end of typescript. Report in 1–3 months. Rejected manuscripts returned with S.A.S.E.

Payment: 2 tearsheets. Offprints of articles can be purchased.

Indexed In: MLA International Bibliography, and others.

Copyright: By the Board of Trustees of the University of Illinois. Authors can reprint in books or collections of their own essays after receiving permission from the University of Illinois Press.

JOURNAL OF ENGLISH STUDIES

Department of English, Scott Christian College, Nagercoil 629 003, South India. Founded 1978. Sponsored by Scott Christian College, Post-Graduate Department of English. Published annually.

Major Field(s) of Interest: Articles on all aspects of English literature and language as well as Indo-Anglian literature.

Manuscript Information: Articles of 8–10 typescript pages. Style: MLA. 2 copies of manuscript required. Report in 1–3 months. Rejected manuscript returned with S.A.S.E.

Payment: Copies.

Copyright: By the journal.

*JOURNAL OF MEDIEVAL AND RENAISSANCE STUDIES

4666 Duke Station, Duke University, Durham, NC 27706. Founded 1971. Sponsored by the Duke University Press. Published 2 times per year (Spring and Fall).

Major Field(s) of Interest: Scholarly articles on any matters pertinent to the process of change observable in late Medieval and Renaissance culture. The journal examines general problems as well as specific issues and accomplishments in art, history, literature, music, philosophy, and theology. The journal is especially interested in interdisciplinary or comparative studies of thought, expressions, and institutions. It is also interested in articles on more limited topics or on particular figures which throw light on the problems of transition. Journal reviews books.

Manuscript Information: Articles of 20–35 pages plus notes. Style: MLA. Report in 2 months. Rejected manuscripts returned.

Payment: Offprints.

Copyright: By Duke University Press.

*JOURNAL OF MODERN LITERATURE

921 Anderson Hall, Temple University, Philadelphia, PA 19122. Rates: $16 per year individuals. $20 per year institutions. Founded 1970. Sponsored by Temple University. Published 3 times per year.

Major Field(s) of Interest: Scholarly studies of all literatures in the twentieth century. The journal also considers literatures from other languages as well as works in English and is particularly interested in scholarship involving manuscripts and letters and comparative music and arts. Journal reviews books.

Manuscript Information: Articles of 20–30 pages. Notes of 5–15 pages. Book reviews up to 250 words. Style: *MLA Style Sheet* (1965 edition). 2 copies of manuscript preferred. Report in 8–12 weeks. Rejected manuscripts returned with S.A.S.E.

Payment: 3 copies of the issue.

Indexed In: MLA International Bibliography, MHRA, and others.

Copyright: By Temple University. Authors may reprint with permission.

*JOURNAL OF NARRATIVE TECHNIQUE

Department of English, Eastern Michigan University, Ypsilanti, MI 48197. Rates: $10 per year individuals (includes membership in the Society for the Study of Narrative Literature). $20 per year institutions. Founded 1971. Sponsored by the Society for the Study of Narrative Literature and Eastern Michigan University. Published 3 times per year.

Major Field(s) of Interest: The journal publishes manuscripts in English dealing with narrative literature in any language. Subject matter may be drawn from all periods and literary genres, provided that in each instance the focus is on the author's management of narrative elements and the narrative movement of the work. Journal reviews books.

Manuscript Information: Articles of 20-35 manuscript pages. Notes of 10–15 pages. Book reviews of 500–1,000 words. Style: MLA with endnotes. 2 copies of manuscript preferred. Report in 3–4 months. Rejected manuscripts returned with S.A.S.E.

Payment: 3 copies of the journal.
Indexed In: MLA International Bibliography.
Copyright: By the journal. Authors may reprint with permission.

THE JOURNAL OF PRE-RAPHAELITE STUDIES

School of Art, Arizona State University, Tempe, AZ 85287–1505. Rates: $25 per year individuals. $40 per year institutions. Founded 1977. Sponsored by Arizona State University. Published 2 times per year.

Major Field(s) of Interest: The journal is interested in interdisciplinary subjects, and publishes articles and pictorial material bearing on the Pre-Raphaelite movements, its antecedents and sequelae, as well as material on literature, art history, and drama. Journal reviews books.

Manuscript Information: No length restrictions on articles or notes. Book reviews up to 800 words. Style: MLA. Illustrations must be glossy black and white photographs. 2 copies of manuscript required. Report in 6 months. Rejected manuscripts returned with S.A.S.E.

Payment: 2 copies. Offprints are available for a fee.
Indexed In: MLA International Bibliography.
Copyright: By the author.

JOURNAL OF THE HISTORY OF IDEAS

Rutgers University, 88 College Avenue, New Brunswick, NJ 08903–5059. Rates: $15 per year individuals. $25 per year institutions. Founded 1940. Mainly self-supporting. Sponsored in part by Rutgers University and Temple University. Published quarterly.

Major Field(s) of Interest: The journal publishes articles in the history of philosophy, history of literature, history of the arts, history of natural and social sciences, history of religion, history of political and social movements. Articles should emphasize the interrelations of several fields of study. Journal reviews books, but book reviews are solicited.

Manuscript Information: Articles up to 9,000 words. No set length for notes. Book reviews up to 9,000 words. Style: Chicago. Contributors should consult a current issue of the journal for form. 3 copies of manuscript required. Report in 3 months. Rejected manuscripts returned with S.A.S.E.

Payment: 1 copy of the issue in which articles appears plus offprints.
Indexed In: Review-Articles are indexed in *Book Review Index.* Articles are indexed in *Abstracts of English Studies, The Philosopher's Index.*
Copyright: By the journal. Authors may reprint their own articles free of charge. Reprint fee for others: $10 per page.

THE JOURNAL OF THE MIDWEST MODERN LANGUAGE ASSOCIATION
302 English/Philosophy Building, University of Iowa, Iowa City, IA
52242–1408. Rates: $12 per year individuals. Founded 1968. Sponsored
by The Midwest Modern Language Association. Published twice annually.

Major Field(s) of Interest: Articles and essays on the study and teaching of language and literature, particularly in relation to political, historical, and cultural issues, are especially welcome, as are studies in critical
methodology, literary history, and theory of language. Journal reviews
books. Authors must be members of M/MLA.

Manuscript Information: Articles should not exceed 8,000 words.
Book reviews should not exceed 1,000 words. Style: *MLA Handbook for
Writers of Research Papers* (1984). 2 "blind" copies of manuscript re-
quired. Report in 6–8 weeks.

Payment: Offprints.

Copyright: By the M/MLA. Authors must contact M/MLA for
permission to reprint.

*JOURNAL OF THE ROCKY MOUNTAIN MEDIEVAL
AND RENAISSANCE ASSOCIATION
Department of English, Brigham Young University, Provo, UT 84602.
Rates: $15 per year individuals. $20 per year institutions. Founded 1980.
Sponsored by the Rocky Mountain Medieval and Renaissance Associa-
tion. Published annually.

Major Field(s) of Interest: Provides a forum for scholars of the Middle Ages or Renaissance to publish articles on all aspects of the Medieval
and Renaissance periods: literature, art, and history. Journal reviews
books, but book reviews are solicited.

Manuscript Information: Articles and essays from 20–30 double-
spaced manuscript pages. Notes up to 10 pages. Book reviews up to 500
words. Style: Chicago. All articles are carefully source-checked. Report in
6–8 weeks. Rejected manuscripts returned with S.A.S.E.

Payment: 10 copies.

Indexed In: MLA International Bibliography, ABC Clio, Leeds,
MHRA, Medieval Bibliography.

Copyright: By the journal. Right to reprint is retained by the author.

*JOURNAL OF THE SHORT STORY IN ENGLISH
Faculté des Lettres, Langues et Sciences Humaines, 49045 Angers Cedex,
2, rue Lakanal, Centre D'Études et de Rechereches sur la Nouvelle en
Langue Anglaise, Université d'Angers, France. Rates: France: 140 Francs
per year. Other countries: 165 Francs per year. Mainly self-supporting:

partially sponsored by the Conseil Scientifique de l'Université d'Angers."
Published biyearly.

Major Field(s) of Interest: The nineteenth and twentieth century short story in English, studied from a historical, literary, or textual point-of-view. Essays on the poetics of the short story are also welcome and original interviews of short story writers are regularly published. Special issues treat either specific aspects of the short story, the words of one author or group of authors, or report on the proceedings of colloquiums held at the Faculté des Lettres, Langues et Sciences Humaines of Angers on the short story. Journal reviews books.

Manuscript Information: Articles of 12–20 pages. Book reviews of 2–3 pages. Style: MLA. 2 copies of manuscript required. Report in 1–2 months. Rejected manuscripts returned with S.A.S.E.

Payment: 1 copy of the issue and 20 offprints.

Indexed In: MLA International Bibliography, The Year's Work in English Studies—Annual Bibliography of English Literature, Etudes Anglaises.

Copyright: By the University of Angers. Authors are freely granted permission to reprint with usual credit line.

JOYCE STUDIES ANNUAL

Harry Ransom Humanities Research Center, P. O. Box 7213, University Station, The University of Texas at Austin, Austin, TX 78713. Rates: $35.00 per year individuals. $35 per year institutions. Founded 1990. Sponsored by the Harry Ransom Research Center and the University of Texas Press. Published annually.

Major Field(s) of Interest: The journal invites contributions of significance on James Joyce and closely related topics. It is especially interested in essays in the areas of historical, textual, and comparative criticism. The journal publishes the annual James Joyce Checklist, and scholars are urged to send a citation of any publication regarding Joyce to the journal.

Manuscript Information: Articles up to 50 double-spaced manuscript pages. Style: Chicago. Report in 3 months. Rejected manuscripts returned with S.A.S.E.

Payment: 1 copy of the journal.

Copyright: By the University of Texas Press.

KEATS-SHELLEY JOURNAL

Department of English, Bennett Hall D–1, University of Pennsylvania, Philadelphia, PA 19104–6273. Rates: $20 per year individuals. $30 per year institutions and foreign. Founded 1952. Sponsored by the Keats-Shelley Association of America, Inc. Published annually.

Major Field(s) of Interest: The journal publishes articles on Keats, Shelley, Byron, Hunt, and their circles. Journal reviews books.

Manuscript Information: Articles of 20–30 double-spaced typed pages. Notes of 1–10 pages. Book reviews up to 5 pages. Style: Chicago with numbered endnotes. Report in 3–6 months. Rejected manuscripts returned with S.A.S.E.

Payment: 2 copies of the journal.

Copyright: By the Keats-Shelley Association of America, Inc.

LAMAR JOURNAL OF THE HUMANITIES

Lamar University, P. O. Box 10023, Beaumont, TX 77710. Rates: $6 per year. Founded 1973. Sponsored by Lamar University, College of Arts & Sciences. Published 2 times per year.

Major Field(s) of Interest: Interdisciplinary or general interest humanities subjects from all scholarly disciplines. The journal is especially interested in philosophy, art, music, and popular culture. Journal reviews books.

Manuscript Information: Articles of 3,000–7,000 words. Notes of 500–2,000 words. Book reviews up to 750 words. Style: Chicago. Report in 90 days. Rejected manuscripts returned with S.A.S.E.

Payment: 6 copies.

Indexed In: MLA International Bibliography, America: History and Life, Abstracts of English Studies.

Copyright: By the journal. Reprinting allowed with permission.

THE LANGSTON HUGHES REVIEW

Box 1904, Brown University, Providence, RI 02912. Rates: $10 per year individuals. $14 per year institutions and foreign. Founded 1982. Sponsored by the Langston Hughes Society and Brown University, Afro-American Studies Program. Published 2 times per year.

Major Field(s) of Interest: The journal is broadly concerned with the life and writings of Langston Hughes and any ideas and information that are relevant to the critical study of the Hughesian tradition. Sometimes special issues are set aside for specific articles on a specific theme. The basis for article selection varies. Contributions are restricted to subscribers. Journal reviews books.

Manuscript Information: Articles of 3,000–5,000 words in length. Book reviews up to 1,000 words. Notes of 250–750 words. Style: MLA. Report in 60 days. Rejected manuscripts returned with S.A.S.E.

Payment: Copies.

Copyright: By the Langston Hughes Society. Author maintains copyright.

*LEGACY: A JOURNAL OF NINETEENTH-CENTURY
AMERICAN WOMEN WRITERS
Department of English, Bartlett Hall, University of Massachusetts, Amherst, MA 01003. Rates: $15 per year individuals. $18 per year institutions. Founded 1983 (as a newsletter); 1985 (as a journal). Sponsored by the University of Massachusetts at Amherst. Published semiannually.

Major Field(s) of Interest: The journal welcomes critical, biographical, historical articles on nineteenth-century and some early twentieth-century American women writers, speakers, diarists, letter-writers, etc. The journal especially welcomes articles and biographical profiles on black, native American, and immigrant/ethnic women. Journal reviews books, but reviews are commissioned.

Manuscript Information: Articles up to 30 pages. Profiles up to 2,000 words. Book reviews up to 1,500 words. Style: MLA (1985). Content notes only. Use works cited format. 2 copies of manuscript required. Report in 3–5 months. Rejected manuscripts with S.A.S.E.

Payment: 2 copies of journal and 20 offprints.

Indexed In: Abstracts of English Studies, American Literary Scholarship, American History & Life, Book Review in the Humanities, Feminist Periodicals, Information American, MLA International Bibliography, Literary Criticism Register, Recently Published Articles—American History Association, Studies in Women Abstracts.

Copyright: By the journal. Copyright can be transferred to author upon written request.

THE LIBRARY CHRONICLE OF THE UNIVERSITY OF TEXAS AT AUSTIN
Harry Ransom Humanities Research Center, Box 7219, Austin, TX 78713. Founded 1944. New Series in 1970. Sponsored by the Harry Ransom Humanities Research Center and the General Libraries, the University of Texas at Austin. Published quarterly.

Major Field(s) of Interest: The journal publishes articles that are based on the special collections libraries at the University of Texas, primarily those of the Harry Ransom Humanities Research Center. The journal publishes studies in literature, photography, film, iconography, theatre arts, and book arts. All articles must be significantly related to the holdings at the HRHR Center. Authors should obtain permission to quote from unpublished materials in the Center's collections.

Manuscript Information: Articles up to 21 pages. Style: Chicago and MLA with footnotes at the end of article. Report in 1 month. Rejected manuscripts returned with S.A.S.E.

Payment: 6 copies.

Indexed In: Humanities Index, Institute for Scientific Information.

Copyright: By the author. Reprints must give credit to the Journal.

THE LION AND THE UNICORN:
A CRITICAL JOURNAL OF CHILDREN'S LITERATURE

Department of English, Brooklyn College, CUNY, Brooklyn NY 11210. Rates: $15 yearly (individuals); $26 yearly (institutions). Founded 1977. Sponsored by Department of English, Brooklyn College, CUNY.

Major Field(s) of Interest: The Lion and the Unicorn is a theme and genre-centered journal in children's literature. It is a critical journal and publishes essays and interviews with authors in the field.

Manuscript Information: Length 5–35 double-spaced pages. *MLA Handbook* style and footnote form. Report varies in length of time.

Payment: 2 copies of the issue free.

Indexed In: Arts and Humanities Citation Index, Current Contents, MLA International Bibliography.

Copyright: By the Johns Hopkins University Press.

THE LITERARY CRITERION

Dhvanyaloka, Mysore–6, India. Rates: $12 per year. Founded 1952. Sponsored by Literary Criterion Centre, Mysore. Published 4 times per year.

Major Field(s) of Interest: The close study of significant works, authors, and movements in English, American, and Commonwealth literatures. Journal reviews books.

Manuscript Information: Articles of 3,000–4,000 words. Notes up to 250 words. Book reviews up to 500 words. Style: MLA. 2 copies of manuscript required. Submit original typescript. Report in 1–2 months. Rejected manuscripts not returned.

Payment: Copies.

Copyright: By the journal.

*LITERARY RESEARCH: A JOURNAL OF
SCHOLARLY METHOD AND TECHNIQUE

Department of English, The University of Maryland, College Park, MD 20742. Rates: $15 per year individuals. $20 per year institutions. Founded 1976. Sponsored by the Research Center for Arts and Humanities, the

Department of English, The University of Maryland, and the College of Arts and Humanities, the University of Maryland. Published quarterly (January, April, July, October).

Major Field(s) of Interest: Articles and notes on all aspects of research (practical, pedagogical, theoretical) in modern literature, including literary scholarship and methods, bibliography, and textual studies. Journal reviews books.

Manuscript Information: No length restrictions on articles, notes, or book reviews. Style: *MLA Handbook.* The journal is published using an IBM (MS DOS 3.1), WordPerfect 5.1 software, and an HP Laser Jet Series II. 2 copies of manuscript required. Send a hard copy with the disk, along with technical information about the hardware and software used in its production. Report in less than 6 months. Rejected manuscripts returned with S.A.S.E.

Payment: Copies.

Indexed In: Abstracts of English Studies, American Humanities Index, American Literary Scholarship, Annual Bibliography of English Language and Literature, Arts and Humanities Citation Index, Current Contents/Arts and Humanities, Literary Criticism Register, MLA International Bibliography, The Year's Work in English Studies.

Copyright: By the journal.

*LITERATURE AND HISTORY

Department of English, Ohio State University, 164 West 17th Avenue, Columbus, OH 43210-1370. Rates: $21 per year individuals. $29 per year institutions. Founded 1975; new series 1990. Sponsored by King Alfred's College, U.K., Southern Oregon State College, and Ohio State University. Published biannually.

Major Field(s) of Interest: The journal focuses on the relations between writing, history, and ideology, and it limits material to cross-disciplinary articles on literature and history or the interdisciplinary interests of historians and literary critics and scholars. Journal reviews books, but book reviews are solicited.

Manuscript Information: Articles of 10–25 pages. Book reviews of 500–1,000 words. Style: MLA with notes at end of article. 2 copies of manuscript required. Report in 2–3 months. Rejected manuscripts returned with S.A.S.E.

Payment: None.

Indexed In: MLA International Bibliography.

Copyright: By the journal. Reprint possible on request.

*Literature and Medicine

Institute for the Medical Humanities, University of Texas Medical Branch, Galveston, TX 77550. Rates: $16.50 per year individuals. $27.00 per year institutions. Founded 1982. Sponsored by the Institute for the Medical Humanities, University of Texas Medical Branch, Galveston, TX. Published semiannually.

Major Field(s) of Interest: The journal fosters a dialogue between medical practitioners and literary scholars. It publishes one thematic issue and one general issue each year. Articles on any aspect of literature and medicine may be submitted that explore the various relationships between literature and medicine, such as images of healers, physician-writers, psychiatry and literature, use and abuse of literary concepts in medicine, literature and biomedical ethics, etc. Journal reviews books, but book reviews are solicited.

Manuscript Information: Articles of 15–40 double-spaced manuscripts including notes. Book reviews of 4–6 pages. Style: Chicago with endnotes. 2 copies of manuscript required. Submit original typescript and 1 copy. Use nonsexist language. Report in 8–12 weeks. Rejected manuscripts returned with S.A.S.E.

Payment: 2 copies of the issue. Offprints available at modest fee.

Indexed In: Arts and Humanities Citation Index, Current Contents, MEDLARS, MLA International Bibliography.

Copyright: By the Johns Hopkins University Press. Authors may republish their articles without charge in any volume consisting wholly of their own work, providing that each use acknowledge the original publication in *Literature and Medicine.*

*Literature and Theology

Oxford Journals, Oxford University Press, Walton Street, Oxford, OX2 6DP, England. Rates £30 UK. $60 North America. Founded 1987. Sponsored by the Oxford University Press, Oxford, England. Published 3 times per year.

Major Field(s) of Interest: Interdisciplinary study of literature and theology, narrative hermeneutics, cultural contexts, language, semiotics. The journal is neither a journal of theology nor a journal of literary studies, but exists within the creative tension between the two disciplines. Journal reviews books.

Manuscript Information: Articles of 3,000–5,000 words. Book reviews of 300–500 words. Style: Modified MLA and Chicago. Footnotes at the end of essay. 3 copies of manuscript required. Report in 1–2 months. Rejected manuscripts returned with S.A.S.E.

Payment: 30 offprints.

Indexed In: *Religion Index One, Periodicals (RIO), Index to Book Reviews in Religion, Religious and Theological Abstracts.*
Copyright: By Oxford University Press.

*THE MALCOLM LOWRY REVIEW

Department of English, Wilfrid Laurier University, Waterloo, Ontario, N2L 3C5, Canada. Rates: $25 per year individuals. $50 per year institutions. Founded 1977. Sponsored by the Department of English, Wilfrid Laurier University. Published twice a year.

Major Field(s) of Interest: Scholarly articles, notes, interviews, and reviews related to the life and works of Malcolm Lowry (1909–1957). Journal publishes an annual bibliography each Fall and reviews books.

Manuscript Information: Articles of any length. Reviews of any length. Book reviews of any length. Style: Any style. Report in 2–5 months. Rejected manuscripts returned with S.A.S.E.

Payment: None.

Indexed In: MLA International Bibliography.

Copyright: By the author.

MALEDICTA: THE INTERNATIONAL JOURNAL OF VERBAL AGGRESSION

Maledicta Press, P. O. Box 14123, Santa Rosa, CA 95402–6123. Rates: $20 per year individuals. $26 per year institutions. Founded 1977. Sponsored by the International Maledicta Society. Published biannually.

Major Field(s) of Interest: The journal specializes in uncensored glossaries and studies of all offensive and negatively-valued words and expressions, in all languages and from all cultures, past and present. Main areas of interest are the origin, etymology, meaning, use, and influence of Verbal Aggression and Verbal Abuse of any kind (swearwords, insults, epithets, terms of abuse; damnations, curses; threats; nicknames; racial, religious, ethnic, sexual slurs and stereotypes); words usually considered "vulgar," "profane" or "obscene" (blasphemy, scatology, sexual and excretory body parts and activities), as well as derogatory proverbs, similes, metaphors, exclamations, slang and jargon of all subgroups, offensive gestures, graffiti, and other maledicta.

Manuscript Information: Articles of 3–30 pages. Notes of 1–2 pages. No length restrictions on book reviews. Style: MLA with endnotes or within article and Chicago. Submit original manuscript. Report in 1–2 weeks. Rejected manuscripts returned with S.A.S.E.

Payment: 20 copies. Offprints available.

Copyright: By the journal. Copyright reverts to author after publication.

Mark Twain Circular

English Department, The Citadel, Charleston, SC 29409. Rates: $7 per year ($8 for foreign address) and includes membership in Mark Twain Circle. Founded 1987. Sponsored by the Mark Twain Circle of America. Published quarterly.

Major Field(s) of Interest: The journal publishes articles and notes relating to the life and/or work of Mark Twain. A continuing annotated bibliography "About Mark Twain" is included in each issue.

Manuscript Information: Articles of 1–5 pages. Notes of 1–5 pages. Style: MLA. Report in 2 weeks. Rejected manuscripts returned with S.A.S.E.

Payment: 3 copies.

Indexed In: Modern Humanities Research Association, MLA International Bibliography, American Literary Scholarship, Literary Criticism Register, Checklist of Scholarship on Southern Literature.

Copyright: All rights remain with author.

*Mark Twain Journal

c/o Department of English, The College of Charleston, Charleston, SC 29424. Rates: $15 per year ($5 discount for members of Mark Twain Circle). Founded 1936. Independent South Carolina nonprofit corporation.

Major Field(s) of Interest: Articles on Mark Twain's life and works with emphasis on original materials rather than subjective interpretations. Journal welcomes submissions that can be documented from Twain's own time and on contemporary sources.

Manuscript Information: Articles of 2–30 two-column pages. Notes of ½–2 pages. Style: MLA or Chicago. Report in 1 month. Rejected manuscripts returned with S.A.S.E., except for foreign submissions.

Payment: 10 copies of issue. Additional copies of issue can be ordered before printing.

Indexed In: MLA International Bibliography, MHRA, AES, Literary Criticism Register.

Copyright: By the journal, except when agreement is made otherwise. Generally, permission to reprint is granted.

Massachusetts Studies in English

Department of English, Bartlett Hall, University of Massachusetts, Amherst, MA 01003. Rates: $8 individuals. $12 libraries. Sponsored by the Department of English and the Graduate Program in English, the University of Massachusetts at Amherst. Published semiannually.

Major Field(s) of Interest: MSE is a generalist journal open to the study of all aspects of English and American literature. Special issues are devoted to the study of selected genres of nonfiction, psychoanalytical approaches to literature, feminist criticism, American Realism, and Victorian Studies. Each issue includes notification of the journal's future interest and the deadline for submission. Queries are appreciated.

Manuscript Information: Articles up to 7,000 words. Notes of 750–1,000 words. 3 copies of manuscript required. Style: *MLA Style Manual* (1985). Report in 8–12 weeks. Rejected manuscripts returned with S.A.S.E.

Payment: 2 copies of the issue.

Indexed In: MLA International Bibliography.

Copyright: By the journal. Authors are freely granted permission to reprint with usual credit line.

MEDIAEVAL STUDIES

Pontifical Institute of Mediaeval Studies, 59 Queen's Park Crescent E, Toronto, Ontario, M5S 2C4, Canada. Rates: $30 Canadian per year. Founded 1939. Sponsored by the Pontifica Institute of Mediaeval Studies. Published annually.

Major Field(s) of Interest: Publishes research on the Middle Ages, including that which deals with hitherto unedited manuscripts and/or archival material.

Manuscript Information: No restrictions on length of articles or notes. Style: Chicago and journal. 2 copies of manuscript required. Submit typescript and microfilm or xerox reproduction of medieval manuscripts being edited. Report in 4–5 months. Rejected manuscripts returned.

Payment: None.

Copyright: By the journal.

MEDIAEVALIA: A JOURNAL OF MEDIAEVAL STUDIES

Center for Medieval & Early Renaissance Studies, State University of New York, Binghamton, NY 13901. Founded 1975. Sponsored by the State University of New York, Binghamton, Center for Medieval & Early Renaissance Studies. Published annually.

Major Field(s) of Interest: Interdisciplinary articles on the Middle Ages as well as articles on history, literature, art history, and philosophy that, though not strictly interdisciplinary in themselves, may lead to interdisciplinary applications. Journal reviews books, but book reviews are by invitation only.

Manuscript Information: Articles up to 25 pages. Style: MLA. 2 copies of manuscript required. Report in 3 months. Rejected manuscripts returned with S.A.S.E.

Payment: Offprints.
Copyright: By the Center for Medieval & Early Renaissance Studies.

MEDIEVALIA ET HUMANISTICA: STUDIES IN
MEDIEVAL AND RENAISSANCE CULTURE
P. O. Box 13827, North Texas Station, Denton, TX 76203. Rates: $39.96 per year. Founded 1943. Sponsored by the Modern Language Association. Published annually.

Major Field(s) of Interest: Articles in all areas of medieval and Renaissance studies. Articles should: (1) make a marked contribution to knowledge or understanding; or (2) employ an interdisciplinary approach of importance to the understanding of the subject; or (3) treat a broad theme or topic; or (4) discuss new directions in humanistic scholarship; or (5) review major areas of current concern within particular fields. Journal reviews books.

Manuscript Information: Articles of 2,500–9,000 words. Style: Chicago or MLA. 2 copies of manuscript required. Submit original typescript. Report in 2 months. Rejected manuscripts returned with S.A.S.E.

Payment: 25 free offprints.

Indexed In: Art Index, Book Review Index, Humanities Index, International Bibliography of Periodical Literature, International Medieval Bibliography.

Copyright: By the Medieval and Renaissance Society.

MEDIUM AEVUM
University College, Oxford, OX1 4BH, United Kingdom. Rates: $45 per year. Founded 1932. Sponsored by the Society for the Study of Mediaeval Languages and Literatures. Published 2 times per year.

Major Field(s) of Interest: Articles on Mediaeval European languages and literatures. Journal reviews books.

Manuscript Information: Articles up to 12,000 words. Notes up to 4,000 words. Book reviews up to 800 words. Style: MLA, Chicago, and MHRA. 2 copies of manuscript required. Report in 1–4 months. Rejected manuscripts returned with S.A.S.E.

Payment: 10 copies.

Indexed In: Abstracts of English Studies, Indice Historico Espanol, Arts & Humanities Citation Index, MLA International Bibliography.

Copyright: By the Society. Permission normally granted subject to author's agreement.

*MELVILLE SOCIETY EXTRACTS

Department of English, Hofstra University, Hemstead, NY 11550. Rates: $7 per year individuals. $10 per year institutions. Founded 1969. Sponsored by the Melville Society of America. Published quarterly.

Major Field(s) of Interest: Short articles, notes, and miscellany concerning the life, times, writings, and reputation of Herman Melville (1819–1891). Studies of nineteenth-century figures or movements, as they relate to Melville, are also considered. Journal reviews books.

Manuscript Information: Articles up to 20 pages. Notes up to 10 pages. Book reviews up to 500 words. Style: Old *MLA Style Sheet.* 2 copies of manuscripts required. Report in 6–8 weeks. Rejected manuscripts returned with S.A.S.E.

Payment: Copies.

Indexed In: MLA International Bibliography.

Copyright: By the Melville Society of America. Authors may reprint with permission and credit line.

MENCKENIANA: A QUARTERLY REVIEW

Publications, Enoch Pratt Free Library, 400 Cathedral Street, Baltimore, MD 21201–4484. Rates: $12 per year. Founded 1962. Sponsored by the Enoch Pratt Free Library. Published quarterly.

Major Field(s) of Interest: All material must have some connection to the works and/or life of H. L. Mencken. Journal occasionally reviews books.

Manuscript Information: Articles of 300–2,000 words. Notes up to 1,000 words. Book reviews up to 500 words. Style: Chicago. Report in 3 months. Rejected manuscripts returned with S.A.S.E.

Payment: 3 copies of the issue.

Indexed In: Arts and Humanities Index, American Humanities Index.

Copyright: By the Pratt Free Library. Liberal permission, upon request, to reprint.

MICHIGAN QUARTERLY REVIEW

3032 Rackham Building, University of Michigan, Ann Arbor, MI 48109. Rates: $13 per year. Founded 1962. Sponsored by the University of Michigan. Published quarterly.

Major Field(s) of Interest: The journal is an interdisciplinary publication with special interest in literature and the humanities. The journal publishes essays on literary subjects, more often on authors and careers and issues than readings of specific texts. It also publishes essays on film, poetry, and fiction. Journal reviews books.

Manuscript Information: Articles of 15–25 pages. Book reviews of 8–10 pages. Style: Chicago. Report in 4–6 weeks. In summer, report in 6–8 weeks. Rejected manuscripts returned with S.A.S.E.

Payment: 2 copies plus $10 per page.

Copyright: All rights revert to the author after publication.

MICHIGAN STUDIES IN THE HUMANITIES

3040 MLB, Slavic Department, University of Michigan, Ann Arbor, MI 48109–1275. Founded 1980. Sponsored by the University of Michigan Slavic Department. Published irregularly.

Major Field(s) of Interest: Articles in the humanities, literary theory, and linguistics. Journal reviews books.

Manuscript Information: No restrictions on length of articles or book reviews. Style: MLA or Chicago. Report in 1–3 months. Rejected manuscripts not returned.

Payment: Copies.

Copyright: By the University of Michigan.

*MILTON QUARTERLY

378 Ellis Hall, Ohio University, Athens, OH 45701. Rates: $15 per year individuals. $24 per year institutions. Founded in 1967 as the MILTON NEWSLETTER; changed to the MILTON QUARTERLY in 1970. Sponsored by the Ohio University and the Milton Society of America. Published quarterly (March, May, October, and December).

Major Field(s) of Interest: The journal solicits letters containing news interesting to Miltonists. It will make an effort to print any legitimate query. It will also accept feature articles and notes (critical, explicatory, exegetical) focused on Milton and related Renaissance topics for which a letter of inquiry is advisable. Journal reviews books.

Manuscript Information: No set length for articles, notes, and book reviews. Style: 1985 *MLA Style Manual.* 2 copies of manuscript required. A 200–word abstract should accompany all manuscripts. Report in 2–3 months. Rejected manuscripts returned with comments. Include S.A.S.E.

Payment: 5 copies for each article. 2 copies for each note, query, or review.

Indexed In: Arts and Humanities Citation Index, the *American Humanities Index.*

Copyright: By the editor.

Milton Studies

Attention James D. Simmonds, Department of English, University of Western Australia, Nedlands, Perth, W. A., 6009, Australia. Rates: $9.95. Published annually. Founded 1969. Subscriptions should be sent to Sales and Promotion Manager, University of Pittsburgh Press, Pittsburgh. Pa. 15213.

Major Field(s) of Interest: Milton and Milton scholarship and criticism. Articles on subjects broadly related to Milton are also welcomed.

Manuscript Information: Articles over 3,000 words preferred. Style: MLA style sheet with footnotes printed at the end of the essay. Submit original typescript. Report in 3–4 months. Rejected manuscripts returned with S.A.S.E.

Payment: 1 free copy. Others may be purchased at 40% discount.

Copyright: By the University of Pittsburgh Press.

*Modern Drama

Editorial Offices: Erindale College, University of Toronto, Mississauga, Ontario, L5L 1C6, Canada. Rates: $20.00 per year individuals. $14.00 per year students. $37.50 per year institutions. Founded 1958. Sponsored by the University of Toronto Graduate Center for Study of Drama. Published quarterly.

Major Field(s) of Interest: Critical studies in dramatic literature of the modern period, from 1850 to the present. Journal reviews books. Annual International Bibliography in June issue.

Manuscript Information: Articles up to 4,000 words. Notes up to 1,000 words. Book reviews up to 500 words. Style: Modified MLA and Chicago. Endnotes. 2 copies of manuscript required. Report in 3 months. Rejected manuscripts returned with S.A.S.E. International Reply Coupons for countries outside Canada.

Payment: 3 copies of journal.

Indexed In: Canadian Periodical Index.

Copyright: By the journal. Permission required for any reprinting.

*Modern Fiction Studies

Department of English, Heavilon Hall, Purdue University, West Lafayette, IN 47907. Rates: $15 per year individuals. Founded 1955. Sponsored by the Department of English, Purdue University. Published quarterly.

Major Field(s) of Interest: Criticism, scholarship, and bibliography of fiction in all languages from 1880 to the present. Articles are solicited that use any legitimate approach that illuminates a work of fiction, a writer, or a problem in fictional technique. The journal also welcomes studies of an author's total work and of the forms, techniques, styles, and uses of various other disciplines within the study of fiction. Two issues each year are devoted to individual writers, groups of writers, or specific topics. Future special numbers are listed on the inside back cover of each issue. Journal reviews books, but all book reviews are solicited.

Manuscript Information: Articles up to 25 pages. Notes up to 15 pages. Book reviews up to 500 words. Style: MLA (1985) with endnotes. Report in 1 month. Rejected manuscripts returned with S.A.S.E.

Payment: 2 copies of the journal plus offprints.

Indexed In: MLA International Bibliography.

Copyright: By the Purdue Research Foundation. Authors have right of republication without charge, subject to acknowledgement of original publication. Reprint fees are shared with authors 50/50.

*MODERN LANGUAGE QUARTERLY

Department of English, University of Washington, Seattle, WA 98105. Rates: $16 per year individuals. $26 per year institutions. Founded 1940. Sponsored by the University of Washington. Published quarterly.

Major Field(s) of Interest: The journal publishes scholarly and critical articles dealing with post-classical texts and contexts in English, American, Germanic, Romance, and comparative literatures. Journal reviews books, but all book reviews are solicited.

Manuscript Information: Articles of 4,500–8,000 words. Book reviews of 900–2,500 words. Style: Chicago with endnotes. Report in 6 weeks to 3 months. Rejected manuscripts returned with S.A.S.E.

Payment: 3 copies of journal issue. Offprints are available.

Indexed In: Current Contents, Humanities Index, Academic Index, MLA International Bibliography, Arts & Humanites Citation Index, Abstracts of English Studies, and others.

Copyright: By the University of Washington. No charge for reuse by author. Reprint in other work, $100 split with author.

*THE MODERN LANGUAGE REVIEW

c/o Professor R. M. Walker (Editor), Birkbeck College, Malet Street, London, WC1E 7HX, England. Price: £13 (US $25) to members of MHRA. Published quarterly. Founded 1905. Sponsored and published by the Modern Humanities Research Association and is the official journal of the association.

Major Field(s) of Interest: Research and criticism on English, Romance, Germanic, and Slavonic language and literature, also hitherto unprinted texts and documents, and reviews of books in these fields.

Manuscript Information: Articles in English, preferably not exceeding 12,500 words. *MHRA Style Book*, Third Edition. Footnotes at end of typescript. Report as soon as possible.

Payment: 20 offprints of articles; more available at cost. 10 offprints of reviews.

Copyright: MHRA retains copyright. Reprint request to be addressed to the Editor.

*MODERN PHILOLOGY: A JOURNAL DEVOTED TO RESEARCH IN MEDIEVAL AND MODERN LITERATURE

1050 East 59th Street, Chicago, IL 60637. Rates: $25 per year individuals. $40 per year institutions. $15 per year students and MLA members. Founded 1903. Independent journal published by the University of Chicago Press. Published quarterly: February, May, August, November.

Major Field(s) of Interest: By its own definition, the publication is "a journal devoted to research in medieval and modern literature." The journal has a tradition of publishing multicultural and comparativist scholarship with a strong historical orientation. It publishes essays on literary history, literary criticism, and articles documenting primary sources for literary works. While its primary emphasis is on American, British, and European literatures, the journal also publishes material on Continental, Eastern European, and Latin American subjects. It is interested in all significant developments in the fields of literary study and in major Western languages. Short notes are published only when they are of exceptional importance. Journal reviews books, but book reviews and review-articles are solicited.

Manuscript Information: Articles of 15–30 pages. Notes of 7–30 pages. Book reviews of 4–8 pages. Style: Chicago with complete bibliographical data double-spaced at end of text. Report in 90 days. Rejected manuscripts returned with S.A.S.E.

Payment: 5 copies of issue or 1 year's subscription for articles. 2 copies for reviews. Offprints available for a small fee.

Indexed In: Arts and Humanities Citation Index, Current Contents: Arts and Humanities, Humanities Abstracts, Humanities Index, MLA International Bibliography.

Copyright: By the University of Chicago Press. Permission to reprint must be obtained.

MOSAIC: A JOURNAL FOR THE INTERDISCIPLINARY STUDY OF LITERATURE

208 Tier Building, University of Manitoba, Winnipeg, Manitoba R3T 2N2, Canada. Rates: $19.50 per year individuals. $29.00 per year institutions. Founded 1967. Sponsored by the University of Manitoba.

Major Field(s) of Interest: The journal publishes articles of an interdisciplinary nature that illuminate the study of literature from all periods and nationalities. One of the four yearly issues is a special issue on specific themes. The journal publishes either in English or French. Abstract in English and French required.

Manuscript Information: Articles of 15–25 manuscript pages. Style: MLA with essential notes only. 2 copies of manuscript required. Report in 3–5 months. Rejected manuscripts returned with return envelope and unattached postage.

Payment: 2 copies of issue and 25 offprints.

Indexed In: Canadian Magazine Index, Gale Directory of Periodicals, MLA International Bibliography, American Humanities Index, Librarians' Handbook.

Copyright: By the journal. Academic reprinting granted to the author. Commercial reprinting requires permission and payment of fee.

*THE NABOKOVIAN

Department of Slavic Languages, University of Kansas, Lawrence, KS 66045. Rates: $9 per year individuals. $11 per year institutions. Founded 1978. Sponsored by the Vladimir Nabokov Society. Published semiannually (Spring and Fall).

Major Field(s) of Interest: The journal serves to report and stimulate Nabokov scholarship and to create a link between Nabokov scholars in the United States and elsewhere.

Manuscript Information: No restrictions on length of articles. Notes up to 1,000 words. Style: MLA. No footnotes. Report in 30 days. Rejected manuscripts returned.

Payment: Copies.

Copyright: Not copyright protected.

THE NATHANIEL HAWTHORNE REVIEW

English Department, Clemson University, Clemson, SC 29634. Rates: $6 per year (includes membership in the Nathaniel Hawthorne Society). Founded 1989. Sponsored by the Nathaniel Hawthorne Society, Clemson University, and Bowdoin College. Published 2 times per year.

Major Field(s) of Interest: Short and medium-length articles, lists of conference papers, brief book reviews, notes and queries, notices of research in progress, Hawthorne Society news items, and annual bibliography.

Manuscript Information: Articles up to 3,500 words. Notes up to 1,000 words. Book reviews up to 250 words. Style: MLA. Submit original typescript. Report in 6 weeks. Rejected manuscripts returned.

Payment: Copies.
Copyright: By the author.

THE NEW YORK REVIEW OF BOOKS

250 West 57th Street, New York, NY 10107. Rates: $39 per year. Founded 1963. Published 21 times per year (biweekly except monthly in January, July, August, and September).

Major Field(s) of Interest: Critical articles on politics, culture, literature, and the arts which shape the standards and thinking of American intellectual life. Journal reviews books.

Manuscript Information: Articles up to 3,000 words. Book reviews up to 1,000 words. Journal publishes material in a variety of styles. It accepts no responsibility for unsolicited manuscripts.

Payment: Copies.
Copyright: By the journal.

*NINETEENTH-CENTURY CONTEXTS

Department of Philosophy, Temple University, Philadelphia, PA 19122. Rates: $20 per year (2 issues). Individuals receive membership in the parent organization, Interdisciplinary Nineteenth-Century Studies (INCS). Institutions do not. Founded 1980 (as ROMANTICISM PAST AND PRESENT). Sponsored by INCS, Northeastern University College of Arts and Sciences, and Temple University. Published semiannually.

Major Field(s) of Interest: The journal welcomes articles on all aspects of nineteenth-century culture, especially those that are interdisciplinary and/or of major interest to a wide range of disciplines. Forum contributions are solicited, and contributions are restricted to members of INCS. Journal reviews books, but contributors should query editor before submitting.

Manuscript Information: Articles up to 10,000 words. Notes up to 2,000 words. Book reviews of 500–2,000 words. Style: Chicago and MLA with endnotes. 2 copies of manuscript required. Submit original typescript. Report in 4–6 months. Rejected manuscripts returned with S.A.S.E.

Payment: 5 free copies of the journal.
Indexed In: America: History and Life, Historical Abstracts.
Copyright: By the journal. Journal will assign permission to reprint upon written request free of charge.

*NINETEENTH-CENTURY LITERATURE

Department of English, 405 Hilgard Avenue, University of California. Los Angeles, CA 90024-1530. Rates: $19 per year individuals. $33 per year institutions. Founded 1945. Sponsored by the University of California Press, 2120 Berkeley Way, Berkeley, CA 94720 and the Department of English UCLA. Published quarterly.

Major Field(s) of Interest: Scholarly and critical articles on British and American English-language literature of the nineteenth century, both fiction and nonfiction. Journal reviews scholarly and critical books of the period 1800–1900, but all book reviews are solicited.

Manuscript Information: Articles of 25–35 pages. Notes of 8–12 pages. Book reviews up to 4 pages. Style: *MLA Style Manual* 5.8 (not *PMLA* style). Report in 6–8 weeks. Rejected manuscripts returned with S.A.S.E.

Payment: 2 copies of the journal plus 25 offprints for articles and notes. 1 copy of the journal for reviews.

Copyright: By the Regents of the University of California. Authors may use their own articles without charge in any book of which they are the editor or the author.

*NINETEENTH-CENTURY PROSE

Department of Language & Literature, Mesa State College, Grand Junction, CO 81502. Rates: $11 per year individuals. $25 per year institutions. Founded 1973 (As THE ARNOLD NEWSLETTER, later THE ARNOLDIAN). Sponsored by Mesa State College. Published semiannually.

Major Field(s) of Interest: The journal accepts articles, notes, bibliographical items, and essay-reviews on Victorian nonfiction prose, writers, and historical and cultural contexts of those writers. Journal reviews books, but book reviews are solicited.

Manuscript Information: Articles of 2,000–4,000 words. Notes of 300–1,500 words. Book reviews of 1,000–2,000 words. Style: MLA with endnotes and list of Works Cited. 2 copies of manuscript required. Report in 2–4 months. Rejected manuscripts returned with S.A.S.E.

Payment: 2 copies.

Indexed In: MLA *International Bibliography, Abstracts of English Studies.*

Copyright: By the author. Reprints authorized upon request.

*NINETEENTH-CENTURY STUDIES

English Department, The Citadel, Charleston, SC 29409. Rates: $15 per year individuals. $25 per year institutions. Founded 1987. Sponsored by the Southeastern Nineteenth-Century Studies Association. Published annually.

Major Field(s) of Interest: NCS is an interdisciplinary journal, accepting scholarly articles on all aspects of nineteenth-century culture from all disciplines: literature, modern languages, history, art, architecture, social science, philosophy, religion, music, etc. Journal reviews books.

Manuscript Information: Articles of 15–30 pages. Book reviews of 5–10 pages. Style: MLA. Footnotes should be parenthetical. 2 copies of manuscript required. Report in 3 months. Rejected manuscripts returned with S.A.S.E.

Payment: 3 copies of journal.

Indexed In: MLA International Bibliography.

Copyright: By the Southeastern Nineteenth-Century Studies Association. Reprinting policy determined on an individual basis.

*NINETEENTH CENTURY THEATRE

Department of English, University of Massachusetts, Amherst, MA 01003. Rates: $12 per year individuals. $20 per year institutions. Founded 1973. Sponsored by the Department of English and the Graduate School and Five Colleges, Inc. Published twice yearly: Summer and Winter.

Major Field(s) of Interest: Articles, review essays, book reviews, bibliographies, and other research-related documents on all aspects of English-speaking and European theater for the years 1792–1914. Illustrated articles are welcome.

Manuscript Information: Articles up to 8,000 words. Notes up to 500 words. Book reviews up to 1,000 words. Style: MLA. 3 copies of manuscript required. Report in 8 weeks. Rejected manuscripts returned with S.A.S.E.

Payment: 2 copies of the journal.

Indexed In: International Bibliography of Theatre, YWES, MLA International Bibliography.

Copyright: By the journal. Reprint permission granted.

NMAL: NOTES ON MODERN AMERICAN LITERATURE

English Department, St. John's University, Jamaica, NY 11439. Founded 1976. Sponsored by the Editors. Published 3 times per year.

Major Field(s) of Interest: Articles on modern American literature, 1900 to the present.

Manuscript Information: Articles of 500–1,500 words. Notes of 500–1,500 words. Style: MLA. Submit typescript. Report in 2 months. Rejected manuscripts returned with S.A.S.E.

Payment: Copies.

Copyright: By the editors.

Notes and Queries

Pembroke College, Oxford, OX1 1DW, England. Rates: £26 or US $52 per annum. Founded 1849. Published by the Oxford University Press.

Major Field(s) of Interest: Literary and historical notes of any type: source materials, bibliographical notes, genealogy, lexicography, textual emendations, literary parallels, and readers' queries and answers. Emphasis is on the factual rather than the speculative. Reviews books. Articles selected on editorial and/or peer review.

Manuscript Information: Articles should be brief. A style sheet is available; use *Hart's Rules* and *Oxford Dictionary for Writers and Editors.* Report in 2–3 months.

Payment: None.

Copyright: Copyright belongs to the publisher; permission to reprint must be sought from them and is usually obtained.

Notes on Contemporary Literature

c/o Department of English, West Georgia College, Carrollton, GA 30118. Rates: $5 per year individuals. $10 per year institutions. Founded 1971. Sponsored by the editor: W. S. Doxey. Published 5 times per year (January, March, May, September, November).

Major Field(s) of Interest: Articles on contemporary literature from 1940 to the present. Journal reviews books.

Manuscript Information: Articles up to 1,000 words. Notes up to 1,000 words. Book reviews up to 1,000 words. Style: None. Place notes in text. Report in 2 weeks. Rejected manuscripts returned with S.A.S.E.

Payment: Cash plus 2 copies of the issue.

Indexed In: MLA International Bibliography.

Copyright: By the editor. Reassigned to the author on request.

*Papers of the Bibliographical Society of America

Department of English, University of Maryland, College Park, MD 20742. Rates: $30 per year (through membership in the Society). Founded 1904. Sponsored by the Bibliographical Society of America. Published quarterly.

Major Field(s) of Interest: Articles and notes that deal with books and manuscripts in any field, but they should involve consideration of the book or manuscript (the physical object) as historical evidence, whether for establishing a text or illuminating the history of book production, publication, distribution, or collecting, or for other purposes. Studies of the printing, publishing, and allied trades are also welcome. Journal reviews books.

Manuscript Information: No maximum length for articles. Notes up to 12 typescript pages. Book reviews of 1–4 pages. Style: Chicago Footnotes: Old MLA Style (modified). Report in 4 months. Rejected manuscripts returned with S.A.S.E.

Payment: 40 copies of articles; 20 copies of reviews.

Indexed In: MLA International Bibliography.

Copyright: By the Bibliographical Society of America. Permission to reprint freely granted to author.

*PAPERS ON LANGUAGE AND LITERATURE: A JOURNAL FOR SCHOLARS AND CRITICS OF LANGUAGE AND LITERATURE

Southern Illinois University, Edwardsville, IL 62026–1434. Rates: $12 per year individuals. $24 per year institutions. Founded 1965. Sponsored by Board of Trustees, Southern Illinois University. Published quarterly.

Major Field(s) of Interest: Articles devoted to literary history, theory, analysis, stylistics, interpretation, and evaluation. The journal also publishes essays dealing with or relating to writings in English, American, French, German, Spanish, Russian, and other languages. Brief notes and review essays are included.

Manuscript Information: Articles up to 30 double-spaced pages. Notes of 4–8 pages. Style: *MLA Style Manual* (1985) with endnotes. 2 copies of manuscript required. Report in 3–5 months. 1 copy of rejected manuscripts returned with S.A.S.E.

Payment: 2 copies.

Copyright: By Southern Illinois University, Edwardsville.

PAR RAPPORT: A JOURNAL OF THE HUMANITIES

English Department, Illinois College, Jacksonville, IL 62650. Rates: $8 per year. Founded 1978. Sponsored by Illinois College. Published annually.

Major Field(s) of Interest: Articles in all areas of the humanities and scientific theory with a main emphasis on literature. Journal reviews books and publishes review articles, but review articles are solicited.

Manuscript Information: Articles of 10–12 typescript pages. For length of book reviews, query editor. No length restrictions on notes. Style: MLA. Report in 2–3 months. Rejected manuscripts returned with S.A.S.E.

Payment: Copies.

Copyright: By the author.

*PERSUASIONS: JOURNAL OF THE
JANE AUSTEN SOCIETY OF NORTH AMERICA

Department of English, University of Arizona, Tucson, AZ 85721. Rates: $5 per year individuals. $10 per year institutions. Founded 1979. Sponsored by the Jane Austen Society of North America. Published annually.

Major Field(s) of Interest: Contributions are invited on any aspect of Jane Austen, her family, her art, or her times.

Manuscript Information: Articles of 1,000–3,000 words. Notes of 300–750 words. Style: MLA. Old or New with endnotes. Journal appreciates a lucid style and tries to avoid scholarly jargon. Rejected manuscripts returned with S.A.S.E.

Payment: 6 copies of the journal.

Indexed In: MLA International Bibliography.

Copyright: By the author.

*PHILOLOGICAL QUARTERLY

311 English/Philosophy Building, University of Iowa, Iowa City, IA 52242. Founded 1922. Sponsored by the University of Iowa. Published 4 times per year.

Major Field(s) of Interest: Articles in classical and modern languages and literatures. Journal reviews books.

Manuscript Information: Articles up to 8,000 words. Notes up to 2,500 words. Book review up to 1,500 words. Style: Chicago. Computer-accessible articles have priority for publication. Report in 2 months. Rejected manuscripts returned with S.A.S.E.

Payment: Copies.

Copyright: By the University of Iowa.

PHOENIX

Department of English, Liberal Arts College, Korea University, 1, 5–ka, Anam-dong, Sungbuk-ku, Seoul 136, Korea. Founded 1955. Sponsored by the Department of English, Korea University. Published annually.

Major Field(s) of Interest: Articles and reviews in English language and literature (American literature included). Contributors must be members of the English Literature Society of Korea University. Journal reviews books.

Manuscript Information: Articles of 10–20 printed pages. Notes of 800–1,000 words. Book reviews of 3–4 pages. Style: MLA. Submit original manuscript. Report in 3 months. Rejected manuscripts returned with S.A.S.E.

Payment: 1 copy of the journal plus 30 offprints.

Copyright: By the author.

*PMLA: PUBLICATIONS OF THE MODERN LANGUAGE ASSOCIATION OF AMERICA

10 Astor Place, New York, NY 10003-6981. Annual dues, which include subscription to PMLA, are based on members' incomes. Subscription price for libraries and other institutions $100. Founded 1884. Sponsored by the Modern Language Association. Published 6 times a year (January, March, May, September, October, and November).

Major Field(s) of Interest: PMLA welcomes essays of interest to those concerned with the study of language and literature. As the publication of a large and heterogeneous association, the journal is receptive to a variety of topics, whether general or specific, and to all scholarly methods and theoretical perspectives. The ideal PMLA essay exemplifies the best of its kind, whatever the kind; addresses a significant problem; draws out clearly the implications of its findings; and engages the attention of its audience through a concise, readable presentation. The PMLA urges its contributors to be sensitive to the social implications of language and to seek wording free of discriminatory overtones. Only members of the association may submit articles to PMLA.

Manuscript Information: Articles of 2,500-9,000 words including notes. No limitation on notes. Style: MLA. Report in 8-10 weeks. Rejected manuscripts returned with S.A.S.E. If article is accepted, a 150 word abstract is required.

Payment: 25 sets of tearsheets.

Indexed In: Humanities Index, MLA International Bibliography.

Copyright: By the journal. Right to reprint can be obtained with permission and credit line.

POE STUDIES/DARK ROMANTICISM: HISTORY, THEORY, INTERPRETATION

Department of English, Washington State University, Pullman, WA 99164-5020. Rates: $8 per year individuals. $12 per year institutions. Founded 1968. Sponsored by the Department of English, Washington State University. Published 2 times per year with occasional supplements.

Major Field(s) of Interest: The journal provides a forum that seeks to promote informed, rigorous, cumulative dialogue about Poe and about the modes and traditions of Dark Romanticism to which he is linked. The journal invites submissions of relevant articles and notes from any critical, historical, or scholarly approach, welcomes reasoned rebuttals to arguments appearing here or elsewhere, and encourages proposals, submissions and projects. Journal reviews books, but reviews are solicited.

Manuscript Information: Articles up to 25 manuscript pages. Notes are restricted to 1,000 words or less. Style: Chicago. 2 copies of manuscript required. Manuscripts must be typed on IBM Selectric or be printed on a letter-quality printer in letter gothic, courier, or prestige elite typeface with unjustified right margins preferred. Report in 2–4 months. Rejected manuscripts returned with S.A.S.E.

Payment: 3–10 copies, depending on the type of article.

Indexed In: Literary Criticism Register, MLA International Bibliography, ALS.

Copyright: By the journal. Free use for authors.

*PROSE STUDIES: HISTORY, THEORY, CRITICISM

Department of English, Kent State University, Kent, OH 44242–0001. Rates: $40 per year individuals. $75 per year institutions. Founded 1977. Sponsored by Frank Cass & Co., Ltd., London. Published 3 times per year.

Major Field(s) of Interest: The journal is a forum for the discussion of all forms of autobiography, biography, political, social, and philosophical treatises, theological writings, essays, diaries, letters. etc. Articles are invited on individual texts, genres, literary theory, literary history, rhetorical theory, major figures, and criticism of nonfictional prose. Articles on non-English language writers are appropriate, but the articles must be submitted in English. Journal reviews books.

Manuscript Information: No length limitations on articles. Notes of 1,500–3,000 words. Book reviews of 1,000–1,500 words. Style: Chicago. 2 copies of manuscript required. Report in 4–8 weeks. Rejected manuscripts returned with S.A.S.E.

Payment: 2 copies of the issue and 25 free offprints.

Indexed In: MLA International Bibliography.

Copyright: By Frank Cass & Co., Ltd. Authors are freely granted permission to reprint with usual credit line.

*PROTEUS: A JOURNAL OF IDEAS

Office of Public Relations, 302 Old Main, Shippensburg University, Shippensburg, PA 17257. Rates: $10 per year. Founded 1983. Sponsored by Shippensburg University. Published semiannually (March and October).

Major Field(s) of Interest: The journal provides an interdisciplinary approach to ideas and literature with each issue devoted to a single theme, highlighted by an article written by an authority in the field. Calls for papers are published in *The Chronicle of Higher Education.* Journal publishes book reviews occasionally.

Manuscript Information: Articles up to 5,000 words. Book reviews up to 3,000 words. Style: MLA or Chicago. Footnotes in text. 4 copies of manuscript required. Report in June and late January or early February. Rejected manuscripts returned with S.A.S.E.

Payment: Usually 4 copies of the journal. More upon request.

Indexed In: MCA, PAIS, America: History and Life, Current Contents, Arts and Humanities Citation Index, Historical Abstracts, MLA International Bibliography.

Copyright: By the journal. Reprint with permission and credit line.

*PYNCHON NOTES

c/o John M. Krafft, English Department, Miami University, Hamilton Campus, 1601 Peck Blvd., Hamilton, OH 45011. Rates: $9 per year. Founded 1979. Sponsored in part by the English Department, Miami University and the University of Wisconsin-Eau Claire. Published every 2 years.

Major Field(s) of Interest: Essays and notes on all aspects of Thomas Pynchon's work considered from any critical perspective in the context of contemporary American or comparative literature. Also, contemporary, modern, twentieth century, American literary theory. Journal includes current bibliography and reviews books.

Manuscript Information: Articles of any length. Notes of any length. Book reviews of any length. Style: MLA (New or old). Endnotes preferred (1984 MLA). 1–3 manuscripts required. Report in 4–12 weeks. Rejected manuscripts returned with S.A.S.E.

Payment: In copies.

Indexed In: MLA International Bibliography, Literary Criticism Register, Year's Work in English Studies, American Literary Scholarship, Abstracts of English Studies.

Copyright: By the editors but is not proprietary.

*QUEEN'S QUARTERLY

Queen's University, Kingston, Ontario, K7L 3N6, Canada. Rates: US $22 per year individuals outside Canada. $20 per year in Canada. $25 per year institutions. Sponsored by the *Queen's Quarterly* Committee of Queen's University. Published quarterly.

Major Field(s) of Interest: A multidisciplinary journal that publishes articles on literature, history, the humanities, politics, culture, foreign affairs, science, and arts and letters. Authors should be specialists but write for the general educated reader. The journal also publishes some poetry and fiction as well as review articles. It contains an extensive new book section, and publishes book reviews, reviews of gallery exhibitions, musicals, and dramatic performances. Book reviews, however, are usually commissioned.

Manuscript Information: Articles of 3,000–8,000 words. Book reviews up to 800 words. Style: MLA (1988). See recent issues for style and format. 3 copies of manuscript required. Report in 3 months. Rejected manuscripts returned with S.A.S.E.

Payment: 1 year's subscription and 25 offprints for articles. 2 copies of the issue and offprints for reviews.

Indexed In: Canadian Periodical Index, Arts & Humanities Citation Index, Current Contents, MLA International Bibliography, Abstracts of English Studies, Historical Abstracts, America: History and Life, International Political Science Abstracts, Canadian Literature Index, A Guide to Periodicals, Book Review Index, Canadian Magazine Index.

Copyright: By the author. Journal retains first North American rights only.

RE: ARTES LIBERALES

School of Liberal Arts, Stephen F. Austin State University, P. O. Box 13007, SFA Station, Nacogdoches, TX 75962. Rates: $4 per year. Founded 1974. Sponsored by Stephen F. Austin State University, School of Liberal Arts. Published 2 times per year (Fall and Spring).

Major Field(s) of Interest: Articles in the following disciplines are invited: anthropology, geography, history, languages, literature, philosophy, political science, psychology, religion, and sociology. The journal also invites original poetry and short works of drama and fiction.

Manuscript Information: Articles up to 5,000 words. Notes of 500–1,000 words. Style: *MLA Handbook.* 2 copies of manuscript required. Report in 1 month. Rejected manuscripts returned with S.A.S.E.

Payment: Copies.

Copyright: By the author.

READING MEDIEVAL STUDIES

Department of History, University of Reading, Berkshire, RG6 2AA, Reading, England. Rates: £7.00 per year plus postage. Founded 1975. Sponsored by the University of Reading, Graduate Center for Medieval Studies and the British Academy. Published annually.

Major Field(s) of Interest: Articles on medieval studies, including history, literature (Latin or vernacular), philosophy, archaeology, and art. Journal reviews books.

Manuscript Information: No length restrictions on articles, notes, or book reviews. Style: MLA with endnotes. Report in 3 months. Rejected manuscripts returned with S.A.S.E.

Payment: 6 free copies of volume. Others at half price.

Copyright: By the University of Reading, Graduate Center for Medieval Studies. Reprint rights are dealt with individually, but generally the journal is cooperative in return for due acknowledgement.

RECORDS OF EARLY ENGLISH DRAMA NEWSLETTER

English Department, Erindale College, University of Toronto in Mississauga, Mississauga, Ontario, L5L lC6, Canada. Rates: $7.50 (£4.00) per year. Founded 1976. Sponsored by Erindale College, University of Toronto. Published semiannually.

Major Field(s) of Interest: Articles and notes dealing with records and external evidence of early English drama and minstrelsy to 1642. Journal reviews books.

Manuscript Information: No length restrictions on articles, notes, or book reviews. Style: Journal. Report in 1 month. Rejected manuscripts are not returned.

Payment: 2 copies.

Copyright: By the journal. No reprints without permission.

*RELIGION AND LITERATURE

Department of English, University of Notre Dame, Notre Dame, IN 46556. Rates: $15 per year individuals. $18 per year institutions. Founded 1978. Sponsored by the Department of English, University of Notre Dame. Published 3 times per year.

Major Field(s) of Interest: Critical and scholarly articles concerning the relations between religion in any form and literature in any genre. Journal reviews books, but book reviews are commissioned.

Manuscript Information: Articles up to 30 typed pages. Notes up to 2 typed pages. Book reviews up to 8 typed pages. Style: Chicago. 3 copies of manuscript required.

Payment: 2 copies and 6 offprints.

Indexed In: Abstracts of English Studies, American Humanities Index, American Literature, The Catholic Periodical & Literature Index, Christianity & Literature, MLA International Bibliography, MHRA.

Copyright: By the journal. Authors must request permission to reprint.

*RENAISSANCE AND REFORMATION/RENAISSANCE ET RÉFORME

Victoria College, University of Toronto, Toronto, Ontario, M5S 1K7, Canada. Rates: $15 individuals. $30 institutions. Founded 1964. Sponsored by the Toronto Renaissance and Reformation Colloquium, Victoria Center for Reformation and Renaissance Studies, Canadian Society for

Renaissance Studies, and Pacific Northwest Conference. Published quarterly.

Major Field(s) of Interest: Original research in all areas and on all aspects of the Renaissance and the Reformation. Journal reviews books. Manuscripts accepted in either English or French.

Manuscript Information: No limit on articles (within reason). Notes should be as brief as possible. No limit on book reviews. Style: MLA. 2 copies of manuscript required. Report in 6 weeks. Rejected manuscripts returned with S.A.S.E.

Payment: Copies.

Indexed In: Bowker, MLA International Bibliography.

Copyright: By the journal. Reprint rights with permission.

RENAISSANCE DRAMA

Newberry Library, 60 West Walton Street, Chicago, IL 60610. Rates: $45.95 per year. Founded 1956. Sponsored by the Newberry Library Center for Renaissance Studies and Northwestern University. Published annually (Spring).

Major Field(s) of Interest: Essays are encouraged that explore the relationship of Renaissance dramatic traditions to their precursors and successors; have an interdisciplinary orientation; explore the relationship of drama to society and history; examine the impact of new forms of interpretation on Renaissance drama; and raise fresh questions about the texts and performances of Renaissance plays. The journal is devoted to the understanding of drama of all nations in the fifteenth, sixteenth, and seventeenth centuries as a central feature of Renaissance culture.

Manuscript Information: No restrictions on length of articles or notes. Style: MLA. Report in 3–5 months. Rejected manuscripts returned.

Payment: Offprints.

Copyright: By Northwestern University Press and the Newberry Library Center for Renaissance Studies. Reprinting with permission.

*RENAISSANCE PAPERS

323 Allen Building, Duke University, Durham, NC 27706. Rates: $20 per year. Founded 1956. Sponsored by the Southeastern Renaissance Conference. Published annually.

Major Field(s) of Interest: Publishes selected papers presented at the Annual Meetings of the Southeastern Renaissance Conference. Contributors must be a member of the Southeastern Renaissance Society.

Manuscript Information: Articles up to 10 pages. Style: MLA. Report in 2 months. Rejected manuscripts returned.

Payment: Offprints.
Copyright: By the journal and by the author.

*RENAISSANCE QUARTERLY

Renaissance Society of America, Inc., 1161 Amsterdam Avenue, New York, NY 10027. Rates: $35 per year. Founded 1948. Sponsored by the Renaissance Society of America. Published 4 times per year.

Major Field(s) of Interest: Articles, book reviews, news and notes, and a bibliography on subjects involving all aspects (literary, historical, artistic) of the Renaissance. Journal reviews books.

Manuscript Information: Articles of 2,000–12,500 words. Book reviews of 500–800 words. Style: MLA. 2 copies of manuscript required. Submit double-spaced typescript. Author's name and affiliation should be on cover sheet or separate sheet only. Report in 1–6 months. Rejected manuscripts returned with S.A.S.E.

Payment: Offprints.
Copyright: By the journal.

*RENASCENCE: ESSAYS ON VALUES IN LITERATURE

Brooks Hall, Marquette University, Milwaukee, WI 53233. Rates: $20 per year. Founded 1948. Sponsored by Marquette University Press. Published quarterly.

Major Field(s) of Interest: Elucidates the Christian perspective as a way of looking at literature and discovering the meaning of values in literature. The journal is interested in exploring the relation between criticism and values and accepts manuscripts on world literature from any historical period. The editorial policy defines a perspective rather than a subject matter.

Manuscript Information: Articles of 3,000–7,500 words. Style: *MLA Style Sheet.* 2 copies of manuscript preferred. Submit original typescript with full bibliographical information in the "Works Cited" and a minimum of endnotes. Report in 3–5 months. Rejected manuscripts returned only with S.A.S.E.

Payment: 2 copies of the issue. Offprints of the article are available at a modest fee.

Copyright: By the journal. Authors are freely granted permission to reprint with conventional credit line.

RES PUBLICA LITTERARUM:
CLASSICAL, MEDIEVAL, RENAISSANCE STUDIES

c/o Professor Sesto Prete, Editor, Via dell'Abbazia, 40, 61032, Fano, PS 61032, Italy or Department of Classics, University of Kansas, Lawrence,

KS 66045 USA. Rates: $40 per year. Founded 1978. Sponsored by Istituto Intern. di Studi Piceni. Published annually.

Major Field(s) of Interest: Articles from different humanistic disciplines that touch upon or relate to the Classical, Medieval, and Renaissance periods. Journal reviews books.

Manuscript Information: Articles up to 20 manuscript pages. Notes up to 4 pages. Book reviews up to 2 pages. Style: MLA. 2 copies of manuscript required. Report in 6 months. Rejected manuscripts returned with S.A.S.E.

Payment: Copies may be acquired from the printer.

Copyright: By the journal. Permission to reprint may be requested from the editor.

RESEARCH OPPORTUNITIES IN RENAISSANCE DRAMA

English Department, University of Kansas, Lawrence, KS 66045. Founded 1956. Sponsored by the Editor: David M. Bergeron. Published annually.

Major Field(s) of Interest: The journal reports on the MLA Sessions on Renaissance and Medieval Drama; it includes bibliographies and research articles. Journal reviews books.

Manuscript Information: Articles of 30–40 pages. Book reviews up to 2,500 words. Style: MLA. Report in 2 months. Rejected manuscripts returned.

Payment: Copies.

Copyright: By the editor.

*RESOURCES FOR AMERICAN LITERARY STUDY

Department of English, University of Maryland, College Park, MD 20742. Rates: $15 per year US. $18 per year elsewhere. Founded 1971. Sponsored by the English Department, University of Maryland. Published twice yearly (Spring and Fall).

Major Field(s) of Interest: (1) annotated and evaluative checklists of critical and biographical scholarship on the significant works of major authors or the total work of minor authors; (2) evaluative bibliographical essays on major authors, works, genres, trends, and periods; (3) informative accounts or catalogues of significant collections of research materials of literary and cultural interest available in archives and libraries, with special attention to recent acquisitions; and (4) edited correspondence, personal papers, unpublished materials, and other documents and essays of interest to literary scholars and cultural historians.

Manuscript Information: Articles up to 20–25 pages. Notes from 1–5 pages. Reviews from 1–5 pages. Style: MLA. 2 copies of manuscript required. Report in 2 months. Rejected manuscripts returned with S.A.S.E.

Payment: None.
Indexed In: MLA International Bibliography.
Copyright: By the journal. Reprint with permission for fee.

*RESTORATION: STUDIES IN ENGLISH LITERARY CULTURE, 1660–1700

Department of English, University of Tennessee, Knoxville, TN 37996–0430. Rates: $8 per year individuals and institutions. Sponsored by the Better English Fund established by John C. Hodges at the University of Tennessee, Knoxville. Published semiannually.

Major Field(s) of Interest: Articles focused on British and British Colonial culture in the later Stuart period, including literature, philosophy, theology, fine arts, theater, drama, science, and history. Current bibliography in each issue.

Manuscript Information: Articles of 3,000–7,000 words. Notes up to 3,000 words. Style: *MLA Style Manual* (1985). 2 copies of manuscript required. Report in 4 weeks. Rejected manuscripts returned with S.A.S.E.

Payment: 10 copies of the issue.

Indexed In: MLA International Bibliography, ECCB, and others.

Copyright: By the University of Tennessee. Permission for authors to use their material elsewhere is readily extended.

RESTORATION AND 18TH CENTURY THEATRE RESEARCH

c/o English Department, Loyola University of Chicago, 6525 North Sheridan Road, Chicago, IL 60626. Rates: $8 per year. Founded 1961. Sponsored by Loyola University of Chicago. Published twice yearly.

Major Field(s) of Interest: Articles on Restoration and Eighteenth-Century British theater. Journal reviews books.

Manuscript Information: No length restrictions on articles and notes. Book reviews up to 900 words. Style: MLA with endnotes. 2 copies of manuscript required. Report in 4–6 months. Rejected manuscripts returned with S.A.S.E.

Payment: 5 copies of the journal.

Copyright: By the journal.

*REVIEW

Department of English, 110 Williams Hall, Virginia Polytechnical Institute and State University, Blacksburg, VA 24061 and Department of English, Pennsylvania State University, University Park, PA 16802. Rates: $28 per year. Founded 1977. Sponsored by Virginia Tech Foundation and Pennsylvania State University. Published annually.

Major Field(s) of Interest: The journal publishes essays and reviews of scholarly work in all periods, fields, and genres of English and American literature and language. Contributors are encouraged to write broadly about the current state of affairs in an entire field as well as about the value of the particular works or groups of works under review.

Manuscript Information: No limit on length of articles, notes, or reviews. Give complete bibliographical data and list notes at end of manuscript. 2 copies of manuscript required. Report in 1 month. Rejected manuscripts returned with S.A.S.E.

Payment: 50 copies.

Copyright: By the journal. Authors are freely granted permission to reprint with usual credit line.

THE REVIEW OF CONTEMPORARY FICTION

5700 College Road, Lisle, IL 60532. Rates: $15 per year individuals. $22 per year institutions. Founded 1981. No sponsor. Published 3 times per year.

Major Field(s) of Interest: The journal is interested in jargonless criticism that focuses on contemporary fiction. It includes selections from works-in-progress and interviews as well as a lengthy book review section. Each issue is devoted to two or three contemporary novelists. Occasionally, the journal publishes a special issue on a specific topic. Contributor's school library must be a current subscriber. Journal reviews books.

Manuscript Information: Articles of 3,000–4,000 words. Notes of 500–1,000 words. Book reviews up to 350 words. Style: Chicago with endnotes. Report in 1 month. Rejected manuscripts returned with S.A.S.E.

Payment: 1 copy of the issue.

Indexed In: MLA International Bibliography, American Humanities Index, International Bibliography of Periodical Literature, Book Review Index, Abstracts of English Studies.

Copyright: By the journal. Rights revert to author upon request.

THE REVIEW OF ENGLISH STUDIES: A QUARTERLY JOURNAL OF ENGLISH LITERATURE AND THE ENGLISH LANGUAGE

Academic Publishing Division, Oxford University Press, Walton Street, Oxford, OX2 6DP, England. Rates: $19 per year individuals. $66 per year institutions. Founded 1925. Sponsored by Oxford University Press. Published quarterly.

Major Field(s) of Interest: The journal is concerned with English literature and the English language from the earliest period to the present day. The emphasis in the articles and notes is on historical scholarship rather than interpretative criticism, but it is hoped that the discovery of new facts or material (or the reconsideration of known facts and material) will modify criticism of a writer or a work, and sometimes lead to a fresh evaluation or interpretation. Journal reviews books.

Manuscript Information: Articles of 8,000–10,000 words. Notes of c. 2,000–3,000 words. Book reviews up to 750 words. Style: OUP House Style with consecutive footnotes at the bottom of the page. Report in 8–12 weeks. Rejected manuscripts returned with S.A.S.E.

Payment: 25 free offprints.

Copyright: By Oxford University Press. Permission usually granted for reprinting.

*RHETORIC REVIEW

Department of English, Modern Languages Building #67, The University of Arizona, Tucson, AZ 85721. Rates: $12 per year individuals. $15 per year institutions. Founded 1982. Mainly self-supporting. Published twice yearly (Fall and Spring).

Major Field(s) of Interest: The journal is a generalist organ of rhetoric and composition. It publishes studies on the history of rhetoric, personal essays on writing, the teaching of writing, rhetorical studies of individual authors, essays on the profession, and essays on the theory of rhetoric. Journal reviews books.

Manuscript Information: Articles of 15–25 pages. Some historical and theoretical articles may be longer. Book reviews up to 1,500 words. Style: MLA with endnotes. 3 copies of manuscript required. Report in 2 months. Rejected manuscripts returned with S.A.S.E.

Payment: 1 complimentary issue.

Indexed In: MLA International Bibliography, Sociological Abstracts.

Copyright: By the journal. Permission to reprint carries a fee.

*RHETORIC SOCIETY QUARTERLY

Department of Philosophy, St. Cloud State University, St. Cloud, MN 56301. Founded 1968. Sponsored by the Rhetoric Society of America. Published quarterly.

Major Field(s) of Interest: Articles on rhetorical theory, rhetorical criticism, history of rhetoric, rhetorical pedagogy, rhetorical research, bibliographies, notes and information on rhetorical programs and conferences, reports on new developments in rhetoric, and book reviews.

Manuscript Information: No restrictions on length for articles, notes, or book reviews. Style: MLA. 3 copies of manuscript required. Submit 1 double-spaced manuscript that may be on computer paper. Report in 6 months. Rejected manuscripts not returned.

Payment: Copies.

Copyright: By the journal.

*RHETORICA: A JOURNAL OF THE HISTORY OF RHETORIC

School of Speech, Department of Communication Studies, 1815 Chicago Avenue, Northwestern University, Evanston, IL 60208–1340. Rates: $30 per year individuals (includes membership in the International Society for the History of Rhetoric). $45 per year institutions. Founded 1983. Sponsored by the International Society for the History of Rhetoric. Published quarterly.

Major Field(s) of Interest: The journal publishes articles on any aspect of the history, theory, and practice of rhetoric in all periods and cultures. Articles are accepted in all four of the Society's official languages: English, French, Italian, and German. Journal reviews books.

Manuscript Information: Articles of 15–40 pages. Book reviews up to 10 pages. Style: Chicago. Submit author's name, address, and manuscript title on a separate page. 3 copies of manuscript required with an abstract of 100 words or less in English and French. Report in 5 months. Rejected manuscripts returned with S.A.S.E.

Payment: 3 copies. Reprints can be purchased.

Copyright: By the Journal. Reprint allowed with permission.

ROBINSON JEFFERS NEWSLETTER

Department of English, California State University at Long Beach, 1250 Bellflower Boulevard, Long Beach, CA 90840. Rates: $10 per year. Founded 1963. Sponsored by Occidental College and the Robinson Jeffers Committee. Published quarterly.

Major Field(s) of Interest: News notes, abstracts, reviews, bibliographic studies, manuscript resources, short articles, memoirs, letters by or about Robinson Jeffers and some photo-reproductions. Journal reviews books.

Manuscript Information: Articles of 400–1,000 words, Notes of 400–800 words. Book reviews of 200–400 words. Style: MLA. Keep footnotes to a minimum. Report in 1 month. Rejected manuscripts returned.

Payment: Copies.

Copyright: By Occidental College. Reprints by permission.

*Rocky Mountain Review of Language and Literature
Department of English, Boise State University, Boise, ID 83725. Rates: $15 per year individual. $20 per year libraries. Founded 1946. Sponsored by the Rocky Mountain Modern Language Association. Published quarterly.

Major Field(s) of Interest: Critical and descriptive articles on modern and ancient languages and literatures and pedagogy, directed toward an audience of scholars, writers, and teachers in the fields of English and foreign languages. Poetry, short stories, translations also published. Journal reviews books.

Manuscript Information: Articles 15–24 pages. Book reviews of 300–600 words. Style: New MLA (1985). Other notes at end of manuscript. 2 copies of manuscript required. Submit original manuscript. Do not include author's name on manuscript. Report in 3–4 months. Rejected manuscripts returned with anonymous referee comments with S.A.S.E.

Payment: Offprints may be purchased as well as additional copies of full journal.

Indexed In: MLA International Bibliography, MHRA Annual Bibliography, LLBA, NCTE Abstracts of English Studies, Book Review Index.

Copyright: By the journal. Author retains right to use article without charge in any book author writes, edits, or contributes to, subject only to giving proper credit to RMMLA. Otherwise, minimal fee charged for reprinting rights.

Romantic Review

518 Philosophy Hall, Columbia University, New York, NY 10027. Founded 1909. Sponsored by Columbia University, Department of French and Romance Philology. Published quarterly.

Major Field(s) of Interest: Journal publishes work in all areas of Romantic literature. It is especially interested in material deriving from the new critical methods (structuralist, post-structuralist, neo-Marxist, sociological, semiological). Journal reviews books.

Manuscript Information: No length restrictions on articles or book reviews. Style: MLA. Footnotes are not acceptable. Use doublespaced endnotes. Report in 60 days Rejected manuscripts returned with S.A.S.E.

Payment: Copies.

Copyright: By Columbia University.

The Romantist

F. Marion Crawford Memorial Society, Saracinesca House, 3610 Meadowbrook Avenue, Nashville, TN 37205. Rates: $12.50 per year. Founded

1975. Sponsored by the F. Marion Crawford Memorial Society. Published irregularly (approximately annually).

Major Field(s) of Interest: The journal is in the tradition of the pre–1920 literary reviews. It publishes articles on the modern manifestations of the aesthetic and imaginative aspects of the Romantic tradition (1850–1950) in literature and the arts with a special section on Francis Marion Crawford (1854–1909). Preference is for work about neglected, overlooked, and lesser known authors not currently favored by academic and other "establishment" critics. The journal publishes critical, bibliographical, and biographical studies and occasional articles on artists and musicians. Journal reviews books.

Manuscript Information: No length restrictions on articles, notes, or book reviews. Style: None. Notes at end of text. References should contain full bibliographical information. Query editors before submitting an article or book review. Report in 2 months. Rejected manuscripts returned with S.A.S.E.

Payment: 1 copy and 50% discount.

Indexed In: MLA International Bibliography.

Copyright: By the F. Marion Crawford Memorial Society. Permission freely granted for republication elsewhere if acknowledgment is given to the society.

ROOM OF ONE'S OWN:
A FEMINIST JOURNAL OF LITERATURE AND CRITICISM
P. O. Box 46160, Station G, Vancouver, British Columbia, V6R 4G5, Canada, Rates: Canadian $10 per year individuals Canada. $11 per year individuals elsewhere. Canadian $14 per year institutions. Founded 1975. Sponsored by the Growing Room Collective. Published quarterly.

Major Field(s) of Interest: Articles of criticism and reviews of work by women or of feminist concern. The emphasis is on literature rather than on ideology. The journal also publishes original poetry and prose by women.

Manuscript Information: Articles up to 4,000 words. Book reviews up to 1,500 words. Style: None. Report in 6 months. Rejected manuscripts returned with S.A.S.E.

Payment: Copies.

Copyright: By the author.

*SAUL BELLOW JOURNAL
6533 Post Oak Drive, West Bloomfield, MI 48322. Rates: $12 per year individuals. $20 per year institutions. Founded 1981. Independent. Published twice yearly.

Major Field(s) of Interest: The journal publishes critical and scholarly essays on the works of Saul Bellow as well as biographical articles relevant to Bellow. Journal reviews scholarly books on Saul Bellow and his works.

Manuscript Information: Articles up to 30 pages. Notes of 3–5 pages. Book reviews of 2–4 pages. Style: MLA with internal documentation. Report in 60 days. Rejected manuscripts returned with S.A.S.E.

Payment: 1 copy of the journal.

Indexed In: MLA International Bibliography, Abstracts of English Studies.

Copyright: By the journal. Permission to reprint granted to author upon request.

*SCHOLARLY PUBLISHING:
A JOURNAL FOR AUTHORS AND PUBLISHERS

University of Toronto Press, 10 St. Mary Street, Suite 700, Toronto, ON M4Y 2W8, Canada. Rates: $22.00 per year individuals. $14.00 per year students. $41.50 per year institutions. Founded 1969. Sponsored by the University of Toronto Press. Published quarterly.

Major Field(s) of Interest: Any material related to the publishing of scholarly works. The journal is devoted to publishing essays that discuss the writing and publishing of serious nonfiction by university and commercial presses at all stages. Journal reviews books.

Manuscript Information: Articles of 3,000–5,000 words. Book reviews of 250–450 words. Style: Modified Chicago. Oxford spelling. Report in 30 days. Rejected manuscripts returned.

Payment: In copies.

Copyright: By the journal. Request permission for reprint or standard academic "Fair use."

SCIENCE FICTION: A REVIEW OF SPECULATIVE LITERATURE

Department of English, University of Western Australia, Nedlands, W.A. 6009, Australia. Rates: Australian $24 per year. Founded 1977. Sponsored by the University of Western Australia. Published quarterly.

Major Field(s) of Interest: The journal publishes articles, essays, interviews, and less formal, more personalized discussion pertaining to science fiction and fantasy (mainly contemporary and modern). Journal reviews books.

Manuscript Information: Articles of 2,000–4,000 words. Notes of 400–1,000 words. Book reviews of 500–1,500 words. Style: MLA. 2 copies of manuscript required. Report in 3–4 months. Rejected manuscripts returned with S.A.S.E.

Payment: 3 free copies plus 1 year subscription.
Copyright: Journal takes first Australian Serial Rights, one use only. Reprinting allowed with prior notification.

*SCIENCE-FICTION STUDIES

English Department, Concordia University, 7141 Sherbrooke Street West, Montreal, Quebec, H4B 1R6, Canada. Rates: $12.50 per year individuals. $19.00 per year institutions. Founded 1973. Sponsored by Social Sciences and Humanities Research Council of Canada. Published 3 times per year.

Major Field(s) of Interest: Journal looks for articles in any area of science fiction, including utopian fiction, but not, except for purposes of comparison and contrast, supernatural or mythological fantasy. Journal favors essays that are wide-ranging and make a theoretical point.

Manuscript Information: No restriction on the length of articles. Notes up to 3,000 words. Book reviews are by express commission only. Potential contributors are advised to consult any recent issue of *SFS* for the format of articles or to write for the journal's style sheet. A letter covering word-processed essays should include information about the hardware and software being employed. 2 copies of manuscript required. Report in 60–90 days. Rejected manuscripts are returned if accompanied by unaffixed postage (or a check for the appropriate sum). Authors should be aware that meter or non-Canadian postage stamps are useless to *SFS* for return mail purposes. Abstracts of articles required.

Payment: 20 offprints.

Indexed In: Abstracts of English Studies, Current Contents, MLA International Bibliography.

Copyright: SFS asks for copyright. Author may reprint in his or her own work.

*THE SCRIBLERIAN AND THE KIT-CATS:
A NEWSJOURNAL DEVOTED TO POPE, SWIFT, AND THEIR CIRCLE

Department of English, Temple University, Philadelphia, PA 19122 or Department of English, Northeastern University, Boston, MA 02115. Rates: $7 per year individuals. $9 per year institutions. Founded 1968. Sponsored by Temple University, Philadelphia, PA, Northeastern University, Boston, MA, Goldsmith's College, University of London, London, England, Queen's University, Kingston, Ontario, Canada, and University of Florida, Gainesville, FL. Published semiannually (Spring and Autumn).

Major Field(s) of Interest: The journal reviews scholarly articles and books on English literature 1660–1750, including Dryden, Swift, Pope, Arbuthnot, Behn, Bentley, Berkeley, Blackmore, Cibber, Collier, Congreve,

Montagu, Richardson, Rochester, Settle, Shadwell, etc. The journal is also interested in short articles, notes, and book reviews of eighteenth-century plays and operas. No long articles. Book reviews are usually solicited.

Manuscript Information: Articles of 1–5 pages. Notes of 1–2 pages. Book reviews up to 10 pages. Style: MLA. Report in 6 months. Rejected manuscripts returned with S.A.S.E.

Payment: 2 copies.

Copyright: By the journal. Authors are freely granted permission to reprint with usual credit line.

*SEL: STUDIES IN ENGLISH LITERATURE: 1500–1900

P. O. Box 1892, Rice University, Houston, TX 77251–1892. Rates: $15 per year individuals. $20 per year institutions US. $25 per year institutions foreign. Founded 1960. Sponsored by Rice University. Published quarterly.

Major Field(s) of Interest: Historical and critical studies that make significant contributions to the understanding of English literature. Each issue is devoted to a specific period. Winter: English Renaissance; Spring: Elizabethan and Jacobean Drama; Summer: Restoration and Eighteenth Century; Autumn: Nineteenth Century Romantic and Victorian. Journal reviews books, but unsolicited book reviews are not accepted.

Manuscript Information: Articles of 10–25 double-spaced pages including endnotes. Book reviews up to 12,000 words. Style: Chicago with endnotes. Submit original typescript. Report in 3 months. Rejected manuscripts returned with S.A.S.E.

Payment: 1 copy. Offprints and additional copies may be purchased.

Indexed In: MLA International Bibliography, Review of English Studies, and others.

Copyright: By Rice University. Permission is readily granted to reprint.

THE SEVENTEENTH CENTURY

Centre for Seventeenth-Century Studies, University Library, Palace Green, Durham, DH1 1LA, England. Rates: £10 per year individuals. £15 per year institutions. Founded 1986. Sponsored by the Durham Centre for Seventeenth-Century Studies. Published 2 times per year (Spring and Autumn).

Major Field(s) of Interest: An interdisciplinary journal that aims to encourage the study of the period in a way that looks beyond national boundaries or the limits of narrow intellectual approaches. The intentions of the journal are twofold: to serve as a forum for interdisciplinary approaches to seventeenth-century studies, and at the same time to offer to a multidisciplinary readership stimulating specialist studies on a wide range of subjects. All articles should be accessible to scholars who are not specialists in the field concerned. Subjects covered include literature, political and economic history, social history, theology, philosophy, colonial history, natural sciences, music, and the visual arts. There is a general preference for articles embodying original research. There are no regular book reviews, but instead review articles and surveys of recent research. From time to time, special issues will be devoted to one theme or topic.

Manuscript Informaton: Articles up to 10,000 words. Style: *MHRA Style Book.* Notes at end of article. Contributors should consult a copy of the journal for guidance. 2 copies of manuscript preferred. Report in 3 months. Rejected manuscripts returned with S.A.S.E.

Payment: 25 offprints of article.

Copyright: By the journal. Permission to reprint freely given, subject to acknowledgment.

*SEVENTEENTH-CENTURY NEWS (including NEO-LATIN NEWS)
English Department, Texas A&M University, College Station, TX 77843. Price: $10 per year ($15 foreign). Founded 1941. Sponsored by The Milton Society, Texas A&M University, University of Wisconsin-Milwaukee, The Pennsylvania State University, University of Rochester, Oklahoma State University, Bowling Green University, University of Michigan-Dearborn, University of Southern Mississippi, University of Pittsburgh, University of Akron, Baruch College, C.U.N.Y. Published quarterly.

Major Field(s) of Interest: All aspects of seventeenth-century culture, English, American, and European, with emphasis on literature and history. *SCN* publishes articles and reviews on Donne, Milton, and Dryden; Bacon, Browne, and Burton; the dramatists (except Shakespeare); the most recent work on the Metaphysicals and the Cavaliers; Meditative Poetry and Mannerism; the Baroque and Scientific Movements; and all other aspects, major and minor, of seventeenth-century life and thought. *Neo-Latin News* covers all scholarship on literature and ideas in Latin from 1500 to the present. Journal reviews books, but all reviews are commissioned. Articles are selected by peer review (by specialist scholars and by editors).

Manuscript Information: Articles 2,500–5,000 words in length. Notes of 1,000 words. Book reviews of 700–1,000 words. Style: MLA (1985). In-text footnotes preferred; endnotes when necessary. 2 copies of manuscript required. Report in 1–2 months. Rejected manuscripts returned with S.A.S.E.

Payment: None.

Indexed In: MLA International Bibliography, Arts & Humanities Citation Index, Annual Bibliography of English Language and Literature (MHRA).

Copyright: Rests with the author and journal. *SCN* retains approval rights for any reprinting.

*SHAKESPEARE BULLETIN

Department of English, Lafayette College, Easton, PA 18042–1781. Rates: $10 per year. Founded 1982. Sponsored by Lafayette College. Published 6 times a year (every other month).

Major Field(s) of Interest: The journal is a publication of the New York Shakespeare Society. It publishes performance-oriented articles on Shakespeare and his contemporaries and Renaissance drama. Journal reviews theatre productions and books, but theatre and book reviews are commissioned.

Manuscript Information: Articles up to 12 pages. Theatre reviews up to 1,000 words. Book reviews up to 750 words. Style: MLA. Submit original double-spaced typescript or IBM disk. Report in 3 months. Rejected manuscripts returned with S.A.S.E.

Payment: 3 copies of issue.

Indexed In: MLA International Bibliography, World Shakespeare Bibliography, Abstracts of English Studies.

Copyright: By the journal. *Shakespeare Bulletin* will grant permission to reprint on request.

*THE SHAKESPEARE NEWSLETTER

1217 Ashland Avenue, Evanston, IL 60202. Rates: $12 per year. Founded 1951. Sponsored by Louis Marder, Editor. Published quarterly.

Major Field(s) of Interest: Survey of scholarly and popular Shakespeareana, including digests of articles, lectures, dissertations, book news, brief original articles, and Shakespearean Festival programs. Journal reviews books. Journal is interested in any material relating to Shakespeare.

Manuscript Information: Articles up to 1,500 words. Notes up to 1,500 words. Book reviews: 500 words maximum. Style: MLA. Footnotes: Include in article where possible. Report in 6–12 months. Rejected manuscripts returned with S.A.S.E.

Payment: In copies.

Indexed In: Literary Criticism Register, World Shakespeare Bibliography.

Copyright: No copyright. Author can reprint with reference to THE SHAKESPEARE NEWSLETTER.

*SHAKESPEARE QUARTERLY

The Folger Shakespeare Library, 201 East Capitol Street, Washington, D.C. 20003–1094. Individual Price: $25 for *Quarterly;* $8 for "World Shakespeare Bibliography." Institutional Price: $40 for five issues. Add $5 for foreign postage. Founded 1950. Sponsored by The Folger Shakespeare Library.

Major Field(s) of Interest: Publishes critical articles and notes on Shakespeare in a variety of intellectual, social, artistic and historical contexts, including book and theater reviews of current scholarship, interviews with actors and directors, and critics, and the annual *World Shakespeare Bibliography.*

Manuscript Information: Articles 15–20 pages in length; notes 3–7 typed pages. Reviews variable. Follow *The MLA Style Sheet* (Second Edition) for manuscripts and footnotes. Report in 2–6 months.

Payment: None. 5 copies for articles and notes; 3 for reviews.

Indexed In: The Humanities Index, MLA International Bibliography.

Copyright: By The Folger Shakespeare Library.

*SHAKESPEARE STUDIES

Department of English, University of New Mexico, Albuquerque, NM 87131. Rates: $40 per year. Founded 1965. Sponsored by the University of New Mexico. Published annually.

Major Field(s) of Interest: An annual gathering of research, criticism. and reviews on Shakespeare. Journal reviews books, but book reviews are solicited.

Manuscript Information: No length restrictions on articles or book reviews. Style: MLA with endnotes. Submit original typescript. Report in 3–6 months. Rejected manuscripts returned with S.A.S.E.

Payment: 20 offprints.

Indexed in: MLA International Bibliography.

Copyright: By the journal. Payment required for reprinting.

SHAKESPEARE SURVEY: AN ANNUAL SURVEY OF
SHAKESPEARIAN STUDY AND PRODUCTIONS

Cambridge University Press, Edinburgh Building, Shaftsbury Road, Cambridge, CB2 2RU, England. Founded 1948. Sponsored by Cambridge University Press. Published annually.

Major Field(s) of Interest: Scholarly and critical articles on all aspects of Shakespeare's work with an emphasis on literary criticism and scholarship. Also includes review articles on the previous year's publications in the field and a review of selected productions including the Royal Shakespeare Company's previous Stratford season. Journal reviews books, but book reviews are commissioned.

Manuscript Information: Articles up to 5,000 words. Style: Journal. Report in 3 months. Rejected manuscripts returned. Include International Reply Coupons.

Payment: Copies.

Copyright: By the Cambridge University Press.

THE SHAVIAN: THE JOURNAL OF BERNARD SHAW

Shaw Society, High Orchard, 125 Markyate Road, Dagenham, Essex, RM8 2LB, England. Founded 1946. Sponsored by the Bernard Shaw Society. Published annually.

Major Field(s) of Interest: Articles on the life, works, and times of Bernard Shaw and his contemporaries. Journal reviews books.

Manuscript Information: Articles up to 1,000 words. Notes up to 250 words. Book reviews up to 500 words. Style: MLA or Chicago. 2 copies of manuscript required. The journal will accept submissions in languages other than English if accompanied by English translations. Submit camera-ready copy, A5 format. Report in 3 months. Rejected manuscripts returned with S.A.S.E.

Payment: Copies.

Copyright: Reverts to the author after publication.

SHAW: THE ANNUAL OF BERNARD SHAW STUDIES

Department of English, Central Michigan University, Mt. Pleasant, MI 48859. Rates: $35 per year. Founded 1951 (as *Shaw Bulletin*); superseded by *Shaw Review* January 1959); superseded by SHAW (1981). Sponsored by The Pennsylvania State University Press. Published annually (March/April).

Major Field(s) of Interest: SHAW's perspective is Bernard Shaw and his milieu—its personalities, works, relevance to his age and ours. As 'his life, work, and friends'—the subtitle to a biography of G. B. S.—indicates, it is impossible to study the life, thought, and work of a major literary figure in a vacuum. Issues and men, economics, politics, religion, theatre and literature and journalism—the entirety of the two half-centuries the life of G. B. S. spanned was his assumed province. SHAW . . . welcomes articles that either explicitly or implicitly add to or alter our understanding of Shaw and his milieu.'' Alternative issues of SHAW focus on themes. These themes are advertised in advance. Journal reviews books.

Manuscript Information: Articles of 20–25 typed pages. Notes of

1–8 pages. Book reviews of 4–6 pages. Style: *MLA Style Sheet*. Refer to recent volumes for format. 3 copies of manuscript required. Report in 6–8 weeks. Rejected manuscripts returned with S.A.S.E.

Payment: 1 copy of the journal plus offprints. $50 for articles. $25 for notes.

Indexed In: MLA International Bibliography, International Directory of Little Magazines and Small Presses, Small Press Directory.

Copyright: By The Pennsylvania State University Press. Authors are freely granted permission to reprint with usual credit line.

SIDNEY NEWSLETTER

Department of English, University of Guelph, Guelph, Ontario, N1G 2W1, Canada. Rates: $6.25 per year individuals. $12.50 per year institutions. Founded 1980. Sponsored by the editors: Gerald Rubio and C. S. Hunter. Published 2 times per year (Spring and Fall).

Major Field(s) of Interest: Articles on Sir Philip Sidney, his circle and milieu. Journal reviews books.

Manuscript Information: Articles up to 2,000 words. Notes up to 800 words. Book reviews up to 1,000 words. Style: MLA. Report in 1–3 months. Rejected manuscripts returned with S.A.S.E.

Payment: Copies.

Copyright: By the journal or by the author.

*THE SIXTEENTH CENTURY JOURNAL

Northeast Missouri State University, LB 115, Kirksville, MO 63501. Rates: $35 per year individuals. $35 per year institutions. Founded 1970. Sponsored by the Sixteenth-Century Conference. Published quarterly.

Major Field(s) of Interest: The journal is interdisciplinary in scope, covering the period 1450–1660. It is not Eurocentric, and it publishes articles in literature, theology, demography, history, music, and art history. Journal reviews books.

Manuscript Information: Articles up to 25 double-spaced pages. Reviews up to 600 words. Style: Chicago. 2 copies of manuscript required. Submit original typescript and 1 copy. 150 word abstract is required with each article. Report in 3 months. Rejected manuscripts returned with comments. Include S.A.S.E.

Payment: 20 free copies to authors of articles.

Indexed In: Humanities Index, CERDIX, ABC CLIO, MLA International Bibliography, Art History Index, Religion Index One.

Copyright: By the journal. Permission required for reprinting or reuse by author.

*THE SOUTH ATLANTIC QUARTERLY

304-H Allen Building, Duke University, Durham, NC 27706. Rates: $14 per year individuals. $24 per year institutions. Founded 1901. Sponsored by Duke University Press. Published quarterly.

Major Field(s) of Interest: Articles in the humanities, social sciences, and general pieces of current interest. Journal reviews books.

Manuscript Information: Articles up to 30 pages. Notes up to 2,500 words. Book reviews up to 5,000 words. Style: Chicago. Write to journal for style sheet. 2 copies of manuscript required. Report in 4–8 weeks. Rejected manuscripts returned with S.A.S.E.

Payment: 10 copies.

Indexed In: Abstracts of English Studies, America: History and Life, American Humanities Index, Arts and Humanities Citation Index, Book Review Index, Current Contents, Humanities Index, Index to Book Reviews.

Copyright: By Duke University Press. Upon request, copyright assigned to author.

*SOUTH ATLANTIC REVIEW

120 Dey Hall, University of North Carolina, Chapel Hill, NC 27599–3530. Rates: $12 per year individuals. $20 per year institutions. Founded 1935 (as SOUTH ATLANTIC BULLETIN). Sponsored by South Atlantic Modern Language Association. Published quarterly.

Major Field(s) of Interest: Essays and articles on the modern languages and literatures (English and foreign).

Manuscript Information: Articles of 4,000–6,000 words. Book reviews up to 1,000 words. Style: MLA with endnotes. 2 copies of manuscript required. Submit original typescript and photocopy. Report in 6–8 weeks. Rejected manuscripts returned with S.A.S.E.

Payment: 10 complimentary offprints for articles.

Indexed In: MLA International Bibliography.

Copyright: By South Atlantic MLA. Permission granted for a small fee.

*SOUTH CENTRAL REVIEW: THE JOURNAL
OF THE SOUTH CENTRAL MODERN LANGUAGE ASSOCIATION

Department of English, Texas A&M University, College Station, TX 77843–4227. Rates: $15 per year individuals. $25 per year institutions. $5 per year for graduate students and retirees. Founded 1984. Sponsored by the South Central Modern Language Association. Published quarterly.

Major Field(s) of Interest: Research and scholarship on any aspect of literature, literary theory, and language. Journal reviews books.

Manuscript Information: Articles of 10–20 pages. Book reviews of 1,000–1,500 words. Style: *MLA Style Manual* (1985) with endnotes. 2 copies of manuscript required with author's name only on cover letter. Report in 3 months. If a manuscript is accepted, the journal asks the author to join SCMLA. The journal reviews all manuscripts regardless of the membership status of the author. Rejected manuscripts returned with S.A.S.E.

Payment: Offprints.

Copyright: By the journal.

SPECULUM: A JOURNAL OF MEDIEVAL STUDIES

Medieval Academy of America, 1430 Massachusetts Avenue, Cambridge, MA 02138. Rates: $35 per year individual members. $45 per year contributing members. $60 per year institutions. $20 per year student and retired members. Founded 1925. Sponsored by the Medieval Academy of America. Published quarterly.

Major Field(s) of Interest: Articles on medieval architecture, art, archaeology, armor, fine arts, geography, heraldry, history, law, literature, music, numismatics, philosophy, science, social and economic institutions, and all other aspects of the civilization of the Middle Ages. Journal reviews books, but unsolicited book reviews are not accepted.

Manuscript Information: Articles up to 15,000 words. Notes up to 2,500 words. Book reviews up to 1,200 words. Style: Chicago. 2 copies of manuscripts preferred. Report in 4–6 months. Rejected manuscripts returned with S.A.S.E.

Payment: Offprints.

Copyright: By the Medieval Academy of America.

SPENSER STUDIES: A RENAISSANCE POETRY ANNUAL

Department of English, Princeton University, Princeton, NJ 08540. Rates: $45 per year. Founded 1980. Published annually.

Major Field(s) of Interest: Articles on all sixteenth-century English poets with emphasis on Spenser and Sidney. Also publishes articles on the literary/historical/intellectual context and influence of sixteenth-century English poetry, as well as occasional articles of general interest on Renaissance subjects. Journal reviews books.

Manuscript Information: No length restrictions on articles. Notes to 3,000 words. Style: MLA. 2 copies of manuscript required. Report as quickly as possible; usually within one month. Rejected manuscripts returned with S.A.S.E. Abstract to be submitted with each article.

Payment: 25 offprints.
Indexed In: MLA International Bibliography.
Copyright: By AMS Press. Authors may use their work in their own books.

*STEINBECK QUARTERLY

English Department, Ball State University, Muncie, IN 47306. Rates: $20 per year. Founded 1968. Sponsored by the International John Steinbeck Society and Ball State University. Published quarterly: 2 combined issues.

Major Field(s) of Interest: Critical and biographical articles on John Steinbeck and related subjects. Journal reviews books.

Manuscript Information: Articles 10–15 double-spaced pages. Notes 2–3 pages. Book reviews up to 3 pages. Style: Chicago. Endnotes. 2 copies of manuscripts required. Report in 2 months. Rejected manuscripts returned with S.A.S.E. Contributors must be members in good standing of the International Steinbeck Society.

Payment: 3 copies of journal for articles. 1 copy for reviews.
Copyright: By the journal. Authors may reprint for a fee.

*STUDIA MYSTICA

Department of English, Texas A&M University, College Station, TX 77843–4227. Rates: $14 per year individuals. $18 per year institutions. Founded 1978. Sponsored by Texas A&M University. Published quarterly.

Major Field(s) of Interest: Articles on the interrelationship of mystical experience and aesthetic experience in literature, visual arts, music, philosophy, and religion. Speculative theology not welcome. Journal reviews books.

Manuscript Information: Articles of 15–25 pages. Notes of 1,500–2,000 words. Book reviews of 3–5 pages. Style: MLA. 2 copies of manuscript required. Report in 2–3 weeks. Rejected manuscripts returned with S.A.S.E.

Payment: 25 offprints plus 2 copies of journal.
Indexed In: MLA International Bibliography.
Copyright: By the journal. Rights revert to author.

STUDIES IN BIBLIOGRAPHY: PAPERS OF THE BIBLIOGRAPHICAL SOCIETY OF THE UNIVERSITY OF VIRGINIA

2537 Holkham Drive, Charlottesville, VA 22901. Rates: $25 per year. Founded 1948. Sponsored by the Bibliographical Society of the University of Virginia.

Major Field(s) of Interest: Articles and notes on analytical bibliography, textual criticism, manuscript study, the history of printing and publishing, as well as related matters of method and evidence.

Manuscript Information: Articles of any length. Notes up to 1,500 words. Style: Modified MLA. Report in 1 month. Rejected manuscripts returned with S.A.S.E.

Payment: Free reprints.

Indexed In: The Library, Literary Criticism Register.

Copyright: By the University of Virginia Rectors. Permission to reprint granted with credit.

*STUDIES IN BROWNING AND HIS CIRCLE:
A JOURNAL OF CRITICISM, HISTORY, AND BIBLIOGRAPHY

P. O. Box 6336, Baylor University, Waco, TX 76706. Rates: $15 per year. Founded 1973. Sponsored by Baylor University, Armstrong Browning Library. Published 2 times per year.

Major Field(s) of Interest: Articles and scholarship related to the life and/or works of Robert and Elizabeth Barrett Browning. Journal reviews books.

Manuscript Information: Articles of 2,500–5,000 words. Notes of 800–1,000 words. Book reviews of 600–800 words Style: MLA. 2 copies of manuscript required. Report in 3 months. Rejected manuscripts returned with S.A.S.E.

Payment: Copies.

Copyright: By the author.

STUDIES IN CONTEMPORARY SATIRE:
A CREATIVE AND CRITICAL JOURNAL

Department of English, Clarion University of Pennsylvania, Clarion, PA 16255. Rates: $3 per year. Founded 1974. Sponsored by the English Department, Clarion University. Published annually.

Major Field(s) of Interest: Critical articles on contemporary satiric fiction, poetry, drama, cinema, television, and graphic art. The journal is also interested in original satiric prose and verse. Journal reviews books.

Manuscript Information: Articles of 9–10 pages. Notes of 2–3 pages. Book reviews of 2–3 pages. Style: MLA. 1 copy of manuscript required. Include a short (5–7 line) biographical piece including publications for "Notes on Contributors" section. Report in 3–6 months. Rejected manuscripts returned with S.A.S.E.

Payment: 2 copies.

Indexed In: Abstracts of English Studies, MLA International Bibliography.

Copyright: By the author.

STUDIES IN ENGLISH LITERATURE

501 Kenkyusha Building, 9 Surugadai 2–Chome, Kanda, Chiyoda-Ku, Tokyo 101, Japan. Rates: 6,000 yen per year. Payment for subscription should be in Japanese money. Founded 1920. Sponsored by the English Literary Society of Japan. Published 3 times per year (1 issue is special, consisting of articles all written in English, the other 2 mostly in Japanese).

Major Field(s) of Interest: Publishes articles of all kinds in the fields of English and American literature, language, philology, and linguistics. Contributors must be members of the English Literary Society of Japan. Journal reviews books.

Manuscript Information: Articles up to 25 double-spaced pages. Book reviews of 10–15 double-spaced pages. Style: MLA with endnotes. 3 copies of manuscript required. Enclose brief author biography. Report in 2 months. Rejected manuscripts returned with S.A.S.E.

Payment: 20 offprints.

Copyright: By the English Literary Society of Japan. Authors are granted permission to reprint with usual credit line.

STUDIES IN ICONOGRAPHY

School of Art, Arizona State University, Tempe, AZ 85287–1505. Rates: $15 per year individuals. $29 per year institutions. Founded 1975. Sponsored by the Art History Faculty, Arizona State University School of Art, and Arizona State University. Published annually.

Major Field(s) of Interest: The journal is interdisciplinary and accepts articles dealing with the meaning of form and content in all the arts. It is also interested in articles on iconographical problems in art and literature from any historical period. Journal reviews books.

Manuscript Information: Articles of 20–30 pages. Notes of 3–5 pages. Book reviews of 2–5 pages. Style: Chicago. Follow the *Modified Art Bulletin* for footnote form. 2 copies of manuscript required. Report in 2–3 months. Rejected manuscripts returned with S.A.S.E.

Payment: Copies and currency.

Indexed In: Scientific Information.

Copyright: By the journal.

*STUDIES IN MEDIEVALISM

520 College Avenue, Holland, MI 49423. Founded 1979. Sponsored by the Society for the Study of Medievalism. Published irregularly.

Major Field(s) of Interest: The journal provides an interdisciplinary medium for scholars in all fields, including the visual and other arts, concerned with any aspect of the post-medieval idea and the study of the Middle Ages. It includes articles on the influence, both scholarly and popular, of this study on Western society after 1500.

Manuscript Information: Articles of 2,000–7,500 words. Notes up to 1,000 words. Book reviews up to 1,000 words. Style: MLA. 2 copies of manuscript required. Submit original typescript, 1 copy and an abstract. Report in 3 months. Rejected manuscripts returned with S.A.S.E.

Payment: Copies.

Copyright: By the journal.

STUDIES IN PHILOLOGY

Department of English, University of North Carolina at Chapel Hill, Greenlaw Hall, 066 A, Chapel Hill, NC 27514. Rates: $15 per year individuals. $20 per year institutions. Founded 1906. Sponsored by the University of North Carolina, Chapel Hill, Departments of Languages and Literatures. Published quarterly.

Major Field(s) of Interest: Articles on classical, medieval, and modern literature with emphasis upon the Middle Ages and the Renaissance.

Manuscript Information: Articles of 20–30 typescript pages. Style: Chicago. Report in 3–6 months. Rejected manuscripts returned.

Payment: Offprints.

Copyright: By the University of North Carolina Press.

*STUDIES IN ROMANTICISM

236 Bay State Road, Boston, MA 02215. $20.00 per year individuals. $49.50 per year institutions. Founded 1961. Sponsored by the Trustees of Boston University. Published quarterly.

Major Field(s) of Interest: An interdisciplinary journal interested in articles on literature, art, and music produced in the Romantic period in England, America, and the Continent. Some issues are devoted to a specifically announced topic. Occasionally, the journal carries limited bibliographical articles. Journal reviews books.

Manuscript Information: Articles of 20–35 pages. Book reviews of 3–6 pages. Style: MLA. 2 copies of manuscript required. Submit original typescript. Quotations in all modern European languages are permitted if English translations are provided. Report in 2–4 months. Rejected manuscripts returned with S.A.S.E. Abstracts are required.

Payment: 4 complimentary copies. Offprints for a modest fee.

Copyright: By the journal. Authors freely granted permission to reprint with credit line.

*STUDIES IN SHORT FICTION

Newberry College, Newberry, SC 29108. Rates: $18 individuals. $21 institutions. Founded 1963. Sponsored by Newberry College. Published quarterly.

Major Field(s) of Interest: SSF welcomes serious commentary on short fiction of all countries and periods as the focus of article-length manuscripts. Notes are likewise devoted exclusively to short fiction and may be in the form of unpublished letters, *explication de texte,* textual criticism, etc. Journal reviews books.

Manuscript Information: Articles up to 3,750 words. Notes up to 1,250 words. Book reviews are solicited. Style: *MLA Style Manual* (1985). Report in 6–8 months. Rejected manuscripts returned with S.A.S.E.

Payment: 1 copy of journal and tearsheets.

Copyright: By Newberry College. Reprint rights granted upon request but fee charged.

STUDIES IN WEIRD FICTION

281 4th Street, #3, Jersey City, NJ 07302. Rates: $5 per issue. Founded 1979. Sponsored by the Editor: S. T. Joshi. Published 2 times per year.

Major Field(s) of Interest: The journal focuses on the criticism of fantasy, horror, and supernatural fiction subsequent to Poe. Journal reviews books, but book reviews are solicited.

Manuscript Information: Articles of 2,000–6,000 words. Notes of 250–500 words. Book reviews of 500–1,500 words. Style: Chicago. 4 copies of manuscript required. Report in 4–10 months. Rejected manuscripts returned with S.A.S.E.

Payment: Copies.

Copyright: By the journal. Copyright reverts to author after 1 year.

*STUDIES IN THE AGE OF CHAUCER

Department of English, University of Tennessee, Knoxville, TN 37996–0430. Rates: $30 per year. Founded 1979. Sponsored by The New Chaucer Society. Published annually.

Major Field(s) of Interest: The journal publishes articles on the art of Chaucer and his contemporaries, their literary relationships and reputations, and the artistic, economic, intellectual, religious, scientific, social, and historical backgrounds to their work. Each issue contains a limited number of substantial articles, reviews of books on Chaucer and related topics, and an annotated Chaucer Bibliography. Journal reviews book, but unsolicited book reviews are not accepted.

Manuscript Information: Articles of 10,000–15,000 words. Book reviews up to 1,000 words. Style: Chicago. 2 copies of manuscript required. Report in 2 months. Rejected manuscripts returned with S.A.S.E.

Payment: 20 offprints for articles. 10 offprints for reviews.

Copyright: By the New Chaucer Society.

STUDIES IN THE AMERICAN RENAISSANCE

Department of English, University of South Carolina, Columbia, SC 29208. Rates: $40 per year. Founded 1977. Sponsored by the University Press of Virginia. Published annually.

Major Field(s) of Interest: Examines the lives and works of mid-nineteenth-century American authors and the circumstances in which they wrote, published, and were received. The editor welcomes biographical, historical, and bibliographical articles on the literature, history, philosophy, art, religion, and general culture of America during the period 1830–1860. Journal reviews books.

Manuscript Information: No length restrictions on articles, notes, or book reviews. Style: Journal. 2 copies of manuscript required. Report in 4–6 weeks. Rejected manuscripts returned with S.A.S.E.

Payment: 1 copy plus 25 offprints.

Indexed In: America: History and Life, American Humanities Index, American Literary Scholarship / An Annual, American Literature, Historical Abstracts, Literary Criticism Register, MLA International Bibliography.

Copyright: By the journal. Authors freely granted permission to reprint.

*STUDIES IN THE HUMANITIES

110 Leonard Hall, Indiana University of Pennsylvania, Indiana, PA 15705. Rates: $5 per year individuals. $12 per year institutions. Founded 1969. Sponsored by the Indiana University of Pennsylvania. Published 2 times per year (June and December).

Major Field(s) of Interest: In addition to articles employing traditional approaches, the journal encourages the submission of work that reaches across disciplines and cultures to deepen our understanding of an artist, a work, or a genre. Journal also welcomes studies which place artists or their works in the context of ideas of their times. Journal will consider papers that offer a scholarly treatment of material not found in the usually academic categories. Articles are reviewed by members of the journal's national editorial advisory board.

Manuscript Information: No limit on length of articles. Book reviews of 2–6 pages. Style: MLA. Report in 6 weeks. Rejected manuscripts returned with S.A.S.E.

Payment: 3 copies of journal.

Indexed In: MLA International Bibliography, Film Literature Index, American Humanities Index, Index to Book Reviews in the Humanities.

Copyright: Indiana University of Pennsylvania. Permission to reprint freely given.

STUDIES IN THE LITERARY IMAGINATION

Department of English, Georgia State University, Atlanta, GA 30303–3083. Rates: $5 per year individuals. Free to US Institutions. Founded 1968. Sponsored by the Department of English, Georgia State University. Published biannually.

Major Field(s) of Interest: Each issue of the journal is devoted to a special topic in English and American literature. Topics are selected by the faculty members who then solicit manuscripts.

Manuscript Information: Articles of 15–20 pages. Style: MLA with endnotes. Report in 2 months. Rejected manuscripts returned.

Payment: Copies of the journal.

Copyright: By Georgia State University.

*STUDIES IN THE NOVEL

University of North Texas, P. O. Box 13706, Denton, TX 76203. Rates: $10 per year individuals. $20 per year universities and libraries. All foreign: $25. Founded 1969. Sponsored by University of North Texas. Published quarterly.

Major Field(s) of Interest: Publishes studies of novels, novelists, and literary theory. Material on minor or fairly recent novels is not generally included. Journal reviews books, but book reviews are commissioned.

Manuscript Information: Articles of 20–25 pages. Book reviews of 3–6 pages. Style: Chicago. Endnotes. 2 copies of manuscript required. Report in 90 days. Rejected manuscripts returned with S.A.S.E.

Payment: 2 copies of issue and 15–20 tearsheet copies.

Copyright: By the journal. Split fee with contributors.

STUDIES ON VOLTAIRE AND THE EIGHTEENTH CENTURY

Voltaire Foundation, Taylor Institution, St. Giles', Oxford, OX1 3NA, England. Rates: £5. Founded 1954. Sponsored by the Voltaire Foundation. Published 10–12 times per year.

Major Field(s) of Interest: Articles on eighteenth-century studies in the humanities and social sciences.

Manuscript Information: No length restrictions on articles. Submit original typescript. Style: Journal. Report in 3 months. Rejected manuscripts returned with S.A.S.E.

Payment: 25 copies.
Copyright: By the Voltaire Foundation.

SWIFT STUDIES: THE ANNUAL OF THE EHRENPREIS CENTER
Department of English, Johannisstr. 12–20, Westfälische Wilhelms-Universität, 4400 Münster, Germany. Rates: DM67.50 per year. Founded 1986. Sponsored by Friends of the Ehrenpreis Center. Published annually.

Major Field(s) of Interest: Articles and notes dealing with the textual criticism, annotation, and interpretation of the works of Jonathan Swift.
Manuscript Information: Articles of 3,000–6,000 words. Notes of 800–1,500 words. Style: MLA. (2nd edition). Notes at bottom of page. 3 copies of manuscript required. Report in 2–3 months. Rejected manuscripts returned with S.A.S.E.

Payment: Cheque and 20 offprints.
Indexed In: MLA International Bibliography, YWES.
Copyright: By the editor (Professor H. J. Real).

SYDNEY STUDIES IN ENGLISH
Department of English, University of Sydney, N.S.W. 2006, Australia. Rates: Australian $6.50 par year. Published annually.

Major Field(s) of Interest: Publishes criticism and scholarship in English literature and drama. Journal reviews books.
Manuscript Information: Articles up to 5,000 words. Style: MLA. Report in 2 months. Rejected manuscripts returned with S.A.S.E.

Payment: Copies.
Copyright: By the author.

TAMARACK: JOURNAL OF THE EDNA ST. VINCENT MILLAY SOCIETY
Edna St. Vincent Millay Society, Steepletop, Austerliz, NY 12017. Founded 1981. Sponsored by the Edna St. Vincent Millay Society. Published annually.

Major Field(s) of Interest: Concentrates on Edna St. Vincent Millay and her work. Includes articles and reviews of her contemporaries as well as the work of present day poets. Journal reviews books.
Manuscript Information: 5–10 double-spaced typescript pages for articles. Book reviews of 700–1,000 words. Style: Chicago. 2 copies of manuscript required. Cite source of quoted material. Report in 2 months. Rejected manuscripts returned with S.A.S.E.

Payment: Copies.
Copyright: By the journal.

Tennessee Williams Journal

Box 70495, New Orleans, LA or Department of English, University of New Orleans, Lakefront, New Orleans, LA 70148. Rates: $30 for 2 years, individuals. $40 for 2 years, institutions. Founded 1989. Sponsored by Tennessee Williams Journals, Inc. Published biannually.

Major Field(s) of Interest: The journal is devoted to the study of the life and works of Tennessee Williams. It publishes articles, notes, exhibits, calendars of productions, and other material related to Tennessee Williams. A bibliography is included in each issue. Journal reviews books.

Manuscript Information: Articles of 15–25 pages. Notes of 4–5 pages. Book reviews up 4 pages. Style: MLA. 2 copies of manuscripts required. Report in 6 months. Rejected manuscripts returned with S.A.S.E.

Payment: 3 copies of articles.

Copyright: First rights retained by the journal. Permission to reprint from the editor is required with credit line.

The Tennyson Research Bulletin

Department of English Literature, University of Edinburgh, David Hume Tower, George Square, Edinburgh, EH8 9JX, England. Founded 1967. Sponsored by the Tennyson Society. Published annually.

Major Field(s) of Interest: New material on Tennyson, his life, his works, and his contemporaries. Journal reviews books, but reviews are commissioned.

Manuscript Information: Articles of 4,000–8,000 words. Notes of 500–2,000 words. Book reviews of 1,000–2,000 words. Style: MLA. 2 copies of manuscript required. Report in 3 months. Rejected manuscripts returned.

Payment: Copies.

Copyright: By the author.

*Texas Studies in Literature and Language: A Journal of the Humanities

Department of English, Parlin Hall, University of Texas, Austin, TX 78712–1164. Rates: $20 per year individuals. $32 per year institutions. Founded 1911. Sponsored by the University of Texas Press. Published quarterly.

Major Field(s) of Interest: Articles of significance in all areas of English and American literature. Journal publishes review essays.

Manuscript Information: Articles of 20 to 100 pages. Style: Chicago. If photocopy of manuscript is submitted, author must state whether other journals are considering the essay. Report in 3–4 months. Rejected manuscripts returned with S.A.S.E.

Payment: Copies.

Indexed In: Abstracts of English Studies, Current Contents, MLA International Bibliography, MHRA.

Copyright: By the University of Texas Press. Authors may reprint free.

TEXT & PRESENTATION

Classics Department, 3-C Dauer Hall, University of Florida, Gainesville, FL 32611-2005. Rates: $20 per year. Founded 1982 as COMPARATIVE DRAMA CONFERENCE PAPERS; 1991 in its present format. Sponsored by the University of Florida, Department of Classics. Published annually.

Major Field(s) of Interest: Papers and articles are submitted from the annual TEXT & PRESENTATION conference on drama and theater history, reviewed by editorial board, and published annually. Topics include all aspects of drama and production.

Manuscript Information: Artlcles of 10-20 pages. Style: Chicago. Footnotes at bottom of page. 2 copies of manuscript required. Report in 3 months. Submissions restricted to papers presented at the annual conference. Rejected manuscripts returned with S.A.S.E.

Payment: None.

Copyright: By University Press of North America.

TEXT: TRANSACTIONS OF THE SOCIETY FOR
TEXTUAL SCHOLARSHIP

AMS Press, Inc., 56 East 13th Street, New York, N.Y. 10003. Rates: $45 per year. Founded 1984. Sponsored by The Society for Textual Scholarship. Published yearly.

Major Field(s) of Interest: An interdisciplinary journal having to do with any kind of bibliographical exploration in any field.

Manuscript Information: No restrictions as to length. Style: Varies according to the practice of the discipline of the writer. Report as quickly as possible; usually within a month.

Payment: 25 offprints.

Indexed In: MLA International Bibliography.

Copyright: By AMS Press. Authors may use their work in their own books.

*THALIA: STUDIES IN LITERARY HUMOR

c/o Jacqueline Tavernier-Courbin, Department of English, University of Ottawa, Ottawa, Ontario, K1N 6N5, Canada. Rates: $15 individuals. $28 institutions. Founded 1977. Sponsored by Thalia: Association for the Study of Literary Humor. Published 2 times per year.

Major Field(s) of Interest: Articles and notes on literary humor, popular culture, and visual arts, as well as occasional literary parodies. Journal reviews books, but reviews are usually solicited.

Manuscript Information: Articles from 15–25 pages. Notes of 3–4 pages. Book reviews of 3–4 pages. Style: former MLA. Endnotes. 3 copies of manuscript required. Report in 3 to 4 months. Rejected manuscripts returned with S.A.S.E.

Payment: Offprints.

Indexed In: MLA International Bibliography.

Copyright: By the journal. Authors are granted permission to reprint with usual credit line and modest fee if reprint is in book form.

THEATER

222 York Street, New Haven, CT 06520. Rates: $18 per year. Founded 1968. Sponsored by the Yale School of Drama and Yale Repertory Theater. Published 3 times per year.

Major Field(s) of Interest: Writing on diverse theater events throughout America and abroad, particularly on groups, playwrights, and plays. Welcomes essays, interviews, and retrospectives that locate theatrical events in a greater cultural, social, or aesthetic context, and not simply documentations that are time-bound to particular productions. Journal also publishes new plays. Journal reviews books. Most articles and plays are solicited.

Manuscript Information: No length restrictions on articles. Book reviews of 1,000–2,000 words. 2 copies of manuscript required. Report in 3 months. Rejected manuscripts returned with S.A.S.E.

Payment: Copies.

Copyright: Varies.

*THEATRE ANNUAL

School of Theatre Arts, The University of Akron, Akron, OH 44325–1005. Rates: $8 per year. Founded 1945. Sponsored by The University of Akron. Published annually.

Major Field(s) of Interest: The journal is devoted to the arts of the theatre, including theory, criticism, performance technique, design/technology, and arts management. Scholarly manuscripts which focus on subjects of an international nature are welcome. Scholars are encouraged to submit iconographic documentation with manuscripts. Special issues are devoted to American musical theatre, Women in Theatre, and Eugene O'Neill.

Manuscript Information: Articles of 8–15 pages. Style: MLA with endnotes and Chicago preferred. 3 copies of manuscript required. Report in 3-4 months. Rejected manuscripts with comments returned with S.A.S.E.

Payment: 2 copies. Offprints are available at a small fee.

Indexed In: Abstracts of English Studies, Arts & Humanities Citation Index, MLA International Bibliography, Current Contents.

Copyright: By the journal. Permission to reprint is free with written permission.

THEATRE HISTORY STUDIES

Theatre Arts Department, Box 8182, University of North Dakota, Grand Forks, ND 58202. Rates: $6 per year individuals. $10 per year institutions. Founded 1981. Sponsored by the Mid-America Theatre Conference, Inc. and the University of North Dakota. Published annually.

Major Field(s) of Interest: Journal is devoted to research and excellence in all areas of theater history and in diverse national and international fields of interest. Journal reviews books, but book reviews are commissioned by the editor.

Manuscript Information: No length restrictions on articles. Notes up to 1,200 words. Book reviews up to 900 words. Style: MLA. Report in 2 months. Rejected manuscripts returned with S.A.S.E.

Payment: Copies.

Copyright: By the University of North Dakota.

THEATRE NOTEBOOK: A JOURNAL OF THE HISTORY AND TECHNIQUE OF THE BRITISH THEATRE

The Shakespeare Institute, University of Birmingham, Birmingham, B15 2RX, England. Rates: $26 per year combined with membership in The Society for Theatre Research. Founded 1945. Sponsored by the Society for Theatre Research. Published 3 times per year.

Major Field(s) of Interest: The history and technique of the British theater from the earliest times to the recent past. The journal welcomes scholarly articles from nonacademics. Journal reviews books.

Manuscript Information: Articles of 1,000-5,000 words. No length restrictions on notes. Book reviews of 400-900 words. Style: Oxford. Notes at end of article. 3 copies of manuscript required. Report in 3 months. Rejected manuscripts returned with S.A.S.E.

Payment: 6 copies.

Copyright: By the journal and by the author.

*THEATRE STUDIES

Lawrence and Lee Theatre Research Institute of Ohio State University, 1430 Lincoln Tower, 1800 Cannon Drive, Columbus, OH 43210. Rates:

$8 individuals. $10 institutions. Founded 1954. Sponsored by the Ohio State University Department of Theatre. Published 2 times a year.

Major Field(s) of Interest: Articles in the area of theatre history, literature, criticism, and theory by graduate students in accredited graduate theatre programs. Selection is by editors and board of editors advisors, each teaching theatre on the graduate level. All book reviews are done by graduate students.

Manuscript Information: Articles up to 20 pages. Book reviews of 5–6 pages. Style: Chicago. Complete bibliographical information required. 3 copies of manuscripts required. Report in 3–6 months. Rejected manuscripts returned with S.A.S.E.

Payment: Copies.

Indexed In: Guide to the Performing Arts, MHRA.

Copyright: By the journal. Permission to reprint required.

*THEATRE SURVEY: THE AMERICAN JOURNAL OF THEATRE HISTORY
The Graduate School and University Center of the City University of New York, Ph.D. Program in Theatre, Box 355, Graduate Center, 33 West 42 Street, New York, NY 10036–8099. Rates: $30 per year. Founded 1960. Sponsored by the American Society for Theatre Research. Published 2 times per year.

Major Field(s) of Interest: The journal welcomes submission of scholarly articles with an historical bent on a wide range of subjects, including American, African, Asian, British, European theatre. Unsolicited articles are welcome from independent scholars and from theatre historians at any academic level. The journal publishes the best work it receives, whether the methodology employed be traditional, historicist, new historicist, feminist, marxist, structuralist, semiotic, or whatever. The journal willingly prints illustrations. Potential contributors should note that the journal does not ordinarily consider analyses of single plays. Journal reviews books, but book reviews are solicited.

Manuscript Information: Articles of 15–50 pages. Book reviews of 500–1,500 words. Style: Chicago with notes at bottom of page. 3 copies of manuscript required. Once accepted, articles available in compatible electronic form will receive priority in the print queue. Journal uses WordPerfect, but will accept convertible files in other files, or ASCII files. Report in 1–3 months. Rejected manuscripts returned with S.A.S.E.

Payment: Offprints.

Copyright: By the American Society of Theatre Research. Permission to reprint required.

THE THOMAS HARDY JOURNAL

23 Braunston Road, Oakham, Rutland, LE15 6LD, England. Rates: £15 per year individuals. £20 per year institutions. Founded 1985. Sponsored by the Thomas Hardy Society. Published 3 times per year.

Major Field(s) of Interest: Articles, reviews, and letters related to the work and life of Thomas Hardy. Journal reviews books.

Manuscript Information: Articles up to 4,000 words. Notes up to 200 words. Book reviews up to 800 words. Style: MLA. Notes at end of article. Report in 3 months. Rejected manuscripts returned with S.A.S.E.

Payment: 4 copies.

Copyright: By the author.

THE THOMAS HARDY YEARBOOK

Saravia, Delancey Park, St. Sampson, Guernsey, CI, England. Rates: £5. Founded 1970. Sponsored by the Toucan Press. Published annually.

Major Field(s) of Interest: Publishes essays and articles about the life, times, and works of Thomas Hardy including his environment, both physical and cultural, and on Somerset and Dorset writers, especially those of the nineteenth century. Journal reviews books.

Manuscript Information: Articles of 500–8,000 words. Book reviews of 500–3,000 words. Style: MLA preferred. Submit original typescript. Report in 1 week. Rejected manuscripts returned with S.A.S.E.

Payment: 20 copies.

Copyright: By the Toucan Press and by the author.

*THE THOMAS WOLFE REVIEW

Department of English, University of Akron, Akron, OH 44325. Rates: $3 per year. Founded 1977. Sponsored by the Department of English, University of Akron. Published semiannually (Spring and Fall).

Major Field(s) of Interest: Critical articles dealing with all aspects of the life and work of Thomas Wolfe (1900–1938): reminiscences (particularly those casting new light on him), criticism, bibliography, queries, forthcoming publications about him, and news of interest to those interested in Wolfe. Occasionally the journal publishes poetry about Wolfe and short fiction involving him.

Manuscript Information: Articles up to 5,000 words. Notes up to 2,000 words. Style: MLA with endnotes. Report in 2–3 weeks. Rejected manuscripts returned with S.A.S.E.

Payment: 4 copies of the journal.

Indexed In: Abstracts of English Studies, American Humanities Index, Arts and Humanities Citation Index.

THE THOREAU SOCIETY BULLETIN

The Thoreau Society, Inc., State University College, Geneseo, NY 14454. Rates: $20 per year (includes membership in The Thoreau Society). Founded 1941. Sponsored by The Thoreau Society, Inc. Published quarterly.

Major Field(s) of Interest: The journal publishes articles on Henry David Thoreau, and all material accepted pertains to Thoreau. A bibliography is published in each issue. Journal reviews books, but book reviews are assigned.

Manuscript Information: Articles 200–1,200 words. Notes of 200–500 words. Book reviews of 200–1,000 words. Style: MLA. Report in 1 month. Rejected manuscripts returned with S.A.S.E.

Payment: 5 copies of the issue.

Indexed In: MLA International Bibliography, American Humanities Index.

Copyright: No copyright.

TRANSACTIONS OF THE SAMUEL JOHNSON SOCIETY
OF THE NORTHWEST

Samuel Johnson Society, English Department, University of Calgary, 2500 University Drive N,W.. Calgary, Alberta, T2N 1N4, Canada. Founded 1951. Sponsored by the Samuel Johnson Society of the Northwest. Published irregularly.

Major Field(s) of Interest: Publishes papers on Samuel Johnson and eighteenth-century literature read at the society's meetings.

Manuscript Information: Articles up to 5,000 words. Style: MLA. Submit camera-ready copy for all illustrations. Report in 3–4 months. Rejected manuscripts returned with S.A.S.E.

Payment: Copies.

Copyright: By the journal.

*TRISTANIA: A JOURNAL DEVOTED TO TRISTAN STUDIES

Department of Foreign Languages, University of Tennessee at Chattanooga, 615 McCallie Avenue, Chattanooga, TN 37402. Rates: $9.95 per year individuals. $19.95 per year institutions. Founded 1976. Sponsored partially by the University of Tennessee at Chattanooga. Published yearly.

Major Field(s) of Interest: Journal is devoted to the study of all aspects of the Tristan legend materials. Traditional, nontraditional, comparatist, and interdisciplinary approaches are welcome as well as notes and essays on origins, the story itself, and influence at all periods of time. Journal reviews books, but reviews are solicited.

Manuscript information: Articles up to 20 pages including notes. Book reviews up to 1,000 pages. Style: MLA. 2 copies of manuscripts required. Manuscripts should be triple-spaced on 8½ x 11 inch paper. Include a 1-page abstract. Report in 3 months. Rejected manuscripts returned with S.A.S.E.

Payment: 1 copy.

Indexed In: MLA International Bibliography, International Medieval Bibliography.

Copyright: By the journal. Reprinting allowed with permission.

TSE: TULANE STUDIES IN ENGLISH

Department of English, Tulane University, New Orleans, LA 70118. Founded 1949. Sponsored by the Tulane University, Department of English. Published irregularly.

Major Field(s) of Interest: Articles on or related to English and American literature and language. Contributors must have or had had an affiliation with Tulane University.

Manuscript Information: Articles of 2,500–5,000 words. Style: MLA. Minor variations permitted. 2 copies of manuscript required. Good photocopies are acceptable. Multiple submission is discouraged. Report in 3–6 months. Rejected manuscripts returned with S.A.S.E.

Payment: Copies.

Copyright: By the journal.

*TURN-OF-THE-CENTURY WOMEN

Department of English, Georgetown University, Washington, DC 20057. Rates: $10 per year. Founded 1984. Published twice a year.

Major Field(s) of Interest: Articles on the lives and accomplishments, literary, artistic, theatrical, social and political, of British and American women in the period 1880–1920. Journal reviews books.

Manuscript Information: Articles of 10–15 pages. Notes of 4–8 pages. Book reviews up to 3 pages. Style: MLA (old style preferred). Report in 3 months. Rejected manuscripts returned with S.A.S.E.

Payment: 2 copies of journal.

Indexed In: MLA International Bibliography.

Copyright: By the journal.

*TWENTIETH CENTURY LITERATURE:
A SCHOLARLY AND CRITICAL JOURNAL

Department of English, Hofstra University, Hempstead, NY 11550. Rates: $20 per year individuals. $24 per year for institutions. Founded 1954. Sponsored by Hofstra University. Published quarterly.

Major Field(s) of Interest: Manuscripts on all aspects of modern and contemporary literature including articles in English on writers in other languages. Articles selected by 2 referees. Annual prize of $500 awarded to outstanding critical essay.

Manuscript Information: Articles of 18–24 pages. Notes of 3–4 pages. No book reviews. Style: *MLA Style Sheet* (2nd edition, 1970). 3 copies of manuscript required. Report in 2–3 months. Rejected manuscripts returned with S.A.S.E.

Payment: 2 copies of journal plus 20 offprints.

Indexed In: Humanities Index, Bibliographic Index, MLA International Bibliography.

Copyright: By the journal.

TWENTIETH CENTURY VIEWS

Prentice Hall Press, One Gulf & Western Plaza, New York, NY 10023. Founded 1979. Sponsored by Prentice Hall Press. Published irregularly.

Major Field(s) of Interest: Publishes contemporary critical opinions on major authors, providing a twentieth-century perspective on their changing status in an era of profound revelation.

Manuscript Information: Articles up to 7,500 words. Style: MLA. Report in 3–4 months. Rejected manuscripts returned.

Payment: Copies.

Copyright: By Prentice Hall Press.

*THE UNIVERSITY OF MISSISSIPPI STUDIES IN ENGLISH

P. O. Box 941, Oxford, MS 38655. Rates: $20 per year. Founded 1961. Sponsored by the University of Mississippi. Published annually.

Major Field(s) of Interest: The journal is interested in any variety of study about British and American literature: bibliographical, biographical, critical, edited letters, and manuscripts.

Manuscript Information: Articles up to 50 pages. No set length for notes. Book review-essays up to 7 pages. Style: MLA and Chicago. Endnotes "House Style." See copy of journal for example. 2 copies of manuscript required. Report in 1–6 months. If a manuscript is accepted, the journal requests that it be placed on Macintosh disk in Microsoft Word. Rejected manuscripts returned with S.A.S.E.

Payment: 2 copies of the journal (no offprints).

Indexed In: MLA *International Bibliography, MHRA, American Literature, Victorian Studies, Mississippi Quarterly.*

Copyright: By the journal. Reprint permission granted by the editor with no charge.

*UNIVERSITY OF TORONTO QUARTERLY: A CANADIAN JOURNAL OF THE HUMANITIES

University of Toronto Press, Editorial Department, 10 St. Mary Street, Suite 700, Toronto, Ontario, M4Y 2W8, Canada. Rates: Canadian $23 per year individuals. Canadian $43 per year institutions. Founded 1933. Sponsored by the University of Toronto. Published quarterly.

Major Field(s) of Interest: The journal welcomes contributions in all areas of the humanities: literature, philosophy, fine arts, music, the history of ideas. It favors articles that cross either periods or disciplines and that appeal to a broad readership. The journal does not normally print thematically oriented criticism or the results of highly specialized research. Articles on Canadian subjects are welcomed, though these should harmonize with the international character of the journal. The journal does not publish fiction or poetry. Journal reviews books, but book reviews are assigned.

Manuscript Information: No length restrictions on articles or book reviews. Style: Modified MLA with endnotes. Include bibliographical information in notes at end of article. 1 copy of the manuscript required. Editor prefers a photocopy which does not have to be returned. Report in 3 months. Rejected manuscripts returned upon request. Include S.A.S.E. or International Reply Coupons.

Payment: $40 for articles plus 2 copies of the journal.

Copyright: By the University of Toronto Press. Fees split with author on reprinting.

THE UPSTART CROW: A SHAKESPEARE JOURNAL

Department of English, Clemson University, Clemson, SC 29634–1503. Rates: $7 per year. $12 for 2 years. Founded 1977. Sponsored by Clemson University and Drury College. Published annually.

Major Field(s) of Interest: The journal publishes short articles and notes on the editing, producing, teaching, and interpretation of Shakespeare's poetry and plays. The journal encourages new approaches and original ideas that would stimulate thinking or rethinking, and the journal publishes a poem per issue that is Shakespeare-related as well as occasional art and photos.

Manuscript Information: Articles of 20–25 double-spaced pages. Notes up to 1,500 words. Style: Chicago with notes at bottom of page. 2 copies of manuscript required. Prefer abstract. Quotations should be single-spaced in typescript. Submit original typescript. Report in 4 months. Rejected manuscripts returned with S.A.S.E.

Payment: 2 copies of journal and 15 offprints.

Indexed In: MLA International Bibliography, World Shakespeare Bibliography.

Copyright: By Clemson University.

VIATOR: MEDIEVAL AND RENAISSANCE STUDIES

Center for Medieval and Renaissance Studies, 212 Royce Hall, UCLA, 405 Hilgard Avenue, Los Angeles, CA 90024–1485. Rates: $47 per year. Founded 1970. Sponsored by the Center for Medieval and Renaissance Studies, UCLA. Published annually.

Major Field(s) of Interest: Articles on all aspects of the period from late antiquity through the northern Renaissance (AD 350 to AD 1650). Subjects may include the West, Byzantium, the Orthodox Slavs, or topics related to societies that had ties with the West during the above defined period. The journal places special emphasis on intercultural and interdisciplinary studies concerning the West.

Manuscript Information: Articles of 25–100 pages. Style: Chicago with footnotes doubled-spaced, numbered consecutively, following the text. Prefer 2 manuscripts. Report in 3–4 months. Rejected manuscripts returned with S.A.S.E. Submit 200–word Abstract.

Payment: 75 free offprints.

Indexed In: MLA International Bibliography, American Bibliography of Slavic and East European Studies, British Archaelogical Abstracts, Geological Abstracts, RILA, ABC-CLIO, Historical Abstracts, America: History and Life.

Copyright: By the University of California Board of Regents. Authors may republish with permission from the University of California Press provided acknowledgment is given.

VICTORIAN LITERATURE AND CULTURE

Department of English, NYU, 19 University Plaza, Room 235, New York, NY 10003 or Department of English, SUNY/Stony Brook, Stony Brook, NY 11794. Rates: $25 per year individuals. $30 per year institutions. Includes membership in the Browning Institute. Founded 1971 as BROWNING INSTITUTE STUDIES: AN ANNUAL OF VICTORIAN LITERARY AND CULTURAL HISTORY. Sponsored by the Browning Institute. Published annually.

Major Field(s) of Interest: The journal publishes articles, chapters of works in progress on all aspects of Victorian literature and culture with emphasis on Robert and Elizabeth Barrett Browning and other literary and artistic figures associated with them. Biographical, critical, bibliographical as well as articles using a contemporary perspective will be considered. Journal reviews books. Review-essays are solicited.

Manuscript Information: No limit on length of manuscripts for articles. No notes. Book reviews of 3–5 pages. Style: MLA with endnotes and list of works cited. 2 copies of manuscript required. Report in 3 months (except summers). Rejected manuscripts returned with S.A.S.E.

Payment: 1 copy of volume.

Indexed In: MLA International Bibliography, Literary Criticism Register.

Copyright: Author retains republishing rights.

VICTORIAN NEWSLETTER

FAC 200, Western Kentucky University, Bowling Green, KY 42101. Rates: $5 per year individuals. $6 per year foreign. Founded 1952. Sponsored by the Victorian Group, Modern Language Association and Western Kentucky University. Published 2 times per year.

Major Field(s) of Interest: Articles and notes on British Victorian literature. Book notices only.

Manuscript Information: Articles up to 25 pages. Notes of 6–8 pages. Style: MLA (2nd Edition). Report in 3 months. Rejected manuscripts returned with S.A.S.E.

Payment: 5 copies of the journal plus tearsheets.

Indexed In: Abstracts of English Studies, Literary Criticism Register, Institute for Scientific Information, The English Association.

Copyright: By the journal. Authors are granted the right to reprint with the permission of the author and the journal.

*VICTORIAN PERIODICALS REVIEW

Department of English, Southern Illinois University at Edwardsville, Edwardsville, IL 62026. Rates: $13 per year individual. $18 per year institutions. Founded 1968. Sponsored by the Research Society for Victorian Periodicals. Published quarterly.

Major Field(s) of Interest: Articles or notes with a historical, critical, or bibliographical emphasis on the editorial and publishing history of Victorian periodicals (newspapers, magazines, or reviews) or on the importance of periodicals for an understanding of the history and culture of Victorian Britain, Ireland, and the Empire. Journal welcomes brief informal reports of work in progress. Journal reviews books.

Manuscript Information: Articles up to 30 pages. Notes of 3–5 pages. Book reviews of 2–5 pages. Style: MLA preferred with notes in text and list of Works Cited. 2 copies of manuscript required. Report in 6–9 months. Rejected manuscripts returned with S.A.S.E.

Payment: 1 copy of the issue and reduced price for extra copies.

Indexed In: MLA International Bibliography, American Humanities Index.

Copyright: By the journal. Requests to reprint must be submitted in writing.

VICTORIAN POETRY

Department of English, West Virginia University, Morgantown, WV 26506. Rates: $15 per year individuals. $25 per year institutions. Founded 1963. Sponsored by West Virginia University. Published quarterly.

Major Field(s) of Interest: Articles on English literature of the 1830–1914 period. The journal focuses primarily on the aesthetic consideration of nineteenth-century poetry, mostly British, with occasional study of poetry in social, historical, and philosophical contexts. Appropriate critical studies of prose, especially in its aesthetic or rhetorical aspects, are also published. Journal reviews books, but book reviews are solicited.

Manuscript Information: Articles of 15–25 pages. Notes of 4–10 pages. Book reviews of 2–6 pages. Style: Chicago with endnotes. 2 copies of manuscript required. IBM compatible disc requested. Report in 3 months. Rejected manuscripts returned with S.A.S.E.

Payment: None.

Copyright: By West Virginia University. Request permission for reprints.

VICTORIAN STUDIES:
A JOURNAL OF THE HUMANITIES, ARTS AND SCIENCES

Ballantine Hall, 338, Indiana University, Bloomington, IN 47401. Rates: $16 per year individuals. $20 per year institutions. $12 per year students. Founded 1958. Sponsored by the Trustees of Indiana University. Published quarterly.

Major Field(s) of Interest: Interdisciplinary articles focused on the literature, arts, and sciences of Victorian England (1820–1910). Special emphasis is placed on cultural studies of this time period. Journal reviews books, but book reviews are commissioned.

Manuscript Information: Articles up to 25 pages. Book reviews of 800–1,500 words. Style: MLA. 2 copies of manuscript required. Report in 3 months. Rejected manuscripts are not returned.

Payment: Offprints.
Copyright: By the Indiana University Trustees.

*VICTORIANS INSTITUTE JOURNAL
Department of English, East Carolina University, Greenville, NC 27858.
Rates: $10 per year individuals. $14 per year institutions. Founded 1971.
Sponsored by the Victorians Institute and East Carolina University. Published annually.

Major Field(s) of Interest: Publishes work on Victorian literature, art, history, culture, and ideas. Journal reviews books.

Manuscript Information: Articles of 10–20 pages. Notes of 500–2,000 words. Book reviews of 500–1,500 words. Style: MLA with endnotes and parenthetical references. 2 copies of manuscript required. Report in 3–6 months. Rejected manuscripts returned with S.A.S.E.

Payment: 1 copy of issue and 12 offprints.

Copyright: By East Carolina University Publications. Permission granted to reprint upon request to ECU Publications.

VIRGINIA QUARTERLY REVIEW:
A NATIONAL JOURNAL OF LITERATURE AND DISCUSSION
1 West Range, Charlottesville, VA 22903. Rates: $15 per year individuals. $22 per year institutions. Founded 1925. Sponsored by the University of Virginia. Published quarterly.

Major Field(s) of Interest: Articles and discussion on contemporary literature. Journal reviews books.

Manuscript Information: Articles of 3,000–4,000 words. Book reviews of 1,000–3,000 words for essay reviews. Style: Chicago. Report in 6 weeks. Rejected manuscripts returned with S.A.S.E.

Payment: Copies.

Copyright: By the journal.

*VIRGINIA WOOLF MISCELLANY
Department of English, Sonoma State University, Rohnert Park, CA 94928. Rates: Free to individuals. Founded 1973. Sponsored by the Departments of English, Stanford University and Sonoma State University. Published 2 times per year (Fall and Spring).

Major Field(s) of Interest: The journal publishes scholarly articles on all subjects directly related to Virginia Woolf studies. Journal reviews books.

Manuscript Information: Articles up to 1,000 words. Notes up to 500 words. Book reviews up to 1,000 words. Style: MLA. 2 copies of manuscript required. Report in 4–6 weeks. Rejected manuscripts returned with S.A.S.E.

Payment: 5 copies.

Copyright: By the journal. Permission to reprint is required.

The Visionary Company: A Magazine of the Twenties

Mercy College, Dobbs Ferry, NY 10522. Rates: $6 per year. Founded 1981. Sponsored by Mercy College. Published annually.

Major Field(s) of Interest: The journal encourages the study and appreciation of the lives and works of American writers of the 1920s and their relevance to the post-modern world. Journal reviews books.

Manuscript Information: Articles of 15–20 pages. Notes of 1 page. Book reviews of 3–4 pages. Style: MLA. 2 copies of manuscript required. Report in 6–12 months. Rejected manuscripts returned with S.A.S.E.

Payment: Copies.

Indexed In: MLA International Bibliography.

Copyright: By the journal.

*The Wallace Stevens Journal

Clarkson University, Potsdam, NY 13699–5750. Rates: $20 per year individuals. $25 per year institutions. Subscription price includes membership in the Wallace Stevens Society. Founded 1977. Sponsored by the Wallace Stevens Society, Inc. Published biannually.

Major Field(s) of Interest: Scholarly articles on the poetry or life of Wallace Stevens. The journal also carries poems that reflect Stevens's influence, themes, and style or material related to Stevens in some way. Articles comparing Stevens with other authors are also accepted. Journal reviews books.

Manuscript Information: Articles of 20–40 pages, but the journal has no special length limitations. Book reviews up to 1,200 words. Style: Chicago. Either old or new footnote form accepted, at end of article. 2 copies of manuscript required. Computer disk files are requested for accepted manuscripts. Report in 6–9 weeks. Rejected manuscripts returned with S.A.S.E.

Payment: 3 copies of the issue.

Bibliographical Issue: The Spring issue contains a current bibliography.

Indexed In: MLA International Bibliography, Abstracts of English Studies, Arts & Humanities Citation Index, Current Citations, IBR, IBZ, MHRA.

Copyright: By the journal. Rights revert to author upon request with appropriate credit line.

*WALT WHITMAN QUARTERLY REVIEW

308 English-Philosophy Building, University of Iowa, Iowa City, IA 52242. Rates: $12 per year individuals. $15 per year institutions. Founded 1983. Sponsored by the Graduate College and the Department of English, University of Iowa. Published quarterly.

Major Field(s) of Interest: Publishes biographical, textual, and interpretive essays on Whitman, his work, influence, cultural context, and relation to his times. Journal reviews books and publishes bibliographies.

Manuscript Information: Articles of 15–35 pages. Notes of 1–10 pages. Book reviews of 3–15 pages. Style: MLA (2nd edition) or Chicago. Consult "Guidelines for Contributors" published in each issue. 2 copies of manuscript required. Report in 2 months. Rejected manuscripts returned with S.A.S.E.

Payment: 2 free copies.

Indexed In: MLA International Bibliography, Current Contents, American Literary Scholarship.

Copyright: By the journal. Permission to reprint with usual credit line.

THE WELLSIAN

c/o The H. G. Wells Society, English Department, Nene College, Moulton Park, Northampton, NN2 7AL, England. Founded 1960. Current series since 1976. Sponsored by the H. G. Wells Society. Published annually.

Major Field(s) of Interest: Articles on the work, thought, and life of H. G. Wells. Journal reviews books.

Manuscript Information: Articles of 2,000–9,000 words. No length restrictions on notes. Book reviews up to 1,000 words. Style: MLA with endnotes. Report in 60 days. Rejected manuscripts returned with S.A.S.E.

Payment: 2 copies.

Copyright: By the author. The journal appreciates a credit when reprinting.

*WESTERN HUMANITIES REVIEW

Department of English, University of Utah, Salt Lake City, UT 84112. Rates: $15 per year individuals. $20 per year institutions. Founded 1947. Sponsored by the University of Utah, Department of English. Published quarterly.

Major Field(s) of Interest: Articles on any aspect of the humanities, including fiction and poetry of merit and book reviews of critical works.

Manuscript Information: Articles up to 2,000 words. Notes up to

800 words. Book reviews up to 1,000 words. Style: None. Report in 1 month. Rejected manuscripts returned with S.A.S E.

Payment: Copies.

Copyright: By the journal.

WILLA CATHER PIONEER MEMORIAL NEWSLETTER

326 North Webster, Red Cloud, NE 68970. Rates: $10 per year. Founded 1957. Sponsored by the Willa Cather Pioneer Memorial & Educational Foundation. Published quarterly.

Major Field(s) of Interest: Promotes and assists in the development and preservation of the art, literature, and historical collection relating to the life, time, and work of Willa Cather. Journal reviews books.

Manuscript Information: Articles up to 1,000 words. Book reviews up to 50 words. Style: None. Report in 6 months. Rejected manuscripts returned.

Payment: Copies.

Copyright: By the Willa Cather Pioneer Memorial & Educational Foundation.

*WILLIAM CARLOS WILLIAMS REVIEW

Department of English, Swarthmore College, Swarthmore, PA 19081–1397. Rates: $8 per year individuals. $10 per year institutions. Founded 1975 under its current name. From 1975–1979, the journal was entitled the WILLIAM CARLOS WILLIAMS NEWSLETTER. Sponsored by the William Carlos Williams Society affiliated with the Modern Language Association. Published 2 times per year (Spring and Fall).

Major Field(s) of Interest: The life and art of the American poet William Carlos Williams (1883–1963). The journal publishes previously unpublished Williams documents, scholarly articles, notes, and book reviews, announcements, current bibliographic listings, and other pertinent material relating to William Carlos Williams.

Manuscript Information: Articles up to 10,000 words. Notes of 500–1000 words. Book reviews of 1,500–2,000 words. Style: *MLA Style Manual.* Computer disks are requested for articles that have been accepted for publication. Report in 6 months. Rejected manuscripts returned with S.A.S.E.

Payment: Issue copies.

Indexed In: MLA International Bibliography, American Humanities Index, Abstracts of English Studies, Arts and Humanities Index, Literary Criticism Register.

Copyright: By Peter Schmidt for the journal.

THE WINESBURG EAGLE:

THE OFFICIAL PUBLICATION OF THE SHERWOOD ANDERSON SOCIETY
Department of English, Virginia Polytechnic Institute and State University, Blacksburg, VA 24061-0112. Rates: $8 per year ($9 overseas). Founded 1975. Sponsored by the Sherwood Anderson Society. Published 2 times per year (November and April).

Major Field(s) of Interest: Articles dealing with the life and works of Sherwood Anderson. Contributions are not limited, but priority is given to the scholarship of the members of the Sherwood Anderson Society. Journal reviews books.

Manuscript Information: No set length on articles. Notes up to 500 words. Book reviews up to 750 words. Style: MLA with endnotes. Report in 4-6 weeks. Rejected manuscripts returned with S.A.S.E.

Payment: 2 copies of the issue.

Copyright: By the Sherwood Anderson Society. Authors are freely granted permission to reprint, except for edited texts, with usual credit line.

WOMEN'S STUDIES: AN INTERDISCIPLINARY JOURNAL
Department of English, Queens College, City University of New York, Flushing, NY 11367. Founded 1972. Sponsored by the National Women's Studies Association. Published 3 times per year.

Major Field(s) of Interest: A forum for the presentation of scholarship and criticism about women in the fields of literature, history, art, sociology, law, political science, economics, anthropology, and the sciences. Also publishes poetry, short fiction, film, and book reviews.

Manuscript Information: Articles of 15-20 pages. Book reviews of 500-1,000 words. Style: MLA. 2 copies of manuscript required. Submit double-spaced typescript and include a 100-150 word abstract. Report in 3 months. Rejected manuscripts returned with S.A.S.E.

Payment: Copies.

Copyright: By Gordon & Breach Science Publishers, Ltd.

THE WORDSWORTH CIRCLE
Department of English, Temple University, Philadelphia, PA 19122. Rates: $15 per year. Founded 1970. Sponsored by the Department of English, Temple University. Published quarterly.

Major Field(s) of Interest: The journal is an international quarterly founded to improve communication among colleagues interested in the lives, works, and times of the English Romantic writers: Wordsworth, Coleridge, Blake, Hazlitt, De Quincey, Lamb, Southey, Byron, Shelley, Keats, Sir Walter Scott, Jane Austen, and the minor and popular writers such as James Hogg, Maria Edgeworth, Leigh Hunt, and Walter Savage Landor. Representing the diversity and range of contemporary professional activity, the journal publishes all forms of legitimate studies in the field: bibliography, textual and historical scholarship, biography, interpretive criticism, interdisciplinary and comparative studies, critical theory, as well as special issues on individual writers, topics, or works, and news of special events, library collections, and conference proceedings, including papers delivered at the annual Wordsworth Summer Conference in Grasmere. The third number (Summer) is devoted to reviews of all works published on English, American, or Continental Romanticism during the previous year.

Manuscript Information: Articles of 5,000–10,000 words. Notes up to 1,500 words. Book reviews up to 2,500 words. Style: MLA. 2 copies of manuscript required. Report in 3 months. Rejected manuscripts returned.

Payment: Copies.

Copyright: By the author.

WORLD LITERATURE TODAY:

A LITERARY QUARTERLY OF THE UNIVERSITY OF OKLAHOMA

630 Parrington Oval, Room 110, University of Oklahoma, Norman, OK 73019–0375. Rates: $24 per year individuals. $36 per year institutions. Founded 1927 (original name: BOOKS ABROAD: 1927–1976). Sponsored by the University of Oklahoma. Published quarterly.

Major Field(s) of Interest: An international literary quarterly devoted to contemporary writers and literary movements in foreign countries, the journal publishes literary criticism, creative writing, and related topics from any area of the world and in any language. Articles are aimed at a literate general audience rather than at specialists. Articles should be critical, biographical, or comparative in nature. Emphasis is on European, African, Asian, and Middle Eastern writing rather than Anglo-American literature. Journal reviews books.

Manuscript Information: Articles of 3,000–4,500 words. Notes of 500–3,000 words. Book reviews of 300–500 words. Style: Chicago. Footnotes should be kept to a minimum. Report in 4–6 weeks. Rejected manuscripts returned with S.A.S.E.

Payment: 3 copies and 25 offprints for articles.

Indexed In: Book Review Index, Arts & Humanities Citation Index, Social Science & Humanities Index, International Bibliography of Book Reviews.

Copyright: By the University of Oklahoma Press. Permission to reprint required.

*WORLD LITERATURE WRITTEN IN ENGLISH

Department of English, University of Guelph, Guelph, Ontario, N1G 2W1, Canada. Rates: $15 per year individuals. $25 per year institutions. Sponsored by the University of Guelph. Published 2 times per year.

Major Field(s) of Interest: The journal focuses on commonwealth and post-colonial literatures in English: African, Caribbean, Australian, New Zealand, Canadian, and South Pacific. The journal is interested in postcolonial theory and publishes fiction, drama, and poetry. Journal reviews books.

Manuscript Information: Articles up to 5,000 words. Notes up to 250 words. Book reviews up to 1,000 words. Style: MLA with parenthetical citation. 2 copies of manuscript required. Report in 2–3 months. Rejected manuscripts returned with S.A.S.E.

Payment: 1 copy of the journal.

Copyright: By the journal and the author. Permission granted to reprint with credit line.

*THE WRITING CENTER JOURNAL

Department of Humanities, Michigan Technological University, Houghton, MI 49931. Rates: $10 per year. Founded 1980. Sponsored by the National Writing Centers Association. Published 2 times per year: Fall/Winter and Spring/Summer.

Major Field(s) of Interest: The journal is the official publication of the National Writing Centers Association. It publishes research on critical theory and writing center instruction, politics of writing center instruction, students' perspectives of the writing center, cultural diversity in writing center instruction, collaborative learning and the writing center, theories of learning and writing center instruction, writing centers and community involvement, and literacy programs in the writing center. Journal reviews books.

Manuscript Information: Articles up to 20 pages. Book reviews up to 5 pages. Style: MLA. 4 copies of manuscript required. Name and identifying information should appear on title page only. Report in 6 weeks. Rejected manuscripts returned with S.A.S.E.

Payment: 2 copies of the journal.

Copyright: By the journal. Authors are freely granted permission to reprint with usual credit line.

*YEATS: AN ANNUAL OF CRITICAL AND TEXTUAL STUDIES

Department of English, University of Tennessee, Knoxville, TN 37996–0430. Rates: vary per issue. Founded 1981. Sponsored by the University of Michigan Press and the Department of English, University of Tennessee. Published annually.

Major Field(s) of Interest: Articles and notes on any aspect of Yeats studies. The journal is interested in editions of unpublished or uncollected materials. Each issue contains an Annual Bibliography of Criticism. Journal reviews books, but unsolicited reviews are not accepted.

Manuscript Information: No restrictions on length of articles, notes, or book reviews. Style: "Old MLA." See journal Style Sheet. Report in 1–3 months. Rejected manuscripts returned with S.A.S.E.

Payment: 2 copies of the journal. 1 copy for reviews.

Indexed In: MLA International Bibliography.

Copyright: By the University of Michigan Press. Reprint without fee as long as original publication is acknowledged.

YEATS ELIOT REVIEW: A JOURNAL OF CRITICISM AND SCHOLARSHIP
Department of English, University of Arkansas at Little Rock, Little Rock, AR 72204. Founded 1974. Sponsored by the University of Arkansas at Little Rock. Published 2 times per year.

Major Field(s) of Interest: Research-based papers and notes on all aspects of Yeats and Eliot studies. Journal also includes bibliographical update, book reviews, review articles, and notes.

Manuscript Information: Articles up to 15 pages. Book reviews up to 1,000 words. Style: MLA. Employ Canadian/British usage in spelling. 2 copies of manuscript required. Report in 90 days. Rejected manuscripts returned with S.A.S.E.

Payment: Offprints.

Copyright: Retained by the author.

II. Criticism and Theory Journals

THE AMERICAN JOURNAL OF SEMIOTICS

Department of Comparative Literature, University of California at Davis, Davis, CA 95616. Rates: $30 per year individuals. $40 per year institutions. Founded 1981. Sponsored by the Semiotic Society of America. Published quarterly.

Major Field(s) of Interest: The journal is interested in scholarship that analyzes texts, groups, events, cultural and natural objects utilizing a semiotic methodology. It is also interested in the theory and methods of academic disciplines in relationship to semiotics. Contributors must be members of the Semiotic Society of America. Journal reviews books.

Manuscript Information: No length restrictions on articles or book reviews. Style: SSA Style Guide. Type double-spaced manuscripts on 8½ x 11 inch paper divided into the following sections: Title page, Text, Notes, References, Tables, Figure Captions, and Figures. Each section begins on a new page. 3 copies of manuscript required. Report in 3 months. Rejected manuscripts returned with S.A.S.E.

Payment: Copies.

Copyright: By the author.

APPROACHES TO SEMIOTICS

Mouton Publishers, 200 Saw Mill River Road, Hawthorne, NY 10532. Founded 1983. Sponsored by the editor: Thomas A. Sebeok. Published irregularly.

Major Field(s) of Interest: Articles in the humanities, the social and behavioral sciences, and the life sciences which deal with signification and interpretation in, or communication and interaction among and between, human beings and the speechless creatures.

Manuscript Information: Articles up to 5,000 words. Style: MLA. Report in 3 months. Rejected manuscripts returned.

Payment: Copies.

Copyright: By Mouton Publishers.

*THE ARIZONA QUARTERLY:
A JOURNAL OF AMERICAN LITERATURE, CULTURE, AND THEORY

Main Library B–451, University of Arizona, Tucson, AZ 95721. Rates: $10 per year individuals. $15 per year institutions. Founded 1945. Sponsored by the University of Arizona, Department of English. Published quarterly.

Major Field(s) of Interest: The journal publishes articles that offer theoretical, historical, and cultural approaches to the canonical and non-canonical texts of American literature. It also publishes short stories and poems. Journal reviews books on American literature and criticism.

Manuscript Information: No length restrictions on articles. Book reviews of 2,500–10,000 words. Style: MLA with some modification. Consult journal for style. 2 copies of manuscript preferred. Submit original typescript. Report in 30–60 days. Rejected manuscripts returned with S.A.S.E.

Payment: 2 copies of the journal.

Copyright: By the Arizona Board of Regents. Authors are freely granted permission to reprint with usual credit line.

BRITISH JOURNAL OF AESTHETICS

University of Sussex, School of Cultural and Community Studies, Arts Building, Falmer, Brighton, BN1 9QN, England. Rates: $24 per year individuals. $55 per year institutions. Founded 1960. Sponsored by the British Society of Aesthetics. Published 4 times per year.

Major Field(s) of Interest: The journal promotes research, study, and discussion in aesthetics as a theoretical study of the arts and related kinds of experience, predominantly from a philosophical point of view, but psychological, sociological, scientific, historical, critical, or educational viewpoints are also admitted. Journal reviews books, but unsolicited book reviews are not accepted.

Manuscript Information: Articles up to 5,500 words. Book reviews up to 900 words. Style: Journal. Double-spaced typescript including indented quotations and references. Report in 3 months. Rejected manuscripts returned with S.A.S.E.

Payment: Copies.

Copyright: By Oxford University Press, Walton Street, Oxford OX2 6DP, England.

*COMPARATIVE LITERATURE

223 Friendly Hall, University of Oregon, Eugene, OR 97403–1233. Rates: $12.50 per year individuals. $19.00 per year institutions. Founded 1949. Sponsored by the American Comparative Literature Association. Published quarterly.

Major Field(s) of Interest: Articles that explore important problems of literary theory and literary history not confined to a single national literature. A broad range of theoretical and critical approaches is encouraged. Journal reviews books, but unsolicited book reviews are not accepted.

Manuscript Information: Articles of 5,000–12,000 words. Book reviews up to 1,200 words. Style: MLA (1985). Submit original typescript or a photocopy with assurance that manuscript is not being submitted elsewhere. Report in 2 months. Rejected manuscripts returned.

Payment: Copies.

Copyright: By the author.

*CRITICAL INQUIRY

The University of Chicago Press, 5720 South Woodlawn Avenue, Chicago, IL 60637. Rates: $29 per year individuals. $62 per year institutions. Founded 1974. Sponsored by the University of Chicago Press. Published quarterly.

Major Field(s) of Interest: An interdisciplinary journal devoted to publishing the best critical thought in the arts and humanities, the journal publishes articles dealing with theory, method, and critical principles that explore the fields of criticism, literature, history, music, film, philosophy, and the fine arts.

Manuscript Information: Articles up to 30 pages. Notes up to 5 pages. Style: Chicago. 2 copies of manuscript required. Submit original double-spaced typescript. Report in 6 weeks. Rejected manuscripts returned with S.A.S.E.

Payment: Copies.

Indexed In: MLA Abstracts, Sociological Abstracts, Arts and Humanities Citation Index, Current Contents: Arts and Humanities, Humanities Index.

Copyright: By the University of Chicago Press.

*CRITICAL TEXTS: A REVIEW OF THEORY AND CRITICISM

Department of English and Comparative Literature, 602 Philosophy Hall, Columbia University, New York, NY 10027. Rates: $9 per year individuals. $15 per year institutions. $20 per year foreign. Founded 1982. Mainly self-supporting. Partially sponsored by the Department of English and Comparative Literature, Columbia University. Published 3 times per year.

Major Field(s) of Interest: Interviews with leading critics, articles and reviews on theoretical issues in literature, art, film, music, and language, and translations of articles unavailable in English. Journal reviews books and is interested in publishing reviews of new work of theoretical interest in the humanities and social sciences.

Manuscript Information: Articles of 15–25 pages. Reviews of 8–12 pages. Style: MLA. 2 copies of manuscript required. Report in 6–12 weeks. Rejected manuscripts returned with S.A.S.E.

Payment: 1 complimentary copy of issue.

Indexed In: Philosopher's Index, Serials Directory, American Humanities Index, Literary Criticism Register, MLA Guide to Periodicals, MLA International Bibliography.

Copyright: By the journal. *CritT* freely grants permission to reprint with the usual credit line. but authors must request permission.

*CRITICISM: A QUARTERLY FOR LITERATURE AND THE ARTS

Department of English, Wayne State University, Detroit, MI 48202. Rates: $28 individuals. $42 libraries. Founded 1959. Published quarterly.

Major Field(s) of Interest: Criticism is designed to advance the study of literature and the other arts; it is a medium for the scholarly analysis and evaluation of artists and their works. Formal aesthetics and the more technical studies in philology and linguistics are not within its scope. It examines the arts and literatures of all periods and nations, either individually or in their interrelationships and the critical theory regarding them.

Manuscript Information: Articles 20–30 pages. Notes 3–5 pages. Book reviews 3–5 pages. Style: *MLA Style Sheet* (1970). Submit original typescript. Report in 1–3 months. Rejected manuscripts returned with S.A.S.E.

Payment: 2 copies of the issue.

Copyright: By the Wayne State University Press. Permission to reprint routinely given.

DIACRITICS: A REVIEW OF CONTEMPORARY CRITICISM

Department of Romance Studies, 283 Goldwin Smith Hall, Cornell University, Ithaca, NY 14853. Rates: $19 per year individuals. $42 per year institutions. Founded 1971. Sponsored by the Department of Romance Studies, Cornell University. Published quarterly.

Major Field(s) of Interest: Contemporary criticism in literature, cinema, and the arts as well as a preview of important work in progress. Journal invites speculation and debate about criticism from all quarters— its grounds, achievements, and current problems in theory and practice. While the journal is concerned primarily with the problems of criticism, the editors have adopted no formal policy governing the choice of books to be reviewed or critical perspectives to be explored. Diacritical discussion entails distinguishing the methodological and ideological issues that critics encounter and setting forth a critical position in relation to them. Review articles, which are the principal component of each issue, should both provide a serious account of the work(s) under consideration and allow the reviewer to respond by developing his own ideas or positions.

Manuscript Information: Articles up to 15 typewritten pages. Style:

MLA. Footnotes on separate page. 2 copies of manuscript required. Report in 180 days. Rejected manuscripts returned with S.A.S.E. Correspondence with editors prior to submission of manuscripts is recommended.

Payment: 2 copies of journal. Reprints can be ordered.

Indexed In: American Humanities Index, Arts and Humanities Citation Index.

Copyright: By the Johns Hopkins University Press.

DISCOURSE: JOURNAL FOR THEORETICAL STUDIES IN MEDIA AND CULTURE

Center for Twentieth Century Studies, P. O. Box 413, University of Wisconsin-Milwaukee, Milwaukee, WI 53201. Rates: $12 per year individuals. $24 per year institutions. Founded 1978. Sponsored by the University of Wisconsin-Milwaukee Center for Twentieth Century Studies. Published 2 times per year (Spring-Summer and Fall-Winter).

Major Field(s) of Interest: Discourse explores a variety of topics in cultural criticism, continental philosophy, theories of media and literature, and the politics of sexuality, including questions of language and psychoanalysis. Journal reviews books.

Manuscript Information: Articles of 18–22 pages. Book reviews of 5–7 pages. Style: MLA. With endnotes. 2 copies of manuscript required. Report time is variable. Rejected manuscripts returned with S.A.S.E.

Payment: 2 copies.

Indexed In: MLA International Bibliography.

Copyright: By the Regents of the University of Wisconsin. After publication, rights revert to the journal.

*THE EIGHTEENTH CENTURY: THEORY AND INTERPRETATION

Texas Tech University Press, Lubbock, TX 79409–1037. Rates: $16 per year individuals. $28 per year institutions. Founded 1959. Sponsored by Texas Tech University. Published 3 times per year (Fall, Winter, Spring).

Major Field(s) of Interest: All aspects of British, American, and Continental culture, 1660–1800, including literature, history, fine arts, science, music, history of ideas, and popular culture. The editors take special interest in essays concerned with the application of twentieth-century theory and methodology to the eighteenth-century. The editors invite commentaries on essays published in the journal or on other matters of concern to its readers. Journal reviews books.

Manuscript Information: Articles of 4,000–10,000 words. Book reviews of 2,500–3,000 words. Style: Chicago. 2 copies of manuscript should be submitted in hard copy as well as on IBM-compatible disks, preferably as ASCII files. Report in 4 months. Rejected manuscripts returned with S.A.S.E.

Payment: 4 copies of journal for articles, 2 for reviews.

Indexed In: MLA International Bibliography.

Copyright: By the Texas Tech University Press.

ENCLITIC

P. O. Box 36098, Los Angeles, CA 90036-0098. Rates: $16 per year individuals. $36 per year institutions. Founded 1976. Published quarterly.

Major Field(s) of Interest: Articles on contemporary literature, politics, critical theories, and film. ENCLITIC is dedicated to finding and preserving what is experimental and innovative in American cultural and political life. It is devoted to the task of constantly monitoring the mass media, visual and printed information, and the institutions of culture and politics that influence and engulf modern life. Journal reviews books.

Manuscript Information: Articles of 2,500-5,000 words. Book reviews of 500-1,500 words. Style: *MLA Style Sheet.* 3 copies of manuscript required. Report in 2-3 months. Rejected manuscripts returned with S.A.S.E.

Payment: In copies.

Indexed In: Sociological Abstracts, MLA International Bibliography, International Index to Film Periodicals. Film-Literature Index, Social Sciences and Humanities Index, PAIS.

Copyright: By the journal. Permission to reprint granted.

ESSAYS IN CRITICISM:
A QUARTERLY JOURNAL OF LITERARY CRITICISM

6a Rawlingson Road, Oxford, OX2 6UE, England. Rates: $64 per year. Founded 1951. Sponsored by Oxford University. Published quarterly.

Major Field(s) of Interest: Journal publishes articles in English literature from all periods. The journal has an English bias, but suitable articles from abroad are welcome. Journal reviews books, but unsolicited book reviews are not accepted.

Manuscript Information: Articles of 7,000-8,000 words. Book reviews of 3,000-4,000 words. Style: Footnotes at end of article. Report in 1 month. Rejected manuscripts returned with S.A.S.E.

Payment: 12 offprints.

Copyright: By the journal and by the author. Permission fees are shared 50/50 with the author.

*ESSAYS IN LITERATURE

114 Simpkins Hall, Western Illinois University, Macomb, IL 61455. Rates: $5 per year individuals. $9 per year libraries. Founded 1973. Sponsored by the College of Arts & Sciences, Western Illinois University. Published semiannually (Spring and Fall).

Major Field(s) of Interest: Literature and literary theory in the British and American traditions and the modern European languages. The journal welcomes studies concerning any literary theory or pedagogical applications of theory. Articles selected on the basis of peer review.

Manuscript Information: Articles from 20–35 pages. Notes from 8–12 pages. Style: MLA 1985 with endnotes. Report in 2–3 months. Rejected manuscripts returned with S.A.S.E.

Payment: 3 complimentary copies of issue.

Indexed In: MLA International Bibliography, Humanities Index.

Copyright: By the journal. Authors permitted to reprint in other forums without charge, but authors must request permission.

ESSAYS IN THEATRE

Department of Drama, University of Guelph, Guelph, Ontario N1G 2W1, Canada. Rates: Canada $12 per year individuals. Canada $15 per year institutions. Founded 1982. Sponsored by the University of Guelph, Drama Department. Published 2 times per year.

Major Field(s) of Interest: Articles on dramatic theory, aesthetics, literature, theater history, and production. Journal reviews books, but book reviews are commissioned.

Manuscript Information: Articles up to 5,000 words. Book reviews up to 1,000 words. Style: MLA. 2 copies of manuscript required. Report in 2 months. Rejected manuscripts returned.

Payment: Copies.

Copyright: By the author.

ÉTUDES LITTÉRAIRES

c/o Secretaire à la Rédaction, Faculté des Lettres, Université of Laval, Quebec, G1K 7P4, Canada. Rates: Canada $23 per year. Foreign $26 per year. Institutions: $38 per year. Founded 1968. Sponsored by the Département des Littératures, Université Laval. Published 3 times per year.

Major Field(s) of Interest: The journal publishes articles in French (English articles may be translated if very interesting) on literary theory, genre, cinema, theater, and individual authors. Journal reviews books, but book reviews are solicited.

Manuscript Information: Articles up to 20 pages with abstract in

French and English. Book reviews up to 5 pages. Style: MLA with complete bibliographic data at the end of article. Write for "Protocole de redaction." Submit original typescript. If possible, submit floppy disk on MicroSoft Word 4. Report in 3 months. Rejected manuscripts are not returned.

Payment: 20 offprints for articles, 1 for reviews.

Copyright: By the journal.

*EXEMPLARIA: A JOURNAL OF THEORY IN MEDIEVAL AND RENAISSANCE STUDIES

Department of English, University of Florida, 4008 Turlington Hall, Gainesville, FL 32611–2036. Rates: $18 per year individuals. $30 per year institutions. Founded 1987 (first published 1989). Sponsored by the University of Florida, Loyola University of New Orleans, and Medieval and Renaissance Texts and Studies of SUNY Binghamton, NY. 13902–6000. Published biannually.

Major Field(s) of Interest: Multidisciplinary in concept, the journal is devoted to studies concerned with theoretical and experimental approaches to medieval and Renaissance culture. The goal of the journal is to promote conversation among the many languages of criticism and theory now being heard in medieval and Renaissance studies in North America and abroad. The journal provides a forum where different methods, different terminologies, different approaches can communicate without sacrificing any of their distinctiveness.

Manuscript Information: Articles of 25–45 pages. Style: Chicago with complete footnotes. 2 copies of manuscript required preferably with a diskette version in any word-processing program. Articles in French, German, or Italian must be accompanied by a 500–word abstract. Report in 2–3 months. Rejected manuscripts returned with S.A.S.E.

Payment: 1 copy of the journal and 40 offprints at cost.

Indexed In: MLA International Bibliography.

Copyright: By the Medieval and Renaissance Texts and Studies. Authors may reprint with permission and due acknowledgment.

FEMINIST STUDIES

c/o Women's Studies Program, University of Maryland, College Park, MD 20742. Rates: $24 per year individuals. $48 per year institutions. Founded 1974. Sponsored by the Women's Studies Program, the University of Maryland. Published 3 times per year.

Major Field(s) of Interest: Articles on all areas of feminist debate, theory, and discussion. Journal reviews books, but book reviews are commissioned.

Manuscript Information: Articles up to 35 double-spaced pages including notes. An abstract is required when submitting articles for consideration that is used for circulation purposes only, not published. Book reviews of 12–15 double-spaced pages. Style: Chicago. 3 copies of manuscript required. Report in 4 months. Rejected manuscript not returned.

Payment: 2 copies and 10 tearsheets.

Indexed In: Alternative Press Index, America: History and Life.

Copyright: By the journal or by the author.

GLYPH: TEXTUAL STUDIES

University of Minnesota Press, 2037 University Avenue, S.E., Minneapolis, MN 55414. Founded 1977. Sponsored by the University of Minnesota Press. Published annually.

Major Field(s) of Interest: Publishes articles on the problems of representation and textuality contributing to the confrontation between American and Continental critical scenes. Each issue has a subject focus.

Manuscript Information: Articles of 20–40 pages. Style: Chicago. 2 copies of manuscript required. Report in 3 months. Rejected manuscripts returned with S.A.S.E.

Payment: Copies.

Copyright: By the journal.

*JOURNAL OF ADVANCED COMPOSITION

English Department, University of South Florida, Tampa, FL 33620–5550. Rates: $15 per year. Founded 1980. Sponsored by the Association of Teachers of Advanced Composition. Published semiannually.

Major Field(s) of Interest: The journal focuses on scholarship in composition theory and advanced writing. It provides a forum for scholars of rhetoric and composition theory, especially those interested in the general field of advanced composition, including advanced expository, business and technical writing, and writing across the curriculum. The journal is especially interested in research and theoretical discussions examining cognition, discourse theory, epistemology, gender, ideology, research methods in composition, rhetoric, style, and the connections between contemporary criticism and composition theory.

Manuscript Information: Articles of 3,000–7,500 words. Book reviews up to 1,250 words. Style: MLA. 3 copies of manuscript required. Submit original typescript. Print name and affiliation on a cover sheet, not on the article. Report in 2 months. Rejected manuscripts returned with S.A.S.E.

Payment: 2 copies.

Indexed In: MLA International Bibliography, LLBA, American Humanities Index.

Copyright: By the journal. Journal will surrender ownership upon request of author.

JOURNAL OF AESTHETICS AND ART CRITICISM

5145 H. C. White Hall, the University of Wisconsin-Madison, 600 N. Park Street, Madison, WI 53706. Rates: $25 per year individuals. $30 per year institutions. Founded 1942. Sponsored by the American Society for Aesthetics. Published quarterly.

Major Field(s) of Interest: The journal publishes current research articles and timely reviews of books in aesthetics and the arts. The "arts" include not only traditional forms, such as music, literature, architecture, landscape architecture, dance, sculpture, and the visual arts, but also more recent additions including film, photography, earthworks, performance art, and the crafts or decorative arts. The journal also publishes work dealing with the theoretical interfaces of the arts and other disciplines, both humanistic and scientific. Journal reviews books, but book reviews are solicited only by invitation.

Manuscript Information: Articles up to 35 typed pages. Notes up to 12 typed pages. Book reviews of 1,500–3,000 words. Style: Chicago. 2 copies of manuscript required. Report in 3 months. Rejected manuscripts returned with S.A.S.E.

Payment: 50 reprints of article.

Copyright: By the journal. Reprinting without fee permitted for classroom use and as part of monograph by author.

JOURNAL OF COMPARATIVE LITERATURE AND AESTHETICS

B8 Jyoti Vihar: 768019, Sambalpur, Orissa, India. Rates: $9 per year (seamail). $12 (air mail). Founded 1978. Sponsored by Vishvanatha Kaviraja Institute. Published 2 times per year (Summer and Winter).

Major Field(s) of Interest: Articles on comparative studies in literature, general aesthetics, literary theory, philosophy, religion, culture, film theory, and fine arts. Journal reviews books.

Manuscript Information: Articles of 5,000–25,000 words. Notes of 200–500 words. Book reviews of 500–1,000 words. Style: MLA with endnotes. Report in 6 months. Rejected manuscripts returned. Send International Reply Coupons.

Payment: U.S. Dollars or Sterling Pounds.

JOURNAL OF DRAMATIC THEORY AND CRITICISM

Department of Theatre and Film, 356 Murphy Hall, The University of Kansas, Lawrence, KS 66045–2175. Rates: $10 per year individuals. $18 per year institutions. $8 per year students. Founded 1986. Sponsored by the Joyce and Elizabeth Center for the Humanities and the Department of Theatre and Film, The University of Kansas. Published twice yearly (Spring and Fall).

Major Field(s) of Interest: New theories and methodologies of performance, performance criticism, performance reviews, book reviews, and commentaries about theories, methods, criticism, and exploration of dramatic terms as used outside the fields of the performing arts. The journal is also interested in historical investigations of any of the above subjects and studies that raise issues of importance to dramatic theory and criticism, particularly those which enter poststructuralist discourse.

Manuscript Information: Articles up to 25 pages exclusive of footnotes. Book reviews up to 1,500 words. Style: MLA. 3 copies of manuscript required: Original and 2 copies (copies should not have the author's name on them). Report in 6 weeks. Rejected manuscripts returned with S.A.S.E.

Payment: None.

Copyright: By the journal. Scholars may, without prior permission, quote from the journal to document their own work. Requests for permission to reprint should be made to the publisher.

LIT: LITERATURE INTERPRETATION THEORY

Department of English, University of Connecticut, Storrs, CT 06268. Rates: $38 per year individuals. $74 per year institutions. Founded 1989. Sponsored by Gordon and Breach Publishers. Published quarterly.

Major Field(s) of Interest: The journal publishes vigorous theoretical and critical essays that center on literature and culture. The journal encourages authors to take strong stands on controversial themes. It publishes essays that span historical periods and critical schools. It welcomes essays on cultural and social criticism from the point of view of Marxism and other political criticism, as well as formalism, structuralism, semiotic criticism, and hermenteutics. It also welcomes studies on feminist and gender issues, on ethnic criticism as well as on new historicism and old.

Manuscript Information: No length restrictions on articles, notes, or book reviews. Style: MLA with endnotes. 3 copies of manuscript required. Report in 3 months. Rejected manuscripts returned with S.A.S.E.

Payment: 1 copy.

Indexed In: MLA International Bibliography, MHRA Bibliography, Literary Criticism Register.

Copyright: By the journal. It freely grants permission to reprint.

THE LITERARY ENDEAVOUR:
A QUARTERLY JOURNAL DEVOTED TO ENGLISH STUDIES

Flat 3, Block 6, H.I.G.I Stage, Opp. Water Tank, Baghlingampalli, Hyderabad 500044, India. Rates: $12 per year. Founded 1979. Sponsored by the editor: L. Adinarayana. Published quarterly.

Major Field(s) of Interest: Journal aims to promote an awareness of modern creative trends and critical approaches to literature in English. Journal reviews books.

Manuscript Information: Articles up to 3,000 words. Notes up to 300 words. Book reviews up to 1,000 words. Style: MLA. 2 copies of manuscript required. Manuscripts should include a declaration that they are original, previously unpublished work. Report in 3 months. Rejected manuscripts returned with S.A.S.E.

Payment: Copies.

Copyright: By the journal. Copyright reverts from journal to author after 1 year.

*LITERATURE AND BELIEF

3134 Jesse Knight Humanities Building, Brigham Young University, Provo, UT 84602. Rates: $5 per year in USA. $7 per year outside USA. Founded 1981. Sponsored by Brigham Young University, Center for the Study of Christian Values in Literature. Published annually.

Major Field(s) of Interest: Articles that focus on the moral/religious/ethical considerations of literature or that provide a critical theory of literary analysis based on those considerations. Journal reviews books.

Manuscript Information: Articles of 2,500–5,000 words. No length restrictions on book reviews. Style: MLA with notes in text or end notes. 2 copies of manuscript required. Report in 4–6 months. Rejected manuscripts returned with S.A.S.E.

Payment: 2 complete copies of the journal plus 10 reprints.

Indexed In: MLA International Bibliography, Literary Criticism Register, Abstracts of English Studies.

Copyright: By the journal. It is generous with reprinting permission.

LITERATURE AND PSYCHOLOGY

Department of English, Rhode Island College, Providence, RI 02908. Rates: $12 per year individuals. $18 per year institutions. Founded 1950. Sponsored by the National Association for Psychoanalytic Criticism and Rhode Island College. Published quarterly.

Major Field(s) of Interest: Publishes articles, notes, comments, and reviews pertaining to literary criticism as informed by depth psychology. The journal welcomes more theoretical articles for inclusion in special issues. It particularly encourages the submission of essays on such subjects as psychoanalysis and other modes of critical theory.

Manuscript Information: No restrictions as to length of articles, notes, or books reviews. Style: MLA. 2 copies of manuscript required. Report in 4 months. Rejected manuscripts returned with S.A.S.E.

Payment: Copies.

Copyright: By the journal.

*NEW LITERARY HISTORY:

A JOURNAL OF THEORY AND INTERPRETATION

Department of English, 234 Wilson Hall, University of Virginia, Charlottesville, VA 22903. Rates: $22 per year individuals. $68 per year institutions. Founded 1968. Self-supporting. Published quarterly (February, May, August, November).

Major Field(s) of Interest: The journal is interested in theory and interpretation—the reasons for literary change, the definitions of periods, and the evolution of styles, conventions, and genre. It also publishes articles from other disciplines that help interpret or define the problems of literary study.

Manuscript Information: Articles up to 5,000 words. Style: Chicago. Provide complete bibliographical data in notes and list notes at end of article. Report in 3 months. Rejected manuscripts returned with S.A.S.E.

Payment: 1 copy of the journal plus 25 offprints.

Indexed In: Abstracts of English Studies, America: History and Life, Annual Bibliography of English Language and Literature, Arts and Humanities Citation Index, Current Contents, Historical Abstracts, Humanities Index, Linguistics and Language Behavior Abstracts, Literary Criticism Register, MHRA Annual Bibliography, MLA Abstracts.

Copyright: By Johns Hopkins University Press. Authors may request permission to reprint with usual credit line.

New York Literary Forum

21 E. 79th Street, New York. NY 10021. Founded 1978. Sponsored by City University of New York, Graduate Center. 1 double number published each year.

Major Field(s) of Interest: Publishes contemporary criticism emphasizing interdisciplinary approaches. Contains analytical works by scholars. Each issue deals with 1 topic and emphasizes innovative and controversial studies.

Manuscript Information: Articles up to 3,500 words. Book reviews up to 3,500 words. Style: MLA. 2 copies of manuscript returned. Report in 1–3 months. Rejected manuscripts returned with S.A.S.E.

Payment: Copies.

Copyright: By the journal.

Novel: A Forum on Fiction

Box 1984, Brown University, Providence, RI 02912. Rates: $20 per year individuals. $26 per year institutions. Founded 1966. Sponsored by Brown University. Published 3 times per year (Fall, Winter, Spring).

Major Field(s) of Interest: The journal publishes articles on the history and theory of fiction unrestricted by time, place, or origin. It is interested in reviews of narrative theory, genre, and critical studies of fiction. Besides unsolicited essays, the journal is interested in receiving letters and essays for its "Critical Exchange" and unsolicited reviews of neglected fiction or of books on fiction. In most cases, however, book reviews are solicited.

Manuscript Information: Articles of 10–20 pages. Book reviews of 1–2 pages. Style: Chicago or MLA. 2 copies of manuscript required. Submit original typescript. Quotations in original European languages are not translated. Report in 4 months. Rejected manuscripts returned with S.A.S.E.

Payment: $100 for articles. $35 for reviews. No copies.

Copyright: By the journal. Reprint rights with permission.

The Oxford Literary Review

Department of English, The University, Southhampton, SO9 5NH, England. Rates: $30 per year. Founded 1974. Sponsored by the University. Published annually.

Major Field(s) of Interest: Literary theory, philosophy, psychoanalysis, political theory. Journal reviews books.

Manuscript Information: Articles up to 7,500 words. Book reviews up to 5,000 words. Style: Journal. Write for style sheet or consult a back copy of the journal. 2 copies of manuscript required. Report in 6 months. Rejected manuscripts not returned.

Payment: 5 copies of the journal.

Indexed In: MLA *International Bibliography, Abstracts of English Studies.*

Copyright: By the journal. Authors can reprint with credit line. Reprints require fee split 50% between author and journal.

*PAPERS ON LANGUAGE AND LITERATURE: A JOURNAL FOR SCHOLARS AND CRITICS OF LANGUAGE AND LITERATURE

Southern Illinois University at Edwardsville, Edwardsville, IL 62026–1434. Rates: $12 per year individuals. $24 per year institutions. Founded 1965. Sponsored by the Southern Illinois University at Edwardsville. Published quarterly.

Major Field(s) of Interest: Papers devoted to literary history, analysis, stylistics, theory, and interpretation. Journal publishes original materials relating to belles-lettres, letters, journals, notebooks, and similar documents as well as essays dealing with writings in English, American, French, German, Spanish, Russian, and other languages. Brief notes and review essays are included. Journal reviews books.

Manuscript Information: Articles up to 30 double-spaced typed pages. Notes of 4–8 pages. Book reviews 3–5 pages. Style: *MLA Style Manual* (1985). Endnotes. 2 copies of manuscript required. Report in 3–5 months. Rejected manuscripts (1 only) returned with S.A.S.E.

Payment: 2 copies of the journal.

Copyright: By Southern Illinois University at Edwardsville.

PARAGRAPH: THE JOURNAL OF THE MODERN CRITICAL THEORY GROUP

Oxford University Press, Walton Street, Oxford, OX2 6DP, England. Rates: $30 per year. Founded 1983. Sponsored by the Modern Critical Theory Group. Published 2 times per year.

Major Field(s) of Interest: Articles on modern critical theory. Journal commissions all notes and review-articles.

Manuscript Information: Articles up to 7,000 words. Review-Articles up to 2,000 words. Style: Journal. 2 copies of manuscript required. Articles written in French must be accompanied by an English translation. Report in 15 months. Rejected manuscripts returned with S.A.S.E. or International Reply Coupons.

Payment: Copies.

Copyright: By Oxford University Press.

PAUNCH

123 Woodward Avenue, Buffalo, NY 14214. Founded 1963. Sponsored by Arthur Efron, Editor. 1 double issue published each year.

Major Field(s) of Interest: Articles on the body in literature, problems in aesthetics, particular in relation to Dewey's *Art as Experience* and Pepper's *The Basis of Criticism in the Arts,* literature in relation to the authority, and criminality, of the modern state, reviews, and poetry.

Manuscript Information: No restrictions on length of articles, notes, or reviews. Style: None. Report in 3 months. Rejected manuscripts returned with S.A.S.E.

Payment: None.

Copyright: By the Editor for first serial rights only.

PHILOSOPHY AND LITERATURE

Department of French, Whitman College, Walla Walla, WA 99362. Rates: $17 individuals. $30 institutions. Founded 1977. Sponsored by Whitman College. Published 2 times per year.

Major Field(s) of Interest: Philosophical interpretations of literature, literary investigation of classic works of philosophy, articles on the aesthetics of literature and philosophy of language relevant to literature, the theory of criticism, and the relations between philosophy and the dramatic media of theater and film.

Manuscript Information: Articles up to 7,500 words. Notes up to 2,000 words. Book reviews up to 650 words. Style: Chicago. 2 copies of manuscript required. Report in 4 months. Rejected manuscripts returned with S.A.S.E.

Payment: 25 offprints.

Indexed In: American Humanities Index, Arts & Humanities Citation Index, Current Contents, Literary Criticism Register, MLA International Bibliography, Philosopher's Index.

Copyright: By the Johns Hopkins University Press.

PHILOSOPHY AND RHETORIC: A QUARTERLY JOURNAL

Department of Philosophy, 240 Sparks Building, University Park, PA 16802. Rates: $22.50 per year individuals. Founded 1968. Sponsored by the Pennsylvania State University, Departments of Philosophy and Speech Communication. Published quarterly.

Major Field(s) of Interest: The journal publishes papers on theoretical issues involving the relationship between philosophy and rhetoric (including the relationship between formal or informal logic and rhetoric); articles on philosophical aspects of argumentation (including argumentation in philosophy itself); studies of philosophical views on the nature of rhetoric of historical figures and during historical periods; philosophical analyses of the relationship to rhetoric of other areas of human culture and thought; and psychological and sociological studies of rhetoric with a strong philosophical emphasis. Journal reviews books.

Manuscript Information: Articles up to 30 typed double-spaced manuscript pages. Book reviews up to 10 pages. Style: Chicago with double-spaced notes gathered at the end. 3 copies of manuscript required with an abstract not exceeding 250 words. Report in 3 months. Rejected manuscripts are not returned.

Payment: 25 free copies.

Copyright: By the Pennsylvania State University Press. Reprint rights are granted with permission of the publisher.

POETICS: JOURNAL FOR EMPIRICAL RESEARCH ON LITERATURE, MEDIA, AND THE ARTS

Fachbereich Sprach-und Literaturwissenschaften, Universität, GH Siegen, Siegen, West Germany or Cees J. van Rees, Tilburg University, Department of Language and Literature, P. O. Box 90153. 5000 LE Tilberg, The Netherlands. Founded 1971. Sponsored by Elsevier Science Publishers B.V., P. O. Box 211, 1000 AE Amsterdam, The Netherlands. Published 6 times per year.

Major Field(s) of Interest: The journal is devoted to theoretical and empirical research on books, media, and the arts. It welcomes contributions in which major problems in the study of literature and neighboring arts and their performance and history in the media and other fields of culture get a theoretically based and empirically oriented treatment. The journal is interdisciplinary. Some of the topics on which it focuses are experiments in the processing of (literary) texts and other media, the sociology of the producers, distributors and publics of specific forms of art, information, and entertainment, the historical developments and the function of institutions that display, promote and/or judge works of literature, the arts and other media, research techniques current in empirical investigation and relevant to the scope of the journal, the theoretical and philosophical foundations of empirical research in the fields of art and culture, contributions from neighboring disciplines such as sociology, cognitive psychology, linguistics, discourse studies, historiography, economics, media research of statistics.

Manuscript Information: Articles of 5–50 pages. Style: Journal. Write for copy of "Instructions to Authors." 3 copies of manuscript required. Include a summary of no more than 200 words. Report in 3 months. Rejected manuscripts are not returned.

Payment: 25 offprints of the article.

Indexed In: Current Contents, Arts & Humanities Citation Index, Abstracts of English Studies, and others.

Copyright: By Elsevier Science Publishers B.V. Authors are granted permission to reprint with usual credit line.

POETICS TODAY

P. O. Box 39085, Tel Aviv, Israel. Rates: $24 per year individuals. $40 per year institutions. Founded 1979. Sponsored by Tel Aviv University, Porter Institute for Poetics and Semiotics. Published quarterly.

Major Field(s) of Interest: Articles on contemporary literary theory, descriptive poetics of specific texts, writers or genres, language in context, and communication in culture. Journal reviews books.

Manuscript Information: No length restrictions on articles or book reviews. Style: Journal. Include references and footnotes on separate sheets. For complete particulars, see *Poetics Today,* 1,iii. Submit a 200–word abstract and a biographical sketch with all manuscripts. Report in 3–6 months. Rejected manuscripts returned with S.A.S.E. or International Reply Coupons.

Payment: Copies.

Copyright: By Israel Science Publishers, Inc.

PRECISELY

P. O. Box 73, Canal Street, New York, NY 10013. Founded 1977. Sponsored by RK Editions. Published 2 times per year.

Major Field(s) of Interest: Publishes literary criticism of experimental literature of the past quarter century.

Manuscript Information: Articles of 300–10,000 words. Style: None. Report in 2 months. Rejected manuscripts returned with S.A.S.E.

Payment: Copies.

Copyright: By the author.

*PRE/TEXT: A JOURNAL OF RHETORICAL THEORY

English Department, Box 19035, The University of Texas, Arlington, TX 76019–0035. Rates: $15 per year individuals. $45 per year institutions. Founded 1980. Privately owned by the editor. Partial support from the Department of English, University of Texas at Arlington. Published quarterly.

Major Field(s) of Interest: Journal is interested in exploratory articles and working papers that deal with rhetorical theory (broadly defined), that are written across traditional, modern and postmodern perspectives and that address the interdisciplinary nature of rhetorical theory and rhetorical metatheory. Journal reviews books, but review articles are solicited.

Manuscript Information: Articles of 20–30 pages, but length is usually open. Notes: no length restrictions. Book reviews: no length restrictions. Style: MLA. 3 copies of manuscript required. Report in 3 months. Rejected manuscripts returned with S.A.S.E. Prospective authors should contact the editor prior to submission.

Payment: 1 copy of the journal.

Indexed In: MLA International Bibliography, Sociological Abstracts.

Copyright: By the journal. Permission to reprint upon request.

RADICAL TEACHER:
A NEWSJOURNAL OF SOCIALIST THEORY AND PRACTICE

P. O. Box 102, Kendall Square Post Office, Cambridge, MA 02142. Rates: $10 per year (single issues $4 each). Founded 1974. Sponsored by Boston Women's Teacher's Group, Inc. Published 3 times per year.

Major Field(s) of Interest: The journal publishes articles on literary theory, classroom life at all levels, the economics of the teaching profession, and the structure and dynamics of cultural issues from a socialist/feminist perspective. Journal reviews books.

Manuscript Information: Articles up of 10–12 pages. Notes up to 400 words. Book reviews of 1,200–2,000 words. Style: MLA with notes in the text. 2 copies of manuscript required. Report in 3 months. Rejected manuscripts returned with S.A.S.E..

Payment: 5 copies of the magazine.

Indexed In: MLA International Bibliography.

Copyright: By the journal. Permission to reprint granted if requested with usual credit line..

*READER: ESSAYS IN READER-ORIENTED THEORY,
CRITICISM, AND PEDAGOGY

Department of Humanities, Michigan Technological University, Houghton, MI 49931. Rates: $8 per year individuals. $10 per year institutions. Founded 1976. Sponsored by Michigan Technological University. Published twice a year: Fall and Spring.

Major Field(s) of Interest: Articles that focus on the readers' reactions to text or reader-oriented textual strategies and reader-response to theory, criticism, and pedagogy. No restrictions on figure, movement, or period. Articles selected by peer review. Journal reviews books.

Manuscript Information: Articles up to 20 pages. Book reviews of 3–4 pages. Style: MLA. 2 copies of manuscript required. Report in 2 months. Rejected manuscripts returned with S.A.S.E.

Payment: 4 copies of issue.

Indexed In: Arts and Humanities Citation Index, Current Contents, Arts and Humanities Citation Index.

Copyright: By Michigan Technological University.

RECOVERING LITERATURE:

A JOURNAL OF CONTEXTUALIST CRITICISM

P. O. Box 805, Alpine, CA 92001. Rates: $6 per year. Founded 1972. Independently owned. Published 1–3 times per year.

Major Field(s) of Interest: Literary criticism from a contextualist point-of-view. Journal encourages criticism that undermines cultural myths and pieties, habitualized perceptions, and cultural attitudes—including leftist or feminist myths and pieties as well as the older ones. Journal reviews books.

Manuscript Information: Articles of any length. Notes of any length. Book reviews from 1–3 pages. Style: Flexible. Report in 3–6 weeks. Rejected manuscripts returned with S.A.S.E.

Payment: Copies.

Indexed In: MLA International Bibliography, Literary Criticism Register.

Copyright: By the journal, but authors can freely reprint.

REPRESENTATIONS

322 Wheeler Hall, University of California, Berkeley, CA 94720. Rates: $24 per year individuals. $48 per year institutions. $16 per year students. Founded 1983. Sponsored by the University of California Press. Published quarterly.

Major Field(s) of Interest: The journal publishes interdisciplinary studies in the humanities and interpretative social sciences, focusing on recent developments in literary criticism, iconography, historiography, and social theory.

Manuscript Information: Articles up to 30 pages. Notes up to 10 pages. Style: Chicago. 2 copies of manuscript required. Manuscripts must be double-spaced typescript with footnotes typed separately and attached to the end of article. Report in 3 months. Rejected manuscripts returned with S.A.S.E.

Payment: 2 copies plus cash.

Indexed In: Modern Language Abstracts, Arts and Humanities: Current Contents, Citation Index, International Repertory of the Literature of Art, MLA International Bibliography.

Copyright: By the University of California Press.

SEMIOTICA: JOURNAL OF THE
INTERNATIONAL ASSOCIATION FOR SEMIOTIC STUDIES
P. O. Box 10, Indiana University, Bloomington, IN 47402-0010. Rates: $181.20 per year individual IASS members. $473.55 per year for institutions. Founded 1969. Sponsored by the International Association for Semiotic Studies. Published monthly, except February and September.

Major Field(s) of Interest: Articles that address semiotic concepts within the lines of their own field of inquiry. Journal reviews books.

Manuscript Information: No length restrictions on articles or on book reviews. Style: *Semiotic* has its own style sheet. 2 copies of manuscript required. Report in 2 months. Rejected manuscripts are not returned.

Payment: 30 offprints. Reduced rate available for additional copies.

Indexed In: Current Contents, Arts and Humanities Citation Index, Language Teaching, Sociological Abstracts.

Copyright: By Mouton de Gruyter Publishers, Genthiner Strasse 13, 1000 Berlin 30, FRG or 200 Saw Mill River Road, Hawthorne, NY 10532.

STANFORD LITERATURE REVIEW
Department of French and Italian, Building 260, Stanford University, Stanford, CA 94305. Rates: $25 per year individuals. $50 per year institutions. Subscription address: ANMA Libri Company, P. O. Box 876, Saratoga, CA 95071. Founded 1984. Sponsored by the Department of French and Italian, Stanford University. Published semiannually (Spring and Fall).

Major Field(s) of Interest: SLR publishes essays in the areas of comparative literature and literary theory with a special emphasis on inter- or metadisciplinary research and speculative criticism. The focus of the journal is comparatist, but in a novel sense: its primary aim is to explore the multiple paths that link literature with other domains of knowledge.

Manuscript Information: Articles of 20–25 pages in length. Notes of 3–5 pages. Style: MLA (1985). 2 copies of manuscript required. Report in approximately 3 months. Rejected manuscripts returned with S.A.S.E.

Payment: 1 copy of journal plus 20 offprints.

Copyright: By the journal. Authors granted permission to reprint with standard credit line.

*STUDIES IN TWENTIETH CENTURY LITERATURE
Department of Modern Languages, Kansas State University, Eisenhower Hall, Manhattan, KS 66506. Rates: $15 per year individuals. $20 per year institutions. Founded 1976. Sponsored by the University of Nebraska, Lincoln and Kansas State University. Published 2 times per year.

Major Field(s) of Interest: Articles written in English devoted to literary theory and practical criticism with exclusive emphasis upon twentieth-century literature written in French, German, Russian, and Spanish (including Latin America). Essays should focus on poetry, prose, drama, or literary theory. Submissions on English or American literature are not accepted. Journal reviews books.

Manuscript Information: Articles of 20–30 typescript pages. Book reviews of 500–750 words. Style: MLA (1985). 4 copies of manuscript required. Submit original typescript and 3 copies. Include a 200–word abstract. Report in 3 months. Rejected manuscripts returned upon request. Include self-addressed envelope and loose return postage.

Payment: 1 free copy and 10 offprints.

Indexed In: MLA International Bibliography, Humanities Index.

Copyright: By the journal. Permission to reprint subsequent to publication will normally be granted.

*STYLE

Department of English, Northern Illinois University, DeKalb, IL 60115–2854. Rates: $20 per year individuals; $25 per year institutions. $12 per year students. Founded 1966. Sponsored by Northern Illinois University. Published quarterly.

Major Field(s) of Interest: STYLE considers articles that analyze stylistic and related features of literature and that propose and discuss methods and theories of analyzing and evaluating style and related features on such traditional subjects as diction, syntax, grammar, metrics, figures of speech, rhetorical figures, and genre/period/author styles. STYLE also welcomes essays examining the theory of literature, hermeneutics, linguistics and literature, conventions, structure, effects, the process of reading, and problems of narratology. Journal also publishes annotated bibliographies on special topics related to stylistics from time to time and book reviews.

Manuscript Information: Articles 15–40 pages in length. Book reviews up to 1,500 words. Style: MLA. 2 copies of manuscript required. Submit a 150 word abstract. Will accept floppy disk with hard copy. Report in 120 days. Rejected manuscripts returned with S.A.S.E.

Payment: None.

Indexed In: Abstracts of English Studies, Annual Bibliography of English Language and Literature (MHRA), *Arts and Humanities Citation Index, Canadian Review of Comparative Literature, An Index to Book Reviews in the Humanities, International Bibliography of Book Reviews* (IBR), *International Bibliography of Periodical Literature* (IBZ),

Language and Language Behavior Abstracts and *MLA International Bibliography.*

Copyright: By the journal. Permission to reprint must be requested in writing.

*SUBSTANCE: A REVIEW OF THEORY AND LITERARY CRITICISM

Department of French and Italian, University of California, Santa Barbara, CA 93106. Rates: $18 per year individuals; $40 per year institutions. Founded 1971. Sponsored by the Department of French and Italian, University of California, Santa Barbara, CA. Published quarterly.

Major Field(s) of Interest: SUBSTANCE is a major interdisciplinary journal which promotes new thought by leading American and European authors. The emphasis is on examining contemporary culture and the disciplines represented include literary theory, philosophy, psychoanalysis, art criticism, film studies, photography, physics, biology, and mathematics.

Manuscript Information: Articles of 18–30 typed pages. Book reviews of 3–6 pages. Style: MLA. 2 copies of manuscript required. Report in 6–8 weeks. Rejected manuscripts returned with S.A.S.E.

Payment: 2 copies. Offprints for small fee.

Copyright: By the journal. No charge, but written permission required.

SYMPOSIUM: A QUARTERLY JOURNAL IN MODERN FOREIGN LITERATURES

210 Crouse Hall, Syracuse University, Syracuse, NY 13210. Rates: $47 per year. Founded 1948. Sponsored by HELDREF Publications, 4000 Albermarle Street, Washington, D. C. 20016. Published quarterly.

Major Field(s) of Interest: The journal welcomes articles written about modern foreign languages and literatures. Articles dealing with English and American literature are published only if a comparative approach is used. Articles dealing with criticism and literary theory are encouraged. Journal reviews books.

Manuscript Information: Articles of 20–30 pages. Book reviews of 2–3 pages. Style: MLA. 2 copies of manuscript required. Abstracts are necessary for articles written in foreign languages. Report in 4–6 weeks. Rejected manuscripts returned with S.A.S.E.

Payment: 2 copies of the journal.

Indexed In: MLA International Bibliography.

Copyright: By HELDREF Publications. Permission to reprint required.

TEXT AND PERFORMANCE QUARTERLY

The Speech Communication Association, 5105 Backlick Road, Suite E, Annandale, VA 22003. Rates: $50 per year for SCA members. $25 per year for undergraduate student members. $90 per year for libraries. Founded 1980 as LITERATURE IN PERFORMANCE. Name changed in 1989. Sponsored by the Speech Communication Association. Published quarterly.

Major Field(s) of Interest: While the journal is particularly interested in the nexus of text and performance, it is also concerned with the whole process from the creation and criticism of text through the creation and criticism of performance, together with the history and theory of both ends of the spectrum. The interest in text covers texts of all kinds, including literature, ethnography, anthropology as well as the usual fields of interpretation and theatre. TPQ welcomes research into the performance of texts of all kinds, not simply literary and written texts. Journal reviews books.

Manuscript Information: No restrictions on length of articles, notes, or book reveiws. Style: MLA with endnotes. 4 copies of manuscript required. Report in 6–8 weeks. Rejected manuscripts returned with S.A.S.E.

Payment: 2 copies of issue plus tearsheets.

Indexed In: MLA International Bibliography.

Copyright: By the Speech Communication Association. Full author right to reprint granted upon request.

*THEATRE JOURNAL

Department of English, University of Michigan, Ann Arbor, MI 48109. Rates: $19 per year individuals. $46 per year institutions. Individual members of the Association for Theatre in Higher Education receive the journal as part of their membership. Founded 1948. Sponsored by the Johns Hopkins University Press and the American Association for Theatre in Higher Education. Published quarterly.

Major Field(s) of Interest: The journal provides an outlet for scholarly articles on criticism in the theatre arts, theatre history, performance criticism, and theory of the drama. All methodologies are welcome, and the journal publishes material from all critical approaches. It is especially interested in social and historical studies, production reviews, and theoretical inquiries that illuminate dramatic texts and productions. Journal reviews theatre productions and books, but all reviews are solicited.

Manuscript Information: Articles of 25–35 pages. Notes up to 1,500 words. Book reviews and theatre reviews up to 750 words. Reviews should be sent to the appropriate review editor. Style: Chicago with endnotes. 3 copies of manuscript required. Report in 3–4 months. Rejected manuscripts returned with S.A.S.E.

Payment: 2 copies of the issue for articles. 1 copy for reviews.

Indexed In: Book Review Index, Current Contents: Social & Behavioral Sciences, Current Index to Journal in Education, Education Index, Humanities Index.

Copyright: By the Johns Hopkins University Press in cooperation with the Association for Theatre in Higher Education.

*TULSA STUDIES IN WOMEN'S LITERATURE

The University of Tulsa, 600 South College Avenue, Tulsa, OK 74104. Rates: $12 individuals. $14 per year institutions. Founded 1982. Sponsored by the University of Tulsa. Published semiannually.

Major Field(s) of Interest: TSWL welcomes the submission of articles, notes, and queries on literature in all time periods and places, including foreign language literature and in every genre: poetry, prose, drama, essays, diaries, memoirs, journalism, and criticism. While articles need not be exclusively concerned with female writers, the focus must be on "women and writing," explicating the specific links between the woman writer and her work. The journal particularly encourages work in feminist critical and literary theory. Journal reviews books. Book reviews are solicited.

Manuscript Information: Articles up to 25 pages, Notes of 6–10 pages. Book reviews up to 500 words. Style: MLA (1977). 3 copies of manuscript required. Report in 3–6 months. Rejected manuscripts returned with S.A.S.E.

Payment: 2 issues of journal and 3 sets of offprints.

Indexed In: MLA International Bibliography, Book Review Index.

Copyright: By the University of Tulsa. Reprinting by permission only.

WOMEN & PERFORMANCE: A JOURNAL OF FEMINIST THEORY

NYU/Tisch School of the Arts, Performance Studies Department, 721 Broadway, 6th Floor, New York, NY 10003. Founded 1983. Sponsored by Women & Performance Project, Inc. Published irregularly.

Major Field(s) of Interest: Articles on feminist issues in dance, theater, film, music, video, and ritual. Journal includes articles on feminist performance, and reviews of both feminist and mainstream performance. The journal also publishes scripts of performance and film. Journal reviews books.

Manuscript Information: Articles of 15–20 double-spaced typescripts. Style: MLA or Chicago. 2 copies of manuscript required. Report in 1–2 months. Rejected manuscripts returned with S.A.S.E.

Payment: Copies.

Copyright: By the author.

*WORKS AND DAYS: ESSAYS IN THE SOCIO-HISTORICAL DIMENSIONS OF LITERATURE AND THE ARTS

Department of English, 110 Leonard Hall, Indiana University of Pennsylvania, Indiana, PA 15705. Rates: $7 per year individuals. $12 per year institutions. Founded 1979. Sponsored by Indiana University of Pennsylvania. Published biannually (Spring and Fall).

Major Field(s) of Interest: Theoretically informed investigations of literature, language, rhetoric, or art in relation to culture, history, politics, race, class, gender, ideology, or power. The journal also publishes articles that deal with the relations of theory to pedagogy. Journal reviews books.

Manuscript Information: Articles of 12 or more pages. Book reviews of 10 or more pages. Style: MLA with endnotes. 2 copies of manuscript required. Report in 3 months. Rejected manuscripts returned with S.A.S.E.

Payment: 2 copies.

Indexed In: MLA International Bibliography, Humanities Index.

Copyright: By the journal. Permission to reprint granted with credit line.

*THE YALE JOURNAL OF CRITICISM

Box 2968 Yale Station, New Haven, CT 06520. Rates: $20 per year individuals. $50 per year institutions. Founded 1986. Published in association with the Whitney Humanities Center. Published 2 times per year.

Major Field(s) of Interest: The journal provides a forum for interdisciplinary criticism in all fields of the humanities. It welcomes essays and approaches that involve acts of confrontation and discovery.

Manuscript Information: Articles of 30–40 pages. Notes up to 5 pages. Style: Chicago with endnotes. 2 copies of manuscript required. Report in 4–6 months. Rejected manuscripts returned with S.A.S.E.

Payment: 1 copy.

Indexed In: MLA International Bibliography, Humanities Research Index, Wilson Quarterly.

Copyright: By Yale University. Reprint permission is always granted.

*Yearbook of Comparative and General Literature
Ballantine Hall 402, Indiana University, Bloomington, IN 47405. Rates: $12.50 per year individuals. $17.50 per year institutions. Founded 1952. Sponsored by the Indiana University Comparative Literature Program, American Comparative Literature Association, and the National Council of Teachers of English. Published annually.

Major Field(s) of Interest: Publishes methodologically oriented research in comparative literature: articles dealing with theory and practice in the study of genres and modes, themes and motifs, periods and movements, as well as other intercultural and interdisciplinary phenomena; also, articles on the theory and history of comparative literature and the teaching of the subject on all levels and in all parts of the world. Emphases: Asian-Western literary relations, the comparative study of arts, film studies with a focus on literature, the theory and practice of translation. Special features: comprehensive reviews of research, comparative reviews of translation into English of important texts, annual bibliography of the relations of literature and other arts. Journal reviews books, but book reviews are commissioned.

Manuscript Information: Articles up to 20 typed pages. Book reviews of 4–5 pages. Style: MLA. 2 copies of manuscript required. Report in 6–8 weeks. Rejected manuscripts returned upon request. Include S.A.S.E.

Payment: 2 copies of issue and 20 offprints for articles. 10 offprints for reviews.

Indexed In: MLA International Bibliography.

Copyright: By the journal. Reprint rights with permission.

III. Film Journals

AMERICAN FILM: JOURNAL OF THE FILM AND TELEVISION ARTS
6671 Sunset Boulevard, Suite 1514, Hollywood, CA 90028. Rates: $28.95 per year (includes membership in the American Film Institute). Founded 1967. Published monthly.

Major Field(s) of Interest: Articles, notes, reviews by professional film critics and reports on film festivals and activities of the American Film Institute.

Manuscript Information: Articles up to 3,500 words. Style: None. Report in 2 months. Rejected manuscripts returned with S.A.S.E.

Payment: Copies.

Indexed In: Arts and Humanities Citation Index, Index to Book Review Humanities.

Copyright: By BPI Communications, Inc., 1515 Broadway, 39th Floor, New York, NY 10036.

THE AMERICAN FILM INSTITUTE MONOGRAPH SERIES
American Film Institute, P.O. Box 27999, 2021 N. Western Avenue, Los Angeles, CA 90027. Price: $25 volume (hardcover); $10 volume (paperback). Founded 1983. Sponsored by the American Film Institute. Published irregularly.

Major Field(s) of Interest: Scholarly essays on major issues in film and television theory.

Manuscript Information: Articles should not exceed 15–20 typed pages. Notes of up to 2 pages. Style: *The Chicago Manual of Style.* Submit 1 copy of manuscript. Report in 9 months.

Payment: None.

Copyright: By the American Film Institute.

CAMERA OBSCURA: A JOURNAL OF FEMINISM AND FILM THEORY
Rush Rhees Library, University of Rochester, Rochester, NY 14627. Rates: $18 per year individuals. $35 per year institutions. Founded 1974. Sponsored by the University of Rochester. Published 3 times per year.

Major Field(s) of Interest: Perspectives on the national and international film scene. Topics ranging from the avant-garde in filmmaking to popular culture and the mass media. Journal reviews books and welcomes book review essays.

Manuscript Information: Articles of 30–40 pages. Book reviews of 10–15 pages. Style: MLA with endnotes. Report in 3–6 months. Rejected manuscripts returned.

Payment: 2 copies of the issue.

Indexed In: Alternative Press Index, Arts and Humanities Citation

Index, Film/Literature Index, International Index to Film Periodicals, Current Contents.

Copyright: By the Johns Hopkins University Press.

CINEASTE: AMERICA'S LEADING MAGAZINE OF THE ART AND POLITICS OF THE CINEMA

P. O. Box 2242, New York, NY 10009. Rates: $13 per year individuals. $21 per year institutions. Founded 1967. Published 4 times per year.

Major Field(s) of Interest: A quarterly magazine that offers a social, political, and esthetic perspective on the cinema, the journal publishes material from various left-of-center perspectives. It is interested in all areas of the cinema: Hollywood films (old and new), American independents (16mm and 35mm), European quality films, and the cinema of the Third World. It rarely publishes material on television or video, although the journal carries an irregular "home video" column. The journal is interested in reviews that deal with recently published books, although recent may mean as much as two years old if the book is important. It also carries in-depth career interviews with major personalities, medium-length interviews on a current production or issue, and very short interviews of a few questions which can be used as side-bar features. The journal also publishes interviews with directors, performers, composers, collectives, producers, distributors, technicians, or anyone else involved in the creative or business end of filmmaking.

Manuscript Information: Feature articles of 3,000–4,000 words. Book reviews of 1,000–1,500 words. Shorter book reviews of 500–750 words. "Book Briefs" of no more than 1 double-spaced page. Film-review essays of 1,500–2,000 words. Shorter film reviews of 500–750 words. Style: None. Whenever possible, sources should be incorporated into the text rather than footnotes. Report in 3 weeks. Rejected manuscripts returned with S.A.S.E.

Payment: Minimum of $12 for reviews and short pieces. Minimum of $20 for feature material. 3 copies of the issue for short pieces and 6 copies for feature pieces.

Indexed In: International Index of Film/TV Periodicals, The Alternative Press Index.

Copyright: By the journal.

CINEMA

Box 398, Outremont Station, Montreal, Quebec, H2V 4N3, Canada. Rates: $3 per issue. Founded 1972. Published monthly.

Major Field(s) of Interest: Articles on Canadian cinema: industry, filmmakers, history, policy, etc. Articles selected on the basis of editor's decision.

Manuscript Information: Articles of 50–80 pages. Style: Tabloid-size magazine (10½ x 14 inches). Journal desires solicited manuscripts only or approval on the basis of outline.

Payment: Modest fees plus copy of the magazine.

Copyright: By the journal.

*CINEMA JOURNAL

University of Illinois Press, 54 East Gregory Drive, Champaigne, IL 61820. Rates: $20 per year individuals. $25 per year institutions. Founded 1959. Sponsored by the Society for Cinema Studies and the University of Illinois Press. Published quarterly.

Major Field(s) of Interest: The journal publishes articles about American and international film and television. It concentrates on areas of screen studies within college programs. The journal is published in cooperation with the Society for Cinema Studies, which is composed of college and university educators, filmmakers, historians, critics, scholars, and others concerned with the moving image. Activities of the society include an annual meeting and the publication of the journal. Members of the society receive the journal as one of the benefits of membership. Contributors must be members of the Society for Cinema Studies.

Manuscript Information: Articles up to 7,500 words in length. Style: Chicago. 3 copies of manuscript required. Author's names should not appear on the manuscript, and frame enlargements or other illustrative materials must be supplied by the authors, who are responsible for obtaining permission to publish them. Report in 1–3 months. Rejected manuscripts returned with S.A.S.E.

Payment: Copies.

Indexed In: Arts and Humanities Citation Index, Film Literature Index, International Index to Film Periodicals, MLA International Bibliography.

Copyright: By the University of Illinois Press.

FILM: MONTHLY JOURNAL OF THE
BRITISH FEDERATION OF FILM SOCIETIES

21 Stephen Street, London, W1P 1PL, England. Rates: £22 per year (U.K.). £22 sterling overseas. Founded 1954. Sponsored by the British Film Institute. Published bimonthly April/May, June/July and monthly the rest of the year.

Major Field(s) of Interest: The journal publishes film reviews, information on UK or worldwide Federation of Film Societies film availability, new releases in the UK, film festivals, information on directors, and letters to the editor.

Manuscript Information: No length restrictions on articles or book reviews. Style: journal. Report in 2–4 months. Rejected manuscripts returned with S.A.S.E.

Payment: 2 copies of magazine for article.

Copyright: By the British Federation of Film Societies.

FILM & HISTORY

The Historians Film Committee, New Jersey Institute of Technology, Newark, NJ 07102. Rates: $12 per year individuals (includes membership in the Historians Film Committee). $20 per year institutions. Published quarterly.

Major Field(s) of Interest: All aspects of film, motion pictures, and television. Factual, critical, esthetic, and philosophical material is accepted.

Manuscript Information: Articles of 2500–10,000 words. Style: None. Only footnotes which amplify a point in the text should be used, not bibliographical notes. Report in 3–4 weeks. Rejected manuscripts returned.

Payment: Copies.

Indexed In: Historical Abstracts, American History and Life, International Index to Film Periodicals, American Historical Association's "Recently Published Articles."

Copyright: By the Historians Film Committee.

FILM COMMENT

The Film Society of Lincoln Center, P. O. Box 3000, Denville, NJ 07834–9925. Rates: $26.95 per year. Founded 1962. Sponsored by the Film Society of Lincoln Center. Published 12 times per year.

Major Field(s) of Interest: Scholarly comments from cultural and historical points of view on every phase of the international motion picture industry: directors, screenwriters, festivals, foreign films, realism, and other-isms. Emphasis is on the best with frequent reviews and interviews. Journal reviews books.

Manuscript Information: Articles of 1,000–5,000 words. Book reviews of 750–1,500 words. Style: None. Footnotes are discouraged. Report in a few days. Rejected manuscripts returned with S.A.S.E.

Payment: Cash plus 4 copies.

Indexed In: Arts and Humanities Citation Index, Book Review Index, Film Literature Index, Humanities Index, Readers' Guide.

Copyright: By the Journal.

*FILM CRITICISM

Box D, Allegheny College, Meadville, PA 16355. Rates: $9 per year individuals. $10 per year institutions. Founded 1976. Sponsored by Allegheny College. Published 3 times per year.

Major Field(s) of Interest: Scholarly articles on all aspects of film criticism, theory, and history. The journal publishes analyses of particular films, genres, and national cinemas. It also reviews books, conducts interviews, and makes festival reports. Journal has a special book review issue periodically.

Manuscript Information: Articles of 15–25 pages. Book reviews of 1–5 pages. Style: MLA (2nd edition). 2 copies of manuscript required. Report in 3 months. Rejected manuscripts are returned with detailed editorial commentary and suggestions for revision.

Payment: 3 copies of the issue.

Indexed In: Film Literature Index, FIAF International Index of Film Periodicals, Humanities Citation Index, MLA International Bibliography, Literary Criticism Register.

Copyright: By the journal.

FILM DOPE

88 Port Arthur Road, Nottingham, NG2 4GE, England. Rates: $17.90 per year. Founded 1971. Sponsored by the British Film Institute. Published 3 times per year.

Major Field(s) of Interest: Journal welcomes contributions on international cinema (the whole period of the 1890s to present) from new writers who are not restricted in any way as to length, style, or approach. Potential contributors should always contact the editor at the above address before sending manuscripts to discover which entries in a predetermined alphabetical scheme are forthcoming. A list of forthcoming inclusions is available on request. The journal publishes interviews on a regular basis. Contributions in this form are welcome, but they must be made by prior arrangement.

Manuscript Information: No length restrictions on contributions. Style: Footnotes are discouraged. 2 copies of manuscript required. Report in 2 months. Rejected manuscripts returned with S.A.S.E. or International Reply Coupons.

Payment: As requested in copies.

Indexed In: FIAF International Index of Film Periodicals.

Copyright: By the author.

FILM QUARTERLY

2120 Berkeley Way, Berkeley, CA 94720. Rates: $14 per year. Founded 1945 (as HOLLYWOOD QUARTERLY). Sponsored by the University of California Press. Published quarterly.

Major Field(s) of Interest: Film criticism, history, theory. Gossip and personality material not accepted. FILMQ prefers retrospective articles on directors, survey articles on film trends, and new developments. Also articles on artistic issues posed by films. FILMQ desires material in any field from scholars "who have something to say about film; however, . . . standards are such that familiarity with film literature is important for aspiring contributors." FILMQ provides an annual review of all English-language film books. Bibliographical issue reviews all English-language film books not covered earlier.

Manuscript Information: Articles generally up to 25 manuscript pages; reviews generally up to 8 manuscript pages. No preferred style sheet. Footnotes at end of article or review. Report in 1–10 weeks. 1 manuscript copy required but S.A.S.E. suggested if return desired. Article selection is made by the Editorial Board.

Payment: Ca. 2¢ per published word.

Indexed In: Art Index, Book Review Index, Film Literature Index, Humanities Index, International Index to Film Periodicals, Monthly Cumulating Periodical Index, Popular Periodical Index.

Copyright: By the University of California Press. No subsidiary use permitted without author's consent.

FILMS IN REVIEW

Box 589, New York, NY 10021. Rates: $18 per year. Founded 1950. Sponsored by the National Board of Review of Motion Pictures. Published monthly except June-July and August-September, when bimonthly.

Major Field(s) of Interest: Journal reviews, classifies, and disseminates all aspects of motion picture and television scholarship as entertainment and as art. Articles on factual, critical, historical, esthetic, and philosophic work are accepted that express the public's opinions about films and their cultural and social effect. Journal reviews books, TV, Films, and Film music.

Manuscript Information: Articles of 2,500–10,000 words. Style: None. Only footnotes which amplify a point should be used. Report in 2–3 weeks. Rejected manuscripts returned.

Payment: "A reasonable number of copies of the issue will be given."

Copyright: By the National Board of Review of Motion Pictures.

IMAGENES: PUBLICATIÓN SEMESTRAL DE TEORÍA, TÉCNICA, CRÍTICA Y EDUCACIÓN ACERCA DE LA IMAGEN EN MOVIMIENTO

Universidad Interamericana de Puerto Rico, Recinto Metropolitano, Decanato de Estudiantes, Apartado 1293, Hato Rey, PR 00919. Rates: $6 per year Puerto Rico; $8 per year US. $10 per year elsewhere. Founded 1985. Sponsored by Inter-American University of Puerto Rico. Published 2 times per year.

Major Field(s) of Interest: Articles on film theory, film history, film technique, and film criticism written in Spanish and English.

Manuscript Information: Articles of 8,000 words in length. Notes of 50 words. Submit 2 copies of manuscript. Style: MLA. Report in 3–6 months. Rejected manuscripts returned with S.A.S.E.

Payment: None.

Copyright: By the journal.

THE JOURNAL OF FILM AND VIDEO

Division of Mass Communication, Emerson College, 100 Beacon Street, Boston, MA 02116. Rates: $12 per year individuals. $20 per year year foreign. Founded 1947. Sponsored by the University of Film Video Association. Published quarterly.

Major Field(s) of Interest: The journal focuses on the problems and substances in teaching in the fields of film and video production, history, theory, criticism, and aesthetics. The journal is also interested in scholarly articles on film and video, the related media, their components and relationships, and about problems of education in these fields and the function of film and video phenomena in society. Journal reviews books.

Manuscript Information: Articles of 12–15 typescript pages. Reviews of 3–5 pages. Style: MLA (1985) with endnotes. 3 copies of manuscript required. Articles should be sent to the Editor, JFV, at the address listed above. Photographs or illustrations should be on glossy stock, preferably 8 x 10, and accompanied by captions, credit lines, and secured permission(s) for reprint. Reviews should be sent in duplicate to Don Fredericksen, Department of Theatre Arts, Cornell University, Ithaca, NY 14853. Report in 6–8 weeks. Rejected manuscripts returned with S.A.S.E.

Payment: 4 copies of the issue.

Copyright: By the journal. Authors are freely granted permission to reprint with usual credit line.

JOURNAL OF POPULAR FILM AND TELEVISION

Popular Culture Center, Bowling Green State University, Bowling Green, OH 43403. Rates: $21 per year individuals. $42 per year institutions.

Founded 1971. Sponsored by HELDREF Publications, 4000 Albermarle Street, N. W., Washington, D. C. 20016. Published quarterly.

Major Field(s) of Interest: The journal is dedicated to popular film and television in the broadest sense. Concentration is on commercial cinema and television including stars, directors, producers, studios, networds, genres, series, and audience. Articles on film and television theory and criticism are invited as well as interviews, filmographies, and bibliographies. No esoteric distinctions between "motion pictures," "films," "cinema," and "movies," nor between "television," "video," "network television," or "public television" control editorial policies. Journal reviews books.

Manuscript Information: Articles of 10-20 pages. Book reviews of 300-600 words. Style: MLA Style Sheet (Revised Edition). 2 copies of manuscript required. Report in 3-4 months. Rejected manuscripts returned with S.A.S.E.

Payment: Copies.

Indexed In: Abstracts of Popular Culture, America: History and Life, Historical Abstracts, International Index to Film Periodicals, International Index to Television Periodicals, Film Literature Index, Media Review Digest, The Explicator, MLA International Bibliography.

Copyright: By the Helen Dwight Reid Education Foundation for Libraries.

JUMP CUT: A REVIEW OF CONTEMPORARY MEDIA
P. O. Box 865, Berkeley, CA 94701. Rates: $14 per year individuals. $20 per year institutions. Founded 1974. Published irregularly 1-2 times per year.

Major Field(s) of Interest: The review publishes material on film, television, video, and related media and cultural analysis. Taking an explicit political stand as a nonsectarian left, feminist, and anti-imperialist publication, JUMP CUT is committed to presenting and developing media criticism which recognizes: (1) media in a social and political context; (2) the political and social needs and perspectives of people struggling for liberation—workers, women, blacks and other oppressed minorities, Third World people, gays and lesbians; (3) the interrelationship of class, race, and gender oppression; (4) new theoretical and analytic perspectives. The review stresses contemporary media, but it is open to publishing material on older films, tapes, and programs when the article involves a significant re-evaluations or uses a well-known example to develop a critical or theoretical point. The range includes all types and forms of media from Hollywoood's commercial dramatic narrative to independent documentary and experimental work. The review is especially interested in neglected areas such as educational media, children's programs, animation, intermedia and mixed media, new technologies, consumer formats, etc., and related cultural analysis such as photography and popular music. Journal reviews books.

Manuscript Information: No length restrictions on articles. Book reviews and notes up to 4 pages. Style: MLA with endnotes. 2 copies of manuscript required. Report in 2–6 months. Rejected manuscripts returned with S.A.S.E.

Payment: Copies.

Indexed In: International Index of Film Periodicals, Alternative Press Index, Film Literature Index.

Copyright: By the journal. No reprint without written permission.

LITERATURE/FILM QUARTERLY

Salisbury State College, Salisbury, MD 21801. Rates: $12 per year individuals. $24 per year institutions. Founded 1973. Sponsored by Salisbury State College. Published quarterly.

Major Field(s) of Interest: (1) Articles on individual movies, on different cinematic adaptations of a single literary work, on a director's style of adaptation, on theories of film adaptation, on the "cinematic" qualities of authors or works, on the reciprocal influence between film and literature, on author's attitudes toward film and film adaptations, on the role of the screenwriters, and on teaching of film. (2) interviews with directors, screenwriters, and literary figures. (3) reviews of current film adaptations of literary works. (4) reviews of books concerning film and the relationship between film and literature. (5) responses to any of the articles and reviews. Journal sometimes publishes specialized bibliographies. Journal discourages the kind of specialized jargon found in some cinema studies publications.

Manuscript Information: Articles up to 3,000 words. Reviews up to 1,500 words. Style: MLA (1985). 2 copies of manuscript required. If possible, supply stills or frame enlargements of the films discussed. Report in 3–4 months. Rejected manuscripts returned with S.A.S.E.

Payment: 2 complimentary copies of the issue plus discounts for additional copies.

Indexed In: FIAF International Index of Film Periodicals, MLA International Bibliography, Humanities Index, Annual Bibliography of English Language and Literature, Abstracts of English Studies.

Copyright: By Salisbury State College.

MONTHLY FILM BULLETIN
British Film Institute, 21 Stephen Street, London, W1 1P1, England. Rates: £15.80 per year. $28 per year. $46 per year in airmail. Founded 1934. Sponsored by the British Film Institute. Published monthly.

Major Field(s) of Interest: Articles, reviews, and interviews on all aspects of contemporary cinema. The journal reviews every new release in Britain and provides a synopsis and full list of cast and technical credits. As both a critical magazine and a journal of record, the main aim is to provide authoritative coverage of every English and foreign film released. A yearly index of all films reviewed is published also. Most articles are commissioned by the editor.

Manuscript Information: Articles of 1,500–2,500 words. Reviews up to 1,500 words. Style: None. Report in 2 months. Rejected manuscripts returned.

Payment: Copies.

Copyright: By the British Film Institute.

*PERFORMING ARTS RESOURCES
Theatre Library Association, 111 Amsterdam Avenue/PARC, New York, NY 10023. Rates: $20 per year with individual membership. $25 per year with institutional membership. Founded 1939. Sponsored by the Theatre Library Association. Published annually.

Major Field(s) of Interest: Provides documentation for theater, film, television, and popular entertainments. Includes articles on storage and use of nonprint resources, studies of curatorship, indexes, bibliographies, subject matter guides to various archives and collections and museums, descriptions of regional holdings in a particular field or subject matter, and surveys of research materials, government holdings, training and programs in the performing arts. While the major portion of each annual volume is devoted to describing and indexing resources for research, some articles treat such issues as historiography, methodology, and states of research in the performing arts.

Manuscript Information: Articles of 10–20 pages. Notes of 4–10 pages. Style: Chicago. 2 copies of manuscript required. Report in 1 month. Rejected manuscripts returned with S.A.S.E.

Payment: 2 copies.

Copyright: By The Theatre Library Association.

POST SCRIPT: ESSAYS IN FILM AND THE HUMANITIES

Jacksonville University, 2800 University Blvd. North, Jacksonville, FL 32211. Rates: $10 per year individuals; $18 per year institutions. Founded 1981. Sponsored by Post Script, Inc. Published 3 times per year.

Major Field(s) of Interest: Manuscripts on film as language and literature (narrative, character, imagery); ensemble acting; the actor as auteur; film music; film as visual art (painting and cinematic style, set design, costuming); film and photography; film history; aesthetics and ontology; the response of film and the humanities to technology; interdisciplinary studies in theme and genre; film and American studies; interviews. Includes bibliography of film studies for the year. Journal reviews books.

Manuscript Information: Articles from 2–20 pages in length. Notes up to 1,000 words. Book reviews from 500–1,000 words. Style: MLA. 2 copies of manuscript required. Black and white photographs or photocopies should accompany article or note. Report in 4–6 weeks. Rejected manuscripts returned with S.A.S.E.

Payment: None.
Copyright: By the journal.

QUARTERLY REVIEW OF FILM STUDIES

Critical Studies Program, School of Cinema-Television, Room 405, University of Southern California, Los Angeles, CA 90089. Founded 1976. Sponsored by the University of Southern California, Division of Humanities & School of Cinema-Television. Published 4 times per year.

Major Field(s) of Interest: Interested in manuscripts that focus on interdisciplinary theory, criticism, and reviews of film and television culture. Journal reviews books. Most reviews are commissioned.

Manuscript Information: Articles up to 30 pages in length. Book reviews of 1,500–25,000 words. Notes of 100 words. Style: Chicago. 2 copies of manuscript required. Manuscripts printed with a dot matrix are not accepted. Author must secure copyright permission for photographs submitted. Report in 6–12 months. Rejected manuscripts returned with S.A.S.E.

Payment: None.
Copyright: By the journal.

SCREEN

The John Logie Baird Centre, University of Glasgow, Glasgow, G12 8QQ, Scotland. Rates: $41 per year North America for individuals. $72 per year North America institutions. Sponsored by The Department of

Theatre, Film and Television Studies, University of Glasgow. Published quarterly.

Major Field(s) of Interest: SCREEN is the leading international journal of film and television studies committed to the development of ethical, theatrical, and historical work within its field of interest. Journal reviews books.

Manuscript Information: Articles up to 5,000 words. Book reviews up to 2,500 words. Style: None. 2 copies of manuscripts required. Report in 3 months. Rejected manuscripts returned with S.A.S.E. or International Reply Coupons.

Payment: 1 copy.

Copyright: By the journal. Reprint fee of £15 per 1,000 words.

SHAKESPEARE ON FILM NEWSLETTER

Department of English, Nassau Community College, Garden City, NY 11530. Rates: $5 per year. Founded 1976. Sponsored by the University of Vermont and Nassau Community College. Published biannually (December and April).

Major Field(s) of Interest: Shakespeare and other authors of the medieval, Renaissance, and early modern period with special reference to visual and audio performance. The journal is also interested in illustrations, paintings, slides, or other visual materials related to early works of literature and drama. The journal also welcomes abstracts of conference papers, abstracts of longer papers published elsewhere, reviews of relevant books, reviews of media productions, reviews of state productions that have a media connection, bibliographies, filmographies, videographies, notes, queries (the journal's speciality is answering queries), lists of holdings at libraries and archives, interviews, responses to previous articles, notes, or reviews, conference news, both announcements and digests. All published articles are approved by the editors.

Manuscript Information: Articles up to 1,300 words. Notes as short as 100 words. Book reviews up to 500 words. Style: MLA with footnotes incorporated within the text of the article. 2 copies of manuscript required. Submissions should be on 800 floppy disk for Macintosh computer in Microsoft Word 4.0 or ASCII accompanied by hard (paper) copy. Report in 3 months. Rejected manuscripts returned with S.A.S.E.

Payment: 2 copies of the newsletter.

Indexed In: MLA International Bibliography, The World Shakespeare Bibliography.

Copyright: By the University of Vermont. Generally there are no objections to reprinting.

VARIETY

475 Park Avenue South, New York, NY 10016. Rates: $100.00 per year
U.S. (single copies $2.50). Foreign subscriptions on request. Founded
1905. Sponsored by Cahners Publishing Company, Newton, MA., a subsidiary of Reed International plc., London. Published weekly.

Major Field(s) of Interest: News about all aspects of film, television
and homevideo, entertainment law, finance, marketing and technology,
legitimate theater, recorded music, and live entertainment worldwide.
Journal reviews films, television programs, homevideos, stage productions,
concerts, live presentations, and entertainment-related books worldwide.

Manuscript Information: Articles from 400–2,000 words. Style:
News English and Associated Press style manual. Footnotes are not required. Report in 30 days, Rejected manuscripts returned with S.A.S.E.

Payment: $100–$350 for articles. Copies.

Copyright: By the journal, strictly enforced worldwide. Reprint rights
often granted with usual credit line.

THE VELVET LIGHT TRAP

Department of Radio-Television-Film, CMA 6. 118, University of Texas,
Austin, TX 78712. Rates: $15 per year individuals. $28 per year institutions. Founded 1971. Sponsored by the University of Texas Press, under
the auspices of the Radio-Television-Film Department, University of
Texas, Austin and the Department of Commercial Arts, and the University of Wisconsin, Madison. Published biannually.

Major Field(s) of Interest: The journal is devoted to investigating historical questions that illuminate the understanding of film, occasionally
expanding its scope to adjacent institutions, related media, and other national cinemas. It is interested in research on neglected areas and objects
of study related to film and other media. The journal issues calls for papers on specific themes; however, the editors will consider all submissions. Journal reviews books.

Manuscript Information: Articles up to 35 pages. No length restrictions on notes and book reviews. Style: MLA (1985) with endnotes and
with Works Cited. 3 copies of manuscript required. Report in approximately 2 months after deadline in call for papers.

Payment: Offprints.

Copyright: By the University of Texas Press. Requests for reprinting
should be sent to Subsidiary Rights Manager, UT Press, Box 7819, Austin, TX 78713.

Wide Angle: A Film Quarterly of
Theory, Criticism, and Practice

P.O. Box 388, Athens, OH 45701. Rates: $19 per year individuals. $41 per year institutions. Founded 1978. Sponsored by the Ohio University, Athens Center for Film and Video. Published 4 times per year.

Major Field(s) of Interest: Film studies on classical and avant-garde films, film theory and interpretations; critical analyses; and coverage of national cinema from the United States, Europe, Japan, and Australia, Latin America, and the Third World. Journal publishes book reviews.

Manuscript Information: Articles up to 4,000 words in length. Reviews up to 2,000 words. Style: MLA. 3 copies of manuscript required. Report in 120 days. Rejected manuscripts are not returned.

Payment: 2 copies of issue.

Indexed In: Arts and Humanities Citation Index, Current Contents, Film and Video International Index to Film Periodicals, Media Review Digest.

Copyright: By Ohio University, Athens Center for Film and Video.

IV. LANGUAGE AND LINGUISTICS JOURNALS

ADFL Bulletin

Association of Departments of Foreign Languages, 10 Astor Place, New York, NY 10003-6981. Rates: $15 individual. $30 institutions. $5 per copy. Subscription is part of departmental membership. Founded 1969. Sponsored by the Association of Departments of Foreign Languages. Published 3 times per year.

Major Field(s) of Interest: Publishes articles on professional and pedagogical issues involving foreign language departments in colleges and universities. Includes articles on curriculum, instruction, methods, career placements, and department objectives.

Manuscript Information: Articles of 12–18 pages, double-spaced. Must conform to the 1985 MLA *Style Sheet* guidelines in both presentation of content and footnote form. Report in 3 or 4 months. Submit manuscripts in triplicate.

Payment: 4 complimentary copies to author.

Indexed In: CIJE, ACTFL *Annual Bibliography of Books and Articles on Pedagogy in Foreign Languages,* ERIC.

Copyright: By the *ADFL Bulletin.*

*American Speech: A Quarterly of Linguistic Usage

English Department, Duke University, Durham, NC 27706. Rates: $20 per year individuals (includes membership in the American Dialect Society). $25 per year institutions. Founded 1925. Sponsored by the American Dialect Society. Published quarterly.

Major Field(s) of Interest: Scholarly studies of the English language in the Western Hemisphere, although contributions dealing with English in other parts of the world, with other languages influenced by it, and with general linguistic theory may also be submitted for consideration. The journal welcomes articles dealing with current usage, dialectology, and the history and structure of English. The journal is not committed to any particular theoretical framework, but preference is given to articles that are likely to be of interest to a wide readership. The "Miscellany" section publishes short notes, and the journal reviews books.

Manuscript Information: Articles from 1 paragraph up to 40 typewritten pages. Book reviews up to 6 pages. Notes up to 4 pages. Style: MLA with in-text citation or paragraph style for footnotes. Use endnotes for informational material. 2 copies of manuscript required (except for reviews). Report in 4–6 weeks. Rejected manuscripts returned with S.A.S.E.

Payment: 250 offprints for articles. 10 offprints for notes and reviews.

Indexed In: MLA International Bibliography.

Copyright: By the American Dialect Society. Authors may republish without cost in any book of their own works.

ANNUAL REVIEW OF APPLIED LINGUISTICS

Department of Linguistics, University of Southern California, Los Angeles, CA 90089–1693. Founded 1980. Sponsored by the Cambridge University Press. Published annually.

Major Field(s) of Interest: Applied linguistics. Unsolicited manuscripts are not accepted.

Manuscript Information: Articles up to 5,000–6,000 words plus up to 20 annotated bibliographic citations and up to 40 other bibliographic citations. Style: Journal. Submit original typescript. Outlines are required 6 months prior to copy deadlines. Report in 6–8 months. Rejected manuscripts are not returned.

Payment: Copies.

Copyright: By Cambridge University Press.

ANTHROPOLOGICAL LINGUISTICS

Rawles Hall 108, Indiana University, Bloomington, IN 47405. Rates: $12 per year individuals. $16 per year institutions. Founded 1959. Sponsored by Indiana University Department of Anthropology. Published quarterly (Spring, Summer, Fall, Winter).

Major Field(s) of Interest: The journal is concerned with language from an anthropological perspective as well as from the perspective of linguistics. It is devoted primarily to the publications of data-oriented papers, particularly on language still spoken but not usually written. In addition to heavily exemplified papers on problems in synchronic and diachronic linguistics, the journal welcomes submissions on such topics as social uses of language in western and nonwestern societies, kinship systems, speech styles and register, conversational analysis, metaphor and semantic anthropology, as well as theoretical and methodological considerations of language and speech. Journal reviews books. Books for review (as well as the reviews themselves) should be sent to the editors for consideration.

Manuscript Information: Articles of 20–40 pages in length. Book reviews up to 10 typed double-spaced pages. Style: See *AL* 24, no. 4. Footnotes should be typed on a separate sheet and numbered consecutively. Contact editor for journal style sheet. 3 copies of manuscript required. All papers must have an abstract. Report in 4 months. Rejected manuscripts returned with S.A.S.E.

Payment: 50 reprints. Additional reprints are available at 50¢ per page per 50 copies.

Indexed In: Institute for Scientific Information, Current Contents, Social Sciences Citation Index, KTO.

Copyright: By the journal and the author.

APPLIED PSYCHOLINGUISTICS

Larsen Hall, 7th Floor, Harvard Graduate School of Education, Cambridge, MA 02138. Rates: $36 per year individuals. $71 per year institutions. Founded 1979. Sponsored by Harvard Graduate School of Education and Cambridge University Press. Published 4 times per year.

Major Field(s) of Interest: Articles on both normal and disordered language and communicative development in children and normal and disordered language and communicative functioning in adults. The journal welcomes submissions as full-length articles (original research, theoretical or methodological studies, issue-oriented literature reviews), short notes, or critical responses to articles previously published. Journal reviews books.

Manuscript Information: Articles up to 50 double-spaced typed pages on 8½ by 11 inch or A4 paper with margins set to accommodate approximately 70 characters per line and 25 lines per page. Book reviews of 4–8 pages. Style: APA. Each element of the article or note should begin on a new page and should be arranged as follows: title page (including title, short title, author's full name and affiliation, including mailing address), abstract, text with tables, interspersed as they occur, appendixes, acknowledgements, footnotes, references (including reference notes for unpublished citations), captions and figures. Each table and figure should be submitted on a separate page. 4 copies of manuscript required. Submit original manuscript plus 3 copies. Report in 1–2 months. Rejected manuscripts returned with S.A.S.E.

Payment: 25 offprints. Additional copies may be purchased if ordered at proof stage.

Copyright: By Cambridge University Press. Authors are responsible for obtaining written permission to publish material (quotations, illustrations, etc.) for which they do not own the copyright.

BABEL: INTERNATIONAL JOURNAL OF TRANSLATION

Akademiai Kiado, Alkotomany u.21, H–1054, Budapest, Hungary. Founded 1955. Sponsored by UNESCO. Published 4 times per year.

Major Field(s) of Interest: Articles on translation and translators, applied linguistics, and terminology. Journal reviews books.

Manuscript Information: Articles up to 6,000 words. Notes up to

150 words. Book reviews up to 300 words. Style: Journal. 2 copies of manuscript required. Report in 4 months. Rejected manuscripts are not returned.

Payment: Copies.

Copyright: By the journal.

THE BILINGUAL REVIEW/LA REVISTA BILINGÜE

Hispanic Research Center, Bilingual Review/Press, Tempe, AZ 85287-2702. Rates: $15 per year individuals; $24 per year institutions. Single copies: $5 individuals; $8 institutions. 3 issues per year. Founded 1974. Sponsored by the Hispanic Research Center, Arizona State University.

Major Field(s) of Interest: Devoted to the linguistics and literatures of bilingualism, particularly Spanish-English, in the United States. Publishes articles related to bilingual education, the linguistics of bilingualism, and literary criticism of United States-Hispanic literature, in addition to short stories and poetry by/about same. Not interested in publishing translations of previously published poems/stories. Book reviews are assigned by the editor.

Manuscript Information: 15–30 pages is average. Since authors come from varying fields, the journal accepts any standard style sheet. Notes or references run at end of article. Report in 8–10 weeks. Desire 2 copies of manuscript. Journal carries creative, nonscholarly material.

Payment: 2 copies to contributors.

Indexed In: LLBA, MLA International Bibliography.

Copyright: Journal holds copyright; authors must request permission to reprint, but permission is freely granted with usual credit line.

BULLETIN OF THE ASSOCIATION FOR
LITERARY AND LINGUISTIC COMPUTING

National Computing Centre Ltd., Oxford Road, Manchester, M13 9PL, England. Founded 1973. Sponsored by the Association for Literary and Linguistic Computing. Published 3 times per year (April, August, and November).

Major Field(s) of Interest: Articles on all aspects of computing as applied to the study of literature, linguistics, and language. Journal reviews books.

Manuscript Information: Articles up to 10 single-spaced pages including diagrams. Submit a 150–word abstract in English and a 75–word autobiographical note. Notes up to 500 words. Book reviews up to 500 words. Style: Modern Humanities Research Association or MLA. Report in 3 months. Rejected manuscripts returned.

Payment: Copies.
Copyright: By the Association for Literary and Linguistic Computing.

CANADIAN JOURNAL OF LINGUISTICS/
REVUE CANADIENNE DE LINGUISTIQUE

Department of Linguistics, Carleton University, Ottawa, Ontario, K1S 5B6, Canada. Rates: $40 Canadian. Founded 1954. Sponsored by the Association Canadienne de Linguistique/Canadian Linguistic Association. Published quarterly.

Major Field(s) of Interest: General and theoretical linguistics. The journal is bilingual and publishes articles and reviews in both English and French.

Manuscript Information: Articles of 20–30 pages. Submit only xerox copies. Style: Should be similar to that utilized by the Linguistic Society of America or Chicago. No bibliographic reference in footnotes. Report in 3–6 months. After an article is accepted, it must be resubmitted on computer disk or sent via electronic mail. Rejected manuscripts are not returned.

Payment: 25 copies.

Copyright: By the Canadian Linguistic Association. Permission to reprint freely granted.

CARLETON PAPERS IN APPLIED LANGUAGE STUDIES

Centre for Applied Language Studies, Carleton University, Room 215 Paterson Hall, Ottawa, K1S 5B6, Canada. Rates $8 (Canadian) within Canada; $8 (US) for foreign mailing. Founded 1984. Sponsored by Carleton University; partially self-supporting.

Major Field(s) of Interest: Approaches to communicative language-teaching, syllabus design, pedagogical implications of research on writing, discourse analysis, and computer-assisted learning. As a working journal, it provides an opportunity to share provisional results in these fields.

Manuscript Information: Should not exceed 25 double-spaced typed pages. Style: A.P.A. Footnotes form: based on the guidelines of *The Publication Manual of the American Psychological Association.* Report within 6 to 8 weeks. Require 3 copies of manuscript.

Payment: None.

Indexed In: Abstracts of articles are published in *Linguistic and Language Behavior Abstracts* (LLBA).

Copyright: No copyright imposed.

COLLEGE LANGUAGE ASSOCIATION JOURNAL

Morehouse College, Atlanta, GA 30314. Rates: $30 per year. Founded 1957. Sponsored by the College Association and Morehouse College. Published quarterly.

Major Field(s) of Interest: Any type of article dealing with language and literature, including bibliographical articles. Articles may be written in English, French, Spanish, or German. Contributors must be members of the College Language Association. Journal reviews books.

Manuscript Information: No specified length for articles, but usually 15–20 typewritten pages. Excessively long articles must be unusually meritorious and timely. Style: MLA with notes at the bottom of the page. 2 copies of manuscript required. Report in 4 months. Rejected manuscripts returned with S.A.S.E.

Payment: No reprints are available.

Copyright: By the journal. Use of material permitted for a fee.

COLUMBIA UNIVERSITY WORKING PAPERS IN LINGUISTICS

Box 708, Casa Italiana, Columbia University, New York, NY 10027. Founded 1975. Sponsored by Columbia University. Published irregularly.

Major Field(s) of Interest: Articles on linguistic research. Contributors must be a member of the linguistic community but not necessarily at Columbia University.

Manuscript Information: No length restrictions for articles. Style: None. 2 copies of manuscript required. Consult with editor prior to submission. Report in 2 months. Rejected manuscripts returned with S.A.S.E.

Payment: Copies.

Copyright: By Columbia University.

THE COMPARATIVE ROMANCE LINGUISTICS NEWSLETTER

Department of Foreign Languages, Literatures & Linguistics, University of Rochester, Rochester, NY 14627. Rates: $6 per year individuals. $8 per year institutions. Founded 1950. Sponsored by the MLA, Comparative Romance Linguistics Discussion Group. Published 2 times per year.

Major Field(s) of Interest: Publishes news in the field of comparative Romance linguistics and bibliography. Journal reviews books.

Manuscript Information: Articles of 10–15 pages. Style: Chicago. Report in 4 months. Rejected manuscripts returned.

Payment: Copies.

Copyright: By the University of Rochester.

COMPUTATIONAL LINGUISTICS

Computer Science Department, University of Rochester, Rochester, NY 14627. Founded 1973. Sponsored by the Association for Computational Linguistics. Published quarterly.

Major Field(s) of Interest: Articles on computational linguistics. Journal reviews books.

Manuscript Information: Articles up to 45 pages. Notes up to 2 pages. Book reviews up to 1 page. Style: None. 5 copies of manuscript required. Manuscripts must be double-spaced including footnotes. Submit 150–200 word abstract. Report in 2–3 months. Rejected manuscripts are discarded.

Payment: Copies.

Copyright: By the Association for Computational Linguistics.

COMPUTERS AND TRANSLATION

Linguistics Research Center, University of Texas, Box 7247, University Station, Austin, TX 78713–7247. Rates: $110 per year. Founded 1986. Sponsored by Paradigm Press, Inc. Published 4 times per year.

Major Field(s) of Interest: Journal is devoted to the study of computer-aided translation, artificial intelligence, and general linguistic studies related to translation. Journal reviews books.

Manuscript Information: Articles up to 3,000 words. Notes up to 500 words. Book reviews up to 1,000 words. Style: Linguistics Society of America. See back cover of journal for additional requirements. 4 copies of manuscript required. Report in 1–6 months. Rejected manuscripts returned with S.A.S.E.

Payment: Copies.

Copyright: By Paradigm Press.

CORNELL WORKING PAPERS IN LINGUISTICS

Department of Modern Languages & Linguistics, Cornell University, Ithaca, NY 14853–4701. Founded 1980. Sponsored by the Cornell University, Department of Modern Languages & Linguistics. Published irregularly.

Major Field(s) of Interest: Publishes papers in linguistics written by faculty members or students at Cornell University or an invited contributor.

Manuscript Information: Articles up to 12 pages. Style: Linguistics Society of America. Submit camera-ready copy and a 100–word abstract. Report in 3 months. Rejected manuscripts returned.

Payment: Copies.

Copyright: By the author.

CUNYFORUM: PAPERS IN LINGUISTICS

The Graduate School and University Center of the City University of New York, Ph.D. Program in Linguistics, Box 455, Graduate Center, 33 West 42 Street, New York, NY 10036-8099. Rates: $7.50 per year. Founded 1976. Sponsored by the Linguistics Department, CUNY Graduate Center. Published annually.

Major Field(s) of Interest: Publishes working studies in all areas of linguistics. Articles on syntax and semantics are especially welcome. Journal reviews books.

Manuscript Information: No length restrictions on articles. Notes up to 250 words. Book reviews up to 300 words. Style: LSA with footnotes at the bottom of the page. 2 copies of manuscript required plus 1 hard disc preferably in WORD. Report in 6-8 weeks. Rejected manuscripts returned with S.A.S.E.

Payment: 1 copy.

Indexed In: MLA International Bibliography.

Copyright: By the author.

DICTIONARIES: JOURNAL OF THE
DICTIONARY SOCIETY OF NORTH AMERICA

Fenn Tower 1214, Cleveland State University, 1983 East 24th Street, Cleveland, OH 44115. Rates: $20 per year (includes membership in the Dictionary Society of North America). Founded 1975. Sponsored by the Dictionary Society of North America and Cleveland State University. Published annually.

Major Field(s) of Interest: The journal publishes essays and reviews in German, French, and English on monolingual and bilingual lexicography in theory and practice, lexicographers, dialects with a lexicographical perspective, pronunciation, etymology, computers and dictionaries, dictionaries in progress, and polylingual dictionaries. Contributors must be a member of the Dictionary Society of North America in the year in which their submission is published. Contributors should send an abstract to the editor before submitting a manuscript.

Manuscript Information: Articles of 3,000-12,000 words. Notes of 400-500 words. Book reviews of 2,500-5,000 words. Style: MLA with endnotes. 2 copies of manuscript required. Report in 2-4 months. Rejected manuscripts returned with S.A.S.E.

Payment: Money plus 2 tearsheets.

Copyright: By the Dictionary Society of North America. Fees for reprinting are divided equally with authors.

THE DISCOURSE ANALYSIS RESEARCH GROUP NEWSLETTER
Education Tower 1428, University Drive N. W., Calgary, Alberta, T2N 1N4, Canada. Rates: $10 per year. Founded 1985. Sponsored partially by the Research Grants Committee, the Special Funds Project, and the Deans of the faculties of Education, General Studies, Humanities and Social Sciences. Published 2 times per year.

Major Field(s) of Interest: The newsletter provides a medium for the dissemination of the latest news about, as well as a forum for scholarly discussion on, a wide range of topics encountered in the study of language as it is used in everyday life. Emphasis is placed on (1) accounts of work-in-progress, (2) commentary on issues arising out of new publications, (3) discussion of innovative courses, (4) news of as well as reports on conferences, seminars, and workshops, and (5) reviews of recent publications. The object in assembling this material is to promote the exchange of information. Journal reviews books.

Manuscript Information: Articles up to 2,000 words or 10 pages of double-spaced type. Style: Consult D.A.R.G. NEWSLETTER. Give complete bibliographical data in reference at the end of article, and run quotations of fewer than 10 lines in the text. 2 copies of manuscripts preferred. Report in 4–6 weeks. Rejected manuscripts returned.

Payment: 5 copies of the issue for articles and 2 copies for book reviews.

Copyright: By the author.

ELT JOURNAL
Oxford University Press, Journals Department, Walton Street, Oxford, OX2 6DP, England. Rates: UK £14. USA $32 per year individuals. £21. USA $48 per year institutions. Founded 1946. Sponsored by Oxford University Press. Published quarterly.

Major Field(s) of Interest: An international journal published in association with The British Council, ELT provides a forum for the exchange of ideas and information on classroom practice, new developments in methodology, language acquisition and the English language itself. Articles about aspects of English language (grammar, vocabulary, pronunciation, use, idioms, etc.) are welcome, so long as they do not require specialized knowledge of linguistics and so long as they deal with specific learning and teaching procedures. The journal also accepts articles that relate current theory and research in fields such as psychology, sociology, and linguistics to actual classroom practice. Reviews are accepted that discuss professional and critical assessments of new publications.

Manuscript Information: Articles of 1,000–3,000 words are preferred.

Book reviews up to 1,500 words. Style: Write for *A Guide For Contributors* (Editor, 2 Smyrna Mansions, Smyrna Road, London NW6 4LU). Report in 30 days. Rejected manuscripts returned with S.A.S.E. or International Reply Coupons.

Payment: £30 for each article and survey review. £20 for each review plus 2 copies of the issue.

Copyright: By the journal. Reprint fees to use copyright material shall be borne by the author.

ETC.: A REVIEW OF GENERAL SEMANTICS

P. O. Box 2469, San Francisco, CA 94126. Rates: $30 per year. Founded 1943. Sponsored by the International Society for General Semantics. Published quarterly.

Major Field(s) of Interest: Focuses on the role of symbols in human behavior and explores the relationships between language, thought, and behavior, and questions of improving human communication. Journal reviews books.

Manuscript Information: Articles of 750–3,000 words. Notes up to 1,000 words. Book reviews of 500–2,000 words. Style: Chicago. 2 copies of manuscript required. Report in 3–9 months. Rejected manuscripts returned with S.A.S.E.

Payment: Copies.

Copyright: By the International Society for General Semantics.

ÉTUDES CELTIQUES

École Pratique des Hautes Études, IVᵉ section, Sorbonne, 45–47 rue des Écoles, 75000 Paris, France. Rates: 300 Francs per year. Founded 1936. Sponsored by the Centre National de la Récherché Scientifique. Published annually.

Major Field(s) of Interest: Articles from various scholarly disciplines that deal with Celtic studies past and present. The journal favors comparative studies in grammar of Celtic languages, etymology, and medieval insular literature, but it also considers ancient and modern linguistics and philology, archaeology, epigraphy, numismatics, and the history of literature, art, law, and religion. The journal includes news items and has a bibliographical section. Journal reviews books.

Manuscript Information: Articles up to 30 pages. Notes of 1–3 pages. Book reviews of 1–5 pages. Style: French. Report in 6–8 months. Rejected manuscripts returned with S.A.S.E.

Payment: 25 offprints.

Copyright: By the Centre National de la Récherché Scientifique.

FOCUS: TEACHING ENGLISH LANGUAGE ARTS
Ellis Hall 114A, Ohio University, Athens, OH 45701. Rates: $10 (membership); single copies when available $5 each. Founded 1973. Sponsored by the Southeastern Ohio Council of Teachers of English.

Major Field(s) of Interest: Short articles and items about the English Language Arts are invited. Issues are thematic with themes generally announced a year in advance.

Manuscript Information: 5 to 8 double-spaced pages. *MLA Style Sheet* (Second Edition). Avoid footnotes whenever possible by including documentation in the text. Report in 1 month.

Payment: One copy of issue.

Copyright: With SOCTE. Reprinting by permission of the editors.

FOLIA PHONIATRICA: INTERNATIONAL JOURNAL OF
PHONIATRICS, SPEECH THERAPY AND COMMUNICATION PATHOLOGY
S. Karger AG, CH–4009 Basel, Switzerland. Rates: $150 per year. Founded 1947. Sponsored by the International Association of Logopedics & Phoniatrics. Published 6 times per year.

Major Field(s) of Interest: Articles concerning experimental and quantitive methods for the study of speech and the vocal organs. Journal reviews books.

Manuscript Information: No length restrictions on articles, notes, or book reviews. Style: Journal. Submit original double-spaced typescript plus 1 copy. Include a 10–line summary in French and German. Consult editor for further details. Report in 6 months. Rejected manuscripts returned.

Payment: Copies.

Copyright: By the journal.

FORUM FOR MODERN LANGUAGE STUDIES
Buchanan Building, University of St. Andrews, Union Street, St. Andrews, KY16 9PH, Scotland, United Kingdom. Price (per annum): Individual subscribers: £15/$37.50. Institutions: £35/$70.00. Founded 1965. Sponsored by the University of St. Andrews.

Major Field(s) of Interest: Articles on all aspects of the language and literature of English, French, German, Italian, Spanish, and Portugese; other modern language and literary studies considered.

Manuscript Information: No particular restrictions on length. For style and footnote requirements, see copies of journal. Advice on presentation is available on request. List footnotes at end of typescript. Report in 4–6 weeks.

Payment: 20 offprints.

Abstracts: Abstracts may be printed with author's permission.

Copyright: Jointly held by journal and the author. Reprint rights readily granted.

FORUM ITALICUM

Center for Italian Studies, State University of New York at Stony Brook, Stony Brook, NY 11794–3359. Rates: $16 per year individuals and retired. $25 per year institutions. Founded 1967. Sponsored by the Center for Italian Studies. Published 2 times per year.

Major Field(s) of Interest: An American journal of Italian studies where scholars, critics, and teachers can present their views on the literature, language, and culture of Italy and other countries in relation to Italy, the journal publishes critical and informative articles, poetry, translation, and fiction. The journal encourages creative writers to offer original poems, stories, and translations of works of merit, and young and hitherto unpublished scholars are encouraged to contribute critical work. Contributions are normally in English and Italian, but manuscripts in French, Portuguese, or Spanish will be considered. Journal reviews books.

Manuscript Information: Articles of 10–30 pages in length. Notes of 3–4 pages. Book reviews of 2–3 pages. Style: MLA. 2 copies of manuscript required. Report in 2–3 months. Rejected manuscripts returned with S.A.S.E.

Payment: Money.

Indexed In: MLA International Bibliography, Sociological Abstracts.

Copyright: By the journal.

FORUM LINGUISTICUM

c/o Jupiter Press, P. O. Box 101, Lake Bluff, IL 60044. Rates: $20 per year individuals. $30 per year institutions. Founded 1976. Sponsored by the Linguistic Association of Canada and the United States. Published 3 times per year (April, August, December).

Major Field(s) of Interest: Articles in all areas of linguistics, both theoretical and descriptive, and its humanistic applications to related disciplines and to the general human condition. Journal reviews books.

Manuscript Information: Articles of 10–20 pages. Notes of 1 page. Book reviews of 2–3 pages. Style: Linguistic Society of America with some modifications. Report in 3 months. Rejected manuscripts returned.

Payment: Copies.

Copyright: By the journal.

*THE FRENCH REVIEW: JOURNAL OF THE
AMERICAN ASSOCIATION OF TEACHERS OF FRENCH

Department of French and Italian, University of California, Santa Barbara, CA 93106. Rates: $27 per year. Founded 1927. Sponsored by the American Association of Teachers of French. Published 6 times per year (October, December, February, March, April, May).

Major Field(s) of Interest: Articles on all aspects of French literature, language, linguistics, cinema, civilization, and film. Journal reviews books, but all book reviews are solicited. All contributors must be members of the American Association of Teachers of French.

Manuscript Information: Articles up to 5,000 words. Notes up to 2,500 words. Book reviews up to 650 words. Style: MLA with endnotes. Contributions may be in English or French. Prospective contributors should consult the *Guide for Authors.* 3 copies of manuscript required. Report in 2–3 months. Rejected manuscripts are not returned.

Payment: None.

Indexed In: MLA International Bibliography.

Copyright: By the journal. Reprinting is allowed in scholarly books with permission.

GENERAL LINGUISTICS

332 Burrowes Building, Pennsylvania State University, University Park, PA 16802. Rates: $28 per year individuals. $34 per year institutions. Founded 1955. Sponsored and published by The Pennsylvania State University Press. Published quarterly.

Major Field(s) of Interest: The journal invites articles in all fields of linguistics, historical, comparative, descriptive, and in allied fields such as sociolinguistics. Journal reviews books but does not accept unsolicited reviews.

Manuscript Information: No length restrictions on articles, notes, or book reviews. Style: MLA. Footnotes at end of article. 2 copies of manuscript required. Submit original typescript. Report in 4–6 months. Rejected manuscripts returned.

Payment: 25 offprints.

Indexed In: Sociological Abstracts.

Copyright: By The Pennsylvania State University Press.

GEOLINGUISTICS: JOURNAL OF THE
AMERICAN SOCIETY OF GEOLINGUISTICS

Department of Modern Languages, North Hall, University of Bridgeport, Bridgeport, CT 06601. Rates: $22 per year. Founded 1974. Sponsored by the American Society of Geolinguistics. Published annually in December.

Major Field(s) of Interest: Articles on the distribution, use, relative practical importance, identification, and interrelationships of present-day languages. Fields of interest include materials in other areas of linguistics, especially languages in contact, sociolinguistics, and language education. Journal reviews books. Preference is given to material submitted by members and invited speakers, but other contributions are welcome.

Manuscript Information: Articles of 5–25 single-spaced typescripts with blank lines between paragraphs and wide margins. Notes of 1,000–3,000 words. Book reviews of 600–1,000 words. Style: MLA. 2 copies of manuscript required. Clear photocopies are acceptable. Do not submit carbon copies. English is the preferred language of publication. Abstract is preferred for unsolicited items. Report in 2 months. Rejected manuscripts returned.

Payment: Copies.

Copyright: By the author

*THE GERMAN QUARTERLY

German Department, Box 1104, Washington University, St. Louis, MO 63130. Rates: Annual Subscription: $35. Free to AATG members. Back issues: $10 each. Founded 1928. Sponsored by the American Association of Teachers of German. Published quarterly.

Major Field(s) of Interest: Articles on all aspects of German literature and language. Submission of articles with an interdisciplinary approach is encouraged. Articles selected on the basis of peer review. Journal reviews books, but unsolicited book reviews are not accepted.

Manuscript Information: Articles not over 25 pages in length. Book reviews not over 3 pages. Style: MLA with endnotes. 2 copies of manuscript required. Report variable (usually 6–8 weeks). Rejected manuscripts returned with S.A.S.E. Articles accepted and printed in English and/or German.

Abstracts: GQ requires abstract in English of about 100 words with each article.

Indexed In: The Education Index.

Copyright: By the American Association of Teachers of German. Permission to reprint granted upon request with credit line.

*GERMANIC REVIEW

Department of Germanic Languages, Columbia University, 319 Hamilton Hall, New York, NY 10027. Rates: $35 per year. $9 per single copy.

Founded 1926. Sponsored by the Helen Dwight Reid Foundation. Published quarterly.

Major Field(s) of Interest: Publishes the results of scholarly research in all areas of German literature from the medieval period to the present, as well as in literary criticism and linguistics. Articles are accepted in English or German. Journal reviews books. Peer review.

Manuscript Information: Articles of 20–30 typed pages. Book reviews of 3–5 typed pages. Style: MLA. 2 copies of manuscript are required. Report in 3 months. Rejected manuscripts returned with S.A.S.E.

Payment: 10 copies of the issue for articles. 2 copies for reviews.

Abstracts: 200 word abstract for MLA database.

Indexed In: MLA International Bibliography.

Copyright: Author retains copyright.

HISPANIC JOURNAL

Department of Spanish & Classical Languages, 456 Sutton Hall, Indiana University of Pennylvania, Indiana, PA 15705. Rates: $8 per year individuals. $12 per year institutions. Founded 1979. Sponsored by Indiana University of Pennsylvania, Graduate School and Department of Spanish and Classical Languages. Published 2 times per year.

Major Field(s) of Interest: Articles on literary criticism, linguistics, and Spanish and Latin American thought and culture. Journal reviews books.

Manuscript Information: Articles of 2,500–7,000 words. Notes of 500–1,200 words. Book reviews of 500–2,000 words. Style: MLA. 2 copies of manuscript required. Report in 1–8 months. Rejected manuscripts returned.

Payment: Copies.

Copyright: By the journal.

HISPANIC REVIEW

512 Williams Hall, University of Pennsylvania, Philadelphia, PA 19104. Rates: $20 per year for individuals. $30 per year institutions. Founded 1933. Sponsored by the University of Pennsylvania and Hispanic Society of America. Published quarterly.

Major Field(s) of Interest: A quarterly journal devoted to research in the Hispanic languages and literatures. Journal reviews books.

Manuscript Information: Manuscripts should not exceed 7,500 words including notes and documentation. Contributors should prepare their manuscripts following *The MLA Style Manual* (New York, 1985), and only original typescripts of articles will be considered. Do not include copies. Unsolicited article manuscripts should be accompanied by self-addressed return envelopes and correct postage in loose stamps or International Reply Coupons. Unsolicited book reviews are not considered for publication. Report in 2–4 weeks.

Payment: None.

Copyright: Trustees of the University of Pennsylvania.

*HISTORIOGRAPHIA LINGUISTICA: INTERNATIONAL JOURNAL FOR THE HISTORY OF THE LANGUAGE SCIENCES

John Benjamins Publishing Company, Amsteldijk 44, P. O. Box 75577, 1070 AN Amsterdam, Holland. Rates: $52 per year individuals. $166 per year institutions. Founded 1973. Sponsored by the Publisher. Published 2 times per year.

Major Field(s) of Interest: The journal serves the scholarly interests of linguists, psycholinguists, historians of ideas and of science, and philosophers of language of divergent persuasions in the history of linguistic thought. Each issue contains at least 3 major articles, 1 review article, and a bibliography devoted to a particular topic in the field. It also contains a number of reviews of recent publications and short book notices. Journal reviews books, but book reviews are solicited.

Manuscript Information: Articles of 25–35 typescript pages. Notes of 1,200–1,500 words. Book reviews up to 3,000 words. Style: LSA with modifications introduced by the journal. 3 copies of manuscript required. Report in 2–3 months. Rejected manuscripts returned with comments with S.A.S.E.

Payment: 1 copy of the journal plus 30 offprints.

Copyright: By the journal.

IN GEARDAGUM: ESSAYS ON OLD AND MIDDLE ENGLISH LANGUAGE AND LITERATURE

Society for New Language Study, P. O. Box 10596, Denver, CO 80210. Rates: $6 per year. Founded 1974. Sponsored by the Society for New Language Study. Published annually.

Major Field(s) of Interest: The journal publishes articles on Old and Middle English literature, language, and poetry. Journal reviews books.

Manuscript Information: Articles up to 5,000 words. Notes of 1,500–2,000 words. Book reviews of 2,000–4,000 words. Style: None. 2 copies of manuscript required. Report in 1 month. Rejected manuscripts returned with S.A.S.E.

Payment: Copies.

Copyright: By the Society for New Language Study.

International Journal of American Linguistics

Linguistics Department, Campus Box 295, University of Colorado, Boulder, CO 80309. Rates: $30 per year individuals. $60 per year institutions. Founded 1917. Sponsored by the University of Chicago Press. Published quarterly.

Major Field(s) of Interest: Devoted to scholarly studies of all the languages native to North, Central, and South America, including Eskimo-Aleut and certain creoles and pidgins of the hemisphere. The journal concentrates on the investigation of linguistic data and on the presentation of grammars, historical reconstruction, grammatical fragments, and other discussions relevant to American Indian languages. Journal reviews books.

Manuscript Information: Articles up to 5,000 words. Notes up to 1,750 words. Book reviews up to 1,750 words. Style: Linguistics Society of America. 3 copies of manuscript required. Report in 4 months. Rejected manuscripts returned.

Payment: Copies.
Copyright: By the journal.

International Journal of Computer and Information Sciences

Center for Information Research, University of Florida, Gainesville, FL 32611. Founded 1972. Sponsored by Plenum Publishing Corporation. Published 6 times per year (January, March, May, September, October, November).

Major Field(s) of Interest: Articles on software engineering, systems programming, pattern recognition, picture processing, computer graphics, information retrieval, computer organization, language processing, automata theory, mathematical linguistics, computer control, data structure and access, management information systems, biomedical information processing.

Manuscript Information: Articles of 15–20 pages. Notes up to half-page. Book reviews of 1 page. Style: Institute of Electrical and Electronics Engineers. 3 copies of manuscript required. Submit original double-spaced typescript and an abstract in English of 150 words. Footnotes should be typed at bottom of page to which they refer. Report in 2–4 months. Rejected manuscripts returned upon request.

Payment: Copies.
Copyright: By Plenum Publishing Corporation.

INTERNATIONAL JOURNAL OF SIGN LINGUISTICS

Multilingual Matters Ltd., Bank House, 8a Hill Road, Clevedon, Avon, BS21 7HH, England. Rates: $38 per year individuals. $110 per year institutions. Founded 1990. Sponsored by The International Sign Linguistics Association. Published 2 times per year.

Major Field(s) of Interest: The aim of the journal is to promote the linguistic study of sign languages. It is intended that contributions reflecting all aspects of sign linguistics should find space in the journal. Articles on neurolinguistics, applied linguistics, theoretical linguistics, sociolinguistics, developmental linguistics, comparative linguistics, psycholinguistics, semiotics, semantics, syntax, morphology, and phonology are all welcome if they bear directly upon the study of sign languages. Papers on natural gesture, or on primate signing, will be included insofar as they illuminate linguistic aspects of sign. Journal reviews books.

Manuscript Information: Articles up to 7,000 words. Notes up to 500 words. Book reviews up to 2,500 words. Style: See "Notes on the Submission of Manuscripts" contained in the journal. 4 Copies required. Submit a 200–word abstract. Report in 3 months. Rejected manuscripts returned with S.A.S.E.

Payment: 10 copies of the journal. Additional copies may be ordered when returning page proofs.

Copyright: By the author who can reproduce his/her article with the usual credit line.

INTERNATIONAL JOURNAL OF THE SOCIOLOGY OF LANGUAGE

Ferkauf Graduate School, Yeshiva University, 1300 Morris Park Avenue, Bronx, NY 10461. Rates: $51.50 per year individuals. $145.00 per year institutions. Founded 1974. Sponsored by Walter de Gruyter & Co. Published 6 times per year.

Major Field(s) of Interest: Articles on the development of the sociology of language in its broadest sense, as a truly international and interdisciplinary field in which various approaches, theoretical and empirical, supplement and complement each other, contributing thereby to the growth of language-related knowledge applications, values, and sensitivities. Most issues are devoted to specific topics and articles appearing in these issues are commissioned or result from a call-for-papers on a particular subject. One issue is comprised of unrelated articles and published annually. Journal reviews books.

Manuscript Information: Articles up to 30 double-spaced typescript pages. Notes up to 2 double-spaced pages. Book reviews up to 6 double-spaced typescript pages. Style: Request Style Sheet or Chicago. 2 copies of manuscript required. Submit abstract in English for articles not written in English. Report in 4–6 months. Rejected manuscripts returned with S.A.S.E.

Payment: 25 offprints.

Indexed In: ASCA Current Contents, Language Teaching, Linguistic Abstracts, Linguistics and Language Behavior Abstracts, Social Science Citation Index, Sociological Abstracts, International Bibliography of the Social Sciences.

Copyright: Mouton de Gruyter. Reprinting permitted after 2 years.

INTERNATIONAL REVIEW OF APPLIED LINGUISTICS IN LANGUAGE TEACHING

P. O. Box 629, 69 Heidelberg, Germany. Rates: $50 per year individuals. $95 per year institutions. Founded 1963. Self-supporting. Published quarterly.

Major Field(s) of Interest: Applied linguistics, language acquisition, contrastive linguistics, error analysis, and language teaching methodology. Journal reviews books.

Manuscript Information: Articles up to 25 double-spaced typescript pages. Notes up to 20 pages. Book reviews up to 3 pages. Style: MLA with notes at end of articles. 2 copies of manuscript required. Provide a one-half page abstract. Report in 3 months. Rejected manuscripts are not returned.

Payment: 1 copy of the issue and 30 free offprints.

Indexed In: ERIC, LLBA, Language Teaching and Linguistics, MLA International Bibliography.

Copyright: By Julius Groos Verlag.

JOURNAL OF CHILD LANGUAGE

Department of Linguistics, University of Manchester, Manchester, MI3 9PL, England. Rates: £28 per year individuals. £63 per year institutions outside the UK. Sponsored by the Cambridge University Press. Published 3 times per year.

Major Field(s) of Interest: Articles on all aspects of language development in children. This includes crying, babbling, auditory-perceptual ability in prelinguistic babies, the development of phonology, intonation, grammer, semantics, pragmatics, and the social and cognitive aspects of language. It also covers the study of related topics like imitation, and parental speech to children. Crosslinguistic comparisons showing language universals and language difference are also included. Studies on the development of sign language, of the language of disabled children and of the development of reading and writing are included where they relate to more general matters of language development. In addition, the journal contains a "Notes and Discussion" section with short pieces of data illustrating points of general theoretical interest. Journal reviews books.

Manuscript Information: Articles up to 20 pages. Notes up to 5 pages. Book reviews of 500–2,000 words. Style: Journal. Consult the back cover of the journal. 3 copies of manuscript required. Report in 3 months. Rejected manuscripts returned upon request.

Payment: Copies.

Copyright: By Cambridge University Press.

*JOURNAL OF COMMUNICATION

University of Pennsylvania, 3620 Walnut Street, Philadelphia, PA 19104–6220. Rates: $30 per year individuals. $65 per year institutions. Founded 1950. Sponsored by the University of Pennsylvania. Published quarterly.

Major Field(s) of Interest: Concerned with the study of communication theory, research, practice, and policy. It is addressed to those in every field who are interested in research and policy developments and in the public impact of communication studies. The editors welcome contributions (articles, brief reports, book reviews, news notes, and other communications) devoted to significant problems and issues in communications and to events and work of wide professional and scholarly interest. Journal reviews books.

Manuscript Information: Articles of 15–25 pages. Book reviews of 3–6 pages. Style: Journal. 3 copies of typed, double-spaced manuscripts should be submitted with a 50-word abstract. Report in 3–6 months. Rejected manuscripts returned with S.A.S.E.

Payment: 1 copy.

Indexed In: Behavioural Abstracts, Communication Abstracts, Current Contents, Current Index of Computer Literature, Education Index, ERIC Current Index to Journals in Education, Film Literature Index, Historical Abstracts and American History and Life, Information Science Abstracts, International Bibliography of Periodical Literature and Book Reviews, International Index to Television Periodicals, Language & Language Behavior Abstracts, MLA International Bibliography, Political Science Abstracts, Psychological Abstracts, Sage Abstracts in Family Studies, Public Administration, Urban Studies, Social Science Citation Index, Sociological Abstracts, Topicator, United States Political Science Documents, Universal Reference System.

Copyright: By Oxford University Press. Reprints of individual articles are available only from the authors.

*Journal of English Linguistics

Department of English, Park Hall, University of Georgia, Athens, GA 30602. Rates: $15 per year individuals. $20 per year institutions. Founded 1967. Independent. Published semiannually (April and October).

Major Field(s) of Interest: Journal publishes articles and reviews of books on the historical and modern periods of the English language. Topics from comparative studies, language contact, pidgins and creoles, stylistics, and other such fields are acceptable as long as they have their focus on the English language. The journal does not restrict the linguistic approach contributors may take, but it insists that all articles be accessible to readers without particular advance theoretical training.

Manuscript Information: Articles of 10–15 typescript pages. Notes of 5–10 pages. Book reviews up to 5 pages. Style: LSA and New MLA. 2 copies of manuscript required. Report in 3 months. Rejected manuscripts returned with S.A.S.E.

Payment: 20 offprints.

Indexed In: MLA International Bibliography, MHRA, A&H Citation Index, Current Contents, International Bibliography of Periodical Literature, International Bibliography of Book Reviews, Linguistics and Language Behavior Abstracts, Linguistics Abstracts.

Copyright: By the journal. Permission to reprint granted without a fee.

Journal of Language and Social Psychology

Multilingual Matters Ltd., Bank House, 8a Hill Road, Clevedon, Avon, BS21 7HH, England. Rates: $49 per year individuals. $143 per year institutions. Founded 1982. Sponsored by the editor: Howard Giles. Published quarterly.

Major Field(s) of Interest: The journal encourages language specialists and language-in-education researchers to organize, construe, and present their material in such a way as to highlight its educational implications, thereby influencing educational theorists and practitioners and therefore educational outcomes for individual children. Articles are drawn from important subject matter and well-communicated implications in the areas of curriculum, pedagogy, or evaluations. Journal reviews books.

Manuscript Information: Articles up to 7,000 words. Notes up to 500 words. Book reviews of 500–2,500 words. Letters to the Editor up to 500 words. Style: Journal. See "Notes on the Submission of Manuscripts." 4 copies of manuscript required. Include a 200–word abstract. Contributions and queries should be sent to the editor: Professor H. Giles, Department of Communication Studies, University of California,

Santa Barbara, CA 93106, USA. Report in 3 months. Rejected manuscripts returned with S.A.S.E.

Payment: 50 free offprints.

Indexed In: Linguistic Abstracts, Multilingual Abstracts, LLBA, Institute for Scientific Information, Modern Language Association Intern, World List of Social Science Periodicals, and others.

Copyright: By the author, who can reproduce his/her article with usual credit line.

THE JOURNAL OF LANGUAGE FOR INTERNATIONAL BUSINESS

American Graduate School of International Management, Department of Modern Languages, Thunderbird Campus, Glendale, AZ 85306. Rates: $15 per year individuals. $25 per year institutions. Founded 1984. Sponsored by the American Graduate School of International Management. Published semiannually.

Major Field(s) of Interest: Articles pertaining to the use of language in business. Journal reviews books.

Manuscript Information: Articles of 12–15 double-spaced typescripts. Style: *MLA Style Sheet.* Report in 3 months. Rejected manuscripts returned.

Payment: None.

Copyright: By the journal.

JOURNAL OF LINGUISTICS

Department of Linguistics, University of Manchester, Manchester, M13 9PL, England. Rates: £39 per year individuals. £75 per year institutions. Sponsored by the Linguistics Association of Great Britain. Founded 1965. Published 2 times per year (March and September).

Major Field(s) of Interest: All areas of linguistics, including phonetics and theoretical linguistics. Preference is for articles that have a general and theoretical interest, but an attempt is made to cover as wide a field as possible and to include articles on a variety of languages. Each issue contains a section devoted to comments arising from recent articles. Journal reviews books.

Manuscript Information: Articles of 10–50 typescript pages. Notes up to 10 typescript pages. Book reviews of 1,000–2,000 words. Style: Linguistic Society of America. Consult "Guide to Contributors" printed in each issue. 3 copies of manuscript required. Report in 2–3 months. Rejected manuscripts returned.

Payment: 25 free offprints.

Copyright: By Cambridge University Press. Reprint rights are usually granted.

Journal of Literary Semantics

Honeywood Cottage, 35 Seaton Avenue, Hythe, Kent, CT21 5HH, England. Rates: DM 68 per year individuals, DM 74 per year institutions. Founded 1972. Sponsored by Academic Headquarters: School of European and Modern Language Studies, University of Kent, Canterbury, England. Published 3 times per year.

Major Field(s) of Interest: Articles on all aspects of literary semantics. The journal concentrates on the endeavors of theoretical linguists upon those texts traditionally classed as literary in the belief that such texts are a central, not a peripheral, concern of linguistics. In order to be of interest to those who work in the field of applied linguistics, the journal publishes articles of a philosophical nature in an attempt to relate the study of literature to other disciplines such as psychology, neurophysiology, mathematics, and history. It also publishes articles dealing with the educational problems inherent in the study of literature. Journal reviews books whose subject matter is germane to literary semantics.

Manuscript Information: No length restrictions on articles, notes, or book reviews. Style: *International Review of Applied Linguistics in Language Teaching.* Footnotes at end of article. Report in 1 month. Rejected manuscripts returned with S.A.S.E.

Payment: 25 free offprints.

Copyright: By Julius Groos Verlag, Hertzstrasse 6, P. O. Box 10 24 23, D–6900 Heidelberg 1, Federal Republic of Germany.

Journal of Memory and Language

Department of Psychology, Carnegie-Mellon University, Pittsburgh, PA 15213. Rates: $83.50 per year individuals. $152.00 per year institutions. Founded 1962. Sponsored by the Academic Press. Published 6 times per year.

Major Field(s) of Interest: Articles concerned with experimental, theoretical, and practical problems of language comprehension and production, human learning and memory, and other related language processes. Editorial evaluations of articles is based on the following criteria: significance of the problem and precision of its statement; linkage of the problem with previous relevant work; credibility of the relation between the stated problem and the experimental design; adequacy of the experiment per se; appropriateness and sufficiency of the data analysis; clarity of the relation between the results and the stated problem; and the importance of the problem-design results package as a whole.

Manuscript Information: No length restrictions on articles. Style: American Psychological Association. 4 copies of manuscript required. Include a 120-word abstract. Report in 3 months. Rejected manuscripts are not returned.

Payment: Copies.

Copyright: By the Academic Press.

JOURNAL OF MULTILINGUAL AND MULTICULTURAL DEVELOPMENT

Multilingual Matters Ltd., Bank House, 8a Hill Road, Clevedon, Avon, BS21 7HH, England. Rates: $49 per year individuals. $143 per year institutions. Founded 1980. Published 6 times per year.

Major Field(s) of Interest: The journal is interested in the many aspects of multilingualism and multiculturalism. It publishes research, studies, and criticism of educational policies and systems, teaching and learning strategies, assessment, bilingualism, rights and obligations of minorities, and interaction between cultures. Journal reviews books.

Manuscript Information: Articles up to 7,000 words. Notes up to 500 words. Book reviews of 500-2,500 words. Style: See "Notes on the Submission of Manuscripts" contained in the journal. 3 copies of manuscript required. Include abstract up to 200-words. Report in 3 months. Rejected manuscripts returned with S.A.S.E.

Payment: 10 copies of the journal.

Indexed In: World List of Social Science Periodicals, Sociology of Education Abstracts, Sociology Abstracts, Multicultural Education Abstracts, Linguistic Abstracts, Multilingual Abstracts, MLA International Bibliography, Institute for Scientific Information, ERIC Clearing for Language and Linguistics.

Copyright: By the author who can reproduce his/her work with usual credit line.

JOURNAL OF PSYCHOLINGUISTIC RESEARCH

John Jay College of Criminal Justice, City University of New York, Room 5113, 444 W. 56th Street, New York, NY 10019. Rates: $60 per year individuals. $215 per year institutions. Founded 1971. Sponsored by the City University of New York. Published 6 times per year.

Major Field(s) of Interest: Original theoretical and experimental papers, critical surveys, and book reviews covering a broad range of approaches to the study of the communicative process, including the social and anthropological bases of communication, development of speech and language, semantics (problems in linguistic meaning), biological foundations, psychopathological aspects, and educational psycholinguistics. Journal reviews books.

Manuscript Information: No length restrictions on articles, notes, or book reviews. Style: American Psychological Association. 4 copies of manuscript required. Include an abstract of 150 words. Report in 1–3 months. Rejected manuscripts returned.

Payment: Copies.

Copyright: By the Plenum Publishing Corporation.

LANGUAGE, CULTURE AND CURRICULUM

Multilingual Matters Ltd., Bank House, 8a Hill Road, Clevedon, Avon, BS21 7HH, England. Rates: $38 per year individuals. $110 per year institutions. Founded 1988. Sponsored by The Linguistic Institute of Ireland. Published 3 times per year.

Major Field(s) of Interest: The journal provides a forum for the discussion of social, cultural, cognitive, and organizational factors relevant to the formulation and implementation of language curricula. Second languages, minority and heritage languages are a special concern. First languages and foreign language studies are also welcome when they have implications for multiculturalism. Journal reviews books.

Manuscript Information: Articles up to 7,000 words. Notes up to 500 words. Book reviews of 500–2,500 words. Style: See "Notes on the Submission of Manuscripts" contained in the journal. 4 copies of manuscript required. 200 word abstract required. Report in 8–12 weeks. Rejected manuscripts returned with S.A.S.E.

Payment: 10 copies of the issue.

Indexed In: MLA International Bibliography, LLBA, Sociology of Abstracts, Content Page in Education.

Copyright: By the author who can reproduce his/her article with the usual credit line.

LANGUAGE: JOURNAL OF THE LINGUISTIC SOCIETY OF AMERICA

Department of Linguistics, University of Pittsburgh, Pittsburgh, PA 15260. Rates: $45 per year individuals. $75 per year institutions. Includes membership in the Linguistic Society of America. Founded 1924. Published quarterly.

Major Field(s) of Interest: Scholarly articles that deal with any subfield of the linguistic sciences and reviews of recently published works.

Manuscript Information: No length restrictions on articles or book reviews. Notes up to 2,500 words. Style: Linguistic Society of America. 3 copies of manuscript required. 100–word abstract required. Report in 3 months. Rejected manuscripts returned with S.A.S.E.

Payment: None.

Copyright: By the Linguistic Society. Permission to reprint must be requested.

LANGUAGE AND EDUCATION: AN INTERNATIONAL JOURNAL
Multilingual Matters Ltd., Bank House, 8a Hill Road, Clevedon, Avon, BS21 7HH, England. Rates: $46 per year individuals. $137 per year institutions. Founded 1987. Published quarterly.

Major Field(s) of Interest: The journal encourages language specialists and language in education researchers to organize, construe, and present their material in such a way as to highlight its educational implications, thereby influencing educational theorists and practitioners and therefore educational outcomes for individual children. The journal publishes articles that draw their subject matter from curriculum, pedagogy, and evaluation in education. Journal reviews books.

Manuscript Information: Articles up to 7,000 words. Notes up to 500 words. Book reviews of 500–2,500 words. Style: See "Notes on the Submission of Manuscripts" contained in the journal. 4 copies of manuscript required. 200–word abstract required. Report in 8–12 weeks. Rejected manuscripts returned with S.A.S.E.

Payment: 10 copies of the issue.

Indexed In: Linguistic and Language Behavior Abstracts, Sociology Abstracts, Content Page in Education World List of Social Science Periodicals.

Copyright: By the author who can reproduce his/her article with the usual credit line.

LANGUAGE AND SPEECH
Department of Linguistics, U–145, Room 230, 341 Mansfield Road, University of Connecticut, Storrs, CT 06268. Rates: $140 per year. Founded 1958. Published 4 times per year (March, June, September, December).

Major Field(s) of Interest: Articles on the production and perception of speech, psycholinguistics, linguistic basis of reading, and sociolinguistics. Experimental approaches are preferred. Journal reviews books, but book reviews are commissioned.

Manuscript Information: Articles of 20–30 double-spaced typescripts. Notes of 8 double-spaced typescripts. Book reviews of 5 double-spaced typescripts. Style: Journal. 3 copies of manuscript required. Submit original typescript. Include a short summary up to 4 keywords, postal address, and title of each co-author. Report in 3 months. Rejected manuscripts returned.

Payment: Copies.
Copyright: By the journal.

LANGUAGE AND STYLE: AN INTERNATIONAL JOURNAL
Department of English, Queens College, CUNY, Flushing, NY 11367.
Rates: $16 per year individuals. $22 per year institutions. Founded 1968.
Sponsored by Queens College of the City University of New York. Published quarterly.

Major Field(s) of Interest: Articles on style in all of its manifestations in all of the arts and in all social and cultural contexts. Articles may be written in English, French, or German. There are no restrictions on theoretical approaches. Any consistent and well-defined system, from mathematical linguistics to traditional rhetorical analysis may be employed. It should be possible to employ the analytical method in each article in a general definition of style.

Manuscript Information: Articles of 4,000–25,000 words. Style: Manuscripts should be typed on one side of unglazed paper, double-spaced (including footnotes, quotations, and bibliography), with margins of not less than 1½ inches. References should be placed at the end of the text in alphabetical order as should all special material such as diagrams, tables, charts, etc. 2 copies of manuscript required. Only complete manuscripts are considered. Report in 4–6 weeks. Abstracts requested after acceptance. Rejected manuscripts returned with S.A.S.E.

Payment: 2 copies of the journal and 25 offprints of the article.
Indexed In: American Humanities Index.
Copyright: By the author.

LANGUAGE IN SOCIETY
Department of Anthropology, University of Virginia, Cabrill Hall, Charlottesville, VA 22903. Rates: $42 per year individuals. $80 per year institutions. Founded 1972. Sponsored by Cambridge University Press. Published quarterly (March, June, September, December).

Major Field(s) of Interest: Articles concerned with all branches of the theoretical and empirical study of speech and language as aspects of social life. Journal reviews books.

Manuscript Information: Articles of 25–30 pages. Notes of 500–750 words. Book reviews of 2,000–2,500 words. Style: Linguistic Society of America and Chicago. Notes at end of manuscript. 2 copies of manuscript required. Report in 2 months. Rejected manuscript returned upon request. Send S.A.S.E.

Payment: Reprints.
Copyright: By Cambridge University Press. Authors may reprint in their own work.

LANGUAGE LEARNING: A JOURNAL OF APPLIED LINGUISTICS
178 Henry S. Frieze Building, The University of Michigan, Ann Arbor,
MI 48109–1285. Rates: $30 per year individuals. $50 per year institutions. Founded 1948. Sponsored by the University of Michigan. Published
quarterly.

Major Field(s) of Interest: The journal publishes research articles in
applied linguistics and the practical aspects of language acquisition to
those concerned with the learning of language. The journal welcomes
studies in psycholinguistics, anthropological linguistics, sociolinguistics,
language behavior, language pedagogy, and second-language acquisition.
Journal reviews books.

Manuscript Information: No length restrictions on articles or book
reviews. Style: APA. 4 copies of manuscript required. Abstract of 100–
200 words required. The journal encourages submission of articles on
disk using MicrosoftWord (Macintosh). Report in 3–4 months. Rejected
manuscripts are not returned.

Payment: 20 free reprints.

*Indexed In: Social Science Citation Index, Language Behavior Ab-
stracts.*

Copyright: By the journal.

LANGUAGE PROBLEMS AND LANGUAGE PLANNING
North American Editor, Humphrey Tonkin, University of Hartford,
West Hartford, CT 06117. Rates: $35 per year individuals. $66 per year
institutions. Founded 1962. Sponsored by the Center for Research and
Documentation on World Language Problems. Published 3 times per year.

Major Field(s) of Interest: The journal publishes articles on political,
sociological, and economic aspects of language and language use. The
journal is especially interested in the relationships between and among
language communities, particularly in international contexts. It welcomes
articles on language policy, language management, and language use in
international organizations, multinational enterprises as well as theoretical studies on global communication, language interaction, and language
conflict. Contributions in languages other than English are encouraged,
and the journal accepts articles in Esperanto, French, Spanish, Portuguese, German, and Italian. Journal reviews books.

Manuscript Information: Articles up to 20 double-spaced pages preferred. Notes up to 10 pages. Book reviews up to 2 pages. Style: Chicago.
2 copies of manuscripts required. Abstract required in language of article
and 1 other language. Report in 2–4 months. Rejected manuscripts returned with S.A.S.E.

Payment: 2 copies of the issue.
Copyright: By John Benjamins Publishing Company, P. O. Box 52519, 1007 Amsterdam, Netherlands.

LANGUAGE TESTING
Department of Linguistic Science, University of Reading, Whiteknights, Reading, RG2 2AA, England. Rates: $33 per year individuals. $47 per year institutions. Founded 1984. Sponsored by Edward Arnold (Publishers) Ltd., Woodlands Park Avenue, Maidenhead, Berkshire, UK. Published 2 times per year (June and December).

Major Field(s) of Interest: The journal provides a forum for the exchange of ideas and information between people working in the fields of first and second language testing and assessment. These include researchers and practitioners in English as a foreign language, mother tongue testing and assessment in child language acquisition and language pathology. Journal reviews books, but unsolicited book reviews are not accepted.

Manuscript Information: Articles of 4,000–8,000 words. Book reviews up to 1,000 words. Style: Harvard. Report in 6 months. Rejected manuscripts returned upon request. Include S.A.S.E.

Payment: Copies.
Copyright: By Edward Arnold Publishers Ltd.

THE LINGUIST
Institute of Linguists, 24a Highbury Grove, London, N5 2EA, England. Rates: £15 per year. Founded 1962. Sponsored by the Institute of Linguists. Published 4 times per year (Winter, Spring, Summer, Fall).

Major Field(s) of Interest: Articles, reviews, and news of interest to the professional linguist. Articles deal with language in general, linguistics, and translation. The journal publishes in all languages using Roman alphabet; other languages are published if camera-ready copy is made available. Journal reviews books.

Manuscript Information: Articles of 3,000–4,000 words. Notes of 500–1,000 words. Book reviews of 500–1,000 words. Style: Journal. 2 copies of manuscript required. Submit double-spaced typescript on size A4 (8¼ inch x 11¾ inch) paper. Report in 1 month. Rejected manuscripts returned.

Payment: Copies.
Copyright: By the Institute of Linguists and by the author.

LINGUISTIC ANALYSIS
P. O. Box 95679, Seattle, WA 98145. Rates: $52.50 per year individuals. $105.00 per year institutions. Independent. Published quarterly.

Major Field(s) of Interest: A research journal devoted to the publication of high quality articles in formal language, the journal is interested in manuscripts on syntax, semantics, and phonology. Journal reviews books.

Manuscript Information: Articles of 10–60 typescript pages. Notes of 3–12 pages. Book reviews of 3–50 pages. Style: LSA. See journal. 3 copies of manuscript required with abstract. Report in 1–3 months. Rejected manuscripts returned with S.A.S.E.

Payment: 5 copies of the journal.

Indexed In: Bowkers and others.

Copyright: By Reynard House.

LINGUISTIC INQUIRY

MIT Building 20D–213, Cambridge, MA 02139. Rates: $27.50 per year individuals. $19.00 per year students and retired. $60.00 per year institutions. Founded 1970. Sponsored by the Massachusetts Institute of Technology. Published quarterly (Winter, Spring, Summer, Fall).

Major Field(s) of Interest: The journal is interested in research on current topics in linguistic theory. It publishes research on new theoretical developments by presenting the latest in international research. It also publishes shorter contributions (squibs and discussion) and more extensive commentary (remarks and replies) as well as full-scale articles.

Manuscript Information: Articles up to 50 pages. Shorter manuscripts, accepted as squibs, should not exceed 5 double-spaced pages. Style: Journal. Contributors should follow the *Linguistic Inquiry* Style Sheet in preparing and typing manuscripts for submission. Copies of the Style Sheet may be obtained from the Editor. The Style Sheet may also be found in *Linguistic Inquiry* 1, Volume 15, 563–567. 3 copies of manuscript required. One of these must be the original typed copy. Report in 4 months. Rejected manuscripts returned, but 1 is retained for files.

Payment: 1 copy of the journal and some offprints.

Indexed In: Arts & Humanities Citation Index, Current Contents / Arts & Humanities, Current Contents / Social & Behavior Sciences, Language Teaching and Linguistics Abstracts, Linguistics and Language Behavior Abstracts, Linguistic Bibliography, MLA International Bibliography.

Copyright: By the Massachussetts Institute of Technology.

LINGUISTICS AND PHILOSOPHY: AN INTERNATIONAL JOURNAL

Department of Linguistics, University of Wisconsin, Madison, WI 53706. Sponsored by D. Reidel Publishing Company. Published 4 times per year.

Major Field(s) of Interest: Focuses on traditional areas of language such as meaning and truth, reference, description, entailment, speech acts and traditional areas of linguistics such as syntax, semantics and pragmatics (when the studies are of sufficient explicitness and generality to be also of philosophical interest); systems of logic with strong connections to natural language; modal logic, tense logic, epistemic logic, intentional logic; philosophical questions raised by linguistics as a science: linguistic methodology, the status of linguistic theories, the nature of linguistic universals; philosophically interesting problems at the intersection of linguistics and other disciplines: language acquisition, language and perception, language as a social convention. Contributions may be in the form of articles, review articles, notes, discussions, or remarks and replies. Reviews of books and monographs are relatively few in number and restricted to those publications of the widest possible interest. Book reviews are commissioned.

Manuscript Information: Articles of 2,500–10,000 words. Notes up to 1,000 words. Book reviews up to 2,500 words. Style: None. 3 copies of manuscript required. Submit double-spaced typescript with footnotes numbered consecutively. Report in 3–4 months. Rejected manuscripts are retained.

Payment: Copies.

Copyright: By D. Reidel Publishing Company.

LITERARY AND LINGUISTIC COMPUTING: JOURNAL OF THE ASSOCIATION FOR LITERARY AND LINGUISTIC COMPUTING

Institute of Advanced Studies, Manchester Polytechnic, All Saints Building, Oxford Road, Manchester, M15 6BH, England. Rates: £40 per year United Kingdom and Europe. $72 per year rest of the world. Founded 1986. Sponsored by the Association for Literary and Linguistic Computing. Published quarterly.

Major Field(s) of Interest: All aspects of computing applied to literature and language. Proposals are sought for papers dealing with the results of research into language and literature computer applications. Papers that deal with hardware and software, computer-assisted language learning, word processing for the humanities and the teaching of computer techniques to language and literature students are also appropriate. Survey papers that introduce computing techniques or papers that cover new linguistic methodologies, new applications, and work in progress are also sought. Journal reviews books.

Manuscript Information: Articles up to 9,000 words. Notes up to 1,000 words. Book reviews up to 2,000 words. Style: See journal. Endnotes only. 2 copies of manuscript required. Submit 200–word or less abstract. Report in 7 weeks. Rejected manuscripts returned with S.A.S.E.

Payment: 30 free offprints for articles.

Copyright: By Oxford University Press. Reprint permitted with due acknowledgement.

THE MODERN LANGUAGE JOURNAL

Department of German, Ohio State University, Columbus, OH 43210. Rates: $15 per year individuals. $35 per year institutions. Founded 1916. Sponsored by the National Federation of Modern Language Teachers Associations. Published 4 times per year.

Major Field(s) of Interest: Devoted primarily to methods, pedagogical research, and topics of professional interest to all language teachers. Publishes articles and reviews in the areas of Italian, Spanish, French, German, and all other foreign languages, applied and general linguistics, foreign language methodology, and research. Journal reviews books.

Manuscript Information: Articles up to 20–30 double-spaced typescript including notes. Book reviews up to 500 words. Style: *MLA Style Manual.* Manuscripts should be prepared for anonymous evaluation, and author identification must be removed. 3 copies of manuscript required. Report in 10–14 weeks. Rejected manuscripts returned. Include $4 in loose postage and S.A.S.E.

Payment: Copies.

Copyright: By the journal.

MLN

The Humanities Center, 114 Gilman Hall, The Johns Hopkins University, Baltimore, MD 21218. Rates: $27 per year individuals. $70 per year institutions. Founded 1886. Sponsored by The Johns Hopkins University Press. Published 5 times per year.

Major Field(s) of Interest: Articles, position papers, symposia, notes, and book reviews covering each of the major Romance and Germanic languages—French, German, Italian, Spanish, and English. Its historical range is from medieval to "post-modern." The first four issues published each year center on discussion of the literary and related critical works of a single language. The fifth issue presents comparative approaches to literary texts and theoretical debates. The comparative literature issue also publishes articles on general critical theory. Journal reviews books, but reviews are commissioned.

Manuscript Information: Articles of 20–35 pages. Notes of 5–8 pages. Book reviews up to 5 pages. Style: MLA with endnotes. 2 copies of manuscript required. Report in 3–6 months. Rejected manuscripts returned with S.A.S.E.

Payment: 25 offprints for articles. 2 copies for reviews.

Indexed In: Abstracts of English Studies, Arts and Humanities Citation Index, Book Review Index, Current Contents, Humanities Index International Index of Periodicals, International Bibliography of Periodical Literature, International Bibliography of Book Reviews, Linguistics and Language Behavior Abstracts, MLA International Bibliography, MLA Abstracts.

Copyright: By The Johns Hopkins University Press. Authors are uniformly granted reprint rights.

THE MODERN LANGUAGE REVIEW

Birkbeck College, University of London, Malet Street. London, WC1E 7HX, England. Rates: $25 per year individuals. $70 per year institutions. Founded 1918. Sponsored by the Modern Humanities Research Association. Published 4 times per year (January, April, July, October).

Major Field(s) of Interest: Articles on language and literature, embodying the results of research or criticism, as well as previously unpublished texts and documents. Journal reviews books.

Manuscript Information: Articles of 6,000–8,000 words. Book reviews of 500–1,000 words. Style: Modern Humanities Research Association. 2 copies of manuscript required. Submit original typescript, preferably on size A4 (8¼ inch x 11¾ inch) paper and 1 copy. Report in 2 months. Rejected manuscripts returned.

Payment: Copies.

Copyright: By the journal.

*MODERN LANGUAGE STUDIES

Department of English, Box 1852, Brown University, Providence, RI 02912. Rates: $25 per year. Founded 1970. Sponsored by the Northeast Modern Language Association and Brown University. Published 4 times per year (Winter, Spring, Summer, Fall).

Major Field(s) of Interest: Articles of interest to teachers and scholars in the areas of English, American, and comparative literatures and modern foreign languages. Journal reviews books, but unsolicited book reviews are not accepted. Contributors must be a member of the Northeast Modern Language Association.

Manuscript Information: Articles of 2,500–5,000 words. Notes up to 1,000 words. Book reviews up to 1,000 words. Style: MLA. 2 copies of manuscript required. Submit original typescript and include a 100–word abstract in English if the article is in a foreign language. Report in 3 months. Rejected manuscripts returned with S.A.S.E.

Payment: Copies.

Copyright: By the Northeast Modern Language Association.

MODERN LANGUAGES: JOURNAL OF THE MODERN LANGUAGE ASSOCIATION

10 Holt Park Way, Leeds, LS16 7QR, England. Rates: $10 per year individuals. $30 per year institutions. Founded 1905. Sponsored by the Modern Language Association of Great Britain. Published 4 times per year.

Major Field(s) of Interest: Articles of literary, linguistic, cultural, and pedagogical interest in modern language. Journal reviews books.

Manuscript Information: Articles up to 3,000 words. Book reviews of 350–700 words. Style: MLA. 2 copies of manuscript required. Report in 2 months. Rejected manuscripts returned.

Payment: Copies.

Copyright: By the Modern Language Association of Great Britain.

NATURAL LANGUAGE & LINGUISTIC THEORY

Linguistics Program, Department of Psychology, Brandeis University, Waltham, MA 02254. Rates: $30 per year. Founded 1983. Sponsored by D. Reidel Publishing Company. Published 4 times per year.

Major Field(s) of Interest: Articles on theoretical research concerning natural language data including syntax, semantics, phonology, and morphology. The journal also publishes survey articles of recent developments and replies to papers. Journal reviews books.

Manuscript Information: Articles up to 50 pages. Notes up to 5 pages. Book reviews up to 1,500 words. Style: Style specifications are available from D. Reidel Publishing Company, Box 17, 3300 AA Dordrecht, Netherlands. 4 copies of manuscript required. Submit author's name and address on separate page, not on manuscript. 4 copies of manuscript required. Report in 4–6 months. Rejected manuscripts are not returned.

Payment: Copies.

Copyright: By D. Reidel Publishing Company.

NEWSLETTER OF THE AMERICAN DIALECT SOCIETY

English Department, MacMurray College, Jacksonville, IL 62650. Rates: $20 per year (includes membership in the American Dialect Society). Founded 1969. Sponsored by the American Dialect Society. Published 3 times per year.

Major Field(s) of Interest: Publishes report of studies of dialects in North America as well as news of the American Dialect Society.

Manuscript Information: No length restrictions on articles. Style: None. Report in 4 months. Rejected manuscripts returned upon request.

Payment: Copies.

Copyright: By the author.

*NINETEENTH-CENTURY FRENCH STUDIES

Department of Foreign Languages & Literatures, SUNY College at Fredonia, Fredonia, NY 14063. Rates: $24 per year individuals. $28 per year institutions. Founded 1972. Sponsored by SUNY College at Fredonia. Published twice a year in two double issues (Fall/Winter; Spring/Summer).

Major Field(s) of Interest: Scholarly articles on all aspects of nineteenth-century French literature and criticism. Studies from a philosophical, psychological, sociological, cultural, historical, or critical point of view are invited. Journal reviews books; reviews include works from a wide variety of disciplines that serve to illuminate the literature of the period.

Manuscript Information: Articles up to 5,000 words. Notes up to 500 words. Book reviews up to 750 words. Style: MLA. Endnotes. 2 copies of manuscript required. Report in 60–90 days. Rejected manuscripts returned with S.A.S.E. 100–150 word abstract required for all accepted articles.

Payment: 25 offprints.

Indexed In: MLA International Bibliography, Romantic Movement Bibliography.

Copyright: By the journal. Permission to reprint always granted.

NOTES ON LINGUISTICS

International Linguistics Center, 7500 West Camp Wisdom Road, Dallas, TX 75236. Rates: $10 per year plus postage. Founded 1977. Sponsored by the Summer Institute of Linguistics. Published 4 times per year (January, April, July, October).

Major Field(s) of Interest: Articles of general interest to linguistic field workers. Journal reviews books.

Manuscript Information: Articles of 2–20 pages. Notes up to 300 words. Book reviews up to 500 words. Style: Linguistic Society of America. Report in 1–3 weeks. Rejected manuscripts returned.

Payment: Copies.

Copyright: By the journal.

NOTES ON TRANSLATION

International Linguistics Center, 7500 West Camp Wisdom Road, Dallas, TX 75236. Rates: $10 per year. Founded 1962. Sponsored by the Summer Institute of Linguistics. Published 6 times per year.

Major Field(s) of Interest: Serves the Summer Institute of Linguistics program of translation by sharing information of a practical or theoretical nature with translators. Journal reviews books.

Manuscript Information: Articles of 8–25 pages. Notes of 1 page. Book reviews of 1–2 pages. Style: Chicago. Report in 6 months. Rejected manuscripts are not returned.

Payment: Copies.

Copyright: By the Summer Institute of Linguistics.

OCEANIC LINGUISTICS

Department of Linguistics, University of Hawaii, 1890 East-West Road, Honolulu, HI 96822. Rates: $12 per year individuals. $14 per year institutions. Founded 1962. Sponsored by the University of Hawaii. Published 2 times per year.

Major Field(s) of Interest: Articles that convey competent information and better communication across national boundaries on current research bearing on the languages of the Oceanic area. "Oceanic" languages for the purposes of the periodical are defined as including Malayo-Polynesian (Austronesian), Papuan, and Australian languages. Journal reviews books.

Manuscript Information: No length restrictions on articles, notes, or reviews. Style: Linguistic Society of America. 2 copies of manuscripts required. Report in 4 months. Rejected manuscripts returned.

Payment: Copies.

Copyright: By the journal.

OLD ENGLISH NEWSLETTER

Center for Medieval & Early Renaissance Studies, State University of New York, Binghamton, NY 13901. Rates: $3 per year individuals; $6 per year institutions. Founded 1967. Sponsored by the State University of New York, Binghamton, Center for Medieval & Early Renaissance Studies, and MLA Old English Division. Published biannually, Fall and Spring. Bibliographical issue in Spring.

Major Field(s) of Interest: Anglo-Saxon Studies: with special reference to Old English literature and language. Includes an annual bibliography and review. Articles selected by peer review and commissions. *OENews* reviews books. Reviews are published by invitation. Journal publishes translations sometimes.

Manuscript Information: Articles of 10 pages single-spaced. Notes of 1 page. Style: Older MLA. Footnote form: Older MLA. 2 copies of manuscripts required. Report in 3–5 months. Rejected manuscripts returned with S.A.S.E.

Payment: Never.

Indexed In: MLA International Bibliography.

Copyright: By the Center for Medieval & Early Renaissance Studies.

PAPERS IN LINGUISTICS: INTERNATIONAL JOURNAL OF
HUMAN COMMUNICATION
P.O. Box 5677, Station "L," Edmonton, Alberta, T6C AG1, Canada.
Founded 1969. Sponsored by the Linguistic Research, Inc. Published 4
time per year.
Major Field(s) of Interest: Articles on human and nonhuman communication theory, interaction of verbal and non-verbal modalities of
human communication, language use in sociocultural and cross-cultural
context, symbolic interaction, social psychology, intra- and inter-personal
communication, semantic and logical foundations of language, theories
of competence and/or performance, biological foundations of language,
neurolinguistics, aphasia and other communicative disorders, mass media
communication and its effect on human beings and their environment,
sociolinguistics, ethnolinguistics, cognitive anthropology, psycholinguistics, language acquisition, acquisition of communicative competence,
historical linguistics, dialectology, contacts of languages and cultures,
pedagogy and applied linguistics. Journal reviews books.

Manuscript Information: Articles up to 100 pages. Notes up to 15
pages. No length restrictions on book reviews. Style: Linguistic Society
of America. 3 copies of manuscript required. Report in 6 months. Rejected manuscripts returned.

Payment: Copies.

Copyright: By the author.

PHONETICA: INTERNATIONAL JOURNAL OF SPEECH SCIENCE
S. Karger AG, P. O. Box CH—4009, Basel, Switzerland or S. Karger
Publishers, Inc. 26 West Avon Road, P. O. Box 529, Farmington, CT
06085. Rates: $72.90 per year individuals. $243.00 per year institutions.
Founded 1957. Published quarterly.
Major Field(s) of Interest: The journal features expert original work
covering all aspects of speech communication, including phonology,
phonetics, speech perception, and production, acoustics, and perception.
The journal is interested in articles which present both theoretical issues
and empirical data, as well as discussions of methods of speech analysis
and synthesis and technical applications in the field of speech and speaker
recognition. Journal reviews books.

Manuscript Information: Manuscripts from North America should
be sent to Randy L. Diehl, Department of Psychology, Mezes Hall 330,
University of Texas at Austin, Austin, TX 78712 (USA). Manuscripts
from all other countries should be sent to Professor Dr. Klaus Kohler, In-
stitut für Phonetik und digitale Sprachverarbeitung, Universität Kiel, Ol-
shausenstrasse 40, D–2300 Kiel (FRG). No length restrictions on articles.

Book reviews of 1–2 pages. Style: Journal. Write for "Instructions to Authors." 3 copies of manuscripts required. Only original papers written in English, French, or German are considered. Submit original typescript plus 2 copies. Each paper requires an abstract in English of up to 10 lines. Papers in French or German must also have a summary in that language of not more than 10 lines. Report in 2 months. Rejected manuscripts are not returned.

Payment: 6 copies of the issue and 50 free reprints.

Indexed In: Current Contents and others.

Copyright: By S. Karger AG. Permission to reprint must be obtained from S. Karger.

PUBLICATIONS OF THE MISSISSIPPI PHILOLOGICAL ASSOCIATION
Southern Station, Box 5037, Hattiesburg, MS 39406–5037. Founded 1982. Sponsored by the Mississippi Philological Association. Published annually.

Major Field(s) of Interest: Articles on linguistics, literature, philology, semantics, and pedagogy related to these fields. The journal publishes only papers read at the annual meetings.

Manuscript Information: Articles of 5–20 pages. Style: MLA with endnotes. Report in 6 months. Rejected manuscripts returned with S.A.S.E.

Payment: 1 copy.

Indexed In: MLA International Bibliography.

Copyright: By the journal. On request, the journal will relinquish to author.

PUBLICATIONS OF THE MISSOURI PHILOLOGICAL ASSOCIATION
Department of English, Central Missouri State University, Warrensburg, MO 64093–5046. Rates: $10 per year. Founded 1975. Sponsored by the Missouri Philological Association. Published annually.

Major Field(s) of Interest: Articles in all areas of language and literature study including poetry and fiction. Submissions must have been read at annual Association meeting. Notes are considered when submitted, but they are not published in every issue.

Manuscript Information: Articles up to 10 typed pages. Notes up to 1,000 words. Style: MLA. 2 copies of manuscript required. Submit original typescript. Report in 2 months. Rejected manuscripts returned with S.A.S.E.

Payment: 2 copies.

Copyright: By the journal. Authors freely given permission to reprint.

The Quarterly Journal of Speech

Department of Speech Communication, 6030 Haley Center, Auburn University, Auburn, AL 36849. Rates: $40 per year. $20 per year for students. Founded 1915. Sponsored by the Speech Communication Association. Published quarterly.

Major Field(s) of Interest: All aspects of human communication. The journal is especially interested in articles with a strong theoretical base and those that analyze, examine, or criticize significant occurrences or problems in human communication. Journal reviews books.

Manuscript Information: Articles of 15–25 pages. 100 word abstract required with submission. Book reviews up to 1,200 words. Style: Chicago or APA with footnotes at end of article. 4 copies of manuscript required. Report in 3 months. Rejected manuscripts are not returned.

Payment: 2 copies of the journal.

Indexed In: Communication Index.

Copyright: By the Speech Communication Association. Reprint rights may be purchased from the Association.

Romance Notes

Department of Romance Languages, 238 Dey Hall, University of North Carolina, Chapel Hill, NC 27514. Rates: $15 per year individuals. $18 per year institutions. Founded 1959. Sponsored by the University of North Carolina, Chapel Hill. Published 3 times per year (Fall, Winter, Spring).

Major Field(s) of Interest: Articles on all aspects of the Romance languages and literatures.

Manuscript Information: Articles of 6–7 pages including footnotes. Style: MLA. 2 copies of manuscript required. Submit original manuscript and a 3–line abstract. Place author's name on separate sheet only. Report in 1–3 months. Computer diskette required upon acceptance. Rejected manuscripts returned with S.A.S.E.

Payment: 50 offprints.

Copyright: By the University of North Carolina.

Romance Philology

Department of French, University of California, Berkeley, CA 94720. Rates: $25 per year individuals. $45 per year institutions. Founded 1947. Sponsored by the University of California Press. Published 4 times per year (August, November, February, May).

Major Field(s) of Interest: Articles on historical Romance linguistics and on medieval literature in the Romance languages. Journal reviews books, but book reviews are commissioned. Contributors must be subscribers, reside outside North America, or be unaffiliated with the field.

Manuscript Information: Articles up to 10,000 words. Notes up to 5,000 words. Book reviews up to 2,500 words. Style: Chicago. All submissions must use the author-date system of documentation, keyed to a reference list. 3 copies of manuscript required. Report in 4 months. Rejected manuscripts returned with S.A.S.E.

Payment: Copies.

Copyright: By the Regents of the University of California.

*ROMANCE QUARTERLY

1173 Patterson Office Tower, University of Kentucky, Lexington, KY 40506-0027. Rates: $18 per year individuals. $28 per year institutions. Founded 1954. Sponsored by the University Press of Kentucky. Published quarterly.

Major Field(s) of Interest: Traditional scholarly articles on historical or interpretative subjects in all areas of Romance scholarship in English, French, and Catalan, Italian, Portuguese, and Spanish. Journal reviews books.

Manuscript Information: Articles up to 25 double-spaced pages. Notes up to 5 pages. Book reviews of 500–600 words. Style: Old MLA. Footnotes Form: Modified Chicago. 2 copies of manuscripts required. Report in 6 weeks. Rejected manuscripts returned with S.A.S.E.

Payment: None.

Indexed In: MLA International Bibliography.

Copyright: By the University Press of Kentucky. Reprinting rights freely granted.

THE SECOL REVIEW: SOUTHEASTERN CONFERENCE ON LINGUISTICS

Box 275, Middle Tennessee State University, Murfreesboro, TN 37132. Rates: $15 per year. Sponsored by the Southeastern Conference on Linguistics and Middle Tennessee State University. Published 3 times per year.

Major Field(s) of Interest: Articles on all aspects of linguistics including literature. Contributors should be members of the Southeastern Conference on Linguistics. Journal reviews books.

Manuscript Information: No length restrictions on articles or book reviews. Notes up to 100 words. Style: MLA or Linguistic Society of America. 3 copies of manuscript required. Report in 4 months. Rejected manuscripts returned upon request.

Payment: Copies.

Copyright: By the journal.

SEMIOTEXT(E)

522 Philosophy Hall, Columbia University, New York, NY 10027. Founded 1974. Sponsored by the National Endowment for the Arts, New York State Council on the Arts, and Coordinating Council of Literary Magazines. Published 3 times per year.

Major Field(s) of Interest: Focus is on analyzing the power mechanisms which produce and maintain the present divisions of knowledge (psychoanalysis, linguistics, literature, philosophy, semiotics).

Manuscript Information: Articles of 10–15 pages. Style: MLA. 2 copies of manuscript required. Report in 3 months. Rejected manuscripts are not returned.

Payment: Copies.

Copyright: By the journal.

SIGN LANGUAGE STUDIES

Linstock Press Inc., 9306 Mintwood Street, Silver Spring, MD 20901–3599. Rates: $40 per year individuals. $55 per year institutions. Founded 1972. Sponsored by the editor: William C. Stokoe.

Major Field(s) of Interest: Anthropological, linguistic, sociological, semiotic studies of the sign languages used by deaf populations and others. The journal welcomes studies of gestural systems and of nonvocal communication generally, facial expression, gesticulation, kinesics, language origins, communication networks, primate communications, proxemics, and semiotic systems. Journal reviews books and videotapes. Contributors must be subscribers or members of subscribing institutions.

Manuscript Information: No restrictions on length of articles, notes, or book reviews. Style: See recent issue. Report in 3 months. Submit abstract and biographical notes. Rejected manuscripts returned with S.A.S.E.

Payment: 2 copies of the issue and 25 offprints.

Indexed In: MLA International Bibliography.

Copyright: By Linstock Press.

SOCIOLINGUISTICS

Department of Sociology, University of Montana, Missoula, MT 59812. Founded 1970. Sponsored by the International Sociological Association, Research Committee on Sociolinguistics. Published 1–2 times per year.

Major Field(s) of Interest: Professional activities of the membership and readership, particularly on new developments in research and teaching in sociolinguistics. The journal hopes to draw attention to the study of language involvements in society. Journal reviews books.

Manuscript Information: Articles of 6–10 pages. Book reviews up to

1 page. Style: American Sociolinguistics Association. Report in 1 month. Rejected manuscripts returned.

Payment: Copies.

Copyright: By the journal.

The Southwest Journal of Linguistics

Department of English, Box 13827, University of North Texas, Denton, TX 76203. Rates: $15 per year individuals. $30 per year institutions. Founded 1975. Sponsored by the Linguistics Association of the Southwest. Published semiannually.

Major Field(s) of Interest: Articles on all aspects of linguistics and in any area of linguistics. Journal reviews books. Contributors must be members of the Linguistics Association of the Southwest.

Manuscript Information: Articles of 15–40 pages. Book reviews of 1,000–5,000 words. Style: Linguistic Society of America. 2 copies of manuscript required. Include a 250–word abstract. Report in 2–3 months. Rejected manuscripts returned.

Payment: 2 copies of the issue.

Indexed In: MLA International Bibliography.

Copyright: By the journal. Reprint by permission required.

Studies in Language Learning: An Interdisciplinary Review of Language Acquisition, Language Pedagogy, Stylistics and Language Planning

Language Learning Laboratory, G70 Foreign Language Building, 707 S. Mathews Street, University of Illinois, Urbana, IL 61801. Founded 1975. Sponsored by the University of Illinois, Language Learning Laboratory. Published 2 times per year (Fall and Spring).

Major Field(s) of Interest: Primarily concerned with applied linguistics and specifically with language acquisition, language pedagogy, stylistics, and language planning. The journal gives preference to contributions of a theoretical and/or methodological interest. It aims at developing interdisciplinary cooperation between faculty and students working in language-related fields in humanities, social sciences, education, and other disciplines. It includes prepublication versions of contributions from faculty and students of the University of Illinois. Invited contributions from non-University of Illinois faculty and students are also included. The journal encourages detailed papers which present the state of the art of various subfields of applied linguistics and focus on current insights and controversies in the language-related fields. Shorter notes and comments are published in the "Notes and Comments" section. One issue each year is devoted to a special topic. Journal reviews books.

Manuscript Information: Articles of 4,000–10,000 words. Notes of 300–750 words. Book reviews of 750–1,000 words. Style: Linguistics Society of America. 2 copies of reviews. 1 copy of short Notices or Publications received. Report in 2 months. Rejected manuscripts returned.

Payment: Copies.

Copyright: By the University of Illinois.

STUDIES IN THE LINGUISTIC SCIENCES

Department of Linguistics, University of Illinois at Urbana-Champaign, 4088 Foreign Languages Building 707 S. Mathews Street, Urbana, IL 61801. Rates: $15 per year. Founded 1971. Sponsored by the University of Illinois, Department of Linguistics and School of Humanities. Published 2 times per year.

Major Field(s) of Interest: Articles on general and specialized linguistics. Contributors must be members of the University of Illinois Department of Linguistics or especially invited. Journal reviews books.

Manuscript Information: Articles of 20 single-spaced typescript pages. Style: Journal. 2 copies of manuscript required. Include a half-page abstract. Report in 2 months. Rejected manuscripts returned.

Payment: Copies.

Copyright: By the author.

*TEACHING ENGLISH TO DEAF AND
SECONDARY-LANGUAGE STUDENTS

Department of English, Gallaudet University, 800 Florida Avenue, N.E., Washington, D. C. 20002. Rates: $10 per year individuals. $15 per year institutions. Founded 1974. Sponsored by the Department of English, Gallaudet University. Published biannually.

Major Field(s) of Interest: This journal examines problems and possible solutions for teaching English to deaf and second language students with emphasis on practical methods. Journal reviews books.

Manuscript Information: Articles of 10–15 pages. Notes of 1–3 pages. Book reviews of 3–10 pages. Style: Sections 1, 4, and 7–9 of TESOL *Quarterly Style Sheet* that appears in the December issue. Footnotes at end of article. 2 copies of manuscript required. Report in 3–4 months. Rejected manuscripts are not returned.

Payment: 2 copies of journal.

Copyright: By the journal.

TEACHING LANGUAGE THROUGH LITERATURE
Fordham University, P. O. Box 707, Bronx, NY 10458. Founded 1961.
Sponsored by Fordham University. Published 2 times per year (Fall and
Spring).

Major Field(s) of Interest: Articles on foreign language pedagogy.
The journal focuses on the presentation of practical classroom and labor-
atory lessons that use literary texts in the teaching of foreign language.
Journal reviews books.

Manuscript Information: Articles of 15–25 pages. Notes up to 1,000
words. Book reviews of 500–1,000 words. Style: MLA. Report in 2
months. Rejected manuscripts returned.

Payment: Copies.

Copyright: By the journal.

TENNESSEE PHILOLOGICAL BULLETIN: PROCEEDINGS OF THE ANNUAL
MEETING OF THE TENNESSEE PHILOLOGICAL ASSOCIATION
Department of English, University of Tennessee at Chattanooga, Chattanooga, TN 37403. Rates: $7.50 per year individuals (includes member-
ship). $5.00 per year institutions.

Major Field(s) of Interest: Articles on modern and classical languages
and literatures. The journal publishes the proceedings of the annual meeting of the Tennessee Philological Association. Contributors must be
members of the Association. Cost of reading a paper at the annual meeting is $15.

Manuscript Information: Articles up to 2,500 words. Submit 300
word abstract. Style: MLA. Report in 3 months. Rejected manuscripts
returned with S.A.S.E.

Payment: Copies.

Copyright: By the author.

*TESOL QUARTERLY
Department of English, GN–30, University of Washington, Seattle, WA
98195. Rates: $42 per year (includes membership dues for TESOL).
Founded 1967. Sponsored by the Organization of Teachers of English to
Speakers of Other Languages (TESOL). Published quarterly (Spring,
Summer, Autumn, Winter).

Major Field(s) of Interest: Anthropology, applied and theoretical linguistics, communication, education, English education, first and second
language acquisition, psycholinguistics, psychology, sociolinguistics, and
sociology as related to teaching as a second language or as a second dialect. Articles must address implications and applications of research to

pedagogical issues. Critical and scholarly articles, reports of research, reviews of materials and books in the field are preferred.

Manuscript Information: Articles up to 20 pages. Brief reports up to 7 pages. Book Reviews up to 1,000 words. Notices up to 500 words. Style: APA with footnotes typed directly below line to which it refers. 3 copies of manuscript required. Report in 4 months. Rejected manuscripts are not returned.

Payment: 25 offprints for full-length articles. 10 offprints for others.

Indexed In: MLA International Bibliography.

Copyright: By the journal. Author's permission is required in order to reprint.

TRANSACTIONS OF THE PHILOLOGICAL SOCIETY

School of European Studies, University of Sussex, Falmer, Brighton, BN1 9QN, England. Rates: $79 per year individuals in North America. $131 per year institutions in North America. Founded 1854. Sponsored by the Philological Society. Published 2 times per year.

Major Field(s) of Interest: The study of the history, strucure, development, and varieties of English. The journal is especially interested in historical and comparative linguistics, philology, and general linguistics. Scholars are invited to submit papers for publication regardless of whether or not the papers have been read to meetings of the Society. Papers should be written so as to be accessible to a philological readership in general and not addressed solely to specialists.

Manuscript Information: No length restrictions on articles or notes. Style: Journal. Write for "Style Sheet." The journal also publishes the "Style Sheet" in the endpapers of each number. 3 copies of manuscript required. Abstracts of 100–words is requested. Report in 8 weeks. Rejected manuscripts are not returned.

Payment: 25 offprints.

Copyright: By the Philological Society. Authors are free to reprint with acknowledgment.

TRANSLATION

The Translation Center, 412 Dodge Hall, Columbia University, New York, NY 10027. Rates: $17 per year. Founded 1973. Sponsored by The Translation Center. Published biannually (April and October).

Major Field(s) of Interest: The journal publishes new translations of prose and poetry, short stories and other literary works. The emphasis is on contemporary literature, but retranslations of older works will also be considered. Translations from lesser-known languages are encouraged.

Manuscript Information: Translations up to 30 typescript pages. Style: Chicago. Contributors must provide the following information with submissions: copies of translated work, copy of original text, 10 line biography of translator, 10 line biography of author, and statement of copyright clearance. Report in 6 months. Rejected manuscripts returned with S.A.S.E.

Payment: 3 copies of the issue. Translators are asked to pass 1 copy to the author.

Copyright: By the journal.

TRANSLATION REVIEW

Translation Center, University of Texas at Dallas, P. O. Box 830688, Richardson, TX 75083–0688. Rates: $15 per year individuals. $20 per year institutions. Founded 1978. Sponsored by the American Literary Translators Association. Published 3 times per year.

Major Field(s) of Interest: The journal publishes reviews of all matters pertaining to literary translation and articles relating to the art and craft of translation. Journal reviews books.

Manuscript Information: No length restrictions on articles or book reviews. Style: Chicago. Report in 3 months. Rejected manuscripts returned with S.A.S.E.

Payment: 2 copies of the issue.

Copyright: By the journal. Permission of the editor required to reprint.

*THE USF LANGUAGE QUARTERLY

University of South Florida, CPR 210, Tampa, FL 33620. Rates: $10 per year individuals. $18 per year libraries. Founded 1962. Sponsored by the University of South Florida Division of Language. 2 double issues published per year (December and June).

Major Field(s) of Interest: The journal publishes papers on linguistic studies, theoretical and applied. It includes linguistic and stylistic studies of literary texts, discourse analysis, translation, and lexicography. The journal is also interested in second and foreign language (including ESL/EFL) acquisition, and computers in language teaching. Papers proposing ad hoc solutions to particular classroom problems are not encouraged.

Manuscript Information: Articles up to 8,000 words. Notes up to 2,500 words. Style: LSA with endnotes. 2 copies of manuscript required. Report in 90 days. Rejected manuscripts returned with S.A.S.E.

Payment: 10 free copies.

Indexed In: MLA International Bibliography, Language & Language Behavior Abstracts, ERIC.

Copyright: Original material only or material originally published in a language other than English.

VERBATIM: THE LANGUAGE QUARTERLY

4 Laurel Heights, Old Lyme, CT 06371. Rates: $16.50 per year. Founded 1974. Sponsored by the editor: Laurence Urdang. Published quarterly.

Major Field(s) of Interest: Articles on all aspects of language, especially English, directed to the intelligent layman. Journal reviews books, but book reviews are by assignment only.

Manuscript Information: Articles up to 1,500 words. Notes up to 300 words. Book reviews up to 1,000 words. Style: No footnotes. Contributors are strongly advised to study one or more issues of the journal to get a good idea of the sort of material it publishes. Report in 3 weeks. Rejected manuscripts returned with S.A.S.E.

Payment: 10 copies for articles, 5 for shorter articles, 2 for shortest pieces and letters.

Copyright: By the journal. Reprinting is prohibited without permission in writing.

VISIBLE LANGUAGE: THE QUARTERLY CONCERNED WITH ALL THAT IS INVOLVED IN OUR BEING LITERATE

Rhode Island School of Design, Graphic Design, 2 College Street, Providence, RI 02903. Rates: $30 per year individuals. $55 per year institutions. Founded 1967. Independent. Published quarterly.

Major Field(s) of Interest: The journal is concerned with research and ideas that help define the unique role and properties of written language. It is a basic premise of the journal that writing and reading form an autonomous form of language expression that must be defined and developed on its own terms. Interest centers on the visible presentation of language—text in all its forms, from poetry to forms design, from handwriting to digital typography. The journal is also interested in manuscripts that are developed visually with appropriate examples or diagrammatic elaboration. Journal reviews books.

Manuscript Information: No length restrictions on articles or notes. Book reviews of 500–2,500 words. Style: Chicago with endnotes. 3 copies of manuscript required. Graphic material must accompany text. Report in 3–4 months. Rejected manuscripts are returned with S.A.S.E.

Payment: 6 copies of the issue plus 1 year subscription.

Indexed In: Current Contents, MLA International Bibliography, Psy-

chological Abstracts, SSCI, Scientific Abstracts, Arts & Humanities Citation Index, Abstracts of English Studies, Artbibliography, Language and Language Behavior Abstracts, Information Science Abstracts, Graphic Arts Literature.

Copyright: By the journal. Permission granted to authors to reprint with credit line.

WORD: JOURNAL OF THE INTERNATIONAL LINGUISTIC ASSOCIATION

3363 Burbank Drive, Ann Arbor, MI 48105. Rates: $35 per year (includes membership in the International Linguistic Association). Founded 1940. Published triannually (April, August, December).

Major Field(s) of Interest: Articles on the structure, function, or historical development of English linguistics, language studies, and related issues in all world languages. The journal is also interested in theoretical questions related to all natural languages. Journal reviews books, but prior permission to review is required.

Manuscript Information: Articles of 10–45 manuscript pages. Notes of 1–5 pages. Book reviews of 5–15 pages. Style: Chicago with endnotes. 4 copies of manuscript required. Abstracts required with submission of article. Report in 2–3 months. Rejected manuscripts returned with S.A.S.E.

Payment: None. Authors may purchase issues at half price.

Indexed In: Linguistic Abstracts.

Copyright: By the International Linguistic Association. Permission is freely given to authors to reprint if no profit is involved.

WORD & IMAGE: A JOURNAL OF VERBAL/VISUAL ENQUIRY

School of English & American Studies, University of East Anglia, Norwich, NR4 7TJ, England. Rates: $80 per year individuals. $160 per year institutions. Founded 1985. Published quarterly.

Major Field(s) of Interest: The journal concerns itself with the study of the encounters, dialogues and mutual collaboration (or hostility) between verbal and visual languages, one of the prime new areas of humanistic criticism. The journal provides a forum for articles that focus exclusively on this special study of the relations between words and images. Journal reviews books, but unsolicited book reviews are not accepted.

Manuscript Information: Articles of 4,000–12,000 words. Notes of 500–2,000 words. Book reviews of 500–2,000 words. Style: MLA. 2 copies of manuscript required. Submit original typescript and 1 copy. Report in 3 months. Rejected manuscripts returned with S.A.S.E.

Payment: 50 offprints.

WORD WAYS: THE JOURNAL OF RECREATIONAL LINGUISTICS
Spring Valley Road, Morristown, NJ 07960. Rates: $17 per year. Founded 1968. Sponsored by the editor: A. Ross Eckler. Published quarterly.

Major Field(s) of Interest: The journal studies the ways in which language may be "played" with: e.g., anagrams, lipograms, palindromes, puns. etc. In general, it treats words as aggregates of letters with little emphasis on etymology or meaning. Its major focus is English, although an occasional article may discuss wordplay in foreign languages. Articles may be serious studies or lighthearted inventions. The journal includes research articles and puzzles. Journal reviews books.

Manuscript Information: Articles of 1–10 pages. Notes of 1/2 page. Book reviews of 1/2 page. Style: Footnotes at end of article. Report in 1 month. Rejected manuscripts returned with S.A.S.E.

Payment: 1 copy.

Copyright: By the journal. Authors may reprint with credit.

V. AMERICAN STUDIES

ALABAMA REVIEW: A QUARTERLY JOURNAL OF ALABAMA HISTORY

P. O. Box CS, University, AL 35486. Founded 1947. Sponsored by the Alabama Historical Association. Published 4 times per year (January, April, July, October).

Major Field(s) of Interest: Articles on the natural, civil, literary, cultural, economic, ecclesiastical, and political history of Alabama. Journal reviews books.

Manuscript Information: Articles of 10–25 pages. Book reviews up to 500 words. Style: Chicago. Submit original double-spaced typescript with footnotes typed double-spaced in a separate section. Report in 6 months. Rejected manuscripts returned with S.A.S.E.

Payment: Copies.

Copyright: By the University of Alabama Press.

AMERICAN INDIAN QUARTERLY

c/o Native American Studies, 3415 Dwinelle Hall, University of California, Berkeley, CA 94720–9989. Rates: $25 per year individuals. $40 per year institutions. Founded 1974. Acquired by the Native American Studies Program in 1982. Sponsored by the Native American Studies Program, University of California. Published quarterly.

Major Field(s) of Interest: An interdisciplinary journal of history, anthropology, literature, and the arts, the journal publishes articles germane to all areas of American Indian research. The journal provides a forum for contemporary scholarship and is especially interested in encouraging contributions by Native Americans. Journal reviews books.

Manuscript Information: Articles of 25–30 pages. Notes of 2–5 pages. Book reviews of 2–5 pages. Style: Chicago with notes at end of text. All material, including bibliography, footnotes, and long quotations, must be double-spaced. Footnotes should be numbered consecutively throughout the article and typed on a separate sheet. 2 copies of manuscript required. Report in 2 months. Rejected manuscripts returned with S.A.S.E.

Payment: 1 copy of the issue and 50 copies of the article.

Copyright: By the University of California Regents. Reprint permission usually granted.

AMERICAN QUARTERLY

Room 4601, National Museum of American History, Smithsonian Institution, Department of Social and Cultural History, Washington, DC 20560. $12 per year. Members of the American Studies Association received AQ free. $45 per year institutions. Founded 1949. Sponsored by the American Studies Association and the Smithsonian Institution—National Museum of American History. Published quarterly.

Major Field(s) of Interest: Interdisciplinary studies of all areas of American culture, past and present, and the relation of those areas to the entire American scene and to world society. Also, articles dealing with all aspects of American life, including literature, history, art, music, politics, folklore, customs, popular culture, women's studies, and minority studies. Journal reviews books.

Manuscript Information: Articles up to 20 pages. Book reviews up to 10 pages. Style: Chicago. Footnotes should be held to a minimum. Report in 6 months. Rejected manuscripts returned with S.A.S.E.

Payment: Copies.

Indexed In: Current Contents, Historical Abstracts, Humanities Index, MLA International Bibliography, Arts and Humanities Citation Index, American History & Life, Abstracts of English Studies.

Copyright: By the journal. Permission to reprint is required.

THE AMERICAN SCHOLAR

1811 Q Street, N.W., Washington, DC 20009. Rates: $20 per year. Founded 1932. Sponsored by the editor: Joseph Epstein. Published 4 times per year.

Major Field(s) of Interest: Articles on the arts, sciences, social sciences, and literature. Articles should be written in nontechnical language for an intelligent audience. The journal seeks to fill the gap between learned journals and good magazines for a popular audience.

Manuscript Information: Articles of 3,500–5,000 words. Book reviews of 1,500–2,000 words. Style: Chicago preferred. Submit original double-spaced typescript. Report in 2–4 weeks. Rejected articles returned with S.A.S.E.

Payment: Copies.

Copyright: By the author.

AMERICAN STUDIES: (formerly MIDCONTINENT AMERICAN STUDIES JOURNAL)

University of Kansas, Lawrence, KS 66045. Rates: $10 per year individuals. $16 per year institutions. Founded 1960. Sponsored jointly by the Mid-American Studies Association and the University of Kansas. Published semiannually.

Major Field(s) of Interest: Studies of American culture through its arts, history, or institutions. The journal accepts articles in the fields of history, literature, political science, sociology, anthropology, art, architecture, and music when these fields are clearly of interest to Americanists in general. Articles of purely literary interest are not accepted. Journal reviews books.

Manuscript Information: Articles of 20–30 typescript pages. Book reviews up to 100 words. Style: MLA with footnotes at the end of article. 2 copies of manuscript required with a 100–word abstract. Authors are asked to assist with the cost of illustrations and footnotes beyond 2 double-spaced pages. Authors are required to submit a signed statement that the article is not being considered elsewhere. Report in 3–8 months. Rejected manuscripts returned with S.A.S.E.

Payment: 3 copies of the issue. Offprints are available at $25 per 100.

Indexed In: Historical Abstracts, Humanities Index, MLA International Bibliography, P.A.I.S., Social Science Index, Abstracts of English Studies, American History & Life, American Humanities Index, LCR.

Copyright: By Mid-America American Studies Association.

AMERICAN STUDIES INTERNATIONAL

George Washington University, 2108 G Street, NW, Washington, DC 20052. Rates: $22 per year individuals. $30 per year institutions and foreign. Founded 1962. Self-supporting. Housed at George Washington University. Published 5 times per year (2 journal issues and 3 newsletters).

Major Field(s) of Interest: ASI publishes both bibliographical articles and those which address subjects related to American studies: history, literature, and politics. All American studies themes and original articles by foreign scholars are solicited. Bibliographical essays are accepted from US scholars. Journal staff writes most book reviews.

Manuscript Information: Articles of 10–25 pages. Notes of 1–5 pages. Book reviews up to 500 words. Style: Chicago. Report in 6–8 weeks. Rejected manuscripts are not returned.

Payment: 2 copies plus offprints. $300 for commissioned work.

Copyright: By the journal. Authors can receive reprint fee.

*THE AMERICAS REVIEW: A REVIEW OF HISPANIC LITERATURE AND ART OF THE USA

Arte Publico Press, University of Houston, Houston, TX 77204–2090. Rates: $15 per year individuals. $20 per year institutions. Founded 1973 (as REVISTA CHICANO RIQUENA). Sponsored by Arte Publico Press. Published triquarterly.

Major Field(s) of Interest: The journal, a review of Hispanic literature and art of the USA, focuses on the artistic expression of US Latinos. It is dedicated to the publication, criticism, and review of Hispanic literature in the United States. The journal also publishes literary criticism and book reviews of Chicano, Puerto Rican, and Latino literature. Journal reviews books, but book reviews are solicited by the editor. Contributors must become subscribers.

Manuscript Information: Articles of 10–20 pages. Short fiction up to 30 pages. Book reviews up to 4 pages. Style: MLA with endnotes. 2 copies of manuscript required. Prefer diskette plus 1 hard copy. Report in 3–4 months. Rejected manuscripts returned with S.A.S.E.

Payment: 5 copies. Money for creative work.

Indexed In: Book Review Index, Chicano Periodical Index, Hispanic American Periodical Index, Index of American Periodical Verse, MLA International Bibliography, Popular Culture Abstracts, Sumario Actual de Revistas.

Copyright: By the journal. 50% reprint fee. No fee for publication in author's own book.

THE ANTIOCH REVIEW

P. O. Box 148, Yellow Springs, OH 45387. Rates: $18 per year individuals. $25 per year institutions and foreign. Founded 1941. Sponsored by Antioch College. Published quarterly.

Major Field(s) of Interest: The journal is a national independent quarterly that prints critical and creative articles of interest to both the liberal scholar and the educated layperson. The journal is interested in articles on social and cultural problems, politics, and the arts as well as new short fiction, poetry, and discussion. The journal prints special issues (about two per year) that bring together a number of writers exploring a particular problem or condition of broad contemporary concern. Journal reviews books.

Manuscript Information: Articles of 2,000–8,000 words. Book reviews up to 750 words. Style: Chicago. Footnotes should be held to a minimum. Report in 4–6 weeks. Rejected manuscripts returned with S.A.S.E.

Payment: $10 per published page.

Indexed In: Social Sciences and Humanities Index, PAIS Bulletin, Historical Abstracts, Sociological Abstracts, Abstracts of English Studies, Book Review Index, The Philosophers Index, Current Index of American Periodical Verse, MLA International Bibliography, America: History and Life, Language and Language Behavior Abstracts.

Copyright: By the journal.

APPALACHIAN JOURNAL: A REGIONAL STUDIES REVIEW

University Hall, Appalachian State University, Boone, NC 28608. Rates: $18 per year. Founded 1972. Sponsored by Appalachian State University and the Center for Appalachian Studies. Published quarterly.

Major Field(s) of Interest: The focus of the journal is the Appalachian region, its past, its present, its politics, culture, history, literature, folklore, economics, religion, music, and art, including Appalachian geology and ecology. The journal is multidisciplinary and narrowly focused on scholarship that deals directly with the region of the Appalachian mountains, from New York to Alabama.

Manuscript Information: No length restrictions on articles, notes, or book reviews. Style: *MLA Style Sheet* with endnotes. 2 copies of manuscript are preferred. Report in 1 month. Rejected manuscripts returned with S.A.S.E.

Payment: 6 copies of the issue for articles.

Indexed In: MLA International Bibliography, Humanities Citation Index, America: History and Life, and others.

Copyright: By Appalachian State University. Rights released subsequently to authors for book publication. Royalties assessed to third parties.

*BLACK AMERICAN LITERATURE FORUM

Parsons Hall 237, Indiana State University, Terre Haute, IN 47809. Rates: $20 per year individuals. $32 per year institutions. Founded 1967. Partially sponsored by Indiana State University. Published quarterly.

Major Field(s) of Interest: BALF is the official publication of the Modern Language Association's Division on Black American Literature and Culture. A quarterly journal, BALF prints essays on black American literature, art, and culture. It also publishes bibliographies, interviews, poems, and book reviews. As a rule, one issue per year features poetry. Journal reviews books.

Manuscript Information: Articles with a minimum manuscript length of 10 pages. Book reviews up to 2,000 words. Style: MLA with endnotes. Prefer references within the text of article and list of works cited at end. 2 copies of manuscript required. Include a brief autobiographical sketch. Report in 3 months. Rejected manuscripts returned with S.A.S.E.

Payment: Money occasionally if grants are available. 2 copies of the issue plus offprints.

Indexed In: ABC-CLIO Library, American Humanities Index, American Literary Scholarship, Annual Index to Poetry in Periodicals, Book Review Index, Index of American Periodical Verse, Index to Periodical Articles by and about Blacks, the MHRA Bibliography, and the *MLA International Bibliography.*

Copyright: By Indiana State University. Reprint with permission.

CALLALOO: A JOURNAL OF AFRO-AMERICAN AND
AFRICAN ARTS AND LETTERS
Department of English, Wilson Hall, University of Virginia, Charlottesville, VA 22903. Rates: $16 per year individuals. $32 per year institutions. Founded 1976. Sponsored by the University of Virginia. Published
quarterly.

Major Field(s) of Interest: The journal publishes original works by
and critical studies of black writers worldwide. It includes critical essays,
cultural studies, interviews, visual, art, fiction, poetry, plays, and an annual annotated bibliography. Journal reviews books.

Manuscript Information: No length restrictions on articles or book
reviews. Style: MLA. 2 copies of manuscript required. Submit original
typescript. Report in 3–6 months. Rejected manuscripts returned with
S.A.S.E.

Payment: 25 offprints and 1 copy of the issue.

*Indexed In: America: History and Life, American Humanities Index,
American Literature, Book Review Index, Historical Abstracts, Index of
American Periodical Verse, MLA International Bibliography.*

Copyright: By the Johns Hopkins University Press. All copyright reverts to the author on publication.

ÉTUDES ANGLAISES: GRANDE-BRETAGNE, ÉTATS-UNIS
2 à 4, quai George Sand, 78360 Montesson, France. Rates: 390 Francs
per year. Founded 1937. Sponsored by the Centre National de la Re-
cherche Scientifique & Centre National des Lettres. Published quarterly.

Major Field(s) of Interest: Articles on American and British studies,
including comparative studies on the history of ideas, history of art, literature, language, and culture in English-speaking countries. Journal reviews books.

Manuscript Information: Articles of 10–12 pages. Notes of 2,500–
3,000 words. No length restrictions on book reviews. Style: MLA. 2 copies of manuscript required. Bilingual abstracts of 100 words in English
required with every article. French translations are provided by the journal. Report in 4–8 weeks. Rejected manuscripts are not returned.

Payment: Copies.

Copyright: By Didier Erudition, 6 rue de la Sorbonne, 750005 Paris,
France.

*EXPLORATIONS IN ETHNIC STUDIES: THE JOURNAL
OF THE NATIONAL ASSOCIATION FOR ETHNIC STUDIES
Department of English, Arizona State University, Tempe, AZ 85287.
Rates: $25 per year individuals. $35 per year institutions. Includes review

supplement EXPLORATIONS IN SIGHTS AND SOUNDS AND NAES NEWSLETTER—THE ETHNIC REPORTER. Founded 1978. Sponsored by the National Association for Ethnic Studies, Inc. Published 2 times per year.

Major Field(s) of Interest: An interdisciplinary journal devoted to the study of ethnicity, ethnic groups, intergroup relations, and the cultural life of ethnic minorities, *EES* serves as an advocate for socially responsible research that demonstrates the integration of theory and practice. The journal is interested in interdisciplinary approaches that are exploratory, and it does not expect articles to present final conclusions. The journal publishes one or more "critiques" with each article, which propose additional directions for research or address the implications of the research. Journal reviews books.

Manuscript Information: Articles of 15–20 pages. Book reviews up to 500 words. Style: Write for Style Sheet. 4 copies of manuscript required. Report in 2 months. Rejected manuscripts returned with S.A.S.E.

Payment: Copies.

Indexed In: American History and Life, MLA International Bibliography.

Copyright: By the National Association for Ethnic Studies, Inc. Permission to reprint is usually given.

FOLKLORE

9 Christchurch Road, Worthing, West Sussex, BN11 1JH, England. Rates: $45 per year. Founded 1989. Sponsored by the Folklore Society. Published 2 times per year (Spring and Fall).

Major Field(s) of Interest: Articles on folklore from any area or period, but preference is given to discussion of British material or that from countries whose traditions are related or parallel to those of Britian. Ethnographic studies of more exotic (e.g., oriental) cultures are only occasionally accepted. Journal reviews books.

Manuscript Information: Articles of 7,000–15,000 words. Notes of 300–1,500 words. Book reviews of 300–700 words. Style: Journal with notes at end of article. 2 copies of manuscript required. Report in 4 weeks. Rejected manuscripts returned with S.A.S.E.

Payment: No free offprints are provided.

Copyright: By the Folklore Society. Requests for reprint (with acknowledgement) freely granted.

FOLKLORE FORUM

504 North Fess Street, Bloomington, IN 47405. Rates: $10 per year. Founded 1969. Sponsored by the Folklore Institute, Indiana University. Published 2 times per year.

Major Field(s) of Interest: The journal publishes articles, notes, translations, and book reviews on topics in popular culture, folklore, folklife, and related areas of anthropology, ethnology, ethnomusicology, sociology, and literature. Book, film, and record reviews may deal with any subject in the field. Journal reviews books.

Manuscript Information: Articles of 5–15 pages. Notes of 2–5 pages. Book reviews up to 2 pages. Style: Chicago with endnotes. 2 copies of manuscript required. Include a short authorial biography. Report in 6 weeks. Rejected manuscripts are not returned.

Payment: 2 copies of the issue.

Indexed In: American Bibliography of Slavic and East European Studies, Historical Abstracts, MLA Abstracts of Folklore Studies.

Copyright: By the journal. Permission to reprint must be obtained.

THE FRENCH AMERICAN REVIEW

P. O. Box 526, Norfolk, CT 06058. Rates: $15 per year individuals. $18 per year foreign. Founded 1919 (formerly LAURELS). Sponsored by the American Society of the French Legion of Honor, Inc. Published semi-annually.

Major Field(s) of Interest: The journal is devoted to French-American culture and to all aspects of French-American relations past and present. Current ideas, trends, and events are of particular interest, and essays and articles may cover subjects on literature, the fine arts, history, sociology, anthropology, philosophy, science, political science, economics, and other topics of interest to the nonspecialist reader. All articles must be written in English, although they may include brief quotations in French. 8 x 10 glossy photographs are especially welcome.

Manuscript Information: Articles of 12–20 typed pages in length, double-spaced. Style: MLA with notes at end of article, but a general "Note on Sources" is preferable to footnotes, although footnotes may be used if limited in number and length. Report in 3 months. Rejected manuscripts returned with S.A.S.E.

Payment: $300 plus 6 copies.

Indexed In: MLA International Bibliography.

Copyright: By the journal. Reprint rights provided on request.

GREAT PLAINS QUARTERLY

1214 Oldfather, University of Nebraska, Lincoln, NE 68588–0313. Rates: $15 per year individuals. $20 per year institutions. Founded 1981. Sponsored by the Center for Great Plains Studies. Published quarterly.

Major Field(s) of Interest: A scholarly interdisciplinary journal, the Quarterly publishes significant research and criticism in the geography, history, literature, anthropology, archaeology, ethnology, folklore, fine arts, sociology, political science, economics, and agriculture of the Great Plains region. It also publishes contributions in the "hard" sciences, such as geology, botany, zoology, climatology, and ecology that illuminate human experience in the region. It is also interested in studies that compare the Great Plains to similar regions in other parts of the world. Journal reviews books.

Manuscript Information: Articles of 10,000–15,000 words. Notes up to 100 words. Book reviews up to 400 words. Style: Chicago. See also the journal's style sheet "Preparation of Manuscripts for Publication." 3 copies of manuscript required. Submit original typescript and 2 photocopies. Report in 2–9 months. Rejected manuscripts returned with S.A.S.E.

Payment: 6 copies.

Indexed In: Humanities Index.

Copyright: By the Center for Great Plains Studies. Authors are free to reprint with courtesy acknowledgment.

GRIOT: OFFICIAL JOURNAL OF THE SOUTHERN CONFERENCE ON AFRO-AMERICAN STUDIES, INC.

Department of English, Box 44691, University of Southwestern Louisiana, Lafayette, LA 70504. Rates: $20 per year. Founded 1981. Sponsored by the Southern Conference on Afro-American Studies, Inc., University of Southwestern Louisiana, Department of English and Berea College. Published 4 times per year.

Major Field(s) of Interest: Articles on Afro-American, African, and Caribbean literatures and folklore. Creative writing and oral tradition materials must be by Blacks.

Manuscript Information: Articles of 15–20 pages. Book reviews of 1–3 pages. Style: MLA. 2 copies of manuscript required. Submit biographical data and English summary if article is not in English. Report in 3–6 months. Rejected manuscripts returned with S.A.S.E.

Payment: Copies.

Copyright: By the journal.

HERITAGE OF THE GREAT PLAINS

1200 Commercial Street, Emporia State University, Emporia, KS 66801. Rates: $7 per year. Founded 1957. Sponsored by the Center for Great Plains Studies. Published quarterly.

Major Field(s) of Interest: Articles on the literature, language, history, folklore, art, music, or life in general in Kansas or the Great Plains. Some poetry and fiction are accepted.

Manuscript Information: Articles up to 20 pages. Style: Chicago. Include contributor's vita. Report in 3 months. Rejected manuscripts are not returned.

Payment: 5 copies.
Copyright: By the journal.

*HUMANITIES IN THE SOUTH: NEWSLETTER OF THE SOUTHERN HUMANITIES CONFERENCE

Division of Humanities, Lander College, Greenwood, SC 29646. Rates: Free to Southern Humanities Conference members. Founded 1945. Sponsored by the Southern Humanities Conference. Published 2 times per year.

Major Field(s) of Interest: Journal is interested in ideas, directions, and methods in the humanities with emphasis on higher education. Journal reviews books.

Manuscript Information: Articles of 750–1,000 words. Book reviews up to 500 words. Style: MLA. Submit original typescript. Report in 1–2 months. Rejected manuscripts returned.

Payment: Copies.
Copyright: By the author.

INTERNATIONAL FOLKLORE REVIEW: FOLKLORE STUDIES FROM OVERSEAS

14 Sloane Terrace Mansions, Sloane Terrace, London, SW1X 9DG, England. Rates: £15 per year. Founded 1981. Sponsored by the New Abbey Pubs. Published annually.

Major Field(s) of Interest: The journal aims to make the work of folklorists throughout the world available to folklorists in England, to show how folklore is studied and interpreted in other countries, and to promote international cooperation and understanding. Only articles by contributors outside the British Isles are accepted. Journal reviews books.

Manuscript Information: No length restrictions on articles, notes, or book reviews. Style: MLA. 3 copies of manuscript required. Report in 1 month. Rejected manuscripts returned.

Payment: Copies.
Copyright: By the New Abbey Pubs. and by the author.

ITALIAN AMERICANA

State University of New York College at Buffalo, 1300 Elmwood Avenue, Buffalo, NY 14222. Founded 1974. Sponsored by the City University of New York, Queens College and State University of New York, Buffalo. Published 2 times per year (Spring/Summer and Fall/Winter).

Major Field(s) of Interest: The journal is a cultural and historical review devoted to the Italian experience in the New World, including studies and commentary in the humanities and social sciences, fiction, poetry, bibliographies, and reviews of significant books, films, plays, and art. Journal reviews books.

Manuscript Information: Articles of 15–20 pages. Book reviews of 2–4 pages. Style: MLA. 2 copies of manuscript required. Submit original manuscript. Report in 2–4 months. Rejected manuscripts returned with S.A.S.E.

Payment: Copies.

Copyright: By the journal.

*JOURNAL OF AMERICAN DRAMA AND THEATRE

The Graduate School and University Center of the City University of New York, Ph.D. Program in Theatre, Box 355, Graduate Center, 33 West 42 Street, New York, NY 10036–8099. Rates: $12 per year. Founded 1989. Sponsored by the Center for Advanced Study in the Theater Arts, CUNY. Published 3 times per year.

Major Field(s) of Interest: Scholarly articles on American theatre, history, literature, and criticism.

Manuscript Information: Articles of 5,000–8,000 words. Notes of 500–1,500 words. Style: Chicago or MLA. 3 copies of manuscript required. Report in 4 months. Rejected manuscripts returned.

Payment: 3 copies.

Copyright: Center for Advanced Study in the Theater Arts.

*JOURNAL OF AMERICAN FOLKLORE

Center For The Humanities, Murkland Hall, University of New Hampshire, Durham, NH 03824–3596. Rates: $50 per year individuals. $50 per year institutions. Founded 1888. Sponsored by the American Folklore Society, Inc. Published quarterly.

Major Field(s) of Interest: Scholarly articles and studies on folklore and folklife. Journal reviews films, videotapes, exhibitions, events, books, and records.

Manuscript Information: No length limitations on articles, notes, or book reviews. Style: Journal A JAF style sheet is available from the editor. 3 copies of manuscript required. Nonmembers of the American Folklore Society include a $15 submission fee. Submit original typescript plus 2 copies. Report in 2–6 months. Rejected manuscripts returned with S.A.S.E.

Payment: Copies.

Indexed In: Social Sciences and Humanities Index to Periodicals, Book Review Index.

JOURNAL OF AMERICAN STUDIES
School of English & American Studies, University of Sussex, Falmer, Brighton, BN1 9QN, England. Founded 1967. Sponsored by the British Association for American Studies. Published 3 times per year.

Major Field(s) of Interest: Articles on American literature, history, politics, geography, and related subjects. Articles that cross the conventional lines of those disciplines are welcome, as are comparative studies of American and other cultures. The journal also disseminates information about work in progress and provides a platform for the exchange of scholarly information and opinion. Journal reviews books.

Manuscript Information: Articles up to 5,000 words. Notes of 1,000–2,000 words. Book reviews up to 400 words. Style: Chicago. Report in 2 months. Rejected manuscripts returned. U.S. submissions returned only if accompanied by International Reply Coupons.

Payment: Copies.

Copyright: By Cambridge University Press.

THE JOURNAL OF BASQUE STUDIES
P. O. Box 13212, Fresno, CA 93705. Rates: $12 per year individuals. $16 per year institutions. Founded 1979. Sponsored by the Basque American Foundation. Published biannually.

Major Field(s) of Interest: Articles on the literature, history, culture, linguistics, and folklore of the Basque people. Journal reviews books.

Manuscript Information: Articles up to 20 pages. Book reviews up to 5 pages. Style: Journal. 2 copies of manuscript required. Submit an abstract in English for articles written in Spanish. Rejected manuscripts returned with S.A.S.E.

Payment: None.

Copyright: By the journal.

JOURNAL OF CULTURAL GEOGRAPHY
Department of Geography, Bowling Green State University, Bowling Green, OH 43403. Rates: $12.50 per year individuals. $15.00 per year institutions. Founded 1980. Self-supporting. Published biannually.

Major Field(s) of Interest: Articles on folklore and material culture. Journal reviews books.

Manuscript Information: Articles up to 20 pages. Commentaries up to 10 pages. Book reviews up to 2 pages. Style: Authors should write for style sheet on the preparation of manuscripts and illustrations. Report in 2 months. Rejected manuscripts returned with readers' comments. Include S.A.S.E.

Payment: 20 reprints.

Indexed In: American Geographical Society.

Copyright: By the journal. Permission required for use of lengthy quotations or reprinting of articles.

*JOURNAL OF FOLKLORE RESEARCH

Folklore Institute, Indiana University, 504 North Fess, Bloomington, IN 47408. Rates: $15 per year individuals. $25 per year institutions. Founded 1964. Sponsored by the Folklore Institute, Indiana University. Published 3 times per year.

Major Field(s) of Interest: Devoted to scholarly articles dealing with writings of high quality by the world community of folklore and ethnomusicology. The journal is interested in articles that investigate a particular problem or assess current scholarship in folklore and folklife, material culture, comparative studies, performance studies, oral traditions, and politics of culture. The journal is dedicated to promoting international dialogue and welcomes submissions from foreign cultures. Journal reviews books.

Manuscript Information: No length restrictions on articles and notes. Book reviews up to 500 words. Style: Chicago with endnotes. 2 copies of manuscript required. Report in 3 months. Rejected manuscripts returned with S.A.S.E.

Payment: 2 copies of the journal.

Indexed In: MLA International Bibliography, Social Sciences Index.

Copyright: By the journal. Authors are granted permission to reprint with usual credit line.

JOURNAL OF NEGRO HISTORY

Box 20, Morehouse College, Atlanta, GA 30314. Rates: $30 per year. Sponsored by the Association for the Study of Afro-American Life and History, Inc. Published quarterly.

Major Field(s) of Interest: The journal publishes articles which focus on the fields of African and African-American history. Journal reviews books.

Manuscript Information: Articles of 10–25 pages. Notes up to 10 pages. Book reviews up to 3 pages. Style: Chicago. 3 copies of manuscripts required. Submit original manuscript. Report in 2 months. Rejected manuscripts returned with S.A.S.E.

Payment: Copies.

Copyright: By the journal. Reprints are not available.

JOURNAL OF POPULAR CULTURE

Center for the Study of Popular Culture, Bowling Green University, Bowling Green, OH 43403. Rates: $29 per year. Founded 1969. Sponsored by the Popular Culture Association. Published quarterly.

Major Field(s) of Interest: Articles on "popular culture" of all ages and all countries. Manuscripts are invited which develop or touch on popular culture in the broadest sense of the term. Journal reviews books.

Manuscript Information: Articles of 10–12 pages. Notes up to 200 words. Book reviews of 150–200 words. Style: MLA. 2 copies of manuscript required. Submit original manuscript. Report in 90 days. Rejected manuscripts returned with S.A.S.E.

Payment: Copies.

Copyright: By the journal. Reprint with fees.

JOURNAL OF REGIONAL CULTURES

Popular Culture Center, Bowling Green State University, Bowling Green, OH 43403. Rates: $14.50 per year. Founded 1985. Sponsored by the Popular Culture Association. Published 2 times per year.

Major Field(s) of Interest: Journal describes and analyzes all aspects of regional cultures, their impact on the larger culture, and its impact on them. Contributors must be subscribers. Journal reviews books.

Manuscript Information: Articles up to 15 pages. Notes up to 150 words. Book reviews up to 100 words. Style: MLA. 2 copies of manuscript required. Report in 3 months. Rejected manuscripts returned with S.A.S.E.

Payment: Copies.

Copyright: By the journal.

JOURNAL OF THE AMERICAN STUDIES ASSOCIATION OF TEXAS

Regional Studies Program, Baylor University, Waco, TX 76798–7400. Rates: $10 per year individuals. $25 per year institutions. Founded 1970. Sponsored by the American Studies Association of Texas and Baylor University. Published annually.

Major Field(s) of Interest: The journal publishes scholarly, critical articles on American life and letters, articles on American studies in Texas, program notes, and the President's message. The journal exists to focus interdisciplinary attention to thematic, methodological, and pedagogical issues in American Studies. The annual focus is adopted by the membership of the American Studies Association of Texas in annual meeting 2 years in advance of publication. Submissions on the theme are encouraged, but other topics receive consideration.

Manuscript Information: Articles of 15–20 pages. Book reviews up to 1,200 words. Style: Chicago. 3 copies of manuscript required. Report in 6–10 weeks. Rejected manuscripts returned with S.A.S.E.

Payment: 2 reprints.

Copyright: By Baylor University. Authors are granted permission to reprint with credit line (requires written request).

JOURNAL OF THE GYPSY LORE SOCIETY

Leicester Polytechnic, Scraptoft Campus, Scraptoft, Leicester, LE7 9SU, England. Founded 1888. Sponsored by the Gypsy Lore Society. Published in 2 double issues per year.

Major Field(s) of Interest: Articles on Gypsy studies. Journal reviews books.

Manuscript Information: Articles of 1,500–5,000 words. Notes of 500–750 words. Book reviews of 500–1,000 words. Style: Journal. See issue 4 of each volume. 2 copies of manuscript required. Report in 2–3 months. Rejected manuscripts returned.

Payment: Copies.

Copyright: By the author.

JOURNAL OF THE SOCIETY OF BASQUE STUDIES IN AMERICA

Department of Modern Languages, University of Bridgeport, Bridgeport, CT 06601. Rates: $20 per year. Free to members of the Society, libraries, and associations. Founded 1980. Sponsored by the Society of Basque Studies in America. Published annually.

Major Field(s) of Interest: The journal publishes articles on a wide range of topics relating to the Basque people, their language, culture, civilization, literature, linguistics, ethnology, folklore, and history. Articles are accepted in English, Spanish, French, and Basque. The journal encourages illustrations within the context of articles. Journal reviews books.

Manuscript Information: Articles of 20–25 pages. Notes of 3–5 pages. Book reviews of 2–3 pages. Style: MLA with notes at end of article. Report in 6–8 weeks. Rejected manuscripts are not returned.

Payment: 1 copy of the journal.

Indexed In: MLA International Bibliography.

Copyright: By the journal. Reprinting permitted with author's consent and usual credit line.

Judaism: A Quarterly Journal of Jewish Life and Thought

American Jewish Congress, 15 East 84th Street, New York, NY 10028. Rates: $20 per year individuals. $35 per year institutions. Founded 1952. Sponsored by the American Jewish Congress. Published quarterly.

Major Field(s) of Interest: Nonpartisan journal dedicated to the discussion and exposition of the religious, moral, and philosophical concepts of Jewish life and thought and their relevance to the problems of modern society. Journal reviews books.

Manuscript Information: Articles up to 7,500 words. Book reviews of 1,500–2,500 words. Style: MLA or Chicago. Notes at end of article. Submit original typescript. Report in 4–6 weeks. Rejected manuscripts returned with S.A.S.E.

Payment: 25 free reprints of published paper.

Indexed In: Religious and Theological Abstracts, Index of Jewish Periodicals.

Copyright: By the journal. Reprinting by permission only.

Kansas Quarterly

Department of English, Denison Hall 122, Kansas State University, Manhattan, KS 66506–0703. Rates: $20 per year. Founded 1968. Sponsored by the Kansas Quarterly Association. Published 4 times per year.

Major Field(s) of Interest: The journal focuses on, but is not restricted to, the art, culture, history, lifestyle, and writing of Mid-America.

Manuscript Information: Articles of 10–25 pages. Style: MLA with endnotes. Submit original typescript. Report in 2–6 months. Rejected manuscripts returned with S.A.S.E.

Payment: Cash for fiction and poetry. 2 copies of journal for articles.

Copyright: By the journal. Reprint rights granted for specific purposes.

Kentucky Folklore Record: A Regional Journal of Folklore and Folklife

Box U–169, Western Kentucky University, Bowling Green, KY 42101. Founded 1955. Sponsored by the Kentucky Folklore Society. Published 2 times per year.

Major Field(s) of Interest: Articles on the folklore and folklife of the Southern United States. Journal reviews books.

Manuscript Information: No length restrictions on articles or book reviews. Style: Chicago. 2 copies of manuscript required. Submit original manuscript plus 1 copy. Report in 6 months. Rejected manuscripts returned with S.A.S.E.

Payment: Copies.

Copyright: By the journal.

THE KENTUCKY REVIEW

204 King Library South, University of Kentucky, Lexington, KY 40506–0039. Rates: $10 per year (includes membership). Founded 1979. Sponsored by the University of Kentucky Library Associates. Published 3 times per year.

Major Field(s) of Interest: American, English, and world literature, history, philosophy, art, architecture, music folklore, typography, cinema. Other topics on any aspect of the humanities, including interviews, are welcome.

Manuscript Information: No length restrictions on articles, notes, or book reviews. Style: Chicago. Report in 3–4 months. Rejected manuscripts returned with S.A.S.E.

Payment: Copies.

Indexed In: MLA International Bibliography.

Copyright: By the journal. Authors may reprint with credit line.

LATIN AMERICAN INDIAN LITERATURES JOURNAL:
A REVIEW OF AMERICAN INDIAN TEXTS AND STUDIES

Department of Spanish, Pennsylvania State University, Box 31, University Drive, McKeesport, PA 15132. Rates: $22 per year individuals. $32 per year institutions. Founded 1977 as LATIN AMERICAN INDIAN LITERATURES. A REVIEW OF AMERICAN INDIAN TEXTS AND STUDIES. Published biannually.

Major Field(s) of Interest: The journal publishes texts and studies on Latin American Indian literatures, article abstracts, and a bibliography. The journal is interested in myths, songs, and other forms of oral literature of Latin American Indians, texts in the original language, short studies on indigenous cultures, and bibliographies. Journal reviews books.

Manuscript Information: Articles of 10–20 pages. Notes of 1–2 pages. Book reviews of 2–4 pages. Style: Chicago. See "Notes to Contributors" in journal. 5 copies of manuscript required. Report in 6 months. Rejected manuscripts returned only with S.A.S.E.

Payment: Copies.

Indexed In: ATLAR, Ulrich's, Hapsi, IBZ, IBR, ISI, MLA International Directory of Periodicals, Religious and Theological Abstracts.

Copyright: By the journal. Reprint by permission only.

*LATIN AMERICAN LITERARY REVIEW

2300 Palmer Street, Pittsburgh, PA 15218. Rates: $19 per year individuals. $33 per year institutions. Founded 1972. Published semiannually.

Major Field(s) of Interest: Articles on literatures of Latin America and Latin American minorities in the United States. The journal contains feature articles of recent literary works and translations of poetry, plays, prose fiction, as well as articles on the arts. Translations require short introduction on the author of the original work and should be accompanied by the author's permission to reprint original text in the case of poetry and permission to translate. Journal reviews books.

Manuscript Information: Articles of 10–30 pages. Notes of 2–5 pages. Reviews of 2–4 pages. Style: MLA with endnotes and Chicago. 2 copies of manuscript required. Report in 6 months. Rejected manuscripts returned with S.A.S.E.

Payment: 2 copies of the journal.

Indexed In: Arts and Humanities Citation Index, Hispanic American Periodicals Index, International Bibliography of Periodical Literature, International Bibliography of Book Reviews, MLA International Bibliography.

Copyright: By the journal. Reprinting allowed with permission.

LATIN AMERICAN THEATRE REVIEW

Center of Latin American Studies, University of Kansas, Lawrence, KS 66045. Rates: $15 per year individuals. $30 per year institutions. Founded 1967. Sponsored by the Center for Latin American Studies. Published 2 times per year (Fall and Spring).

Major Field(s) of Interest: Critical, analytical, historical, bibliographical articles on Latin American theatre. The journal accepts articles on plays, theatre groups, movements of Spanish and Portuguese America. The journal reviews books and summaries of plays.

Manuscript Information: Articles of 15–20 pages. Notes up to 5 pages. Book reviews up to 750 words. Style: MLA. 2 copies of manuscript required. Report in 3 months. Rejected manuscripts returned with S.A.S.E. Abstract in English required for articles.

Payment: 25 free copies.

Copyright: By the Center of Latin American Studies. Reprinting for scholarly purposes on request. For commercial purposes, request rate schedule.

LIVING BLUES: A JOURNAL OF THE
BLACK AMERICAN BLUES TRADITION

Center for the Study of Southern Culture, Sam Hall, The University of Mississippi, University, MS 38677. Rates: $18 per year. Founded 1970. Sponsored by The Center for the Study of Southern Culture. Published bimonthly.

Major Field(s) of Interest: Articles on all aspects of black American traditional and popular music. Journal reviews books.

Manuscript Information: Articles of 2,000–5,000 words. Book reviews up to 200 words. Style: Chicago. Report in 6 weeks. Rejected manuscripts returned with S.A.S.E.

Payment: 5 copies of the journal and $45–75 cash.

Copyright: By the journal.

LORE AND LANGUAGE

Centre for English Cultural Tradition and Language, University of Sheffield, Sheffield, S10 S10, England. Rates: £16.50/$27.50 per year individuals. £50.00/$80.00 per year institutions. Founded 1969. Sponsored by the University of Sheffield, Centre for English Cultural Tradition and Language. Published 2 times per year.

Major Field(s) of Interest: Articles on all aspects of English language, linguistics, folklore (especially British folklore), history (especially social, local, and oral), cultural studies, anthropology, and sociology. Journal reviews books.

Manuscript Information: Articles up to 6,000 words. Notes up to 600 words. No length restrictions on book reviews. Style: Journal. Report in 3–6 months. Rejected manuscripts are not returned.

Payment: Money.

Indexed In: Annual Bibliography of English Language and Literature.

Copyright: By the author and by the publisher. Copyright waived for classroom use.

MARKHAM REVIEW

Horrmann Library, Wagner College, Staten Island, NY 10301. Founded 1968. Sponsored by Wagner College. Published quarterly.

Major Field(s) of Interest: Short articles and notes on American literary figures and aspects of American culture, especially from an interdisciplinary point of view. Journal reviews books.

Manuscript Information: Articles up to 6,000 words. Notes of 700–1,000 words. Book reviews up to 750 words. Style: MLA. Include notes at end of manuscript. 2 copies of manuscript required. Report in 6 weeks. Rejected manuscripts returned with S.A.S.E.

Payment: Copies.

Copyright: By the journal.

MATERIAL CULTURE: JOURNAL OF THE PIONEER AMERICAN SOCIETY

Division of Social Sciences, Transylvania University, Lexington, KY 40508. Rates: $20 per year. Founded 1969. Sponsored by the Pioneer American Society. Published 3 times per year.

Major Field(s) of Interest: Articles on material culture, history, folklife, artifacts, art, and architecture. Journal reviews books.

Manuscript Information: Articles up to 20 pages. Book reviews up to 4 pages. Style: Journal. 3 copies of manuscript required. Report in 3 months. Rejected manuscripts returned.

Payment: Copies.

Copyright: By the Pioneer American Society.

MAWA REVIEW

Morgan State University, Baltimore, MD 21239. Rates: $20 per year. Founded 1979. Sponsored by the Middle-Atlantic Writers Association. Published 2 times per year (June and December).

Major Field(s) of Interest: Articles on African, Pan-African, Afro-American, women's, and minority literatures. Journal reviews books.

Manuscript Information: Articles up to 20 pages. Notes up to 2 pages. Book reviews up to 10 pages. Style: MLA. 2 copies of manuscript required. Include a brief biographical sketch. Report in 2 months. Rejected manuscripts returned with S.A.S.E.

Payment: Copies.

Copyright: By the journal.

*MELUS: THE JOURNAL OF THE SOCIETY FOR THE STUDY OF THE MULTI-ETHNIC LITERATURE OF THE UNITED STATES

272 Bartlett Hall, Department of English, University of Massachusetts at Amherst, Amherst, MA 01003. Rates: $35 per year regular members. $40 per year institutions. $15 per year students and retirees. Founded 1974. Sponsored by the Society for the Study of the Multi-Ethnic Literature of the United States and by the University of Massachusetts at Amherst. Published quarterly.

Major Field(s) of Interest: Essays and interviews of interest to those concerned with multi-ethnic literature of America. As the publication of a society of writers, researchers, and teachers, the journal is open to a broad range of general and specific topics dealing with ethnic literature, belles-lettres, autobiography, biographies, and critical studies, or with ethnicity in music, television, and film. The journal welcomes articles on American literature in translation, but English translations should accompany foreign language titles and quotations in other languages. Only members of the Society may publish in the journal.

Manuscript Information: Essays and articles of 5,000–7,500 words including notes. Book reviews of 1,000–1,200 words. Notes of 2,500–5,000 words. Style: MLA. 3 copies of manuscript required with author's name removed. Report in approximately 3–4 months. Rejected manuscripts returned with S.A.S.E.

Payment: 3 copies of the issue.

Indexed In: Abstracts of English Study, Abstracts in Anthropology, American Bibliography of Slavic and East European Studies, American Humanities Index, Arts and Humanities Citation Index, Current Contents.

Copyright: By the journal. Authors are freely granted permission to reprint with usual credit line.

MID-AMERICA FOLKLORE

Ozark Folklore Center, Mountain View, AR 72560 or Arkansas College, Batesville, AR 72501. Rates: $10 per year. Founded 1973 (as Mid-South Folklore; changed to MAF in 1979). Sponsored by Mid-America Folklore Society and Arkansas College. Published 2 times per year (Spring and Fall).

Major Field(s) of Interest: The journal publishes articles on traditional folklore and cultural studies of the central United States, including Missouri, Illinois, Kansas, Oklahoma, and Arkansas. Journal reviews books.

Manuscript Information: Articles of 20–30 pages. Notes of 3–5 pages. Book reviews of 3–5 pages. Style: MLA with endnotes, but see a current issue for guidelines. Report in 2 months. Rejected manuscripts returned with S.A.S.E.

Payment: 5 copies of issue.

Copyright: By Mid-America Folklore Society. Reprint with permission of editor and author.

MIDWESTERN FOLKLORE

Department of English, Indiana State University, Terre Haute, IN 47809. Rates: $7 per year. Founded 1975. Sponsored by the Hoosier Folklore Society and the Indiana State University. Published 2 times per year (Spring and Fall).

Major Field(s) of Interest: Articles on applied and theoretical folklore, primarily from the Midwest but also from other areas.

Manuscript Information: Articles up to 2,500 words. Notes up to 1,000 words. Style: Chicago with endnotes. Submit original typescript. Report in 6 weeks. Rejected manuscripts returned with S.A.S.E.

Payment: 5 copies of the journal.

Indexed In: Historical Abstracts, America: History and Life, MLA International Bibliography.

Copyright: By the author.

MIDWESTERN MISCELLANY

Society for the Study of Midwestern Literature, Ernst Bessey Hall, Michigan State University, East Lansing, MI 48824. Founded 1974. Sponsored by the Society for the Study of Midwestern Literature. Published annually.

Major Field(s) of Interest: Articles on the entire range of Midwestern literature and culture. Journal reviews books. Contributors must be members of Society for the Study of Midwestern Literature.

Manuscript Information: Articles of 1,500–2,000 words. Book reviews of 500–1,000 words. Style: MLA. Report in 3 months. Rejected manuscripts returned.

Payment: Copies.

Copyright: By the journal. Reverts to author upon request.

MISSISSIPPI FOLKLORE REGISTER

Southern Station, P. O. Box 5037, Hattiesburg, MS 39406-5037. Rates: $6 per year. Founded 1965. Sponsored by the Mississippi Folklore Society and the University of Southern Mississippi. Published 2 times per year.

Major Field(s) of Interest: The journal serves the interests of the Mississippi Folklore Society by encouraging the collection, publication, and interpretation of folkways. The emphasis is on, although not limited to, Mississippi folklore. Journal reviews books.

Manuscript Information: Articles of 5–20 pages. Notes of 1,000–2,000 words. Book reviews up to 1,500 words. Style: MLA. 2 copies of manuscript required. Report in 6–8 months. Rejected manuscripts returned with S.A.S.E.

Payment: Copies.

Copyright: By the Mississippi Folklore Society.

*THE MISSISSIPPI QUARTERLY:
THE JOURNAL OF SOUTHERN CULTURE

P. O. Box 5272, Mississippi State, MS 39762-5272. Rates: $12 per year. $15 per year foreign. Founded 1948. Sponsored by the College of Arts & Sciences, Mississippi State University. Published quarterly.

Major Field(s) of Interest: The journal welcomes contributions in the humanities and social sciences dealing with the South, past and present. Journal reviews books, but book reviews are solicited.

Manuscript Information: Articles up to 4,000 words. Notes up to 500 words. Book reviews up to 1,200 words. Style: *MLA Style Sheet* (1977). Report in 3 months. Rejected manuscripts returned with S.A.S.E.

Payment: 2 copies of the issue plus 20 offprints for articles.

Indexed In: Abstracts of English Studies, Current Contents, Historical Abstracts, Humanities Index, MLA International Bibliography, Sociological Abstracts, American Humanities Index, Arts & Humanities Citation Index, America: History and Life, Literary Criticism Record.

Copyright: By the journal. Authors may reprint with usual credit line.

MISSOURI FOLKLORE SOCIETY JOURNAL

P. O. Box 1757, Columbia, MO 65205 or Department of English, 107 Tate Hall, Columbia, MO 65211. Rates: $12 per year. Founded 1979. Sponsored by the Missouri Folklore Society. Published annually.

Major Field(s) of Interest: Articles on folklore, folk music, and Missouri folklife. Journal reviews books.

Manuscript Information: Articles of 10–25 pages. Notes of 1–6 pages. Book reviews of 1–4 pages. Style: Modified Chicago. 3 copies of manuscript required. Report in 6–12 months. Rejected manuscripts returned with S.A.S.E.

Payment: 10 reprints.

Indexed In: MLA International Bibliography, American Studies Bibliography, and others.

Copyright: By the Missouri Folklore Society. Permission of author required to reprint.

*MOTIF: INTERNATIONAL REVIEW OF
RESEARCH IN FOLKLORE & LITERATURE

Department of English, The Ohio State University, 164 West 17th Street, Columbus, OH 43210. Founded 1981. Sponsored by the Department of English, The Ohio State University. Published 3 times per year (February, June, October).

Major Field(s) of Interest: The journal is devoted primarily to studies in the relationship between folklore and literature from theoretical perspectives, as well as more traditional source studies, explications, annotated bibliographies, review-essays, and checklists. The journal occasionally carries creative work, and poems and fiction will be considered.

Manuscript Information: Articles of 10–25 pages. Notes of 1–9 pages. Book reviews of 1–7 pages. Style: MLA with endnotes. 2 copies of manuscript required. Report in 4–6 weeks. Rejected manuscripts returned with S.A.S.E.

Payment: 2 copies.

Indexed In: MLA International Bibliography.

Copyright: By The Ohio State University. Authors are freely granted permission to reprint with usual credit line.

*THE NEW ENGLAND QUARTERLY: A HISTORICAL REVIEW OF NEW ENGLAND LIFE AND LETTERS

Meserve Hall 243, Northeastern University, 360 Huntington Avenue, Boston, MA 02115. Rates: $20 per year individuals. $25 per year institutions. Founded 1928. Sponsored by The Colonial Society of Massachusetts and Northeastern University. Published quarterly.

Major Field(s) of Interest: A historical review of New England life and letters, the journal publishes articles in the fields of literature, art, history, and culture as well as social, political, economic, and artistic studies. It is also interested in brief memoranda and recently discovered documents. Journal reviews books.

Manuscript Information: Articles of 25–40 pages. Notes of 10–15 pages. Book reviews of 3–5 pages. Style: Chicago. See also the journal's Style Sheet for articles and book reviews. 2 copies of manuscript required. Submit original typescript. Report in 1–2 months. Rejected manuscripts returned with S.A.S.E.

Payment: 1-year free subscription.

Indexed In: American History & Life, MLA International Bibliography.

Copyright: By The New England Quarterly, Inc. Reprint rights granted by journal contingent upon approval by the author.

NEW JERSEY FOLKLIFE

Department of American Studies, Rutgers University, New Brunswick, NJ 08903 or New Jersey Folklore Society, P. O. Box 747, New Brunswick, NJ 08903. Rates: $12.50 per year individuals. $8.50 per year students. $15.00 per year institutions. Founded 1976. Sponsored by the Department of American Studies, Rutgers University and the New Jersey Folklore Society. Published annually.

Major Field(s) of Interest: The journal is the official annual of the New Jersey Folklore Society. It is produced in conjunction with the New Jersey Folk Festival sponsored by Dougless College. There is a sister publication, the *New Jersey Folklore Review,* which publishes shorter articles, notices of upcoming events, letters, discussion, etc. *New Jersey Folklife* publishes well-written articles on folklife, folklore, music, dance, agriculture, cooking, ethnic traditions, maritime traditions, costume, religions, architecture, literature, history, and culture. Membership in the New Jersey Folklore Society includes subscriptions to both publications. Journal reviews books occasionally.

Manuscript Information: Articles of 7–45 pages. Book reviews of 5–10 pages. Style: Chicago with footnotes at end. 2 copies of manuscript required. Report in 3 months. Rejected manuscripts returned with S.A.S.E.

Payment: 2 copies of the journal.

Indexed In: America: History and Life, MLA International Bibliography, Historical Abstracts.

Copyright: By the New Jersey Folklore Society. Reprints rights granted with usual credit line.

New Mexico Humanities Review

Humanities Department, New Mexico Tech, Socorro, NM 87801. Rates: $9 per year. Founded 1978. Sponsored by New Mexico Institute of Mining & Technology. Published 2 times per year.

Major Field(s) of Interest: The journal prefers articles on Southwestern themes or by Southwestern writers, but it will consider anything good. The journal also reviews small press books and fiction dealing with Southwest regionalism.

Manuscript Information: Articles up to 6,250 words. Book reviews of 250–1,000 words. Style: New MLA. Report in 8 weeks. Rejected manuscripts returned with S.A.S.E.

Payment: 1 year subscription to journal.

Indexed In: MLA International Bibliography.

Copyright: By the journal. Reprint with permission and acknowledgment.

*New Scholar: An Americanist Review

South Hall 4607, University of California, Santa Barbara, CA 93106. Rates: $18 per year individuals. $34 per year institutions. Founded 1969. Sponsored by the University of California, Santa Barbara. Published semiannually (Fall and Spring).

Major Field(s) of Interest: The journal provides a multidisciplinary forum for scholars seeking a fuller understanding of the unique human condition and experience in the Americas. Manuscripts which deal creatively with methodology and interpretation are especially encouraged. In addition to individual reviews of recent publications, the journal offers essays on significant developments within the literature of the social sciences and humanities. Reviews of literature, film, and other cultural artifacts are promoted as an important facet of interdisciplinary exchange and learning. Reviews are solicited.

Manuscript Information: Articles of 20–40 pages. Notes up to 3,000 words. Book reviews of 1,200–5,000 words. Style: Chicago with endnotes (kept to a minimum) or American Anthropological Association. See "Note to Contributors" on inside back cover of journal. 3 copies of manuscript required. Send 100–word abstract with manuscript. Rejected manuscripts returned with S.A.S.E.

Payment: 1 copy of the journal plus 10 offprints for articles. 5 offprints for book reviews.

Indexed In: ABC POL SCI, America: History and Life, American Humanities Index, Arts & Humanities Citation Index, Chicano Periodical Index, Current Contents/Arts & Humanities, Hispanic American Periodical Index, Historical Abstracts, MLA International Bibliography, Sociological Abstracts.

Copyright: By the journal. Reprint with credit line permitted.

NORTH CAROLINA FOLKLORE JOURNAL

Folklore Society, Department of English, Appalachian State University, Boone, NC 28608. Rates: $7.50 per year individuals. $10.00 per year institutions. Founded 1948. Sponsored by the North Carolina Folklore Society and Appalachian State University. Published 2 times per year (May and November).

Major Field(s) of Interest: Studies of North Carolina folklore and folklife, analyses of the use of folklore in literature, and articles whose rigorous methodology or innovative approach is pertinent to local folklife study. Journal reviews books, but book reviews are solicited.

Manuscript Information: Articles of 1,000–10,000 words. Notes of 500–1,500 words. Book reviews of 500–1,500 words. Style: MLA. Report in 2 weeks. Rejected manuscripts returned with S.A.S.E.

Payment: 5 copies.

Indexed In: MLA International Bibliography, America: History and Life, and others.

Copyright: By North Carolina Folklore Society. Authors granted permission to reprint with credit line.

*NORTH DAKOTA QUARTERLY

Box 8237, University of North Dakota, Grand Forks, ND 58202–8237. Rates: $15 per year individuals. $20 per year institutions. Founded 1910. Sponsored by the University of North Dakota. Published quarterly.

Major Field(s) of Interest: A journal of the arts and humanities with special interest in American Indian culture, regional studies, interdisciplinary studies, the Northern Plains culture, women's studies, the Colonial mind, and environmental issues. The journal also publishes short fiction and poetry. The journal likes works that are solidly based but not pedantic or academic. Journal reviews books.

Manuscript Information: Articles of 15–25 pages. Book reviews of 5–7 pages. Style: MLA (3rd Edition) with endnotes. Report in 4–10 weeks. Rejected manuscripts returned with S.A.S.E.

Payment: 5 copies of the journal.

Indexed In: Abstracts of English Studies, America: History and Life, American Humanities Index, Index of American Periodical Verse, MLA International Bibliography, Journal of Modern Literature.

Copyright: By the University of North Dakota. Copyright reverts to author upon publication.

NORTHEAST FOLKLORE

Northeast Folklore Society, S. Stevens Hall, University of Maine, Orone, ME 04469. $12 per year. Founded 1958. Sponsored by the University of Maine, Orono, Department of Anthropology, Northeast Archives of Folklore & Oral History, and Northeast Folklore Society. Published annually.

Major Field(s) of Interest: Songs, legends, tales, and other traditions of New England and the maritimes. Annual volumes may be monographs, collections of regional material, comparative studies, or several shorter collections of studies. Topics cover the legends, traditions, and lifestyles of the New England and the Atlantic Provinces of Canada. Query before sending manuscripts.

Manuscript Information: Articles up to 20 pages. Style: Chicago. 2 copies of manuscript required. Report in 1–2 months. Rejected manuscripts returned with S.A.S.E.

Payment: 25 complimentary copies.

Copyright: By Northeast Folklore Society.

NORTHWEST OHIO QUARTERLY

Department of History, Bowling Green State University, Bowling Green, OH 43403–0220. Rates: $15 per year. Founded 1929. Sponsored by Maumee Valley Historical Society. Published quarterly.

Major Field(s) of Interest: Articles on regional history, literature, culture, society, and science. Journal reviews books.

Manuscript Information: Articles of 3,000–8,000 words. Notes of 500–2,000 words. Book reviews of 750–2,000 words. Style: Chicago. 3 copies of manuscript required. Submit double-spaced typescript including notes. Report in 3 months. Rejected manuscripts returned.

Payment: Copies.

Copyright: By the journal.

NORWEGIAN-AMERICAN STUDIES

Norwegian-American Historical Association, St. Olaf College, Northfield, MN 55057. Rates: Individual volumes cost about $15. Sponsored by the Norwegian-American Historical Association. Published on average every other year.

Major Field(s) of Interest: Each volume consists of from eight to twelve contributions on Norwegian-American history and Norwegian emigration from 1800 to present. Short studies and translations related to Norwegian-American life are especially welcome, and Norwegian articles are published occasionally in English translation.

Manuscript Information: Articles of 25–30 pages. Notes of 1–10 pages. Style: MLA or Chicago. Write for the journal's style sheet. Report in 2 months. Rejected manuscripts are not returned.

Payment: 3 copies of the issue.

Copyright: By the Norwegian-American Historical Association. Reprint permitted with proper credit.

NOTES ON MISSISSIPPI WRITERS

P. O. Box 5037, Southern Station, Hattiesburg, MS 39406–5037. Rates: $4 per year domestic. $8 per year foreign. Founded 1968. Sponsored by the English Department, University of Southern Mississippi. Published biannually.

Major Field(s) of Interest: Articles about Mississippi writers of scholarly interest. Journal reviews books.

Manuscript Information: No limits, except reason, on articles, notes, and book reviews. Style: MLA with endnotes. Report in 30 days (longer in summer and December). Rejected manuscripts returned with S.A.S.E.

Payment: 5 copies of the journal.

Indexed In: MLA International Bibliography, Literary Criticism Register.

Copyright: By the journal. Permission to reprint usually granted.

OBSIDIAN II: BLACK LITERATURE IN REVIEW

Department of English, Box 8105, North Carolina State University, Raleigh, NC 27695–8105. Rates: $12 per year individuals. Founded 1975. Sponsored by North Carolina State University, English Department. Published 3 times per year.

Major Field(s) of Interest: Articles devoted to the study and cultivation of works in English by and about black writers worldwide with scholarly attention on all aspects of the literature. The journal includes book reviews, bibliographies, and bibliographical essays, short fiction, poetry, interviews, and very short plays.

Manuscript Information: Articles of 2,500–3,500 words. Book reviews of 1,200–1,400 words. Style: MLA. 2 copies of manuscript required. Report in 4–6 weeks. Rejected manuscripts returned.

Payment: Copies.
Copyright: By the journal. Copyright reverts to author after publication.

*THE OLD NORTHWEST: A JOURNAL OF REGIONAL LIFE AND LETTERS

302 Bachelor Hall, Miami University, Oxford, OH 45056. Rates: $10 per year individuals. $15 per year institutions. Founded 1975. Sponsored by Miami University. Published quarterly.

Major Field(s) of Interest: Articles that examine the history and culture of the Old Northwest Territory and the states which developed from it (Ohio, Indiana, Illinois, Michigan, and Wisconsin) as well as other midwestern states sharing the concerns and culture of this part of the United States.

Manuscript Information: Articles of 10–25 manuscript pages. Book reviews of 600–1,000 words. Style: MLA with endnotes. Report in 1–2 months. Rejected manuscripts returned with S.A.S.E.

Payment: 2 copies of articles, 1 for reviews.

Indexed In: Humanities Index, America: History and Life, MLA International Bibliography.

Copyright: By Miami University.

*ORAL TRADITION

301 Read Hall, University of Missouri, Columbia, MO 65211. Rates: $18 per year individuals. $35 per year institutions. Founded 1985 (first issue 1986). Published 3 times per year.

Major Field(s) of Interest: A triannual journal devoted entirely to the interdisciplinary field of research and scholarship on oral literature and tradition, the journal publishes articles on folklore, literary studies, linguistics, and anthropology. The journal is interested in comparative and interdisciplinary studies in oral literature and formulaic theory and periodically it publishes an annotated bibliography of current scholarship in the field. The journal attempts to provide essay-length book reviews of major new works.

Manuscript Information: Articles up to 12,500 words. Notes of any length. Book reviews of 6–10 pages. Style: see journal. Endnotes only. 2 copies of manuscript required. Report in 90 days. Manuscripts accepted for publication must be prepared on floppy disk using either WordPerfect, Microsoft Word, or WriteNow word-processing software, compatible with Apple Macintosh hardware, and must be accompanied by a hard copy. ORAL TRADITION stylesheets are available upon request. Rejected manuscripts returned with S.A.S.E.

Payment: 2 copies of issue.

Copyright: By the journal. Reprint rights granted with acknowledgment.

PENNSYLVANIA FOLKLIFE

Pennsylvania Folklife Society, Box 92, Collegeville, PA 19426. Rates: $10 per year. Founded 1949. Sponsored by the Pennsylvania Folklife Society. Published 3 times per year (Autumn, Winter, Spring).

Major Field(s) of Interest: The journal publishes articles on history, geography, folklore, and folklife of Pennsylvania from colonial times to the present. The journal places special emphasis on Pennsylvania's German history, culture, folklore, and crafts, and it invites comparisons with other ethnic groups. Articles that include drawings or photo illustrations are encouraged.

Manuscript Information: No length restrictions on articles or notes. Book reviews are published if space permits. Style: Chicago with notes at end of article. Report in 2–4 weeks. Rejected manuscripts returned with S.A.S.E.

Payment: 6 copies of the journal.

Copyright: By the journal. Authors may reprint with usual credit line.

PHYLON: THE ATLANTA UNIVERSITY REVIEW OF RACE AND CULTURE

Atlanta University, 223 James P. Brawley Drive, SW, Atlanta, GA 30314. Rates: $26 per year. Founded 1940. Sponsored by Atlanta University. Published quarterly.

Major Field(s) of Interest: The achievements, problems, and concerns of minorities with emphasis on blacks. Journal reviews books.

Manuscript Information: Articles up to 20 double-spaced typescript pages. Book reviews of 300–900 words. Style: Chicago. 4 copies of manuscript required. Submit original typescript. Report in 4–6 weeks. Rejected manuscripts returned with S.A.S.E.

Payment: Copies.

Copyright: By Atlanta University.

POPULAR CULTURE REVIEW

Department of English, 4505 Maryland Parkway, University of Nevada, Las Vegas, Las Vegas, NV 89154–5011. Rates: $7.50 per year (includes membership in FWPCA/FWACA). Founded 1989. Sponsored by the Far West Popular Cultural Association and by the Department of English, University of Nevada, Las Vegas. Published 2 times per year.

Major Field(s) of Interest: All aspects of popular culture worldwide as well as American culture.

Manuscript Information: Articles up to 16 pages. Style: MLA with endnotes. 3 copies of manuscript required. Report in 3 months. Rejected manuscript returned with S.A.S.E.

Payment: 3 copies of the issue.

Copyright: By FWPCA/FWACA. Authors are freely granted permission to reprint with usual credit line.

PROOFTEXTS: A JOURNAL OF JEWISH LITERARY HISTORY

2106 Jimenez, University of Maryland, College Park, MD 20742. Rates: $19 per year individuals. $43 per year institutions. Founded 1980. Sponsored by the Meyerhoff Center for Jewish Studies, University of Maryland, College Park, MD 20742. Published 3 times per year.

Major Field(s) of Interest: The journal publishes literary studies and approaches to classical Hebrew texts, Yiddish literature, American and European Jewish literature, and Jewish writing in other languages. The journal is interested in and concerned about the significance both of literary traditions and contemporary issues of textuality. Journal reviews books, but book reviews are generally solicited.

Manuscript Information: Articles of 20–40 manuscript pages. Notes of 8–15 manuscript pages. Book reviews of 8–25 manuscript pages. Style: Chicago and MLA with endnotes. 4 copies of manuscript required. Hebrew should be transliterated and conform to journal's style. Report in 2–4 months. Rejected manuscripts are not returned.

Payment: 35 copies.

Indexed In: Abstracts of English Studies, Index to Jewish Periodicals, Religious and Theological Abstracts, Index to American Jewish Studies.

Copyright: By Johns Hopkins University Press. Reprint with permission.

PROSPECTS: AN ANNUAL JOURNAL OF AMERICAN CULTURAL STUDIES

Center for American Studies, Columbia University, 603 Lewisohn Hall, New York, NY 10027. Founded 1975. Sponsored by the Center for American Studies. Published annually.

Major Field(s) of Interest: The journal is a multidisciplinary forum that presents works of criticism and scholarship that elucidate the essential nature of the American character and that explore all aspects of American civilization. Neither partisan nor restrictive, the journal is eclectic in its approach, and its format is free, open, and flexible. Journal reviews books.

Manuscript Information: No length restrictions on articles. Style: MLA. 2 copies of manuscript required. Report in 2 months. Rejected manuscripts returned.

Payment: Copies.

Copyright: By Cambridge University Press.

PUBLICATIONS OF THE TEXAS FOLKLORE SOCIETY

Stephen F. Austin State University, Department of English and Philosophy, P. O. Box 13007 SFA Station, Nacogdoches, TX 75962–3007. Rates: $15 per year individuals. $20 per year institutions. Founded 1909. Sponsored by the Texas Folklore Society. Published annually.

Major Field(s) of Interest: The journal is interested in folklore, particularly of Texas and the Southwest. It publishes many of the papers read at the Society's meetings. Other articles are both volunteered and solicited.

Manuscript Information: No length restrictions on articles. Style: MLA or Chicago. Report in 6 months. Rejected manuscripts returned with S.A.S.E.

Payment: 1 copy.

Copyright: By the journal. Authors are freely granted permission to reprint.

REVISTA DE ESTUDIOS HISPÁNICOS

Box 266, Vassar College, Poughkeepsie, NY 12601. Rates: $21.00 per year individuals. $28.50 per year institutions. Founded 1967. Sponsored by Vassar College. Published 3 times per year (January, May, October).

Major Field(s) of Interest: Articles on all aspects and periods of Spanish and Spanish-American literature. The journal is also interested in literary theory, film studies, interdisciplinary studies, comparative literary studies where these areas of research engage Hispanic studies. Journal reviews books, but unsolicited book reviews are not accepted.

Manuscript Information: Articles of 15–40 pages. Book reviews of 3–5 pages. Style: MLA. 2 copies of manuscript required. Submit original typescript. Report in 6 months. Rejected manuscripts returned with S.A.S.E.

Payment: 20 offprints for articles. 2 copies of issue for book reviews.

Indexed In: MLA International Bibliography.

Copyright: By the journal. Reprint with permission.

REVISTA IBEROAMERICANA

1312 C. L., University of Pittsburgh, Pittsburgh, PA 15260. Founded 1938. Sponsored by the Institute Internacional de Literature Iberoamericana and the University of Pittsburgh. Published 4 times per year.

Major Field(s) of Interest: The journal advances the study of Iberoamerican literature and promotes cultural relations among the peoples of the Americas. Contributors must be members of the Institute Internacional de Literature. Journal reviews books.

Manuscript Information: Articles of 20–30 pages. Notes of 10–19 pages. Book reviews of 3–8 pages. Style: MLA. 2 copies of manuscript required. Submit original typescript. Report in 6 months. Rejected manuscripts returned with S.A.S.E.

Payment: Copies.

Copyright: By the journal.

*SAGE: A SCHOLARLY JOURNAL ON BLACK WOMEN

P. O. Box 42741, Atlanta, GA 30311. Rates: $15 per year individuals. $25 per year institutions. Founded 1983. Sponsored by the Women's Research and Resource Center, 350 Spelman Lane, SW, Atlanta, GA 30314–4399. Published biannually (Spring and Fall).

Major Field(s) of Interest: Articles, critical essays, in-depth interviews, reviews of books, films and exhibits, research reports, resource listings, documents, and announcements which focus on the lives and cultures of black women and women of African descent. Contributors are encouraged to query the editor prior to submission since each issue has a thematic focus.

Manuscript Information: Articles of 25–30 pages. Book reviews of 3–5 pages. Style: MLA. Submit double-spaced manuscripts with one-inch margins at the top, bottom, and sides. Manuscripts must have a title page, which should include the author's name, address, phone number, and a 1–3 sentence bio-sketch. 3 copies of manuscript required. Report in 60 days. Rejected manuscripts returned with S.A.S.E.

Payment: None.

Indexed In: Alternative Press Index, MLA International Bibliography, Women's Studies Abstracts, Feminist Periodical Collections, Sociological Abstracts.

Copyright: By the journal. Permission to reprint required.

SIGNS: JOURNAL OF WOMEN IN CULTURE AND SOCIETY

Center for Advanced Feminist Studies, 495 Ford Hall, University of Minnesota, Minneapolis, MN 55455. Rates: $29 per year individuals.

$21 per year students. $58 per year institutions. Founded 1975. Sponsored by the University of Chicago Press. Published quarterly.

Major Field(s) of Interest: The journal publishes essays and current research about women that cut across disciplines, across various feminist perspectives, and across divisions between academic thought and daily life. It includes feminist interdisciplinary research articles, extensive review essays, book reviews, and commentary. Journal reviews books, but book reviews are solicited.

Manuscript Information: Articles of 20–35 pages with notes. Notes of 100–150 words. Book reviews of 2–8 pages. Style: Chicago. Double-space notes on separate page. 3 copies of manuscript required. Submit original and 2 copies. Omit name and identifying footnotes from manuscript. Abstract up to 150 words to accompany article. Report in 12–16 weeks. Rejected manuscripts returned with S.A.S.E.

Payment: 10 copies or 1 year subscription.

Indexed In: MLA International Bibliography and others.

Copyright: By the University of Chicago Press. Authors may be granted permission to reprint with citation.

*SOUTHERN FOLKLORE

Department of Modern Languages and Intercultural Studies, Western Kentucky University, Bowling Green, KY 42101. Rates: $20 per year individuals. $22 per year outside US. Founded 1912. Sponsored by Western Kentucky University and the University Press of Kentucky. Published 3 times per year.

Major Field(s) of Interest: Articles on the analytical, descriptive, comparative, and historical study of folklore, and on recent developments in the discipline, including the public sector and cultural conservation. Journal reviews books.

Manuscript Information: Articles of 20–30 pages. Notes: Very brief. Book reviews of 3–4 pages. Style: Chicago with internal footnotes. 2 copies of manuscript required. Report in 2 months. Rejected manuscripts returned with S.A.S.E.

Payment: 1 copy of the journal for articles. Multi copies for reviews.

Indexed In: Humanities Index, ERIC, and others.

Copyright: By the University Press of Kentucky. Permission to reprint required.

SOUTHERN LITERARY JOURNAL

Department of English, Greenlaw Hall, University of North Carolina, Chapel Hill, NC 27599–3520. Rates: $10 per year. Founded 1968.

Sponsored by the Department of English, University of North Carolina, Chapel Hill. Published 2 times per year (Fall and Spring).

Major Field(s) of Interest: The journal focuses on the literary and intellectual life of the American South from colonial times to the present day. It includes articles on literary criticism, historical studies, and thematic and interpretative analysis. Each issue contains one or more review essays in which recent books are discussed in terms of the larger issues they raise. Journal reviews books.

Manuscript Information: Articles of 10–35 typewritten pages. No length restrictions on book reviews. Style: MLA. Report in 3 months. Rejected manuscripts returned with S.A.S.E.

Payment: 3–5 copies.

Indexed In: MLA International Bibliography.

Copyright: By the journal.

*THE SOUTHERN QUARTERLY: A JOURNAL OF THE ARTS IN THE SOUTH
University of Southern Mississippi, Southern Station, Box 5078, Hattiesburg, MS 39406–5078. Rates: $9 per year individuals. $20 per year institutions. Sponsored by the University of Southern Mississippi. Published quarterly (Fall, Winter, Spring, and Summer).

Major Field(s) of Interest: The journal publishes articles, essays, interviews, and reviews on Southern literature, both historical and contemporary. It also publishes work on all the arts, including music, theatre, dance, art, architecture, literature, and popular and folk art with special interest in Southern culture and history, and it invites writing that brings an interdisciplinary approach to analysis and critique. Journal reviews books.

Manuscript Information: Articles of 15–18 pages. Book reviews of 500–750 words. Style: MLA with endnotes. 1 copy of manuscript required with disk copy in WordPerfect. Report in 3–6 months. Rejected manuscripts returned with S.A.S.E.

Payment: 2 copies of issue plus 1 year subscription.

Indexed In: Arts and Humanities Citation Index, MLA International Bibliography, International Bibliography of Periodical Literature, International Bibliography of Book Reviews, Current Contents: Arts and Humanities, Abstracts of English Studies, American Humanities Index.

Copyright: By the University of Southern Mississippi. Reprinting by permission only and with full bibliographic citation.

SOUTHERN STUDIES: AN INTERDISCIPLINARY JOURNAL OF THE SOUTH
Northwestern State University, Natchitoches, LA 71497. Founded 1961.

Sponsored by Northwestern State University, Natchitoches, Southern Studies Institute. Published 4 times per year.

Major Field(s) of Interest: The journal publishes studies in various fields that contribute to a greater knowledge and understanding of the South and its regional setting. It is especially interested in Southern history and literature. Journal reviews books.

Manuscript Information: No length restrictions on articles, notes, or book reviews. Style: Chicago. Submit original double-spaced manuscript. Report in 2 months. Rejected manuscripts returned.

Payment: Copies.

Copyright: By the journal.

SOUTHWEST REVIEW

6410 Airline Road, Southern Methodist University, Dallas, TX 75275. Rates: $16 per year individuals. $20 per year institutions. Founded 1915 (as the TEXAS REVIEW). Renamed upon relocation to SMU in 1924). Sponsored by Southern Methodist University. Published quarterly.

Major Field(s) of Interest: The journal is interested in contemporary affairs, history, folklore, literary criticism, fiction, poetry, and interviews. The journal is particularly interested in reviews of books of Southwestern interest, which appear in the regular "Southwest Chronicle" column.

Manuscript Information: Articles of 3,500–7,000 words. Style: Chicago and *MLA Style Sheet.* Use endnotes as sparingly as possible. Submit original typescript. Report in 1 month. Rejected manuscripts returned with S.A.S.E.

Payment: Cash plus 3 free copies.

Indexed In: Humanities Index, American Humanities Index, Annual Bibliography of English Language and Literature, MLA International Bibliography, Book Review Index, Historical Index, Index of American Periodical Verse, An Index to Book Reviews in the Humanities, America: History and Life.

Copyright: By the journal, which requires first North American serial rights. The author retains all literary rights. Journal asks for acknowledgment on reprints.

THE SPHINX: A MAGAZINE OF LITERATURE AND SOCIETY

English Department, University of Regina, Regina, Saskatchewan, S4S 0A2, Canada. Founded 1974. Sponsored by the Sphinx Committee. Published 2 times per year.

Major Field(s) of Interest: The journal explores literature and culture from psychological, sociological, and anthropological perspectives. Journal reviews books.

Manuscript Information: Articles up to 4,000 words. Book reviews of 1,000–2,000 words. Style: MLA. Submit original typescript. Report in 6–8 weeks. Rejected manuscripts returned.

Payment: Copies.

Copyright: By the journal.

*STUDIES IN AMERICAN DRAMA: 1945–PRESENT

Department of English, University of Southern Mississippi, Hattiesburg, MS 39406–8395 or Department of English, University of Mississippi, University, MS 38677. Rates: $15 per year. Founded 1986. Sponsored by Ohio State University Press. Published 2 times per year.

Major Field(s) of Interest: All topics relating to American theater and drama from World War II to the present. Subjects under consideration for future issues includes the collaborative achievements of directors and playwrights; ideology and performance; and Tennessee Williams and Sam Shepherd: Theater Magic in a Postmodern World. The journal also solicits original, unpublished interviews with prominent playwrights, as well as bibliographies of playwrights who have not been the subjects of such studies. Journal reviews books.

Manuscript Information: Articles of 15–30 pages. Book reviews up to 4 pages. Please query editors before sending bibliographies. Style: MLA. 3 copies of manuscript required: original and photocopies. Report in 3–6 months. Rejected manuscripts returned with S.A.S.E.

Payment: 2 copies of the journal.

Copyright: By Ohio State University Press.

STUDIES IN AMERICAN FICTION

Department of English, Northeastern University, Boston, MA 02115. Rates: $6 per year individuals. $9 per year foreign individuals. $10 per year institutions. Founded 1973. Sponsored by Northeastern University, Department of English. Published 2 times per year (May and December).

Major Field(s) of Interest: The journal publishes articles, notes, and reviews on the prose fiction of the United States. The journal is interested in authors, works, movements, and influences in American fiction from its beginnings to the present. Journal reviews books, but book reviews are solicited.

Manuscript Information: Articles of 2,500–6,500 words. Notes up to 250 words. Book reviews up to 750 words. Style: Manuscripts should follow the journal's style in all matters of quotation and documentation.

Submit original typescript. Report in 3 months. Rejected manuscripts returned.

Payment: Copies.

Copyright: By the journal.

STUDIES IN AMERICAN HUMOR

Department of English, Southwest Texas State University, San Marcos, TX 78666-4616. Rates: $10 per year individuals. $15 per year institutions. Founded 1974. Sponsored by the Department of English, Southwest Texas State University. Published annually.

Major Field(s) of Interest: Any scholarly examination of any form of American humor or American literature. Journal reviews books.

Manuscript Information: Articles of 2,500-4,000 words. Notes of 100-300 words. Book reviews of 1,000-1,500 words. Style: Chicago or MLA with endnotes. 2 copies of manuscript required. Include a short biographical sketch. Report in 3-4 months. Rejected manuscripts returned with S.A.S.E.

Payment: 5 copies of journal.

Copyright: By the author. Journal requests acknowledgment.

STUDIES IN AMERICAN INDIAN LITERATURE: THE NEWSLETTER OF THE ASSOCIATION FOR THE STUDY OF AMERICAN INDIAN LITERATURE

Center for American Cultural Studies, 603 Lewisohn Hall, Columbia University, New York, NY 10027. Rates: $8 per year. Founded 1977. Sponsored by the Center for American Cultural Studies. Published quarterly.

Major Field(s) of Interest: The journal publishes scholarly articles on both contemporary American Indian literature and traditional literature, including some transcriptions of native language oral texts. It also publishes book reviews, review-essays, and bibliographies.

Manuscript Information: Articles of 1,200-1,500 words. Notes up to 500 words. Book reviews of 1,200-1,500 words. Style: MLA. Submit original typescript. Report in 1 month. Rejected manuscripts returned with S.A.S.E.

Payment: Copies.

Copyright: By the author.

STUDIES IN AMERICAN JEWISH LITERATURE

Department of English, 117 Burrowes Building, Pennsylvania State University, University Park, PA 16802. Rates: $18 per year individuals. $25 per year institutions. Founded 1975. Sponsored by the Kent State University Press. Published biannually.

Major Field(s) of Interest: The journal is devoted to the American Jewish writer and the American Jewish experience. Articles must deal with the Jewish experience in literature. Journal reviews books.

Manuscript Information: Articles of 10–15 pages. Book reviews up to 1,000 words. Style: new MLA. 2 copies of manuscript required. Submit original typescript and 1 copy. Report in 3–6 months. Rejected manuscripts returned with S.A.S.E.

Payment: 2 copies.

Copyright: By Kent State University Press, Kent OH 44242. Lenient reprint policy.

STUDIES IN FRANK WATERS

1921 East Saint Louis, Las Vegas, NV 89104. Rates: $10 per year (includes Frank Waters Society Newsletter if requested). Founded 1975. Sponsored by The Frank Waters Society. Published annually.

Major Field(s) of Interest: Articles on the fiction and non-fiction of Frank Waters (1920–present). The journal invites essays dealing with Frank Waters's individual works, his times, influence, geographic area, and social milieu. Each current volume contains the papers (determined by annual theme) that will be discussed at that year's annual meeting, usually a conjoint with the Rocky Mountain Modern Language Association. Journal carries essay/book reviews.

Manuscript Information: Articles of 8–15 pages. Essay/book reviews of 8–25 pages. Style: MLA with endnotes. Submit 150 word abstract prior to submission of manuscript. On acceptance, a final manuscript plus copy on disc required. Report in 3 months. Rejected manuscripts returned with S.A.S.E.

Payment: 1 copy of the issue.

Indexed In: MLA International Bibliography, Books of the Southwest, Institute for Scientific Information, Index to Social Studies and Humanities Proceedings.

Copyright: By the Frank Waters Society. Journal is generous as to reprinting rights.

STUDIES IN LATIN AMERICAN POPULAR CULTURE

Department of Spanish and Portuguese, University of Arizona, Tucson, AZ 85721. Rates: $15 per year individuals. $45 per year institutions. $30 per year for patrons. Founded 1981. Partially sponsored by the University of Arizona and the University of Minnesota-Morris. Published annually.

Major Field(s) of Interest: English-language scholarly articles, interviews, and review-essays on all aspects of the theory and practice of popular culture in Latin America. Journal reviews books.

Manuscript Information: Articles of approximately 20 double-spaced typed pages including notes, illustrations, and graphics. Book reviews up to 10 double-spaced typed pages. 3 copies of manuscript required. Submit original manuscript and 2 copies. Style: *Turabian, A Manual for Writers,* 4th edition, which is supplemented by the journal's own style sheet. Report in 1–2 months. Rejected manuscripts returned with S.A.S.E.

Payment: None.

Indexed In: Hispanic American Periodicals Index, MLA International Bibliography, Communications Abstracts, Arts and Humanities Citation Index, Current Contents/Arts and Humanities, Historical Abstracts, America: History and Life, Revista Interamericana de Bibliografia/Interamerican Review of Bibliography, Contents of Periodicals on Latin America.

Copyright: By the journal. Authors are freely granted permission to reprint with usual credit line.

TENNESSEE FOLKLORE SOCIETY BULLETIN

Tennessee Folklore Society, Middle Tennessee State University, Box 529, Murfreesboro, TN 37132. Rates: $10 per year individuals. $12 per year institutions. Founded 1935. Sponsored by the Tennessee Folklore Society. Published quarterly.

Major Field(s) of Interest: Articles on folk life, folk arts, and folk culture as well as aspects of traditional culture, literature, and language that relate to the South and to Tennessee. The journal is also interested in studies of literature and folklore, interpretive and theoretical essays, and the publication of transcriptions, ballads, and other source material. It especially encourages photographs and illustrations, and special interest is directed to articles on applied folklore and accounts óf research or services to the field. Journal reviews books.

Manuscript Information: Articles of 2–50 pages. Notes of 250–750 words. Book reviews of 250–1,500 words. Style: MLA with endnotes and Turabian. Report in 1 month. Rejected manuscripts returned.

Payment: 6 copies of the journal, others at discount.

Indexed In: Historical Abstracts, American History and Life, MLA International Bibliography, Southern Folklore.

Copyright: By the journal. Journal freely grants authors reprint rights.

TINTA

Department of Spanish and Portuguese, University of California at Santa Barbara, Santa Barbara, CA 03106. Rates: $3.50 per year. Sponsored by the University of California at Santa Barbara, Department of Spanish and Portuguese. Published annually.

Major Field(s) of Interest: The journal provides a forum for high quality creative, original, and scholarly contributions written in all periods of Latin American, Hispanic and Luso-Brazilian literature and linguistics. The journal also welcomes contributions in Galician and Catalan or on Galician or Catalan issues. Journal reviews books and publishes bibliographies.

Manuscript Information: Articles of 15–20 pages. Notes up to 2 pages. Book reviews up to 3 pages. Style: MLA with endnotes. 2 copies of manuscript required. Include a short autobiography. Report in 3–6 months. Rejected manuscripts returned with S.A.S.E.

Payment: 2 copies per author.

Copyright: By the journal.

TRANSACTIONS OF THE WISCONSIN ACADEMY OF SCIENCES, ARTS, AND LETTERS

Wisconsin Academy of Sciences, Arts, and Letters, 1922 University Avenue, Madison WI 53705–4099. Rates: $5 per year. Founded 1870. Sponsored by the Wisconsin Academy of Sciences, Arts & Letters. Published annually.

Major Field(s) of Interest: Articles on literature, the arts, and science, often with a Wisconsin focus or by Wisconsin authors.

Manuscript Information: No restrictions on length of articles. Style: Varies with subject matter. 2 copies of manuscript required. Report in 3 months. Rejected manuscripts returned with S.A.S.E.

Payment: Copies.

Copyright: By the Wisconsin Academy of Sciences, Arts, and Letters.

*WESTERN AMERICAN LITERATURE: QUARTERLY JOURNAL OF THE WESTERN LITERATURE ASSOCIATION

English Department, Utah State University, Logan, UT 84322–3200. Rates: $15 per year individual subscription only. $23 per year with membership. $18 per year student. $30 per year institutions. Founded 1966. Sponsored by the Western Literature Association. Published quarterly.

Major Field(s) of Interest: The journal is interested in critical articles that explore any aspect of the literature of the American West. It also publishes book reviews and review-essays that deal with current studies of the American West.

Manuscript Information: Articles up to 25 pages. Notes up to 1 page. Book reviews up to 350 words. Style: Chicago with endnotes. 2

copies of manuscript required. Report in 4 weeks. Rejected manuscripts returned with S.A.S.E.

Payment: Tearsheets.

Copyright: By the Western Literature Association. Authors freely granted permission to reprint.

WESTERN FOLKLORE

Department of Foreign Languages, Lake Forest College, Lake Forest, IL 60045. Rates: $20 per year individuals. $30 per year institutions. Founded 1942. Sponsored by the California Folklore Society and Lake Forest College. Published quarterly.

Major Field(s) of Interest: Folklore in any area from any region. Includes articles on American and world folklore. Articles selected by peer review. Journal reviews books.

Manuscript Information: No restrictions on length, but journal does not publish monographs. Book reviews of 300–500 words. Notes up to 300 words. Style: Chicago, 13th edition. See also style in *Journal of American Folklore.* Endnotes. 2 copies of manuscript required. Report in 6–8 weeks. Rejected manuscripts returned with S.A.S.E.

Payment: None.

Indexed In: Historical Abstracts, Music Index, MLA International Bibliography, Arts and Humanities Citation Index.

Copyright: By the journal. Copyright released to author for any republication with proper credit line.

*WESTERN ILLINOIS REGIONAL STUDIES

Library, Western Illinois University, Macomb, IL 61455. Rates: $4 per year individuals. $6 per year institutions. Founded 1978. Sponsored by Western Illinois University. Published semiannually (Spring and Fall).

Field(s) of Interest: The journal has a geographical focus, which emphasizes the history, culture, and literature of western Illinois and adjacent areas. Among the topics and figures in which the journal is interested are frontier history, the Mormons in Illinois, community history, Carl Sandburg, Edgar Lee Masters, Vachel Lindsay, the Black Hawk War, John Hay, and Illinois River history. Journal reviews books.

Manuscript Information: Articles of 10–35 pages. Notes up to 1,500 words. Book reviews of 500–1,000 words. Style: MLA with endnotes. Report in 60 days. Rejected manuscripts returned with S.A.S.E.

Payment: 3 copies. More upon request.

Indexed In: MLA International Bibliography, America: History and Life.

Copyright: By the journal. Reprint rights are always given to authors.

*The Wicazo SA Review: A Journal of
Native American Studies
Indian Studies #188, Eastern Washington University, Cheney, WA 99004.
Rates: $8 per volume individuals. $15 per volume institutions. Founded
1985. Sponsored by Eastern Washington University. Published semian-
nually.

Major Field(s) of Interest: The journal is devoted to the publication
of Native American Indian studies and their development as an academic
discipline. Journal reviews books.

Manuscript Information: Articles of 6–30 pages. Review-essays up
to 6,000 words. Book reviews up to 600 words. Style: Chicago and
MLA. Report in 3 months. 3 copies of manuscript requested. Report in 3
months. Rejected manuscripts returned with S.A.S.E.

Payment: 3 copies of the journal.

Indexed In: Historical Abstracts, America: History and Life.

Copyright: By Eastern Washington University.

The William and Mary Quarterly: A Magazine of
Early American History and Culture
P. O. Box 220, Williamsburg, VA 23187. Rates: $20 per year. Founded
1892. Sponsored by the Institute of Early American History and Culture.
Published quarterly.

Major Field(s) of Interest: Articles on the history and culture of Co-
lonia America and the early Republic as well as related areas of New
World discovery and colonization to the early nineteenth century. The
journal is also interested in the history of the British Isles, the European
continent, Africa, and other areas of the New World to approximately
1815. Journal reviews books.

Manuscript Information: Articles up to 40 typescript pages including
footnotes. Book reviews up to 900 words. Style: Chicago with house
adaptations (See copy of the journal). 2 copies of manuscript required.
Report in 2–3 months. Rejected manuscripts returned with S.A.S.E.

Payment: None.

Copyright: By the author. Rights of journal pertain only to issue in
which article appears and to any subsequent reprints of issue.

VI. FICTION AND POETRY JOURNALS

ABRAXAS

2518 Gregory Street, Madison, WI 53711. Rates: $12 for 4 issues. Founded 1968. Sponsored by Abraxas Press, Inc. Published irregularly 1–4 times per year.

Major Field(s) of Interest: The journal publishes contemporary poetry, particularly the lyric. The editors are looking for translations of contemporary poetry and critical prose on contemporary literary topics and movements and political influences on same. Query editor before submitting prose. Journal reviews small press books, but it does not accept unsolicited book reviews.

Manuscript Information: Articles of 3–15 pages. Book reviews of 3–6 pages. Up to 5 poems. Style: Any. For poetry quotes of over 3 lines, indent without quotation marks in the text. Endnotes only. Report 1–6 months. Rejected manuscripts returned with S.A.S.E.

Payment: 1 copy of the journal or per special arrangements.

Indexed In: American Humanities Index, Index of American Periodical Verse.

Copyright: Reverts to author upon publication.

AGENDA

Agenda and Editions Charitable Trust [Registered Charity Number 326068], 5 Cranbourne Court, Albert Bridge Road, London, SW II 4PE, England. Rates: £14 ($25) private; £18 ($35) libraries and institutions. Founded 1959. An independent publication but has Arts Council Grant. Published quarterly (but often a double issue).

Major Field(s) of Interest: Poetry "of more than usual emotion, more than usual order." Articles on selected poets. Special issues on individual poets. Poetry reviews and translations. Excellence and interest are the only criterion for selection.

Manuscript Information: No special policy on length, form, or style. Manuscripts must be clear, preferably typed. Report in up to 6 months.

Payment: None.

Copyright: Remains with the author.

ALASKA QUARTERLY REVIEW

University of Alaska-Anchorage, 3211 Providence Drive, Anchorage, AK 99508. Rates: $4.50 single copies. $8.00 for subscriptions. Founded 1980. Sponsored by the College of Arts & Sciences, University of Alaska-Anchorage.

Major Field(s) of Interest: Fiction, poetry, essay.

Manuscript Information: No particular requirements. Report in 2–6 months.

Payment: Complimentary copy.

Copyright: By the journal. Permission to reprint is usually granted.

AMERICAN POETRY

Department of English, University of New Mexico, Albuquerque, NM 87131. Rates: $20 per year. Founded 1983. Sponsored by McFarland & Co., Inc., Box 611, Jefferson, NC 28640. Published 3 times per year.

Major Field(s) of Interest: All aspects of American poetry and poetics from the beginning to the present. Journal reviews books.

Manuscript Information: Articles of 18–25 pages. Notes of 1–10 pages. Book reviews of 500–1,000 words. Style: Chicago. 2 copies of manuscript required. Report in 1–3 months. Rejected manuscripts returned with S.A.S.E.

Payment: Copies.

Indexed In: MLA International Bibliography.

Copyright: By the editor. $50 charge for reprinting, half of which goes to the author.

THE AMERICAN POETRY REVIEW

1616 Walnut Street, Room 405, Philadelphia, PA 19103. Rates: $11 per year. Founded 1972. Published bimonthly.

Major Field(s) of Interest: The journal discusses twentieth-century poetry with special emphasis and perspectives on the interests of poets in contemporary and recent poetry.

Manuscript Information: Articles up to 3,000 words. Reviews up to 3,000 words. Style: Chicago. Report in 8–10 weeks. Rejected manuscripts returned with S.A.S.E.

Payment: $75.00 per *APR* page for prose. $1.25 per line for poetry.

Indexed In: American Periodical Verse.

Copyright: APR takes first serial rights only.

THE ANTIGONISH REVIEW

Box 135, St. Francis Xavier University, Antigonish, Nova Scotia, B2G lC0, Canada. Rates: $18 per year. Founded 1970. Published 4 times per year.

Major Field(s) of Interest: The journal is primarily a literary quarterly rather eclectic in scope. It publishes poetry, short fiction, and light critical articles on modern and contemporary writers. The journal publishes book reviews on both national and international authors.

Manuscript Information: Articles of 1,000–6,000 words. Notes up to 2 pages. Book reviews of 1,000–3,000 words. Style: MLA. Report in 3–4 months. Rejected manuscripts returned with S.A.S.E. or International Reply Coupons.

Payment: 2 copies.

Indexed In: The Canadian Periodical Index, The Index of American Periodical Verse, MLA International Bibliography, Arts and Humanities Citation Index, Abstracts of English Studies, The Canadian Magazine Index, Current Contents in the Social and Behavioural Sciences.

Copyright: By the contributors. Permission to reprint in whole or in part must be obtained from the editor.

THE ARMCHAIR DETECTIVE

129 West 56th Street, New York, NY 10019. Rates: $26 per year. Founded 1967. No sponsor. Published quarterly.

Major Field(s) of Interest: The journal is a quarterly magazine devoted to mystery, detective, and crime fiction. It publishes historical overviews, criticism, book reviews, and short fiction. Every issue contains an interview with a well-known mystery writer and portraits of little known writers. Stories are generally from well-known writers.

Manuscript Information: Articles of 4,000–8,000 words. Book reviews of 250–1,000 words. Style: "Not heavily academic." Manuscripts must be double-spaced. No dot matrix; photostatic copies are acceptable Artwork and photographs are very welcome and are always carefully returned. Report in 3 months. Rejected manuscripts returned with S.A.S.E.

Payment: $10 per printed page.

Copyright: By the journal. Journal splits reprint fee with author.

BLACK WARRIOR REVIEW

P.O. Box 2936, Tuscaloosa, AL 35486–2936. Rates: $6.50 per year individuals. $9.00 per year institutions. 2 issues per year. Founded 1974. Sponsored by the University of Alabama.

Major Field(s) of Interest: Contemporary fiction and poetry, as well as essays, reviews, and interviews related to contemporary literature.

Manuscript Information: None provided. Report in 2–8 weeks.

Payment: $5 to $15 per page.

Indexed In: American Humanities Index, Book Review Index, American Index to Periodical Verse, MLA International Bibliography.

Copyright: Rights revert to author upon publication.

CAROLINA QUARTERLY

510 Greenlaw Hall CB #3520, University of North Carolina, Chapel Hill, NC 27599–3520. Rates: $10 per year individuals. $12 per year institutions. Founded 1948. Sponsored by the University of North Carolina. Published triquarterly.

Major Field(s) of Interest: A literary journal that publishes contemporary fiction and poetry, CAROLINA QUARTERLY welcomes unsolicited stories that are immediately intriguing, yet resonate upon second and third readings. It encourages innovative style, structure, characterization, and point of view, but not at the expense of coherence and completeness. The journal also welcomes poetry and artwork. High-quality photographs, paintings, drawings, or prints are welcome. Poets and fiction writers whose work appears in the journal are eligible for the Charles B. Wood Award for Distinguished Writing, a $500 prize awarded annually by the editors.

Manuscript Information: No length restrictions on short stories, but send no more than 2 stories in any 4 month period. No restrictions on length, form, or substance of poems, but inclusion of work of more than 300 lines is impractical. Submit 2–6 poems. No restrictions on content for artwork. Articles up to 7,500 words. No style sheet preference. Heavily annotated articles are not considered. Report in 4–6 months. Rejected manuscripts returned with S.A.S.E.

Payment: $15 per author per issue plus 2 copies of the journal.

Copyright: Journal buys first North American serial rights. Copyright reverts automatically to the author.

CONJUNCTIONS: BI-ANNUAL VOLUME OF NEW WRITING

Bard College, P. O. Box 115, Annandale-on-Hudson, NY 12504. Rates: $18 per year. Founded 1981. Sponsored by Bard College. Published biannually.

Major Field(s) of Interest: One of America's most distinguished anthologies of prose and poetry, the journal publishes innovative work by both established and emerging writers. The journal focuses on new fiction, poetry, translation, essays, book reviews, and interviews.

Manuscript Information: No length restrictions on fiction or poetry manuscripts. Style: MLA. Report in 1 month. Rejected manuscripts returned with S.A.S.E.

Payment: Copies.

Indexed In: American Humanities Index.

Copyright: By the journal. Reverts to author upon publication.

CREATIVE MOMENT

Poetry Eastwest Publications, P. O. Box 391, Sumter, SC 29150. Founded 1972. Sponsored by the Editor. Syed Amanuddin. Published 2 times per year.

Major Field(s) of Interest: The international poetry scene, especially poetry written in English. Journal reviews books.

Manuscript Information: Submit poetry manuscripts. Report in 1 month. Rejected manuscripts returned.

Payment: Copies.

Copyright: By the author.

CUMBERLAND POETRY REVIEW

P. O. Box 120128, Acklen Station, Nashville, TN 37212. Rates: $12 per year individuals. $15 per year institutions. Founded 1981. Sponsored by Poetics, Inc. Published 2 times per year.

Major Field(s) of Interest: A semiannual publication devoted to poetry and poetry criticism, the journal presents poets of diverse origins to a widespread audience. It places no restrictions on form, subject, or style. Manuscripts are selected on the basis of the writer's perspicuous and compelling means of expression. The journal welcomes translations of high quality poetry. The journal aims to support the poet's effort to keep up the language.

Manuscript Information: No restrictions on length, which varies. Style: MLA. Report in 6 months. Rejected manuscripts returned with S.A.S.E.

Payment: 2 copies of the issue.

Indexed In: Standard Periodical Directory, Dustbooks, Poet's Market, Orange's Index, The Writer, Index of American Periodical Verse.

Copyright: Upon publication, copyright reverts to author.

*THE DENVER QUARTERLY

Department of English, University of Denver, Denver, CO 80208. Rates: $5. Founded 1966. Sponsored by the University of Denver.

Major Field(s) of Interest: Although the subtitle of the journal is "A Journal of Modern Culture," the focus recently has been on original poetry and fiction. The essays and reviews the journal does publish are short and have to do exclusively with twentieth-century subjects. DQ carries creative, non-scholarly material.

Manuscript Information: Works no longer than 3,000 words. DQ is looking for critical rather than scholarly articles. If style manual is required, use *MLA Style Sheet.* Prefer no footnotes Report in 2 months.

Payment: $5 per page.

Copyright: By the DENVER QUARTERLY. N.A. serial rights.

FANTASY REVIEW

College of Humanities, Florida Atlantic University, Boco Raton, FL 33431. Price: $27.95 per year. Founded 1978. Sponsored by the Science Fiction Research Association and International Association for the Fantastic in the Arts. Published 10 times per year.

Major Field(s) of Interest: Articles and author interviews on original fiction and selected nonfiction within or related to the genres of fantasy, science fiction, horror, and the occult. All book reviews and many articles are commissioned.

Manuscript Information: Articles of 2,000–5,000 words. Book reviews of 450 words. Notes up to 500 words. Submit original manuscript. Authors should submit photograph. Report in 2–3 months. Rejected manuscripts returned with S.A.S.E.

Payment: None.

Copyright: By the journal.

FIELD: CONTEMPORARY POETRY & POETICS

Rice Hall, Oberlin College, Oberlin, OH 44074. Price $5 per issue. Founded 1969. Sponsored by Oberlin College. Published twice yearly.

Major Field(s) of Interest: Publishes poetry and essays on poetics by working poets only. Reviews are done only by editors. Articles selected by peer reviews. Poems and translations (must have rights).

Manuscript Information: "Anything goes here." MLA style. Report in 2 weeks. Rejected manuscripts returned with S.A.S.E.

Payment: $25 per page.

Bibliographical Issue: Every tenth issue.

Copyright: Upon publication, reverts to author.

FORMATIONS

P. O. Box 327, Wilmette, IL 60091. Rates: $15 per year individuals. $30 per year institutions. Founded 1984. Sponsored by Formations Inc. Published triquarterly.

Major Field(s) of Interest: The aim of the magazine is to relate current American fiction to broader concerns of world culture. It publishes new American fiction juxtaposed with contemporary fiction in translation, as well as essays in other media (painting, music, theater) and the arts and human rights. The journal also publishes photographs and selected works of arts.

Manuscript Information: Articles of various lengths. Style: MLA or Chicago. Report in 1–3 months. Rejected manuscripts returned with S.A.S.E.

Payment: $100–500 for fiction. $100–300 for essays. Copies.

Indexed In: MLA International Bibliography, American Humanities Periodical Listing, Ulrich Guide.

Copyright: By the magazine. Copyright reverts to author upon publication.

*THE GEORGIA REVIEW

University of Georgia, Athens, GA 30602. Rates: $12 per year. Founded 1947. Sponsored by the University of Georgia. Published quarterly.

Major Field(s) of Interest: Essays in poetry, fiction, art history, film criticism, music, psychology, and philosphy. The journal seeks essays rather than articles that are thesis oriented and broadly conceived and that will appeal across disciplinary lines to educated general readers as well as specialists in various fields. The journal under its current editorship is not a scholarly publication, but a journal of arts and letters devoted to widening the audience for short fiction, poetry, and literate discussion of all fields of study. The journal encourages unsolicited work and new writers.

Manuscript Information: No length restrictions on articles and notes. Style: *MLA Style Sheet* (2nd edition). 2 copies of manuscrpt required. Manuscripts should not be submitted if they are under consideration by another journal. Unsolicited manuscripts should not be submitted during the months of June, July, and August. Report in 1–3 months. Rejected manuscripts returned with S.A.S.E.

Payment: $25 per page for prose and graphics. $2 per line for poetry. Copies.

Indexed In: Abstracts of English Studies, America: History and Life, American Humanities Index, Arts & Humanities Citation Index, Book Review Index, Historical Abstracts, Index of American Periodical Verse, Index to Periodical Fiction, Literary Criticism Register, MLA International Bibliography, Modern Humanities Research Association, Sociological Abstracts.

Copyright: By the University of Georgia. Upon publication, copyright reverts to author.

*THE GETTYSBURG REVIEW

Gettysburg College, Gettysburg, PA 17325–1491. Rates: $12 per year domestic; $16 foreign. Founded 1988. Sponsored by Gettysburg College. Published quarterly.

Major Field(s) of Interest: While interdisciplinary in scope, THE GET-
TYSBURG REVIEW is literary in focus. To complement the poetry and fiction
published in the journal, the editors look for articles and essays on a wide
variety of subjects, including literature, art, film, history, science, and
contemporary thought. The main criterion for selection is quality.

Manuscript Information: Articles of 3,000–7,000 words. Book reviews of 3,000–7,000 words. Style: MLA. Rarely publish footnotes. Report in 1–3 months.

Payment: Poetry: $2 per line; prose: $20 per printed page plus 1 year
subscription.

*Indexed In: American Humanities Index, Index of American Periodi-
cal Verse, Historical Abstracts, American History and Life.*

Copyright: Rights revert to author on publication. The magazine re-
serves the right to reprint in an anniversary anthology. Permission given
to authors to reprint with the appropriate credit line.

HIGH PLAINS LITERARY REVIEW

180 Adams Street. Suite 250, Denver, CO 80206. Rates: $20 per year.
Founded 1986. Sponsored by High Plains Literary Review, Inc. Published 3 times per year.

Major Field(s) of Interest: The journal publishes articles, essays, fiction, and poetry. Journal reviews books.

Manuscript Information: Articles of 3,000–6,000 words. Book reviews of 1,500–3,000 words. Style: MLA. Report in 3 months. Rejected
manuscripts returned with S.A.S.E.

Payment: $5 per page plus 2 copies of the issue.

*Indexed In: MLA International Bibliography, Index of American Pe-
riodical Verse, American Humanities Index.*

Copyright: By the Journal. First North American Serial Rights. Copyright reverts to author upon publication.

HIGGINSON JOURNAL

4508 38th Street, Brentwood, MD 20722. Rates: $80 per year. (*Dickin-
son Studies: Emily Dickinson (1830–86), U.S. Poet* comes free with subscription). Founded 1968. Sponsored by Higginson Press. Published
semiannually. See DICKINSON STUDIES in Section I.

Major Field(s) of Interest: Interests of Col. T. W. Higginson: women
poets, especially Emily Dickinson, social reform, black studies, prosody,
contemporary poets, feminism. The journal also publishes creative nonscholarly material.

Manuscript Information: Articles of 1,000–4,000 words. Style: *MLA*

Style Sheet with endnotes. Report in 2 weeks on average. No acknowledgment of receipt of manuscript.

Payment: None. Copies of $4 each.

Indexed In: MLA International Bibliography.

Copyright: Usually not copyrighted, unless there is a major scholarly article.

THE HOLLINS CRITIC

P. O. Box 9538, Hollins College, VA 24020. Rates: $6.00 per year US. $7.50 elsewhere. Founded 1964. Sponsored by Hollins College. Published 5 times per year (February, April, June, October, December).

Major Field(s) of Interest: The journal publishes brief biographical sketches, publication checklists of contemporary authors, and single essay reviews of new books. The journal also publishes poems and brief book reviews. All essays are solicited in advance. Poems are unsolicited.

Manuscript Information: Articles up to 5,000 words. Book reviews up to 300 words. Style: None. Report in 2 months. Rejected manuscripts returned.

Payment: $200 for essays. $25 for each accepted poem. Copies.

Indexed In: Index of American Periodical Verse.

Copyright: By the journal. Lenient reprinting policy.

THE HUDSON REVIEW

684 Park Avenue, New York, NY 10021. Founded 1948. Sponsored by the Hudson Review, Inc. Published quarterly.

Major Field(s) of Interest: Articles on literary and cultural criticism. Journal reviews books.

Manuscript Information: Articles up to 10,000 words. Book reviews up to 2,000 words. Style: Chicago. Submit previously unpublished typescript. Unsolicited nonfiction is read from 1 January–31 March and 1 October–31 December. Unsolicited poetry is read 1 April–30 September. Unsolicited fiction is read 1 June–30 November. Unsolicited manuscripts received at other times are returned unread. Report in 6 weeks. Rejected manuscripts returned with S.A.S.E.

Payment: Copies.

Copyright: By the author, except work made-for-hire.

INTERIM

Department of English, University of Nevada, Las Vegas, Las Vegas, NV 89154. Rates: $5 per year individuals. $8 per year institutions. Founded 1944 at the University of Washington. Ceased 1955. Revived at UNLV

1986. Sponsored partially the University of Nevada, Las Vegas. Published 2 times per year (Spring and Fall).

Major Field(s) of Interest: The journal publishes short articles, prose, poetry, and short fiction of the highest quality.

Manuscript Information: Poetry, in any form, with no length restrictions. Articles, prose, and short fiction up to 7,500 words. Style: None. Report in 2 months. Rejected manuscripts returned with S.A.S.E.

Payment: Copies plus 2 year subscription.

Indexed In: Index of American Periodical Verse, American Humanities Index.

Copyright: By the journal. With acknowledgment, reprint rights revert to author.

THE IOWA REVIEW

308 EPB, the University of Iowa, Iowa City, IA 52242. Published quarterly. Rates: $6.95 individual copies; $15.00 year subscriptions. Founded 1969. Published by the Department of English and the Graduate College of the University of Iowa.

Major Field(s) of Interest: Poetry, fiction, nonfiction, criticism, reviews. Creative work also used.

Manuscript Information: 10 to 25 pages average length. *MLA Style Sheet* for both form and footnotes. Report with 4 to 8 weeks.

Payment: Prose: $10 per page; poetry: $1 per line.

Indexed In: American Humanities Index.

Copyright: By the University of Iowa. Permission needed for reprint.

IRONWOOD

Box 40907, Tucson, AZ 85717. Rates: $9 per year individuals. $17 per year institutions. Founded 1972. Sponsored by the editors: Michael Cuddihy, et al. Published 2 times per year (Spring and Fall).

Major Field(s) of Interest: The journal seeks to publish the very best in contemporary poetry. Every second issue is devoted to a single poet or single aspect of poetry or poetics. Journal reviews books.

Manuscript Information: Articles of 4,000–7,500 words. Notes of 500–1,500 words. Book reviews of 1,500–4,000 words. Style: Journal. Prefer footnotes at end of article or abbreviated within the text. Manuscripts should be double-spaced with ¾–inch margins. Report in 3–6 months. Rejected manuscripts returned with S.A.S.E.

Payment: Copies.

Copyright: By Ironwood Press.

THE KENYON REVIEW

Kenyon College, Gambier, OH 43022. Rates: $15 per year. Founded 1939. Sponsored by Kenyon College. Published quarterly.

Major Field(s) of Interest: Manuscripts on poetry, fiction, criticism, autobiography, and general essays. No manuscripts are accepted during the months of June, July, and August. Journal reviews books, but most book reviews are solicited.

Manuscript Information: Articles of 5,000–10,000 words. Book reviews of 2,000—3,000 words. Style: Chicago. Report in 90 days. Rejected manuscripts returned with S.A.S.E.

Payment: $15 per printed page for poems and book reviews. $10 per printed page for essays and fiction plus copies.

Copyright: By the author.

KENTUCKY POETRY REVIEW

Bellarmine College, Newburg Road, Louisville, KY 40205. Rates: $5 single copy; $8 year subscription (2 issues). Founded 1964. Sponsored by Bellarmine College.

Major Field(s) of Interest: Occasional articles on contemporary American poets; most of each issue consists of original poetry.

Manuscript Information: 4–6 pages. Style: *MLA Style Sheet* and footnote form. Preferably solicited manuscripts only; best to check with the editor. *KPR* carries creative, nonscholarly material. Report in 1 month. Check with the editor before submitting manuscripts.

Payment: One copy of issue.

Copyright: Rights return to author after publication.

*THE LITERARY REVIEW: AN INTERNATIONAL JOURNAL OF CONTEMPORARY WRITING

Fairleigh Dickinson University, 285 Madison Avenue, Madison, NJ 07940. Rates: $18. Founded 1957. Sponsored by Fairleigh Dickinson University. Published quarterly.

Major Field(s) of Interest: Original fiction and poetry reflecting a keen awareness of literary values; essays and interviews with contemporary world class literary figures; book reviews examining 3–4 works under a common theme or thread. Journal publishes essays dealing with major issues and trends in contemporary American and world literature, interpretive essays on the work of important and neglected figures, and essays on literary theory. Journal reviews books.

Manuscript Information: Articles from 15–30 pages. Book reviews from 6–15 pages. Style: MLA. Please examine a sample copy carefully before submitting. Report in 2–3 months. Rejected manuscripts returned with S.A.S.E.

Payment: 2 copies.

Indexed In: Arts & Humanities Citation Index, MLA International Bibliography, Index of American Periodical Verse, Annual Index of Poetry in Periodicals, Literary Criticism Register.

Copyright: Assigned by author to journal. Author retains all reprint rights.

MID-AMERICAN REVIEW

Department of English, Bowling Green State University, Bowling Green, OH 43403. Rates: $3 per issue. Founded 1980 (Formerly ITINERARY 1972–1980). Published twice yearly. Sponsored by the Department of English, Bowling Green State University.

Major Field(s) of Interest: Contemporary poetry and fiction and criticism. Emphasis on American literature; the REVIEW welcomes an international perspective.

Manuscript Information: Articles: 15–20 pages; book reviews: to 2,000 words. *MLA Style Sheet* as to form and footnotes. Report in 6–8 weeks; no manuscripts read in July-August. All submissions must include S.A.S.E.

Payment: 2 free copies of issue.

Indexed In: MLA International Bibliography, American Humanities Index, Index of American Periodical Verse.

Copyright: All rights revert to author upon publication.

THE MINNESOTA REVIEW

English Department, State University of New York at Stony Brook, Stony Brook, NY 11794–33940. Rates: $14 per year. Founded 1960. Sponsored by the English Department, SUNY Stony Brook. Published semiannually.

Major Field(s) of Interest: The journal publishes fiction, poetry, essays, and reviews, particularly of marxist or feminist orientation. The journal is interested in cultural criticism and original fiction and poetry. Journal reviews books.

Manuscript Information: Articles of 5,000–8,000 words. Style: *MLA Style Sheet* with notes at end of article. Report in 2–4 months. Rejected manuscripts returned with S.A.S.E.

Payment: 3 copies of the journal for articles. 2 copies for a review.

Copyright: By the journal. Acknowledgment of prior publication for any reprinting.

THE NEW CRITERION

850 Seventh Avenue, Suite 503, New York, NY 10019. Rates: $32 per year. Founded 1982. Sponsored by the Foundation for Cultural Review, Inc. Published 10 times per year.

Major Field(s) of Interest: The journal publishes critical essays on art, architecture, criticism, drama, dance, literature, literary criticism, poetry, and the academy. Most articles are staff-written or commissioned by the editors. Query preferred. Journal reviews books and publishes new poems and poems in English translation.

Manuscript Information: Unsolicited articles should be no longer than 6,000 words. Book reviews of 2,000–3,500 words. Shorter notices up to 500 words. Style: Consult magazine. Report with 8 weeks. Rejected manuscripts returned with S.A.S.E.

Payment: 10 cents per word upon publication and 2 copies of the issue.

Copyright: By the Foundation for Cultural Review. Authors are freely granted permission to reprint with usual credit line.

NEW ENGLAND REVIEW AND BREAD LOAF QUARTERLY

Middlebury College, Middlebury, VT 05753. Rates: $12 per year individuals. $18 per year institutions. Founded 1978. Sponsored by Middlebury College. Published quarterly.

Major Field(s) of Interest: Journal publishes contemporary fiction, poetry, translations, literary and personal essays. Journal reviews books.

Manuscript Information: Articles 15–20 pages. Book reviews up to 750 words. Style: MLA or Chicago. Report in 6 weeks. Rejected manuscripts returned with S.A.S.E.

Payment: Copies.

Copyright: By the journal. Copyright reverts to author upon publication.

NEW LAUREL REVIEW

828 Lesseps Street, New Orleans, LA 70117. Rates: $8 per year individuals. $9 per year institutions. Founded 1971. Sponsored by the New Orleans Poetry Forum. Published annually.

Major Field(s) of Interest: The magazine publishes good short fiction and poetry. It also publishes articles on literature that an educated reader may find interesting and engaging. Journal reviews books.

Manuscript Information: Articles of 10–15 pages. Book reviews up to 300 words. Style: MLA. Submit only original manuscripts. No copies. Report in 1–2 months. Rejected manuscripts returned with S.A.S.E.

Payment: Copies.
Copyright: By the journal.

NEW LETTERS: A MAGAZINE OF FINE WRITING
University of Missouri-Kansas City, 5216 Rockhill Road, Kansas City, MO 64110. Founded 1971. Sponsored by the University of Missouri, Kansas City. Published quarterly.

Major Field(s) of Interest: The journal provides a medium for creative writing of all kinds. Journal reviews books.

Manuscript Information: Submit original typescript. Report in 1–2 months. Rejected manuscripts returned with S.A.S.E.

Payment: Copies.
Copyright: By the journal.

NEW ORLEANS REVIEW
Box 195, 6363 Saint Charles Avenue, Loyola University, New Orleans, LA 70118. Rates: $9 per issue; $25 per year (individuals); $30 per year (institutions); $40 per year (foreign). Founded 1968. Sponsored by Loyola University, New Orleans. Published quarterly.

Major Field(s) of Interest: Film criticism, literary criticism and history, literature in translations. Poetry, fiction, essays on any subject. Very broad scope, NOR carries creative, nonscholarly material.

Manuscript Information: articles of 20 to 30 pages in lengh. Follow *The Chicago Manual of Style* or older *MLA Style Sheet.* Prefer notes to be worked into text rather than added as footnotes when possible. Report in 4–6 months.

Payment: Payment for translations, fiction, and poetry only.
Copyright: Happy to let author reprint elsewhere.

THE NORTH AMERICAN REVIEW
University of Northern Iowa, Cedar Falls, IA 50614. Price: $11. Published quarterly. Founded 1815 (revived 1964). Sponsored by the University of Northern Iowa.

Major Field(s) of Interest: Fiction and poetry; reviews; literary, political, and current events subjects; "scholarly" pieces are rarely used. For unsolicited articles, query first; unsolicited creative work welcomed.

Manuscript Information: Style demands only common sense and clarity. Footnotes should be avoided. Report in 1–3 months.

Payment: $10 per published page, minimum; poetry 50¢ a line. Offprints arranged with author at cost.

Copyright: Fiction and poetry, 1st N.A. Serial Rights; others, rights negotiated.

NORTHWEST REVIEW

369 PLC, University of Oregon, Eugene, OR 97403. Rates: $14 per year. Founded 1957. Sponsored by the University of Oregon. Published triannually.

Major Field(s) of Interest: The journal seeks essays, articles, and book reviews focused on current literature, particularly fiction and poetry. It publishes works in translation and criticism of current foreign literature. The journal is especially interested in articles addressing small press publications. All manuscripts must be unpublished and not currently under consideration elsewhere.

Manuscript Information: Articles of 5–10 pages. Book reviews of 3–6 pages. Style: Chicago with notes at end of article. Report in 1–3 months. Rejected manuscripts returned with S.A.S.E.

Payment: 3 copies.

Indexed In: American Humanities Index, Grangers Annual Indexes of Verse, Index of American Periodical Verse, Index to Periodical Fiction, MLA International Bibliography.

Copyright: First North American serial rights. Copyright reverts to author on request for use in book form.

THE OHIO REVIEW

209C Ellis Hall, Ohio University, Athens, OH 45701–2979. Rates: $12 per year. Founded 1971. Sponsored by Ohio University. Published 3 times per year.

Major Field(s) of Interest: A general literary review, the journal is mainly interested in essays on or about contemporary poetry, fiction, or criticism, or some aspects of these genres. Journal reviews books of poetry and fiction.

Manuscript Information: No restrictions on manuscript length. Style: *MLA Style Sheet.* List notes at end of article. Report in 90 days. Rejected manuscripts returned with S.A.S.E.

Payment: $1 per line for poetry. $5 per line for prose.

Copyright: By the journal. Reverts to author upon request.

ONTARIO REVIEW

9 Honey Brook Drive, Princeton, NJ 08540. Rates: $8 per year. Founded 1974. Sponsored by the Editor: Raymond J. Smith, et al. Published 2 times per year.

Major Field(s) of Interest: Poetry, fiction, essays, interviews, and graphics. The journal publishes very few conventional articles.

Manuscript Information: Articles of 2,500–5,000 words. Style: None. Report in 1 month. Rejected manuscripts returned with S.A.S.E.

Payment: Copies.

Copyright: By the journal. Copyright is reassigned to author after publication.

PARNASSUS: POETRY IN REVIEW

41 Union Square West, Room 804, New York, NY 10003. Rates: $18 per year individuals. $36 per year institutions. Founded 1972. Sponsored by Poetry in Review Foundation. Published semiannually.

Major Field(s) of Interest: The journal is devoted to publishing in-depth reviews of poetry as well as essays on poetics. Unsolicited original poetry is rarely accepted for publication, and the journal dislikes academic prose. Journal reviews books.

Manuscript Information: Articles of 15–40 pages. No length restrictions on book reviews. Style: Chicago. Report in 2–4 months. Rejected manuscripts returned with S.A.S.E.

Payment: Copies and money.

Indexed In: MLA International Bibliography, Poetry in the Humanities, Literary Criticism Register.

Copyright: By the journal. Reassigned by the journal to the author by request.

PARTISAN REVIEW

236 Bay State Road, Boston, MA 02215. Rates: $18 per year individuals. $28 per year institutions. Founded 1934. Sponsored by Boston University. Published quarterly.

Major Field(s) of Interest: Creative criticism of current literature, politics, fiction, poetry, and art. The journal publishes new fiction and poetry. Journal reviews books, but generally all book reviews are solicited.

Manuscript Information: No particular length requirements for articles. Book reviews of 1,200–1,500 words. Style: Chicago. Report on poetry and fiction in 4–5 months. Report on nonfiction 2–3 months. Rejected manuscripts returned with S.A.S.E. All unsolicited submissions of poetry, fiction, and essays are read as long as they are accompanied by S.A.S.E.

Payment: Varies.

Indexed In: Reader's Guide to Periodical Literature, American Humanities Index, MLA International Bibliography.

Copyright: Reverts to author upon publication. Reprints by permission only.

PEMBROKE MAGAZINE

Box 60, PSU, Pembroke, NC 28372. Rates: $5 per year. Founded 1969. Sponsored by North Carolina Arts Council, National Endowment for Arts, CCLM, and Pembroke State University. Published annually.

Major Field(s) of Interest: The magazine publishes poetry, short stories, and critical essays. It usually focuses on one writer in each issue. Magazine reviews books.

Manuscript Information: Articles up to 2,500 words. Book reviews up to 500 words. Style: MLA. Submit double-spaced manuscript. Report in 6–8 months. Rejected manuscripts returned with S.A.S.E.

Payment: Copies.

Copyright: By the magazine. Reverts to author after publication.

THE PLATTE VALLEY REVIEW

The University of Nebraska at Kearney, Kearney, NE 68849. Rates: $4 per year. Founded 1973. Sponsored by the University of Nebraska at Kearney Press. Published 2 times per year.

Major Field(s) of Interest: The journal publishes mainly the works of University of Nebraska at Kearney faculty, but it does publish outside authors, both invited and uninvited. It is interested in creative writing, fiction, and poetry, and it includes all disciplines and different publishing styles.

Manuscript Information: Articles of 2,000–4,000 words. Style: Flexible. 3 copies of manuscript required. Report in 2–3 months. Rejected manuscripts returned with S.A.S.E.

Payment: 5 copies of the issue.

Indexed In: MLA International Bibliography.

Copyright: The journal is not copyrighted.

PLOUGHSHARES

P. O. Box 529, Cambridge, MA 02139. Rates: $15 per year individuals. $16 per year institutions. Founded 1971. Sponsored by Ploughshares, Inc. Published quarterly.

Major Field(s) of Interest: The journal tries to publish the highest quality new poetry and fiction, interviews with contemporary writers and critical discussions of their work, and discursive criticism organized into continuing debate about what constitutes good writing. Journal reviews books, but book reviews are solicited.

Manuscript Information: Articles up to 4,000 words. Book reviews up to 1,000 words. Style: None. Query editor prior to submission. Report in 3 months. Rejected manuscripts returned with S.A.S.E.

Payment: Copies.

Copyright: By the journal.

POETRY NATION REVIEW

208–212 Corn Exchange Building, Manchester, M4 3BQ, England. Rates: £21.50 ($45) per year. Founded 1976. Sponsored by the Arts Council of Great Britain. Published bimonthly.

Major Field(s) of Interest: The journal publishes poetry in English, articles on contemporary English poetry and fiction, poetry and fiction in translation, and literary criticism. Journal reviews books.

Manuscript Information: Articles up to 6,000 words. Notes of 50–150 words. Book reviews of 250–1,200 words. Poetry manuscripts of variable length. Style: MLA. Submit original typescript. Report in 4 weeks. Rejected manuscripts returned with S.A.S.E. or International Reply Coupons.

Payment: Copies.

Copyright: By the author.

POETRY REVIEW

Poetry Society, 21 Earls Court Square, London, SW5, England. Rates: £13 per year. Founded 1909. Sponsored by the Poetry Society. Published quarterly.

Major Field(s) of Interest: The journal publishes contemporary poetry and reviews. Send letter of inquiry to editor since most articles and reviews are commissioned.

Manuscript Information: No restrictions as to length on articles. Style: None. Report in 90 days. Rejected manuscripts returned. Include return postage or International Reply Coupons.

Payment: Copies.

Copyright: By the author.

PORTLAND REVIEW

P. O. Box 751, Portland, OR 97207. Rates: $4.95. Founded 1968. Sponsored by Student Incidental Fee Funds of Portland State University.

Major Field(s) of Interest: Experimental writing, poetry, and short stories.

Manuscript Information: No special limitations. Style: *MLA Style Sheet* as to form and footnotes. Report in 2 months.

Payment: 1 free copy to contributors.

Copyright: Author retains copyright.

*PRAIRIE SCHOONER

201 Andrews Hall, University of Nebraska, Lincoln, NE 68588-0334. Rates: $15 per year individuals. $19 per year institutions. Founded 1927. Sponsored by the University of Nebraska Department of English and the University of Nebraska Press. Published quarterly.

Major Field(s) of Interest: The magazine is primarily a literary journal, whose intention is to publish the best writing available, both from beginning and established writers. The magazine publishes short stories, poems, interviews, imaginative essays of general interest, and reviews of current books of poetry and fiction. Scholarly articles requiring footnote references should be submitted to journals of literary scholarship because anything written too "academically" is not accepted.

Manuscript Information: No arbitrary limits set on length for articles, but the journal prefers work of approximately 12-15 pages. No length restrictions on book reviews. Style: Chicago. See also the magazine's "Writer's Guidelines." Report in 3 months. Rejected manuscripts returned with S.A.S.E.

Payment: 3 complimentary copies and 10 tearsheets. Yearly cash prizes of $500 and $1,000 are available for Excellence in Writing.

Indexed By: American Humanities Index, Book Review Index, Index of American Periodical Verse, Current Contents, and Humanities Index.

Copyright: By the magazine. Write for information about reprint fees. Magazine will reassign rights to author upon request after publication.

QRL POETRY SERIES

26 Haslet Avenue, Princeton, NJ 08540. Rates: $20 per year. Founded 1943. Sponsored by the editors. 5 or 6 books published within 1 volume.

Major Field(s) of Interest: QRL POETRY SERIES is a continuation of the *Quarterly Review of Literature.* Manuscripts, which are read in the months of May and October only, may consist of a collection of individual poems, a poetry play, translations of a single poet, or a long poem. The journal also publishes photographs, biographies, and statements about writing by the authors. Selections for publication are made through international competition. A $20 submission fee is requested.

Manuscript Information: Manuscripts of 50-100 pages or a long poem of 35 pages or more. Potential contributors may submit only 1 manuscript per reading period. Report in 3 months. Rejected manuscripts may be revised and resubmitted.

Payment: Copies. Occasionally cash awards up to $5,000 are made to those writers whose selections are included in the publication.

Copyright: By QRL POETRY SERIES.

THE RACKHAM JOURNAL OF THE ARTS AND HUMANITIES
4024 Modern Languages Building, University of Michigan, Ann Arbor, MI 48109. Rates: $3 per year individuals. $5 per year institutions. Founded 1971. Sponsored by the University of Michigan, Graduate School, Departments of Literature and Linguistics. Published annually.

Major Field(s) of Interest: Articles on interdisciplinary and comparative literature studies. Journal invites essays on the language, literature, and art of all cultures, translations, original poetry, drama, and short stories. Contributors are primarily graduate students at the University of Michigan.

Manuscript Information: Articles of 10–25 pages. Style: MLA. 2 copies of manuscript required. Report in 4–6 months. Rejected manuscripts returned with S.A.S.E.

Payment: Copies.

Copyright: By the journal.

RENDEZVOUS: A JOURNAL OF ARTS AND LETTERS
Box 8113, Idaho State University, Pocatello, ID 83209–0009. Rates: $7 per year. Founded 1964. Sponsored by the College of Arts and Sciences, Idaho State University. Published biannually (Fall and Spring).

Major Field(s) of Interest: The journal welcomes submissions of innovative, speculative, and creative work inside and outside of traditional disciplines that will generate thoughtful consideration by the nonspecialist. The journal encourages articles and essays that deal with the arts, sciences, humanities, as well as those dealing with education and public affairs. The journal also publishes poetry and short works of fiction or drama as well as photographs, photo essays, and graphics. The journal welcomes suggestions for entire issues organized around a particular theme or topic. Journal reviews books.

Manuscript Information: Articles of variable length. Book reviews of 250–400 words. Style: MLA. No style for poetry or visual arts. 2 copies of manuscript required. Report in 3–6 months. Rejected manuscripts with S.A.S.E.

Payment: In copies of the journal.

Copyright: By Idaho State University. Authors may reprint upon request.

SAN JOSE STUDIES
Department of English, San Jose State University, San Jose, CA 95192. Rates: $12 per year individuals. $18 per year institutions. Founded 1974. Sponsored by San Jose State University. Published 3 times per year (Winter, Spring, Fall).

Major Field(s) of Interest: Interdisciplinary articles and essays which appeal to the educated layperson. The journal publishes critical, creative, and informative writing in the broad areas of the arts, humanities, sciences, and social sciences, and it is particularly interested in quality fiction and poetry.

Manuscript Information: Articles of 10–20 pages. Style: Chicago with notes at end of article. 2 copies of manuscript preferred. Report in 6–8 weeks. Rejected manuscripts returned with S.A.S.E.

Payment: 2 complimentary copies.

Indexed In: ABC-Clio, Abstracts of English Studies, American Humanities Index, Biological Abstracts, Historical Abstracts, H. W. Wilson Company Indexes, Index to Periodical Fiction, Language and Language Behavior Abstracts, Modern Humanities Research Association Annual Bibliography, MLA International Bibliography, National Index of Literary Periodicals, Sociological Abstracts, Women's Studies Abstracts.

Copyright: First Serial rights to San Jose State University Foundation. Permission usually granted forthwith with credit line.

Sewanee Review

University of the South, Sewanee, TN 37375. Rates: $21 per year. Founded 1892. Sponsored by the University of the South. Published quarterly.

Major Field(s) of Interest: The journal is a literary quarterly devoted to criticism, fiction, and poetry. Journal reviews books, but book reviews are solicited.

Manuscript Information: Articles of 5,000–7,500 words. Review-articles of 1,500–4,000 words. Book reviews up to 900 words. Style: Chicago. Submit original typescript. Report in 3–4 weeks. Rejected manuscripts returned with S.A.S.E.

Payment: Copies.

Copyright: By the journal. Partial rights may be reassigned to the author for creative material.

*South Carolina Review

Department of English, 801 Strode Tower, Clemson University, Clemson, SC 29634–1503. Rates: $7.00 per year domestic. $7.50 per year foreign. Founded 1968. Sponsored by the College of Liberal Arts, Clemson University. Published twice yearly (November and April).

Major Field(s) of Interest: The journal welcomes essays, scholarly articles, criticism, poetry, and stories on literature of all periods, figures and nationalities. Most of the criticism, however, focuses on American literature (particularly of the modern period) and the Southern region written for the general reader rather than the specialist. Each year, the journal publishes a special section of essays on Robert Frost. Journal reviews books.

Manuscript Information: Articles of 3,000–4,000 words. Notes of 1,500–2,000 words. Book reviews of 600–800 words. Style: MLA. Report in 6–9 months. Rejected manuscripts returned with S.A.S.E.

Payment: 5 copies for essays, 2 for reviews.

Indexed In: Index of American Periodical Verse, American Humanities Index, Index to Periodical Fiction, Book Review Index.

Copyright: Journal retains first serial rights.

*SOUTHERN HUMANITIES REVIEW

9088 Haley Center, Auburn University, Auburn, AL 36849. Rates: $12 per year. Founded 1967. Sponsored by Auburn University and the Southern Humanities Council. Published quarterly.

Major Field(s) of Interest: Topics of interest in fiction, poetry, and criticism on the arts, literature, philosophy, religion, and history to a general humanities audience. Journal reviews books.

Manuscript Information: Articles of 3,500–5,000 words. Book reviews of 750–1,000 words. Style: MLA. Report in 60–90 days. Rejected manuscripts returned with S.A.S.E.

Payment: 1 copy of journal. (No copies for book reviewers).

Indexed In: Humanities Index, Book Review Index, MLA International Bibliography, Index of Literary Periodicals, and others.

Copyright: By journal.

THE SOUTHERN REVIEW

43 Allen Hall, Louisiana State University, Baton Rouge, LA 70803–5005. Rates: $15 per year individuals. $30 per year institutions. Founded 1935 Original Series; 1965 New Series. Sponsored by Louisiana State University. Published quarterly.

Major Field(s) of Interest: The journal publishes fiction, poetry, critical essays, interviews, book reviews, short stories, and excerpts from novels in progress with emphasis on contemporary literature in the United States and abroad, and with special interest in southern culture and history. Poems and fiction are selected with careful attention to craftsmanship and technique and to the seriousness of the subject matter. Journal reviews books, but book reviews are commissioned.

Manuscript Information: Articles of 4,000–10,000 words. Book reviews of 1,500–4,000 words. Style: Chicago. Prefer no footnotes. Report in 2 months. Rejected manuscripts returned with S.A.S.E.

Payment: $12 per page for prose. $20 per page for poetry. 2 copies of the journal.

Indexed In: Historical Abstracts, America: History and Life, Index of American Periodical Verse.

Copyright: Journal retains first North American serial rights. Decisions on reprinting are made by the author.

SPIRIT: A MAGAZINE OF POETRY

English Department, Seton Hall University, South Orange, NJ 07079. Founded 1934. Sponsored by Seton Hall University. Published 2 times per year.

Major Field(s) of Interest: The magazine publishes contemporary poetry and articles about poetry and poetics. Magazine reviews books.

Manuscript Information: Articles of 5–8 pages. Book reviews of 250–500 words. Style: MLA. Report in 6–10 months. Rejected manuscripts returned with S.A.S.E.

Payment: Copies.

Copyright: By the author.

THE SPOON RIVER QUARTERLY

Department of English, Illinois State University, Normal, IL 61761–6901. Rates: $10 per year individuals. $12 per year institutions. Founded 1976. Sponsored by the Department of English, Illinois State University. Published quarterly.

Major Field(s) of Interest: A literary magazine which publishes only poetry, SRQ features poems by poets with an Illinois connection, interviews with those poets, some critical perspectives, and an appendix of featured poem drafts for classroom use. Only original poetry submissions are solicited.

Manuscript Information: Regular poetry submissions should contain 3–5 poems. The editors read submissions year round. Submissions to the SRQ Illinois Poets series should contain 16–25 pages of mostly unpublished poems by poets with an Illinois connection. All submissions must be accompanied by S.A.S.E. Report in 8 weeks. Rejected manuscripts returned.

Payment: In copies.

Indexed In: Index of American Periodical Verse, Annual Index to Poetry and Periodicals.

Copyright: By Lucia Cordell Getsi. Upon publication, rights to all poems revert to the authors.

*THE TEXAS REVIEW

Department of English, Sam Houston State University, Huntsville, TX 77341. Rates: $10 per year. Founded 1979. Sponsored by the Department of English, Sam Houston State University. Published 2 times per year.

Major Field(s) of Interest: The journal is interested in any article which deals with literature. It publishes poetry, fiction, criticism, reviews, and interviews.

Manuscript Information: Articles of 3,000–10,000 words. Notes of 100-1,000 words. Book reviews of 500–1,000 words. Style: MLA with endnotes. Report in 3 months. Rejected manuscripts returned with S.A.S.E.

Payment: 2 copies of the journal plus 1 year's free subscription.

Indexed In: MLA International Bibliography, Humanities Index.

Copyright: By the journal. Copyright reverts to author upon publication.

THIRD RAIL: A REVIEW OF INTERNATIONAL ARTS & LITERATURE

P. O. Box 46127, Los Angeles, CA 90046. Rates: $30 for 2 years, individuals. $60 for 2 years, institutions. Founded 1975. Sponsored by the editor: Uri Hertz. Published 2 times per year.

Major Field(s) of Interest: A review of international arts and literature, the magazine publishes original poetry and prose, translations of literary work from foreign languages, interviews, criticism, theatre, and film. The review is interested in the developing currents of literature and the arts and tries to offer critical perspectives on them. Journal reviews books.

Manuscript Information: Articles of 500–2,500 words. Notes of 500–1,000 words. Book reviews of 200–1,500 words. Submit original typescripts. Translations from foreign languages should be accompanied by the original text. Report in 3–6 months. Rejected manuscripts returned with S.A.S.E.

Payment: Copies.

Copyright: By the journal. Copyright reverts to author upon publication.

13TH MOON: A FEMINIST LITERARY MAGAZINE:

Department of English, SUNY Albany, NY 12222. Rates: $8 per year per double-issue. Founded 1973. Sponsored by 13th Moon, Inc. Published annually.

Major Field(s) of Interest: The journal is a feminist literary magazine that publishes short fiction, poetry, novel excerpts, plays, criticism, and articles by women or about women's writing from a feminine perspective. Journal reviews books.

Manuscript Information: Articles of 10–20 pages. Book reviews up to 1,000 words. Style: MLA with endnotes. Report in 4 months. Rejected manuscripts returned with S.A.S.E.

Payment: 2 copies of magazine.

Copyright: Magazine retains first North American Serial rights.

TRIQUARTERLY

2020 Ridge Avenue, Evanston, IL 60208–4302. Rates: $18 per year individuals. $26 per year institutions. Founded 1964. Sponsored by Northwestern University. Published 3 times per year.

Major Field(s) of Interest: The journal publishes contemporary American fiction, poetry, and criticism, topical issues dealing with literature and culture, especially Polish and Spanish literature. It publishes special issues that focus on individual writers. Journal reviews books, but book reviews are solicited.

Manuscript Information: No length restrictions on articles or reviews. Style: Chicago. Report in 2–3 months. Rejected manuscripts returned with S.A.S.E.

Payment: 2 copies of the journal plus $1.50 per line for poetry and $20.00 per printed page.

Copyright: By the author.

WASCANA REVIEW

Department of English, University of Regina, Regina, Saskatchewan, S4S OA2, Canada. Founded 1966. Sponsored by the University of Regina. Published 2 times per year.

Major Field(s) of Interest: The journal publishes American, Canadian, and English literary criticism, fiction, and poetry. Journal reviews books.

Manuscript Information: Articles of 5,000–6,000 words. Book reviews of 3,000–4,000 words. Style: MLA. Report in 4–6 weeks. Rejected manuscripts returned with S.A.S.E.

Payment: Copies.

Copyright: By the journal.

*WEBER STUDIES: AN INTERDISCIPLINARY HUMANITIES JOURNAL

School of Arts and Humanities, Weber State College, Ogden, UT 84408–1214. Rates: $10 per year individuals. $20 per year institutions. Founded 1984. Sponsored by the College of Arts and Humanities, Weber State University. Published 3 times per year.

Major Field(s) of Interest: The journal seeks interdisciplinary articles that give a scholarly overview of an important or latest development in a variety of disciplines: art, literature, history, political science, sociology, philosophy, and science. Topical subject matter is encouraged, and the journal prefers general topics over those that are too technical. Journal reviews books, but book reviews are solicited. The journal also publishes biography, fiction, and poetry.

Manuscript Information: Articles of 4,000–6,000 words. Book reviews of 800–1,000 words. Style: MLA with internal documentation. 3 copies of manuscript required. Report in 3–6 months. Rejected manuscripts returned with S.A.S.E.

Payment: $25 honorarium. 5 copies of the issue for articles. 2 copies of the issue for reviews.

Indexed In: Abstracts of English Studies, American Humanities Index, Index of American Periodical Verse, MLA International Bibliography, Sociological Abstracts.

Copyright: By the author.

WEST COAST REVIEW

Simon Fraser University, Burnaby, British Columbia, V5A 1S6, Canada. Rates: Canada $16 per year. Founded 1966. Sponsored by Simon Fraser University, the Canadian Council, and the Government of British Columbia. Published quarterly.

Major Field(s) of Interest: The journal is a literary quarterly which features drama, essays, fiction, and poetry. Journal reviews books.

Manuscript Information: Articles up to 5,000 words. Book reviews of 1,000–2,000 words. Style: Chicago or MLA. Report in 1–3 months. Rejected manuscripts returned with S.A.S.E.

Payment: Copies.

Copyright: By the journal for authors.

INDEX

Entries are by title under major subject headings. Periodicals listed as GENERAL include journals that publish studies in several (general) fields.

LANGUAGE AND LINGUISTIC PEDAGOGY

LANGUAGES (MODERN FOREIGN)

LANGUAGE THEORY

LAWRENCE, D. H.

LESSING, DORIS

LEWIS, C. S.

LEXICOGRAPHY

LIBRARY

LINGUISTICS and PHILOLOGY (GENERAL)

LINGUISTIC THEORY

LITERATURE (AMERICAN)

LITERATURE (AFRICAN AMERICAN)

LITERATURE (ETHNIC)

POLITICS AND POLITICAL SCIENCE